Lady Charlotte Bury

From a painting by Alexander Blaikley

LADY CHARLOTTE BURY

THE DIARY ILLUSTRATIVE OF THE
TIMES OF GEORGE THE FOURTH
INTERSPERSED WITH ORIGINAL
THE LATE QUEEN CAROLINE
OTHER DISTINGUISHED
ED WITH AN I

EIGHTEEN
PHOTOGRAVURE

YORK : JOHN LANE COMPANY . MCMVIII

THE DIARY OF A LADY-IN-WAITING

BY LADY CHARLOTTE BURY
BEING THE DIARY ILLUSTRATIVE OF
THE TIMES OF GEORGE THE FOURTH
INTERSPERSED WITH ORIGINAL LETTERS
FROM THE LATE QUEEN CAROLINE AND
FROM OTHER DISTINGUISHED PERSONS
EDITED WITH AN INTRODUCTION
BY A. FRANCIS STEUART
WITH EIGHTEEN FULL-PAGE PORTRAITS
TWO IN PHOTOGRAVURE : TWO VOLUMES : VOL. I

LONDON : JOHN LANE, THE BODLEY HEAD
NEW YORK : JOHN LANE COMPANY : MCMVIII

Printed by BALLANTYNE & CO. LIMITED
Tavistock Street, Covent Garden, London

INTRODUCTION

LADY CHARLOTTE SUSAN MARIA CAMPBELL—one of the greatest beauties of her day, whose " Diary Illustrative of the Times of George the Fourth " (which we here reprint) made so much stir in the world when it first appeared in 1838—merits a short biographical notice.

She was born February 18, 1775,* and was the younger daughter of John, 5th Duke of Argyll, and of his wife, Elizabeth Gunning, Duchess of Hamilton, one of the beautiful Irish Gunnings of whom we learn so much from Horace Walpole. For Elizabeth Gunning, though her fair face was her sole fortune, married in succession two Scottish Dukes. By her mother's two marriages Lady Charlotte was half-sister to the 7th and 8th Dukes of Hamilton and to the unhappy Elizabeth, Countess of Derby, and full sister to George, 6th, and John Douglas, 7th Duke of Argyll and to the handsome Lady Augusta Clavering. She received her name from Queen Charlotte, whom her mother had escorted from Germany when betrothed to her future husband King George III. and to whom she was then Lady-in-waiting, and as a duke's daughter was, from her earliest years, naturally placed in the highest society. Horace Walpole, writing of the Argyll family to Miss Berry in 1791, when Lady Charlotte was only sixteen, says, " Everybody admires the youngest daughter's person and understanding." She was much

* The *Edinburgh Advertiser* of February 24, 1775, speaks of the birth occurring " at London on the 18th current."

abroad in France and Italy during early life, owing to the ill-health of her mother (who died in 1790) and she acquired a very considerable knowledge of art and a real love of literature and music. She was presented to King George III. and Queen Charlotte, when about seventeen, and soon astonished London by her beautiful face and handsome presence, and we find her praises sung in many letters and memoirs of the time. Like many another spoiled beauty, however, she did not make a brilliant match, for on June 21, 1796, she married her kinsman, John Campbell, "handsome Jack Campbell," a good-looking young man of twenty-four, "a great fellow," and with only a small income, as was most natural, as he was the eldest of the fourteen children of Walter Campbell of Shawfield.

At first Lady Charlotte and her husband were a good deal in Edinburgh, where she queened it over the literary set and wrote some poems which were published anonymously 1797, and there in 1798 she, "in pride of rank and beauty's bloom," introduced Walter Scott, of whom she had made a friend, to Matthew Lewis, the then celebrated author of "The Monk," whose "Divinity" she was. Another of her friends and correspondents was Charles Kirkpatrick Sharpe, the antiquary, whom some called "the Scottish Walpole;" and a more critical one, Miss Susan Ferrier, the novelist, whose father was agent for the Argyll family and who was a frequent visitor at Inverary Castle, where Lady Charlotte often acted as châtelaine. In 1803 she and her husband made Hartwell, in Bucks, their headquarters, but she was still frequently in Scotland, and in Edinburgh in 1809 her husband died, leaving her, at the age of thirty-four, a widow, "in uneasy circumstances," as she had been since her marriage, with nine children but scantily provided for.

A year after this, whether compelled by poverty or not, she accepted the position of Lady-in-waiting to H.R.H.

Caroline, Princess of Wales, with whom she had sympathised for some years. The situation was not a pleasant
one, as the Princess was separated from her husband,
the powerful and vindictive Prince of Wales, and estranged
by Queen Charlotte's dislike to her, from the Court. To
add more difficulties, she, by her own imprudence, follies
and indiscreet conduct, was continually making her
position and that of her ladies and gentlemen, which
was bad at all times, worse than it might have been.
Deserted by her husband soon after the birth, in 1796, of
their only child, the Princess Charlotte, the Princess of
Wales had been involved in serious charges of adultery
brought against her by two treacherous friends, Sir John
and Lady Douglas, whom she, though knowing little of
their antecedents, had foolishly made much of during
her retirement at Blackheath. Though cleared of the
charges in 1806 by "the Delicate Investigation" of a
Commission of Peers appointed by her uncle the King—
always her friend—she was reproved for levity of manners,
and though allowed to appear at Court, she was coldly
received by the old Queen and debarred from seeing much
of her daughter. The scandal which attached to those
proceedings naturally was reflected on her circle, and as
she still continued to keep with her a child, William
Austin, said, by rumour, to be her own, but whom the
"Delicate Investigation" held to be the child of a poor
woman at Deptford whom the Princess had taken under
her protection, there were still many people who believed
the former scandals, which therefore came to the surface
from time to time, and these timid worthies either avoided
the Princess's Court or at most gave it only *quasi*-recogni-
tion, particularly after her persecuting husband became
Prince Regent in 1811. As she was always pressed for
money, in addition to her Court duties, Lady Charlotte
attempted to make an income by literature. In 1812
she published a novel (the precursor of many others)

called "Self-Indulgence," but in 1813 the affairs of the Princess of Wales involved more of her attention as they took a turn for the worse. She was bearer of a letter in January from the Princess to her husband, now Prince Regent, petitioning for freer intercourse with Princess Charlotte, her daughter, but on account of this embassy she was received in a most insulting manner.* During her term of waiting at the Princess's Court (she was then living at 13 Upper Brook Street and going much into society as well), she kept, as we shall see later, a full Diary and in it recorded her impressions and opinions as well as the foibles of her mistress, the Princess of Wales, for whom, in spite of her undignified conduct, she seems to have had a genuine compassion and a real though contemptuous affection. In 1814, the service of the Princess became, through her exhibition of favouritism, too compromising however, and on the excuse of taking her family to Geneva, Lady Charlotte went abroad, but she still remained on friendly terms with her former mistress and corresponded with the Princess and her suite. In October Lady Charlotte was somewhat surprised to find that the Princess of Wales, who had also gone abroad to seek a freer air, arrived also at Geneva, appeared in a bizarre manner at a ball where she was, and extracted a promise that she would rejoin her later during her journeys on the Continent. She accordingly left Nice for Genoa in April 1815 in the Princess of Wales' frigate, the *Clorinda*, joining the Princess at Genoa and went with her to Milan, not leaving her service finally until May 1815, having remained longer than any other member of her English suite, who could not suffer the favour the Princess showed to her ex-courier Bartolomeo Bergami. Lady Charlotte returned to England, "more eaten up with sentiment than ever," says Miss Ferrier, and going

* Miss Knight's Autobiography, i. 216-7.

abroad again, displeased her family * and friends by
marrying at Florence on March 17, 1818, a young clergyman of good birth who possessed a real taste for Art,
the Rev. Edward John Bury, who had travelled in Italy
with her eldest son, and under the name of Lady Charlotte
Bury she was cited as a witness for the defence at the
trial of Queen Caroline in 1820, and was in England
during her sad last days and death. Her husband's
extravagant tastes as well as her own impecunious circumstances forced Lady Charlotte, now in England, now
abroad, to take up her pen anew, and her novels came thick
and fast. She published " Conduct is Fate " (1822),
" Alla Giornata " (1826), " Flirtation, a Marriage in High
Life " (1828), " The Exclusives," "The Separation" (1830),
" The Disinherited," " The Ensnared " (1834), " The
Devoted " (1836), " The Divorced," " Love " (1837),
" Family Records," " The History of a Flirt " (1840), and
" The Manœuvring Mother " (1842). Her books sold well
and she obtained (says N. P. Willis) as much as £200 for
each of these sentimental tales. In addition she published
a work in verse, " The Three Sanctuaries of Tuscany,"
in 1833, which was, owing to her husband's illustrations,
of real value, and several religious books, the title of
one of which (published also in 1830) " Suspirium Sanc-
torum ; or, Holy Breathings," cannot fail to remind us
of Thackeray's " Heavenly Chords " in his paper on
" The Fashionable Authoress."

Lady Charlotte, after many tempestuous and wandering years, died, still beautiful, and, in spite of what ill-

---

* Her family, some of whom made brilliant marriages, consisted of :
(1) Walter Campbell of Islay ; (2) John ; (3) Eliza, m. Sir William
Cumming, Bart. ; (4) Eleonora, m. Lord Uxbridge, afterwards Marquis
of Anglesey ; (5) Beaujolais, m. Earl of Charleville ; (6) Adelaide
Constance, m. Lord Arthur Lennox ; (7) Emma, m. William Russell,
Esq. ; (8) Julia, m. Langford-Brooke, Esq. She had one surviving
daughter by her second marriage ; (9) Bianca Bury, m. David Lyon,
Esq.

informed writers say, by no means alone and neglectèd,* but lovingly tended by her surviving daughters, Lady Arthur Lennox and Mrs. William Russell, at her own house, 91 Sloane Street, London, on March 31, 1861, having attained to the advanced age of eighty-six.

In 1838 there had been published the book which, now known under her name, was then anonymous and entitled the " Diary Illustrative of the Times of George IV." It is said that Mr. Bury, wanting money,† " took possession of " Lady Charlotte's private journal, never intended for publication, that he " made a few alterations and additions, introducing some remarks on Lady Charlotte by way of disguise, and published it without her knowledge, adding many letters addressed to her." To this were added very pharisaical notes and a few *quasi-*embellishments or disguises, and the whole was printed with many internal evidences of hasty preparation for the Press. It had at once *un succès de scandale* and an immense sale. Of the " Literary Gazette " of Almack's, which indicated some of the characters, 5000 copies alone were sold. It was fiercely attacked in the reviews, which said it was vulgar, untrustworthy, unreliable or vulgar as they chose, and the best-known criticism which tore it to pieces was W. M. Thackeray's satire, " Skimmings from the Diary of George IV.," by C. Yellowplush, Esq. But though Thackeray had nothing too bad to say of the diary itself, this did not prevent him quoting some of its most pregnant passages when he desired to use them as brilliant illustrations of his immortal " Four Georges."

The extent of the Lady Charlotte's complicity in the publication of the Diary has been variously stated,

* *E.g.* " Queens of Beauty," by W. Willmott Dixon. 2 vols. 1907.
† *See* " Three Generations of Fascinating Women," p. 201. by Lady Charlotte Campbell's grand-daughter, Lady Russell of Swallowfield; but as the Rev. Edward John Bury died, aged forty-two, in May 1832, this must mean that he took possession of the journal and letters some time before the book was actually published.

but that the Diary—save for a few disguising facts
—was the work of herself alone cannot possibly be
denied. In spite of the " disguise " every one coupled
her name with it, and indeed the thinness of the veil was
obvious. Tom Hood penned the following lines :

> The poor dear dead have been laid out in vain,
> Turn'd into cash, they are laid out again !
>
> When I resign this world so briery,
>   To have across the Styx my ferrying,
>   O, may I die without a DIARY!
>   And be interr'd without a BURY-ing !

which showed to whom popular rumour attributed the
book. The Earl of Albemarle (1799–1891) quotes it
in his " Fifty Years of My Life," as does Karoline Bauer
in her " Memoirs," as of her authorship. Many of her
friends were indignant when they saw it and did not wish
to meet her, and Charles Kirkpatrick Sharpe, Lady Charlotte's own correspondent, wrote in a natural fury at its
publication. " I cannot express my vexation about the
book you mention . . . in all my reading and experience
I never knew anything of the kind. When I wrote the
silly, impertinent letters in question, between twenty and
thirty years ago, I knew that I was writing to the Duke of
Argyle's daughter, and thought myself safe by all the
common rules of good breeding and morality. But I find
I was extremely deceived. I could say more on this
head, but my gratitude gets the better of my spleen, for I
am eternally bound to remember that Lady Charlotte
Bury is Lady Wemyss' sister-in-law and Mr. Campbell's
mother."

The Diary gives, however, what no other book does, an
account of the curious and undignified Court of Caroline,
Princess of Wales, at home and abroad, and, purged of
many of the unnecessary pharisaical notes which have
disfigured the former editions, we now present it in this

new form. From the facts it records about the life of the Princess, in spite of her continual indiscretions, and feeling the gravest sorrow at the continual persecution she experienced at the hands of the despicable Prince Regent, "the First Gentleman in Europe," we cannot, like the writer herself, help compassionating the unfortunate Princess of Wales, whose Court it describes. Nor do we fail to reprobate his mother, "The Good Queen Charlotte," of whose extraordinarily harsh conduct towards her daughter-in-law and Princess Charlotte we get some very striking instances, entirely on a par with her harsh rule which caused all her sons to revolt and had unedifying results within her family circle itself, which we hope will never be fully chronicled. We are shown not only how the Princess of Wales, whose marriage was inauspicious, and from the start unhappy, was made use of as a tool, first by one political party and then by another, but also how very few politicians had her own cause at heart. In spite of the contemptuous phrases used about her in the Diary, we cannot help thinking that Lady Charlotte Campbell did enact the part of a friend—though a very critical one— towards her mistress at a perilous time.

The character given of the Princess Charlotte is that of a high-spirited girl trying to grope for the right way in the midst of horrible domestic factions, and when we read this, together with what is recorded in the reminiscences of her boy friend, Lord Albemarle, and in the Autobiography of Miss Knight, one of her Ladies-in-waiting, we begin to see how attractive she was and how the nation hoped for a good Queen in the ill-fated daughter of the selfish voluptuary the Prince Regent and his indiscreet consort; a girl who had courage enough to say of her parents, "My mother was wicked, but she would not have turned so wicked had not my father been much more wicked still."

There have been several previous editions of this book, one of which was reviewed as if a new work by a contemporary, so little was it known, but this differs from them all. Besides the omission of the horrible italics and many of the unnecessary and disgusting original notes, which perhaps were inspired by Colburn or John Galt, and the unnecessary account of the " Public Characters " and the " Regency and Reign of George IV.," we have made an important change in the text of the " Diary " itself. The names left blank in the former editions (the more important were always but thinly veiled and often explained in an explanatory foot-note) have, where possible, been filled up (although placed in brackets that the modern addition may be easily noticed) from old annotated copies, and these names will be further filled up, if possible, in future editions. Now that so long a time has elapsed since the Diary was first given to the world this can do no harm, and we hope that the few biographical notes which are added will make the book more interesting to the modern reader of the history of the Regency.

ILLUSTRATIONS

THE DIARY OF A
LADY-IN-WAITING

SECTION I

COURTS are strange, mysterious places :—those who pretend most to despise them seek to gain admittance within their precincts ; those who once obtain an entrance there generally lament their fate, and yet, somehow or other, cannot break their chains. I believe, also, that it makes little difference whether those circles of society, which stand apart from the rest of the world, exist under one form of government, or under another ; whether under Emperors, Kings, Protectors or Consuls. They may vary as to modes and designations ; but courts are courts still, and have been so from the earliest times. Intrigues, jealousies, heart-burnings, lies, dissimulation, thrive in them as mushrooms in a hot-bed. Nevertheless, they are necessary evils, and they afford a great school both for the heart and head. It is utterly impossible, so long as the world exists, that similar societies should not exist also ; and one may as well declaim against every other defect attendant upon human institutions, and endeavour to extirpate crime from the world, as pretend to put down courts and their concomitant evils.

December, 1810.—Lady M[ary] C[oke] called upon me by appointment ; and we went together to Her Royal Highness the Duchess of B[runswic]k.* She thought more of me than she had ever done before, because I was on the road to royal favour ; she herself being in her own estimation an engrafted sprig of royalty.† We rumbled in her old tub all the way to New Street, Spring Gardens, much to the discomfiture of my bones ; for, if the vehicle ever had springs, time has stiffened their joints as completely as it has done those of its soi-disant royal mistress. Lady M[ary] C[oke] was grandly gracious, and gave me dissertations on etiquette, such as it existed in her young days, till we reached our destination. We were ushered into the dirtiest room I ever beheld, empty, and devoid of comfort. A few filthy lamps stood on a sideboard ; common chairs were placed around very dingy walls ; and, in the middle of this empty space, sat the old Duchess, a melancholy specimen of decayed royalty. There is much goodness in her countenance, and a candour and sincerity in her manner, and even in her abrupt and rough conversation, which are invaluable in a person of her rank, whose life must necessarily have been passed in the society of those whose very essence is deceit. Her former friendship for friends very dear to me, of whom she spoke in terms of respect and love, gave an interest to the visit which it could not otherwise have had. I sat, therefore, patiently listening to Lady M[ary] C[oke] and Her Royal

* Augusta, widow of Carl II., Duke of Brunswick. She was Princess Royal of England, daughter of Frederick, Prince of Wales, sister of George III., and mother of Caroline, Princess of Wales. She arrived in England July 7, 1807, and died March 23, 1813.

† If Lady M—— C—— means Lady Mary Coke, it is well known she supposed herself to be the widow of the antecedent Duke of York ; for when her mother one day found the Duke in her apartment, and rated her for the impropriety of her conduct, she drew herself up with ineffable dignity, and replied, " Madam, do you know *whom* you are talking to ? You are talking to the Duchess of York." [Original note.] Lady Mary Coke (1726–1811) was the youngest daughter of John Campbell, Duke of Argyll. She had been unhappily married.

Highness, who talked of lords and ladies of the last century, and wondered at those of the present, and passed trippingly over the peccadillos of their own contemporaries, to vent all their moral indignation upon those of mine.

Old Mr. L[i]vingsto[]ne * was announced : poor man, what did he get by his attendance on royalty ? the ill-will of all parties. He knows many things which, if told, would set London on fire. Soon after his entrance, Lady M[ary] C[oke] arose, and, kicking her train behind her, backed out of the room in capital style. How the heart dilates or closes in the presence of different persons ! It must surely be very unwholesome to be with those in whose society the latter is the case.

Went to Kensington—a great ball—everybody of the highest fashion—Dukes of Portland and Beaufort, Earl Harrowby,† &c., &c. As I always wished the royal hostess well I was glad to observe that the company then frequenting the palace were of the best. I sat down by some old friends, and felt that to be near them was a comfort, surrounded as I was by persons for whom I cared not, and who cared not for me ; but the Princess beckoned to me, and taking my arm, leant upon it, parading me around the apartments. The inner room was set out with refreshments, and a profusion of gold plate ; which, by the way, in after times I never saw. Was it taken away, or was it otherwise disposed of ? Sofas were placed around the tables, and the whole thing was well managed.

Her Royal Highness wished the company to come into

* Mr. Livingstone, the tutor of some of the Princes, a good dull man. [Original note.]

† These noblemen and their wives continued to visit Her Royal Highness the Princess of Wales till the King was declared too ill to reign, and the Prince became in fact Regent ; then those ladies disappeared that moment from Kensington, and were never seen there more. It was the besom of expediency, which swept them all away. [Original note.]

this banquetting room ; but, either out of respect, and not knowing whether they ought to do so or not, or because they preferred the outer room, no one would come in, except Lady O[xfor]d, Lord H. Fitzgerald, and Lord G[owe]r, who was forcibly seized upon by Lady O[xfor]d.* Altogether, in my quality of looker-on, I could not but think that lady was no honour to society ; and it was only surprising to remark in her instance, as well as in that of many others, how well impudence succeeds, even with the mild and the noble, who are often subdued by its arrogant assumption of command.

The Princess complained of the weight of some jewels she wore in her head, and said they gave her the head- ache ; then, turning to a person who was evidently a favourite, asked, " May I not take them off now that the first parade is over ? " He replied in his own doucereux voice, " Your Royal Highness is the best judge ; but, now that you have shown off the magnificence of the ornament, I think it would be cruel that you should condemn yourself to suffer by wearing it longer. In my opinion, you will be just as handsome with- out it."

I was convinced, from the manner in which these words were spoken, that that man loved her. Poor soul ! of all those on whom she conferred benefits, I think he was the only man or woman who could be said to have *loved* her,—and he ought not to have done so.

I dined again at Kensington. There were assembled a company of the very first persons of the realm. I was glad to see that what had been told me of low company was not true.

---

* The beautiful Lady Oxford, whose portrait by Hoppner is in the National Gallery, London. She was Jane Elizabeth, daughter of the Rev. James Scott, Vicar of Itchin, Hants, and had married, in 1794, Edward Harley, 5th Earl of Oxford. Her gallantries with Lord Byron and others were well known, and her children were known as " the Harleian miscellany." She died November 20, 1824.

Wednesday, 9th, 1810.—This day, I found Her Royal Highness sitting for her picture. She received me with her usual graciousness of manner, and desired me to " come and sit," her phrase for feeling comfortable and at one's ease. She informed me that Mr. S[——], the painter engaged upon the picture, was only altering the costume of a portrait taken many years back ; which, she said, was by no means doing his talent justice. Certainly the picture was frightful, and I have often regretted that I never saw a tolerable likeness painted of her. Although during the last years of her life she was bloated and disfigured by sorrow, and by the life she led, the Princess was in her early youth a pretty woman ; fine light hair—very delicately formed features, and a fine complexion—quick, glancing, penetrating eyes, long cut and rather sunk in the head, which gave them much expression—and a remarkably delicately formed mouth. But her head was always too large for her body, and her neck too short ; and, latterly, her whole figure was like a ball, and her countenance became hardened, and an expression of defiance and boldness took possession of it, that was very unpleasant. Nevertheless, when she chose to assume it, she had a very noble air, and I have seen her on more than one occasion put on a dignified carriage, which became her much more than the affectation of girlishness which she generally preferred.

To-day, I received the following letter from my friend " Matt Lewis " :—

(Dated) HOLLAND HOUSE,
December 9th, 1810.

The only news which is likely to be *very* interesting to you is, that I have got a violent cold ; and that, too, can scarcely be called *news*, for I have now had it about a week. Perhaps you may think this a subject of much interest to myself, but of very little to you ; but I can assure you that you are likely to feel the bad effects of it, for it makes me so cross and so stupid that you must not expect to find in this letter the slightest scrap of good nature or the faintest spark of entertainment.

Since you left town, I have been to Brocket Hall, and passed ten very pleasant days there, *en trio*, with William * and Lady Caroline Lamb. I was at Kensington, both Saturday and Sunday last, and dine there again to-morrow. The Princess was quite well; very anxious about the dear good King; talked a great deal about you, and expressed much impatience for a letter from you, giving an account of the wedding, and its antecedents and consequences.

Nothing is talked of but the fluctuations in the King's health, and the probable consequences, till I am wearied to death of the eternal discussion. Sometimes, he is said to be so much better that Parliament is to be immediately prorogued; then he is considerably worse, and the Prince is to be appointed Regent, with full powers, the next day. The King's situation is so doubtful that Perceval is resolved to protract measures as much as possible, and the regal power is at present to be confided to a commission of Lords Justices; then again, the Prince, and the King and the Lords Justices, are all to be laid on the shelf together, and the regency is to be vested in Her Majesty Queen Charlotte.

All these projects in their turns are sifted, and supported, and contradicted, and laid down again, leaving one, at the end of the discussion, just as ignorant and as confused as at the beginning. So that I grow quite wearied and impatient with the subject, and am in the precise situation of Sir Philip Francis, when the Prince was telling him a long prosing story, which still went on and went on, without coming to a conclusion: " Well, Sir ? well, Sir ? " cried Sir Philip, out of all patience—" Well, Sir, well ! and what then, Sir ? what then ? "   At last, the Prince said, " Why, what's the matter with you, Sir Francis ? what do you want ? " " Want, Sir, want ? What's the matter with me ? Sir, I want a *result*."   And this is precisely the only thing now which I want to hear about the Regency.   Moreover, it is at least certain that latterly the King's general health is worse than it was; in particular, he has lately had an internal complaint, which in his peculiar circumstances is said frequently to be the forerunner of idiotcy.

* Afterwards Lord Melbourne.

For my own part, I am for having the Queen at the head of the government. It is certain, that having a man there has as yet produced but little good against Bonaparte, and therefore I should like to try a woman. Who knows, but the Queen may be the very woman mentioned in the Revelations, who is destined to be crowned with glory, and conquer the beast; and, therefore, as soon as she is appointed regent, I would immediately have her send a challenge to Bonaparte; decide the whole dispute by single combat; and, if she will but follow the example of that illustrious heroine, the Princess Rusty Fusty, in setting her back against a tree, and defending herself with her fan and her scissors, I make no doubt she will have the same success, and lay the holy Roman Emperor dead at her feet.

In the midst of all these political speculations, Lord Grey has made the disputants a low bow, and has gone back to Northumberland, to remain there till the middle of January. I asked Lord Lauderdale, if Lord Grey's friends did not find fault with his being out of the way at such a moment. "By no means," answered he with great gravity, "Lady Grey is to be confined very soon, and he sacrifices everything to the consideration of his wife. He was quite in the right. I always do the same thing."

London is very full, and the Duchess of Gordon has had some good assemblies. The Princess of Wales lives quietly; never has above four or five people at dinner, and has quite given up going to the play; though she owns, she considers this a very great privation. I have been teased into promising to put together some showy spectacle for Covent Garden; and the Princess insists on its not being produced before Easter Monday, as she says that, till then, she has no hopes of being allowed to visit the theatre.

I am quite impatient for your return to town, not only because I shall be very glad to see you again, but for your own sake, that you may see La Perouse. I am certain you will be pleased with it, out of all measure. I saw it the other night, and was quite delighted; and I promise myself great pleasure in seeing the pleasure which it will give you. There is besides a new actress, a Miss Booth, who promises to be the greatest acquisition that the stage has made for many years. She plays Mrs. Jordan's characters with great sprightliness:

a very pretty little figure (but *not* a very pretty face, at least, to *my* taste); great intelligence, much appearance of sensibility and *naïveté*, and, above all, a voice very sweet, touching, and so articulate that it can be heard all over the house, even in a whisper. She dances, too, remarkably well, and is very good in pantomime. The only thing in which she fails, is her singing, which is abominable; but I trust, (as she is to set herself to the study of music immediately, with all her might and main,) perhaps, she may mend this deficiency.

How do you like Thalaba? There are always so many nothings to be done in London daily, that I have not read ten lines for the last ten weeks, till I came to Holland House, where I have galloped through two volumes of Madame Du Deffand's Letters, and with much amusement, though the anecdotes are in themselves of no great value; still, being written on the spot, and at the moment, they have a vivacity and interest which make one read letter after letter without weariness. The extracts from Lord Orford's letters contain frequently excellent things; and indeed, in Madame Du Deffand's own general observations, there is much good sense and plain truth; but that sense and truth, being generally grounded upon knowledge of the world, and experience of its inhabitants, it unfortunately follows, of course, that the information which it conveys must be of a disagreeable and humiliating complexion. But what puts me out of all patience, and seems to me quite hard-hearted, is Lord Orford's perpetually torturing the poor old blind woman, upon her vanity and her indiscretion, and producing all her defects before her in terrible array, and that too, in the most unqualified language. Could he expect, that at eighty, she would cure herself of her faults, or that if time had not rendered her discreet, his lectures would!—and if being indiscreet contributed to her amusement, in the name of Heaven, why (situated as she was) should she not be so? I really think that this plain dealing with a poor old blind woman, who had passed her eighty long years in frivolity, vanity and dissipation, something barbarous; and I cannot see any purpose which this opening her eyes to her imperfections could possibly answer, except that of vexing and mortifying her; for, as to correcting her, she must have been long past that, and the idea was ridiculous ; though, to be sure, the poor old soul frequently promises to set about the amendment of her faults, as if she was a little school girl ; which is, in truth, almost as ridiculous as the advice.

Have you read these Letters ? You know, of course, that they were edited by your friend, Miss Berry, who has also written the Preface, the Life, and the Notes, all of which are most outrageously abused by many persons, though, in my opinion, without any just grounds.

Believe me,

Ever yours truly,

(Signed) M. G. LEWIS.

Thursday, December.—This was the Princess's birthday. I went to pay my respects. Her Royal Highness was very injudiciously attired—wrapped in a pink dressing-gown. Lady C[——]n was with her ; she seemed grievously tired of the latter, who in truth appears to be a dull woman, and there is an expression in her features of something very like deceit, and a sneer, which makes me grave in despite of myself. Shortly after her departure, came the Duke of Brunswick. He paid his sister a set compliment, and gave her a ring of no value.— (N.B. All princes and princesses give shabby presents.)

The Duke of Brunswick * is very near being a handsome man. His figure is light and graceful ; and were it not that he carries his head ill, he would be a noble looking person. His eyes are deep sunk in his head, more so than I ever saw in any one, and his brows are remarkably prominent, with shaggy eyebrows. This circumstance gives him a sombre expression, and indeed the whole cast of his countenance is gloomy ; but his features are regular ; and, when he smiles, there is a transitory sweetness which is very striking, by the contrast to his usual severity of

* William, Duke of Brunswick (1771–1815), married Princess Marie of Baden, who died in 1808. Lord Albemarle describes him as " a sad and somewhat stern-looking man with sunken eyes and bushy eyebrows, and, what was then seldom seen in England, a pair of mustaches."

expression. In manner he is very reserved,—stiff and Germanic. He remained some time conversing with his sister in German, eyeing the lady-in-waiting occasionally askance. He seemed glad to take his leave.

Her Royal Highness, the old Duchess of Brunswick, next arrived, and still I was desired to remain. I thought this conference would never end ; and yet it seemed not to delight either party. What a factitious life ! The Duchess appears kind-hearted. The tears rolled down her cheeks as she said the poor Princess Amelia cannot live ; she seemed really affected. I take her to be a kind-hearted upright woman, but not in the least clever ; very slow in her speech and in her comprehension ; whereas her daughter is precisely the reverse, and has no patience with the repetition of phrases, and the lengthiness of histories, for which, in fact, she feels no interest.

To-day, I had the honour of meeting the Princess Charlotte, at her grandmother's. She is very clever, but has at present the manners of a hoyden school girl. She talked all sorts of nonsense to me. She is a fine piece of flesh and blood, but can put on dignity when she chooses, though it seems to sit uneasily upon her. What will be her fate ? It is impossible not to feel an interest in any human being, upon whom such a weight of responsibility is placed.

There is no company at the Duchess of Brunswick's, but the old women of the last century, and naturally the Princess calls this a *dullification*. It is unwise for the old to forget they were once young. This it is which always puts the Princess out of humour when she is there, and she yawns and shows it.

There was a Count Munster sat next to me at dinner, who seems quite ill-placed in a court ; for he appears to me to be a delightful and a particularly sincere person. He expresses himself on many subjects with great enthusiasm, and has all the sentiment of a German. He said

Italy was a country in which one should not live too long. I asked him, " Why ? " His reply was, " It is too delightful." The Princess of Wales told him, that whatever little good she had in her, she owed it to his mother, who had been her governess.

One day, Her Royal Highness said to me, " If I always lived with my cousins, the royal family, and, if they were kind to me, I should like them, and care for them ; but I cannot say, treating me as they do, that I feel that affection for them I should otherwise feel, except indeed for my dear old uncle ; and he, poor dear, is lost to me now. So I confess, all I am afraid of is, lest the Princess Amelia should die ; because I could not then get out to amuse myself." There was a levity in this confession, certainly, but yet there was a sincerity in it, which made me augur well of the ingenuousness of her character.

The royal family had sent her presents on her birthday ; the Queen sent a very handsome aigrette, which the young Princess Charlotte observed was really pretty well, considering who sent it. She then laughed heartily, her own peculiar loud but musical laugh.

To-day, I received the following letter from Her Royal Highness the Princess of Wales :—

Monday, December 10, 1810.

MY DEAR,—I am just on the point of setting out for the Priory, where I don't expect to be much enlivened, but go partly from civility, and partly from curiosity, to make the acquaintance with the " Ida of Athens," which I trust will gratify my search for knowledge, or my taste for quizzing.

There is nothing new here under the sun, since you left the metropolis, and I lead literally the life of a recluse, for still public amusements are prohibited for the present. Thanks to heaven, no Lord Chamberlain has been appointed yet, otherwise the dear operas would have begun by this time, and I should have felt myself obliged to renounce this great amusement. The parties in Hanover Square are not more lively than they were last winter in Spring Gardens, except we miss the galanti show, which was exhibited, of all the " old fograms, since the reign of George the First, which, I suppose, was intended to show the difference that existed between them and the beauties of Charles the Second, painted by Sir Peter Lely. But I am afraid his pencil, as that of Titian, or of Marc [*sic*] Angelo, would never have succeeded in making them rivals of that happy century;—their beauty was much more valued and praised, except there is one precedent, which will remain on record in the Argyll family.* Your letter arrived most welcomely, as there had been various reports about a suspension d'armes, an armistice, or a retreat, resembling that of Massena ; but all this puff must have been merely raised by envy, love of gossip, and newsmongers.

I intend to go to Blackheath, before Christmas, to take in an additional stock of health, and strength, and spirits for the winter campaign, which I suspect will be rather longer than usual, Parliament having met so early. Blackheath will be called Le Palais des . . .†, as the sleep will be the most predominant amusement and relaxation ; otherwise, I would feel myself dans l'ordre de la Trappe, being with my lay sister, Mrs. Lisle, who has taken her resemblance from the living skeleton. If anybody would take the pains to write my biography, they would inform the public that for some secret and dreadful crime this penance was inflicted upon me. This is the way one may vouch for the historian's veracity. But as I flatter myself, that this wonderful production of epistolary punning will remain in the archives of the illustrious family of the ——, that upon record, matter of fact reasons of my absence from Kensington will be known.

Believe me, for ever,

Your most sincere,

(Signed) C. P.

The above letter may convey to posterity an idea of the kind of ill-assorted matter which filled the mind of this unfortunate Princess. But something must be attributed to her want of knowledge of the English

* I suppose Her Royal Highness alluded to Lady Charlotte Campbell, the beauty of the Argyll family of that day. [Original note.]
† This word is illegible in the original letter.

language ; and much indulgence may be extended to a person in Her Royal Highness's situation, who was constantly goaded, publicly and privately, to irritation—a fact, which she was too proud to acknowledge, but which made her take refuge in an affected jocularity, and a pretence to wit.

Mr. Ward is frequently one of the Kensington guests. He is certainly a clever man. Indeed, there is a great and laudable wish on the part of the Princess to attract extraordinary persons around her. This desire properly directed might turn to her own advantage, and that of those who belong to her ; but it evaporates in vanity, and produces no effectual improvement in her society. Mr. Ward * is a man concerning whom great expectations are formed, and various parties look at him as a card which, in their own hands, they might like to play ; but there is something uncertain and wayward about him, which just as one is going to like him, prevents one's doing so ; though I was very near the mark the other night, in favour of what he said of the Moon. The Princess calls Mr. Forbes † *Mr. Fob.* There is something ludicrously appropriate in this mispronunciation, I cannot tell why.

Again, I received a note from Her Royal Highness ; the following is a curious extract from it :—

The only astonishing news I can offer you is, that the Regent is dangerously ill ; still I am not sanguine enough to flatter myself that the period to all my troubles and misfortunes is yet come. Yet one must hope for the best.

Ever yours,
C. P.

This day, dined at Kensington, *en petit comité :* no servants, but dumb waiters. These dinners are peculiarly

* Afterwards Lord Dudley. [Part of original note.]
† Now Minister at Dresden, a remarkably clever, agreeable person. [Original note.]

agreeable—nothing to impede the flow of soul, whatever there may be of the feast of reason. The Princess gave a long detailed account of her marriage, and the circumstances which brought it about. " I,—you know, was the victim of mammon ; the Prince of Wales's debts must be paid, and poor little I's person was the pretence. Parliament would vote supplies for the Heir-Apparent's *marriage ;* the King would help his little help. A Protestant Princess must be found—they fixed upon the Prince's cousin. To tell you God's truth, [a favourite expression,] I always hated it ; but to oblige my father, any thing. But the first moment I saw my *futur* and Lady J[erse]y together, I knew how it all was, and I said to myself, ' Oh, very well ! ' I took my partie—and so it would have been, if—but, Oh, mine God ! " she added, throwing up her head, " I could be the slave of a man I love ; but one whom I love not, and who did not love me, impossible—c'est autre chose." She went on to say :—

" One of the civil things His Royal Highness did just at first, was to find fault with my shoes ; and, as I was very young and lively in those days, I told him to make me a better pair, and bring them to me. I brought letters from all the Princes and Princesses to him, from all the petty courts, and I tossed them to him, and said, ' There— that's to prove I'm not an impostor ! ' "

Lady Oxford observed, " Well, Madam, it is the most surprising thing in the world, that the Prince was not desperately in love with your Royal Highness." " Not at all," she replied ; " in the first place, very few husbands love their wives ; and I confess, the moment one is obliged to marry any person, it is enough to render them hateful. Had I come over here as a Princess, with my father, on a visit, as Mr. Pitt once wanted my father to have done, things might have been very different : but what is done cannot be undone."

" What a delightful court we should have now," said one

of the party, "if Her Royal Highness was Queen!"   "I never wish to be Queen," replied the Princess; "the Queen's mother is enough for me."

Lord Abercorn was, at this time, a great friend of the Princess's; he frequently wrote to her, and was very curious to know how she got on with a new person who had lately come to her court. This lady had once been in his society, but had not seen him for years: "I will not satisfy his curiosity," said the Princess; "let him come and see"; but he came not.

To-day, the Princess was in one of her most communicative humours. Poor thing! she was always looking about for some one to pour out her heart to, and never found one. Some dared not listen to her, others would not, and others again, did so only to answer their own purposes; but, as she was quick at reading characters, she often sent the latter upon a wrong scent, which was amusing enough. In general, when I had the honour of being invited to Kensington, I avoided all questions, and endeavoured neither to deceive nor be deceived; but sometimes it was next to impossible not to ask a question, or make an observation, which the next moment was repented of. For instance, when she inveighed against England and the British Court, I asked her if she had left Brunswick with regret: "Not at all; I was sick, tired of it; but I was sorry to leave my father. I loved my father dearly, better nor any oder person"; and the tears poured over her face. "I will tell you," she went on to say, and she mastered her emotion—"I will tell you, there is none affection more powerful than dat we feel for a good fader; but dere were some unlucky tings in our court, which made my position difficult. My fader was most entirely attached to a lady for thirty years, who in fact was his mistress; she was the beautifullest creature, and the cleverest; but, though my father continued to pay my moder all possible respect, my poor moder could not suffer this attachment ; and de consequence was, I did not know what to do between them ; when I was civil to the one, I was scolded by the other, and was very tired of being shuttlecock between them."

The Princess had a custom, when she drove out, of never giving an order, but pointing to the quarter to which she wished to be driven. The postillion watched her eye, and with wonderful quickness took the direction which it (and it alone, very often) designated. I have wondered sometimes, what this dumb show mystery meant. I can only account for it by believing that royal persons divert themselves with very puerile devices, and that they play at secrets, as children do at hide-and-seek.

The Princess sometimes goes to see the Duke of Bruns- wick's two boys.* She climbs to the very top of a house at Vauxhall, where they are living, and having talked for some time to them, goes away again. These visits do not seem to afford either party much pleasure. She complains that the boys are frightful to look upon.

The Princess often does the most extraordinary things, apparently for no other purpose than to make her atten- dants stare. Very frequently, she will take one of her ladies along with her, to walk in Kensington Gardens— all the party being dressed—[it may be] in a costume very unsuited to the public highway ; and, all of a sudden, she will bolt out at one of the smaller gates, and walk all over Bayswater, and along the Paddington Canal, at the risk of being insulted, or, if known, mobbed—enjoying all the while the terror of the unfortunate attendant who may be destined to walk after her. One day, Her Royal Highness inquired at all the doors of Bayswater and its neighbourhood, if there were any houses to be let, and went into many of them, till at last she came to one, where some children of a friend of hers (Lord H. F.) were placed for change of air ; and she was quite enchanted at being

* Carl, born October 30, 1804 ; and William, born April 25, 1806.

known by them, and at having to boast of her extraordinary mode of walking over the country.

Sometimes, the Princess philosophizes : here is a sample
of her philosophy. She said one day, "Suspense is very
great bore, but we live only de poor beings of de hour—
and we ought always to try to make us happy so long we
do live. To tell you God's truth,"—her favourite expression, not always used appropriately,—" To tell you God's
truth, I have had as many vexations as most people ;
but we must make up *vous* mind to enjoy de good, spite
of de bad ; and I mind now de last no more than dat "—
snapping her fingers.

Princess Charlotte came pretty frequently to Kensington at this epoch. Lady de Clifford was then her governess ; that is to say, so named ; for the Princess is her
own governess.

The Princess of Wales speaks highly of Mrs. Fitzherbert.
She always says, " that is the Prince's true wife ; she is an
excellent woman ; it is a great pity for him he ever broke
vid her. Do you know I know de man who was present
at his marriage, the late Lord B[radfor]d.* He declared
to a friend of mine, that when he went to inform Mrs. Fitzherbert that the Prince had married me, she would not
believe it, for she knew she was herself married to him."

The Princess took great pleasure in explaining the state
of politics and parties. She thought she had it all at her
finger's ends, because she had lived with Canning and
Perceval ; but she saw everything through the mist of her
own passions and prejudices ; and, consequently, saw
everything falsely. She used to say, " the nation will go
safe enough, whoever are de ministers, so long as de King
lives ; but when he dies every ting will be overturned.
You will see—mark my words ! The House of Commons
do now busy themselves with trifles, which they had better
let alone. 'Mais il faut être juste.' Ministers would

* Orlando Bridgman, 1st Earl of Bradford (1762–1825).

never have brought in the Duke of York's business, had he not misled them. Had he told them the truth, confided in them, and said, I have committed a folly, save me from exposure, I will do so no more, he would have been saved, and de constitution, too, perhaps ; for the business would have been hushed up. But no, his friends believed that he was intact ; (our friends do more harm than enemies sometimes ;) they said the more the matter is investigated, the more it will be to his honour. " You saw how de matter turn out,"—and she shrugged her shoulders. " I do assure you—to tell you God's truth,—had those letters been published, which were brought up, they might have produced a revolution ; for they not only told all that is true, but a great deal that is not true."

The Princess was in the way of saying jocularly, " I have nine children." And, when her hearers laughed at the joke as such, she would say, " It is true, upon honour ; dat is to say, I take care of eight boys and one girl. De boys shall serve de king. My good friend, Sir J. B., will take care of some. The girl I took by a very romantic accident. In the time of the disturbances in Ireland, a man and woman, apparently of the better class, left a female infant with a poor old peasant woman, who lives at Blackheath, and with the infant, a sum of money sufficient to support it a certain time. But the time elapsed, the money was spent, and no one came to supply the old woman with means for the babe's future exigencies. So she came to me, and told her story, and asked what she should do. At first I thought of putting the child to the parish ; but somehow I could not bear that ; so it ended in my taking charge of the infant entirely at my own expense. She is now at school at Bath, under the care of a Mrs. Twiss, sister of Mrs. Siddons. I have not seen the child for five years, and do not mean to see her till she is grown up : she is now twelve years old."

" It appears to me," said the Princess, one day, " that

jealousy and politics are untying the knot of Lord A[rchibald] H[amilton]'s * love for Lady O[xfor]d.   It is said that Lady O[xfor]d visits Mr. O'Connell and Sir F[rancis] B[urdet]t every day, and Lord A[rchibal]d does not approve ; but the greater reason still, is, that the Lady prefers Lord G[owe]r."

The Princess's villa at Blackheath is an incongruous piece of patch-work.   It may dazzle for a moment, when lighted up at night ; but it is all glitter, and glare, and trick ; everything is tinsel and trumpery about it ; it is altogether like a bad dream.

One day, the Princess showed me a large book, in which she had written characters of a great many of the leading persons in England.   She read me some of them. They were drawn with spirit, but I could not form any opinion of their justice ; first, because a mere outline, however boldly sketched, cannot convey a faithful portraiture of character ; and, secondly, because many of the persons mentioned therein were unknown to me. Upon the whole, these characters impressed me with a high opinion of her discernment and power of expression. Not that it was good English, but that it was strong sense.   But how dangerous !   If that book exists, it would form a curious episode in the memoirs of those times.

The Princess told one of her friends one day, who repeated it to me, that her life had been an eventful one from her earliest years ; that at one period, she was to have been married to the uncle of the Queen of Prussia ; at another, to the Prince of Orange ; at another, to this Queen's brother :—the latter, she said, was a most agreeable man, not at all ugly, and very pleasant in his manners —that she had liked him very much as a friend, but nothing

* Lord Archibald Hamilton was son of Archibald, 9th Duke of Hamilton, and brother of Lady Anne Hamilton, so often mentioned in this Diary. He was born in 1769 and died in 1827, unmarried.

more.—Prince George of Darmstadt (I think that was the name she gave the Queen of Prussia's uncle) was a very handsome man, tall, slight, yet not too thin. " He turned all de women's heads except mine. I like him very much, but he was very perfide to me—a false perfidious friend. It was he who was the lover of the late Queen of France, and he was the real father of the last Dauphin. Just before I came to this country, I was very unhappy. My father said to me, if I would marry on the continent, he never wished to get rid of me, or to send me away ; but if I was determined to marry, that this situation which presented itself seemed sent by Providence to my advantage, and he would not suffer me to slight it. So, as a drowning wretch catches at a straw, I caught at this crown and sceptre. But, if I had not been miraculously supported, I could not have outlived all I have done : there are moments when one is supernaturally helped." The Princess became very grave after this conversation, and soon retired.

The Princess of Wales is not what I think a female character should be ; but she has a bold and independent mind, which is a principal ingredient in the formation of a great queen, or an illustrious woman.

The Princess Charlotte always dines with her mother on Saturdays. This day her Royal Highness came with Lady de Clifford and the Duke of Brunswick. As soon as she grows intimate with any one, she gives way to her natural feelings, and there is an openness and candour in her conversation, which are very captivating. I pity her that she is born to be a queen. She would be a much happier being if she were a private individual. I cannot make out what the Duke of Brunswick's character really is. The Princess of Wales seems fond of him ; yet, as she never speaks openly of him, I conceive there is something about him which does not please her. A son of Lord H. F[itzgeral]d dined at K[ensingto]n, a boy of about fourteen years of age,* who appeared uncommonly clever and very agreeable. He is being educated at Westminster. I asked him many questions about the school, which he answered most intelligently ; but, from all I have seen, the Etonians are more polished.

Lady de Clifford † seems to be a good natured, commonplace person, and the young Princess appears attached to her, which is a good indication of her ladyship's temper.

The dinner over, which always weighs heavily on the Princess when composed of a family party only, Her Royal Highness recovered her natural gaiety. As soon as she returned to the drawing-room, she began talking eagerly to Lady de Clifford *en tête-à-tête*. The Princess Charlotte ran from one end of the room to the other to fetch herself a chair. I rose and said how shocked I was, that Her Royal Highness had not commanded me to do her bidding. " Oh ! " said her mother, " I assure you she likes it ; it is an amusement for her ; she is kept so very strict, it is like feeling herself at liberty to fly about, —is it not Lady de Clifford ? " To which the latter replied sharply, " I assure your Royal Highness, the Princess Charlotte has liberty enough with me." This retort again produced a stiffness, and the time seemed to drag on heavily, until the Princess Charlotte and the Duke of Brunswick withdrew, when we went to the Opera.

Mr. Ward, Mr. H. F[itzgeral]d, Mr. L[uttre]ll, Mr. Lewis, Mr. North, and Mr. Macdonald came to pay their respects in her box. Mr. Lewis, the author of " The Monk," was not, however, a very suitable attendant upon royalty. Mr. Ward was clever and pleasing ; but her Royal Highness was not, upon the whole, much flattered by her visitors, neither had she much cause to be so.

* Afterwards 23rd Lord de Ros, born September 1, 1797.
† Sophia, daughter of Samuel Campbell of Mount Campbell, eo. Leitrim, married, 1765, the 17th Baron de Clifford. She died 1828.

Sunday.—There was, as is customary on this day, a large party at Kensington ; but it was not so pleasant a dinner as usual, for the Duchess of R[utlan]d and her daughter, with Lady S[——]y and her daughter also, rendered it rather formal, and it troubled the Princess to make herself agreeable to them.

After dinner, there was an addition of Mrs. Poole,* Mrs. Lock,† Lady Dunmore, &c., and professional singers —Pucitti, his wife, Naldi, and Tramezani. The music was procured only for the sake of making a noise ; as it is merely an affair of custom with the Princess to have musicians, in order that it may be said she has had a concert ; cats would do just as well. Lord A[rchibal]d H[amilto]n was in a bad humour with Lady O[xfor]d ; consequently, with everybody else. She is only seeking an excuse to break with him, in order to pursue a new intrigue with Lord G[owe]r. The latter is much too good for her. These wordly intrigues are melancholy proofs of depravity. Long attachments, even when not sanctioned by morality, excite compassion ; but the ephemeral fires of passion, intrigue, interest, and pleasure, are loathsome.

The Princess dined with her mother, the Duchess of Brunswick. The Duchess of R[utlan]d, her two daughters ‡ and the Princess Charlotte, formed the principal part of the company. The Duke of Brunswick was also present. He is very silent, and appears to be somewhat of a misanthrope.

The Princess went to the play ; a resource she always reserves to herself, to escape from a dull dinner. She was accompanied by Lord [Henry] Fitz[geral]d, her lady-

* Lady Maryborough.

† The once beautiful Mrs. Lock [*sic* really Locke,] " La belle Jennings de son temps." [Original note.] She was the daughter of Mr. Jennings-Noel and wife of William Locke the younger, a distinguished amateur artist.

‡ Probably the two elder daughters of John, 5th Duke of Rutland, who afterwards became Lady Elizabeth Drummond and Lady Emmeline Stuart Wortley Mackenzie.

in-waiting, and myself. After the play, I was invited
to sup with her Royal Highness. As usual, she talked
of her own situation, and her previous life. " Judge,"
said she, " what it was to have a drunken husband on
one's wedding-day, and one who passed the greatest part
of his bridal-night under the grate, where he fell, and
where I left him. If anybody say to me at dis moment
—will you pass your life over again, or be killed ? I would
choose death ; for you know, a little sooner or later we
must all die ; but to live a life of wretchedness twice
over,—oh ! mine God, no ! Well, time went on, and de
case was, *I began to be wid child, and all de wise people
said so ;* but I pitied dem, for I no more believed it dan
any ting for long time. At last, Charlotte was born.
Well, *after I lay in,*—je vous jure 'tis true ; upon my
honour, upon my soul 'tis true,—I received a message,
through Lord Cholmondeley, to tell me I never was to
have de great honour of inhabiting de same room wid
my husband again. I said very well—but, as my memory
was short, I begged to have dis polite message in writing
from him. I had it—and vas free—I left Carlton House,
and went to Charlton. Oh ! how happy I was ! Everybody blamed me, but I never repented me of dis step.
Oh ! mine God, what I have suffered ! Luckily, I had
a spirit, or I never should have outlived it."

She said more, but I can never remember *all* she says.
Poor Princess ! she was an ill-treated woman, but a very
wrong-headed one. Had she remained quietly at Carlton
House, and conducted herself with silent dignity, how
different might have been her lot ! It is true, as her
Privy Purse, Miss H[——]n, once told a person of my
acquaintance, she was so insulted whilst there, that
every bit of furniture was taken out of the room she dined
in, except two shabby chairs ; and the pearl bracelets,
which had been given her by the Prince, were taken from
her, to decorate the arms of Lady J[erse]y. Still, had

the Princess had the courage which arises from principle, and not that which is merely the offspring of a daring spirit, she would have sat out the storm, and weathered it.

The Princess, in one of her confidential humours, declared she believed that Lady H[ertfor]d * is a woman of intact virtue—it is only a *liaison* of vanity on her part with my better half—but it will not last long—she is too formal for him." I dined with the Princess and Lady Charlotte Lindsay,† the latter a most amiable and delightful person ; but she is so witty and so very brilliant, so full of repartee, that her society dazzles my duller senses , and, instead of being exhilarated by it, I become lowered. I often say to myself in society, "*Où trouverai-je ma place ?* "—Total retirement, secondary intellect, secondary rank, do not suit me ; yet the world, and the first circles, and the wittiest and the prettiest, suit me not either. This is not affectation, 'tis a melancholy truth.

In speaking of Mr. Ward one day, the Princess said, " I will tell you what Mr. Ward is. He is a man all of vanity—he would marry for money, or Parliamentary interest, or to a very fashionable woman, who would make a fool of him ; but though *il joue le sentiment* sometimes," she said, shaking her head, " I do not believe he has one grain of it in his composition. Did you ever observe how he eats ? just like a hog with his snout sucking in a trough."

*   *   *   *   *

A long lapse in my journal. My own life during this time, has been far more interesting to me than when in the busy scenes of court life ; for I have spent the hours with ——. She left town to-day ; so I had nothing to

* Isabella, daughter and co-heir of Charles Ingram, 9th Viscount Irvine, *d.* 1834, second wife of Francis, 2nd Marquis of Hertford, who died 1822. The " Marchesa " of Moore's verses.

† Lady Charlotte North, daughter of the minister Lord North, the 2nd Earl of Guilford, and sister of Lady Glenbervie, married, 1800, Lieut.-Col. the Hon. John Lindsay. She died October 25, 1849.

do but to take to my books *et je me suis fait raison ;* but
it is hard work, and an ugly manufacture.   Lord
G[lenber]bie paid me a visit, announced Lord G[uilfor]d's
marriage with Miss B[oycott] * I don't know why, but I
felt sorry.   What business has that old drunken man to
marry so late in the day ?

I received Her Royal Highness's commands to dine
with her.   She had been very ill with an *attaque de bile,*
as she called it, and was lying on her sofa.   After some
attempts at conversation, which I had no spirits to keep
up, I asked leave to read to Her Royal Highness, and I
began *Les Malheurs de l'Inconstance.*   At seven, dinner
was announced.   The lady-in-waiting and myself were
the only company ; for every person who had been
invited sent an excuse, except Mr. W., who neither sent
nor came.   How rude !   These indignities were, however,
in a great measure brought down upon herself by her own
conduct.   How true it is, that vulgar familiarity breeds
contempt.   The Princess was very ill during dinner-
time ; nevertheless, she would go to the play, for the sake
of her little protégé *Willikin,* as she called him, whose
birthday it was.   There was nobody at the play in her
box, but Lord H. F[itzgeral]d.   *My* nobody is, however,
somebody's everybody.   What is it makes me find the
hours and days so long ?   Hours and days are coloured
by our fancy, not by the sun, or by the hues of nature.

The next day, I again dined at Kensington.   Sir Harry
Englefield, Mr. Gell,† and Lady O[xfor]d were the only
guests.   I was tired to death—oh, yes, to the death of
all pleasure.

One day, the Princess set out to walk, accompanied by
myself and one of her ladies, round Kensington Gardens.

* Francis, 5th Earl, married, July 16, 1810, Maria, 5th daughter of
Thomas Boycott of Wrexham, and died January 11, 1817.
† Sir William Gell (1777–1836), the archæologist.

At last, being wearied, her Royal Highness sat down on a bench occupied by two old persons, and she conversed with them, to my infinite amusement, they being perfectly ignorant who she was. She asked them all manner of questions about herself, to which they replied favourably. Her lady, I observed, was considerably alarmed, and was obliged to draw her veil over her face, to prevent betraying herself; and every moment I was myself afraid that something not so favourable might be expressed by these good people. Fortunately, this was not the case, and her Royal Highness walked away undiscovered, having informed them that if they would be at such a door, at such an hour, at the palace on any day, they would meet with the Princess of Wales, to see whom they expressed the strongest desire. This Haroun Al-raschid expedition passed off happily, but I own I dreaded its repetition. It is said that listeners hear no good of themselves.

That evening, as the carriage drove up to the door, to take the Princess to the Opera, the box on which the coachman sat, broke, fell upon the horses, frightened them, and threw off the unfortunate man, who in the fall broke his leg. The Princess was shocked, but not sufficiently to prevent her from going to the Opera. Royal nerves are made of tough materials.

Sunday.—As usual to-day, there was a large dinner party. After myself, Lord Rivers was the first arrival; and the Princess, not being yet dressed, we had a *tête-à-tête*. He is a pleasant and an elegant man—one of the last of that race of persons who were the dandies of a former century; and how much preferable were they to those of the present day. In the evening, the family of the C[annin]gs. I know not why, but there is something not altogether pleasant about them, though their talents command a sort of admiration; but too much is done for display. Miss C[anning] sings scientifically ; still her voice is not a *voce di petto*, not a delicious breathing of sentiment, which goes to the soul ;—it is studied—made out—acquired—not, in short, the *Canto che nell' anima si sente*. I think the young man is better, though prim and pragmatical ; but his verses on the dying gladiator are full of spirit, and seem the dictates of a natural gift.

Mr. Brougham was present on this occasion. I am half inclined to like him, yet I feel afraid of him : a mind that accustoms itself always to look at every thing in a ludicrous point of view—everything especially, that has to do with feeling—cannot have one chord in unison with mine.

Mr. Ward I positively dislike. In the ignoble necessity of eating and drinking, as the Princess observed, he renders himself an unpleasant companion at table. Then his person looks so dirty ; and he has such a sneer in his laugh, and is so impious as well as grossly indecent in his conversation, that I cannot like this clever man. The night dragged on heavily, but, as the Princess was not well, she soon dismissed her company.

Tuesday.—The Princess went to see a ship launched— the Queen Charlotte. We were too late for the actual ceremony, but what we did see was one of the finest sights, as a moving picture, that I ever beheld. Innumerable vessels gliding about, or rather driving one against another, filled with people gaily dressed—all appearing pleased with the show. But how false the appearance was in many instances, I myself can testify. Nevertheless the pageant had a temporary effect, in drawing off attention from individual sorrows.

The Princess went on board the Commissioner's yacht, where luncheon was prepared for her Royal Highness and her party, which consisted of Lord Aberdeen, Lord H. F[itzgeral]d, myself, and her ladies. Lord Aberdeen is said to be very wise, but he does not condescend to display his stores.

After spending two or three hours on board the yacht, the Princess said she must take us to see Charlton, where she had passed the happiest moments of her life ; and the tears rolled down her face as she spoke ;—those tears were genuine. We walked accordingly to Charlton. It is a very fine situation, only looking over the low county of Essex, it gives one an idea of marshy land, which makes one suspect it must be unhealthy.

When we returned to dinner at Blackheath, we found Lady O[xfor]d, Mr. Gell, Lord A. H[amilto]n, and Lady Jane Harley,* Sir H. Englefield, Miss Berry, Lord R[ivers], and Lady G[——]d. The latter is a most curious-looking woman, but I think she has sense and originality. I like Mr. Gell more and more every time I see him. He is so good-humoured, so unobtrusive, so ready to oblige, that, with his talents and temper, one overlooks a slight degree of vulgarity in his manners. Lord R[——] is less informed, less amiable ; but in him there is a native elegance, and his voice in singing is most melodious. What a charm there is in perfect high breeding !

To-day, Mr. P[——], an old friend, came to see me, and painfully awoke feelings that had long lain dormant. How seldom after an absence do we meet with any person whose heart makes response to our own ! Either they are colder, or their manners, at least, are different from what they were when we parted with them ; which makes them appear changed to us, whether they are in reality or not. I thought nine years had sadly altered him, and obliterated all remembrance of the past. But nine years efface many things :—it is the melancholy fate of every one who lives any time in the world, to prove this truth. After he was gone, I accompanied her Royal Highness, together with Mr. Craven, Mr. Mercer, and

* Afterwards Lady Langdale, a daughter of Lady Oxford.

Mr. Gell, and the Princess's ladies, to the British Museum. " Now," said the Princess, as she was getting into her carriage, " toss up a guinea, to know which shall be the happy two who are to come with me " ; but we had not a guinea amongst us, and the honour was assigned to Mr. Mercer and Mr. Craven. Mr. Gell, I saw, had rather have been one of them, for he blushed. Away we went. I was interested in walking through the magnificent library, and in looking at the statues ; yet whenever I view these collections my mind is depressed. I devoured with greedy eyes the outside of the volumes, and wished —oh ! how vainly—that their contents were stored in my brain. A whole life of learned labour would not suffice for that ; what chance have I then, in the middle of my days, of accomplishing such a wish ?—Then those beautiful statues, which, even in their mutilated state, testify the glorious conceptions of the minds that formed them ! Yes, they breathe the spirit of departed genius, and will continue to do so, to ages yet unborn ; but I— I shall leave nothing to excite one emulative sigh when I am gone ! I shall die, and nothing will tell of my existence ! But happier far are those who have never indulged a wish for fame. If a few who have loved us in life mourn us when dead, that is the only tribute to our memories which is, in fact, worth seeking for. Down, then, proud thought, of living in after ages ! be that which you are destined to be—fulfil the course which is pointed out by Providence, and be content. I have often wondered whether, to a youthful mind, it were an advantage or otherwise, to be led to view the highest works of art or literature at once, without previous preparation. If persons have great sensibility, I think it might rather be a discouragement. As the eye from which a cataract has been removed, cannot endure the broad beam of day, so a very young and tender mind should be gradually led on, as its own powers develope themselves, to the contemplation of the most sublime objects; not as it were made blind with light.

I was informed that two of Lord H[enry] F[itzgeral]d's children were dying. The Princess went to see him. Poor Lord H[enry] F[itzgerald] was in a state of despair, such as the fondest father only can feel. I like him; he is very amiable; but I regretted that her Royal Highness should have exposed herself and him,* by forcing her presence upon him at such a time. The world failed not to lay hold of the circumstance, and turned it to her disadvantage.

The next day, the Princess commanded me to accompany her to Lord A[berdeen]'s, at the Priory. I had not been at that place for many years. What a change those years had wrought in that family! All the younger branches were grown up; some of them become mothers; and there was *another* Lady A[berdee]n! The present one is reckoned agreeable and clever; but how unlike her predecessor in beauty and charm! Lord A[berdee]n † alone appeared unchanged, though all was changed around him; he sang, stalked about the room, and in short was *toujours lui*. He never will allow, I am told, any person to mention the children he has had the misfortune to lose. Alas! poor man, he does not foresee that soon another will drop into the grave. This wilful blindness to God's will is very awful. Lady M [Alice ?]

* On the Queen's trial, Lady Louisa Stuart wrote of the Princess of Wales's indiscretions : '' Common sense was not against her as it is at present, and the plea of her being deserted, deprived of her proper state and privileges, &c., so monstrous when urged as an excuse for associating with couriers and kitchen-maids, was fair enough to palliate more familiarity than suited a Princess towards Lord Henry Fitzgerald, Sir Sydney Smith, and Captain Manby.''

† George, 4th Earl of Aberdeen (1784–1860). He married, first, Lady Katherine Hamilton, who died 1812, and had three daughters, who all died in early youth, Lady Alice in April, 1829 ; and, secondly 1815, Harriet, Viscountess Hamilton, by whom he had issue. His mother, Catherine, daughter of Oswald Hanson of Wakefield, co. York, and widow of the 3rd Earl, died in 1817.

alone, of all the family, seems blooming and healthy.
I hope she at least will live. Altogether this visit was
not very pleasing to me ; I felt too much like St. Leon.
The trees even had grown out of all proportion to my
remembrance of them ; but that remembrance was
perfectly clear, and distinct ; it had been stamped into
my very being, and only gave a more strange effect to
my present sensations, contrasted as they were with
the actual scene.

July 27.—Slept restlessly and ill.   The past and the
present floated in a turbid stream of thought, and the
current glided so rapidly along, that I could not distinguish
the objects it bore upon its surface. My impression
was that of standing in the midst of a chafing, boiling
current, against which I was vainly endeavouring to
stand upright. The effect of this sort of waking dream
was intensely painful. 'Tis such nights that unfit us
for the days which are to follow.

Mr. T[——] again visited me ; but I sought in vain
for those traces of feeling, or any reference to the past,
which I fancied he would evince—I did not meet with
one. Paid a dull visit—what a pity it is when truth is
not accompanied by any charms ! Miss Smith, I think
it is, who has said, that to be dull and disagreeable is
high treason against virtue. To-day, saw Mrs. L[——]
looking like a rose, and her husband, like a sensitive
plant, sitting near her ; from the *Basse Cour* to the
garden was a delicious change. There is something very
interesting in Mr. L[——] ; but I believe it is because
he takes no interest in anything. Not that he is devoid
of affection for his wife and children ; but the finer
particles of his nature, those evanescent emanations of
spirit which are only cognizable to the very few, and
which thrive not unless under the influence of congenial
feelings, are dried up and withered within himself ; and

I should think can hardly be called to life again by any living object. Perhaps the very woman whom he first truly loved could no longer exercise that power over him which she once possessed, even were there no barriers to their re-union. The fair illusion which presented her all perfect to his fancy, existed only, it may be, in his imagination. When time withdrew that heavenly veil in which he had clothed her, here ended the romance, but not the longing after that, which he was destined never to find. It is to be lamented that no wholesome resolve has sprung up in its place, to recover the waste of life—the listless hours—the effeminacy—which too often succeeded to excitement. There are always honourable pursuits open to an aspiring mind, and there are realities in life which are worthy of the most noble and generous natures.

SECTION II

FEBRUARY 10th, 1811.—Of the many times in which I have commenced writing a journal, some reason or other has prevented its continuance, or at least thrown upon it that check, which diminishes the pleasure of writing, and renders the matter less interesting. If nobody is ever to read what one writes, there is no satisfaction in writing ; and, if any body does see it, mischief ensues. So I will not write a journal, but brief notes of such things as I conceive may be amusing, without incurring danger to myself or others.

I am sorry to observe that the poor Princess is losing ground every day, in the opinion of the public. There is a strong and a bitter party against her ; and she is always irritating some one or other of these persons, and drawing down upon herself an excuse for their malevolence by her imprudence. It is to be lamented that she has no intellectual pursuits ; that is the only safeguard against a love of intrigue. People must do something to amuse themselves ; and when they are not employed in any work worthy of the dignity of human nature, they will do mischief out of mere idleness.

The Princess often read aloud. It was difficult to understand her germanised French, and still more, her composite English. She was particularly amused at the Margravine de Bareith's Memoirs.* This lady was sister of Frederick the Great—Devil. In truth, they

* Harriet Lady Granville writes that she read these memoirs in 1812, and says of the Margravine, "Her descriptions, her abuse and her coarseness, put me much in mind of the Princess of Wales, whose early life was probably spent in much the same way."

33

were amusing, as all memoirs are that merely relate facts. Her Royal Highness told me that if she were to die, her papers would be all examined ; for which reason she had burned a great many, and that the rest—particularly the letters she had received from the Prince, either from himself, or written by his orders, previously to her having left Carlton House,—were in safe custody.

To-day, I had a letter from the most entertaining of all correspondents.* Lord Orford's is a joke to this epistolary phenomenon :—

CHRIST CHURCH, OXFORD, 15th March, 1811.

DEAR [——],—It vexes me extremely to think that I must have appeared so ungrateful to you (provided that you did me the honour to remember that there was such a person in existence) by not sooner performing my promise respecting the drawing which you were so good as to desire, and my gleanings which regard the family of [——]; but the truth is, that what with bad eyes, indifferent health, and a perpetual motion from one set of lodgings to another, I have scarcely been able to wield a pen, or open a book since I left London. Even now, my eyes feel as those of Juno's cow-boy must have done, when fixed upon her peacock's tail ; and my eyelids resemble in comfort a couple of hedgehog skins inverted. You must have seen a pair of dice in red leather dice-boxes ;—my optics exhibit exactly such a spectacle. Then my head aches as if I were *with child of Minerva every other day ;* though, alas ! there is but little of the goddess in that quarter. When I last arrived in Oxford, I found that my rooms had been demolished in my absence, and discovered all my articles of furniture and study in the most chaotic confusion : so I looked out for a new abode, carrying, with much pain and labour, my débris about with me. But here, the sitting-room was too small—there, too large ; in this place the chimney smoked, in that, the housemaid was slovenly, and the cat in love. I could settle with comfort nowhere. My luggage, however, like Æsop's basket, became lighter by degrees, as I left half-a-dozen things behind me at every

* Charles Kirkpatrick Sharpe (1781 ?–1851), the Scottish archæologist and antiquarian.

lodging which I relinquished, and I never could hear tidings of them after. In fine, I am at last fixed—laid by for awhile, like a poor slipper that hath been hunted through many unseemly places. I now send you the first fruits of my repose—a representation of Titania, with that little boy in her arms, concerning whom she hath a feud with her spouse in The Midsummer-Night's Dream. It is a wretched performance, but the best that my slender capacity can furnish; therefore, I beseech you to cast an eye of compassion on its deficiencies.

        *   *   *   *   *

Talking of books, we have lately had a literary Sun shine forth upon us here, before whom our former luminaries must hide their diminished heads—a Mr. Shelley, of University College, who lives upon arsenic, aqua-fortis, half-an-hour's sleep in the night, and is desperately in love with the memory of Margaret Nicholson. He hath published, what he terms, the Posthumous Poems, printed for the benefit of Mr. Peter Finnerty; which, I am grieved to say, though stuffed full of treason, are extremely dull; but the Author is a great genius, and, if he be not clapped up in Bedlam or hanged, will certainly prove one of the sweetest swans on the tuneful margin of the Charwell.

Our College of Christ Church is so full of noblemen at present, that one's eyes require green spectacles to preserve them from the glare of the golden tufts among these peers. The Dukes of Leinster and Dorset are pre-eminent, and both very good men, though the one will never head an Irish rebellion, nor the other write a poem quite so pretty as "To all you ladies now on land." The Irish Duke is much cried up for his beauty; but he does not strike me as being remarkably handsome, because his nose is fashioned like a monkey's, and he hath got what in Ireland is called "clober heels." As to Dorset, he is exactly like a sick Canary bird in a hard frost. All the milliners in the place admire Lord Herbert, while the wives of the Dean and Canons affect to admire Lord Apsley, he is so monstrous genteel and sickly.

Shelley's style is much like that of Moore burlesqued; for Frank is a very foul-mouthed fellow, and Charlotte, one of the most impudent brides that I ever met with in a book. Our Apollo next came out with a prose pamphlet in praise

of atheism, which I have not as yet seen ; and then appeared
a monstrous romance in one volume, called St. Ircoyne, or
the Rosicrucian.—Here is another pearl of price ! all the
heroes are confirmed robbers and causeless murderers ; while
the heroines glide *en chemise* through the streets of Geneva,
tap at the palazzo doors of their sweethearts, and on being
denied admittance leave no cards, but run home to their
warm beds, and kill themselves. If you would like to see
this treasure, I will send it. Shelley's last exhibition is a
Poem on the State of Public Affairs. I fear you will be
quite disgusted with all this stuff, so I shall discreetly make
an end, requesting you to believe me your faithful servant,

C. R.

1811.—The tide of time bears in its flux and reflux
many things away, and brings in others to supply their
place. Thus, as we glide down the current, this life
sometimes resembles a bleak and dreary shore ; at others,
the beautiful margin of some bounded sea, fringed with
wood, and clothed with luxuriant vegetation :—but still
'tis but a shore whose varying aspect, as we drift along,
reminds us that it is no fixed abode. But there is a land
of promise beyond the horizon of time, where time itself
will be as though it ne'er had been. As years fly swiftly
away never to be recalled, it is impossible but that, at
the return of the epoch which marks their flight, every
thinking being should pause, and reflect, and standing
as it were upon the isthmus which separates the past
from the future, trace out the path he has trod, and with
inquiring glance look on to that which he is yet to tread.
Regret, disappointment, misfortune, error, strew the
track of most earthly pilgrimages ; and happy are they
whose thorns and briers have not been self-planted,
and who can, amongst their griefs and sorrows, retain
in memory's store the faithful lineaments of some pure
happiness. To dwell long upon the irrevocable past,
is vain—repentance should be deep and sincere—by its
fruits the tree is known—so should its truth be proved :—

but to sink beneath the overwhelming nature of a gloomy self-reproach, to heap difficulties in our onwatd road, is to mar its best uses.

I draw the veil of private life upon one year. I have little to dwell upon during its progress, that does not bring pain along with it. Since the month of June last, my days have past in one uniform tenor ; but not thus has my mind rested in abeyance. No ! it has pondered deeply, and I find the result of these meditations to be, that religion and a future life are all that is really worth thinking about. The heart which acknowledges within it a hopeless vacuum—which has been disappointed in all its expectations, has burnt out its affections to the very ashes, and from nourishing every feeling to excess is forced to subside in the fixed calmness of indifference, and be content with common life,—such a heart must surely perish from inanition, if it aspire not to the life to come. " *Heureusement, quand les mystères de ce monde finissent, ceux de la mort commencent.*" I henceforth determine to live mentally to myself. My outward life will probably be a busy one ; the worldly characters and worldly vices, and strange stories that I may hear, shall be set down on paper, without many remarks of my own, for which I may have neither time nor inclination. *La vie intérieure* is another thing.

Saturday, the 4th of [——], 1811.—Saw Sir Walter Farquhar.* He had been dining with the Regent, as he had been obliged to do for a week past. He would not say all he *could* have said ; but, from what I gathered, it is evident he thinks as all those must think who have access to know the truth ; namely, that a long course of indulgence has at last undermined his Royal Highness's constitution, both mentally and physically speaking.

* Physician to the Prince Regent. Created a Baronet March 1, 1796 ; died March 21st, 1819.

It is given out that the Regent has got spasms in his arms, owing to his having leaned on his elbows at the time he sprained his arm, to save himself from pressing on his ancle! What egregious nonsense! But the same sort of stuff has always been said concerning Princes, whenever they were to be sick or well, to suit public or private concerns.

    *   *   *   *   *

The Ministers now in power are in fact the Regent. The Regent dares not say nay, even when he secretly disagrees with them, as he knows that if the limitation placed by them were taken off, he would be utterly overwhelmed by the host of persons to whom he has made promises, that he neither can nor will fulfil. For this reason, whenever the Regent has been called upon to come forward and act, the public papers have always made the unfortunate Monarch better, in order that there might be a plausible pretext in bringing forward filial duty, as virtuous forbearance, and making excuses for deferring that which he himself dreads ;—namely, the possession of the power to fulfil promises he has no longer the inclination to keep. I think the party who have looked up so long to him cannot continue to be thus gulled without showing their teeth ;—in fact, the throne totters, and the country which has hitherto supported it, is not steady. In the language of Scripture, it " reels to and fro, and staggers like a drunken man."

To-day, I was again one of the guests at Kensington. The Princess Charlotte was there. She is grown excessively, and has all the fulness of a person of five-and-twenty. She is neither graceful nor elegant, yet she has a peculiar air, *et tous les prestiges de la royauté et du pouvoir*. In spite of the higher powers of reason and of justice, these always cast a dazzling lustre, through which it is difficult to see the individuals as they really are. The Princess Charlotte is above the middle height, extremely spread for her age ; her bosom full, but finely shaped ; her shoulders large, and her whole person voluptuous ; but of a nature to become soon spoiled, and without much care and exercise she will shortly lose all beauty in fat and clumsiness. Her skin is white, but not a transparent white ; there is little or no shade in her face ; but her features are very fine. Their expression, like that of her general demeanour, is noble. Her feet are rather small, and her hands and arms are finely moulded. She has a hesitation in her speech, amounting almost to a stammer ; and additional proof, if any were wanting, of her being her father's own child ; but in every thing, she is his very image. Her voice is flexible, and its tones dulcet, except when she laughs ; then it becomes too loud, but is never unmusical. She seems to wish to be admired more as a lovely woman than as a Queen. Yet she has quickness, both of fancy and penetration, and would fain reign despotically, or I am much mistaken. I fear that she is capricious, self-willed, and obstinate. I think she is kind-hearted, clever and enthusiastic. Her faults have evidently never been checked, nor her virtues fostered. The " generous purpose " may have risen in her breast, but it has never been *fixed there*. How much does every day's experience convince me, that from the crowned head to the labouring peasant, no fine qualities are truly valuable, without a fixed principle, to bind them together and give them stability !

The Princess Charlotte was excessively gracious to me ; the wind blew my way " *wooingly*," but that was all. Never was a truer word spoken by man, than that Princes *are a race à part*.

I cannot conceive why the Princess of Wales should dislike that any friend of hers should become intimate with her mother's lady, Madame de Haeckle. I met the latter to-day, but found that this short visit was all the communication I was ever to have with her, if I desired to retain the favour of her Royal Highness. I conclude, therefore, she knows more than is wished.

Lord L[ucan] has been paying her Royal Highness great court lately. I fear perhaps that when she broke with her former counsellor she made a confidant of this man, and so she has fallen into his power, and he is making a tool of her. I see by the great fuss she has made, and the curiosity she has evinced about the Duke of D[evonshire],* that Lord L[ucan] has been schooling her Royal Highness respecting his Grace. But what a weak man Lord L[ucan] was, to suppose that he will ever marry his daughter to the Duke through her means. The Princess naturally wishes it : first, for the amusement of having something to occupy her ; and, secondly, thinking, I suppose, to gain in her turn, through Lord L[ucan]'s interest, a powerful friend and supporter in the Duke of D[evonshire], should he become the Prince's son-in-law. How little do all these people know of the matter they are fighting about ! I know not much, but I think better of him than to suppose he would be the tool of such machinations. The more I see of courts and of the world, the more I wish to escape their polluting influence. The spirit of intrigue which reigns around, the petty passions and debasing contrivances which take place in them, are apt to deaden the finer qualities, both of heart and head. The danger is, lest they should become wholly crushed and withered.

Her Royal Highness talked a great deal of the D[evonshire]s as a family, knowing nothing at all about them. She abused and denigréd the ladies, and repeated all that Mr. G[——] had once told her of their being false friends. This gossip she related in her favourite way, saying—a person once told *her*, that another person,

* William, 6th Duke of Devonshire (1790–1858). He never married.

a gentleman, a friend of both parties, told *him*, that one of the ladies had spoken very ill of *a lady* she pretends to like. If this is true, it is a pity, and I have other reasons for thinking there may be some truth in the story; but who can aver that they have not themselves been occasionally guilty of saying unkind or pettish things of a friend? If everything was repeated, what would become of society? *Le palais de la vérité* would be a hell upon earth. The Princess further went on to say, that she had been credibly informed, "I tell you God's truth," (her favourite expression) "when the second Duchess of D.* was at C[hiswic]k, she spent about twelve hundred pounds in five weeks, and, on the Duke's man of business representing that measures should be taken to regulate the household, the Duchess took offence, and immediately went away. That was the only way of settling the business. But what is very odd," continued the Princess, "is, that in arranging her future furniture, &c., the family diamonds were not appointed to any one. Sir S[amuel] R[omelly] gave it as his opinion, that they, in consequence, became the Duchess's, being considered as part of her paraphernalia; but the comical part of all the story is that she wrote a letter to the D[uke], saying, for his sake, his sister's sake, and all their sakes, she should take the diamonds, but that if he ever married, her Grace would return them to his wife. Vat did she mean?—tell me dat riddle." Every body laughed at the Princess's amusing way of telling a story.

Mrs. A[preece] and Mr. Davy dined with her Royal Highness. I also was of the party. I had never yet become acquainted with this celebrated man, so I took his superior abilities upon trust. His superior ugliness I know by ocular demonstration.—Mrs. A[preece] seems tinctured with something like love. I wonder if he will

* Lady Elizabeth Foster, *née* Hervey, daughter of the Earl of Bristol, Bishop of Derry.

analyze the sentiment.* In the evening, the Princess went to the Duchess of Brunswick's. I am not permitted to talk to Madame de Haeckle, or I should be very much amused. But no,—that is forbidden ground; and, whenever we attempt conversation, the Royalties interfere, and there is an end of it. If ever I might converse with the old Duchess of Brunswick freely, there is such a pleasure in pleasing, and it is so easy to please an old person, that from that source also I could derive interest. But I must not. There is a hardness of manner in the Princess towards her mother, unlike her general demeanour to others, which sometimes revolts me.

Her Royal Highness once read through the whole of *Candide* to one of her ladies, who told me her opinion of it, which does her honour. She said,—"its character as a work of extreme cleverness has been so long established that to venture in the least to detract from it, is to encounter the ridicule of a multitude. I must say, however, that the persiflage which reigns throughout, and in which its whole essence consists, is not consonant to my taste or understanding. Vicious subjects ought not to be treated lightly; they merit the coarsest clothing, and ought to be arrayed in language which would create abhorrence and disgust. But the whole works seems designed to turn vice into virtue. Either it has no aim or end, or it has one which should be loathed. It must be confessed, however, that the tripping levity of its self-assurance, and the sarcastic drollery of its phrase, excite laughter; but it is a poor prerogative after all, to be the mental buffoon of ages."

Though I, perhaps, have more indulgence for Voltaire, in consideration of his vast talents, than my friend, yet I admired the *woman* who thought and spoke thus; and her Royal Highness is fortunate in having such a friend. But I fear princes and princesses do not suffer

* Afterwards Sir Humphry Davy, and who married Mrs. A[preece].

those who are inclined to be their true friends to be so long.

To-day, I was admitted to the Duchess of Brunswick, to pay my respects in a morning visit, and had a *tête-à-tête* interview. I found her sitting, as usual, in the middle of her empty dull room. It is wonderful how little power *locale* has over some persons, and how much it affects others. She made my heart ache for her, poor old soul, when she said, " I have nothing to love ; no one loves me ! "—Alas !—what a picture of human wretchedness did that short sentence comprise ! I have had too much reason to know since, that she spoke the truth. The heart that thus seeks in vain for some reciprocal affection, must either break or become callous. I know not which is the preferable alternative.

About this time, her Royal Highness the Princess of Wales was introduced, by a very injudicious friend of hers, to a set of low persons, totally unfitting her private society :—viz., three singers, the father, mother, and son ; * and also a number of people belonging to a school, whom her Royal Highness allowed and encouraged to treat her very disrespectfully. This at first originated in her love of ease and indolence, which is indulged by living with persons of inferior rank ; but in after-times I much fear there were other reasons for submitting to such an unworthy set of people.

The Princess sent for me to execute a commission, of selling two enormous unset diamonds. I did not like the office, and cannot understand what could induce her Royal Highness to part with them, or why she should be in difficulty for any sum of money which she can

---

* Italian musicians named Sapio. The father and son are mentioned in this Diary as " The Old Ourang-Outang " and " Chanticleer " respectively. Mme. de Boigne in her Memoirs writes of her lessons with " Sappio, formerly music-master to the Queen of France," and describes him as much being sought after, as was his wife, " a very pleasant little person and a good musician."

reasonably want. Is she then drained by the old [——]
and will her eyes never be opened to his rapaciousness ?
or is there a worse reason ?

I went yesterday to Mrs. N[——], paid a long visit,
and asked to see her children, and admired them by
words, but cared not two-pence for them—poor little
ugly things ! What duplicity does the civilization of
mankind naturally impose ! So I sometimes think,
and turn from myself and others equally disgusted.
But as there must be *de la petite monnaie*—base coin
though it be,—this currency of dross is only received
as it is given :—and besides, as long as we do not do
anything base or wicked in order to please, it *is* amiable
to please, even at the expense of sincerity.

I took the diamonds with which I had been entrusted
to several jewellers ; one man offered only a hundred
and fifty pounds for them. I knew this was ridiculous,
and so I restored them to her Royal Highness :—what
became of them I know not, but this I do know, that one
of the jewellers, by referring to his books, declared that
they were jewels belonging to the Crown.

Received an invitation from her Royal Highness to
go to Brandenburgh House. When I arrived, I found
her walking in her garden with Lord L[——]. Shortly
after, he went away, and her Royal Highness talked
over the present state of politics and royal feuds. She
was low, but not subdued in spirit ; wounded, but not
malignant. She related with great spirit and drollery
the visit of the Queen to the Duchess of Brunswick, and
told me that when she, the Princess of Wales, was at
her mother's the other day, the old lady * said in her
blunt way, " Madame de Haeckle, you may have a day

---

* It is difficult to understand how a mother could like to affront
her own child ; but such are the unnatural discrepancies in the human
character, in that of princes particularly ; for on the whole the Duchess
of Brunswick was a kind-hearted woman. [Original note.]

to yourself on Wednesday next, for the Prince has invited me to dine at Carlton House, and he will not suffer any lady-attendants to go there ; and, as my son accompanies me, I shall not want you." This speech astonished all present except her daughter, who had been apprised by the Duke of Kent that such an invitation would take place. It was so unfeeling to announce this with an air of triumph to the Princess of Wales, that but for the poor Duchess being very weak, and easily gulled, one must have conceived her to be devoid of all heart. This speech was followed by a general cessation of all conversation, Madame de Haeckle only looking dismayed. The Duchess of Brunswick first broke silence by turning suddenly to her daughter and saying, " Do you think I should be carried upstairs on my cushion ? " To which the Princess replied with great coolness, " There is no upstairs, I believe ;—the apartments are all on one floor." " Oh, charming, that is delightful ! " rejoined the Duchess ; and with a few more queries, to which the Princess always replied with the greatest self-possession and sang-froid, as though she was not in the least hurt, this strange royal farce ended.

The Duke of Brunswick, however, came to the Princess his sister, and said, " This must not be. You must not suffer her to think of going." Accordingly, Lady G[——] was despatched the next morning, with a long letter written by the Princess to her mother, explaining to her that if she went to Carlton House, her presence there would seem like a tacit acknowledgment that she was satisfied with the Prince's conduct to her daughter ; that he was in the right ; and that she, the Princess, merited the treatment he gave her. Lady G[——] read the letter to the Duchess, then by word of mouth confirmed the contents, and further commented thereon ; but the Duchess was immoveable in her intention, and persisted in going. " No," said she, " I see the business quite in another point of view from what you do ; I love my daughter above all things, and would do any thing in the world for her ; but I must go to Carlton House." Lady G[——] continued in earnest converse and entreaty with her for two hours, but nothing appeared to move the old lady from her determination. When weary and worn, the ambassadress was about to depart, the Duchess cried out—" No, no ; tell her I love her of all things, but give her no hopes on this subject. The Princess has a jewel in you; you have done your embassy well; but give her no hopes."

" *Eh bien !* " said the Princess, continuing her narration of this curious scene, and drawing her breath as she usually does when she is angry, " I gave the matter up, and thought that, like many other things, it could not be helped ; when the next day I received a letter from my mother saying, ' Far be it from me to do anything contrary to your interests ; and hearing that there is a doubt upon the subject, I shall not go to Carlton House.' This resolve astonished me as much as my mother's previous determination, and I immediately wrote to say how grateful I was to her ; in proof of which, I begged to dine with her the next day, and added that I should take no notice of what had passed." " Accordingly," she continued, " nothing was said upon the subject, and there the business ended ; but was there ever such an idea entered a mother's head ! " added the Princess. " It was so evidently a trap, that was set to inveigle the poor old Duchess into a tacit condemnation of *me !* "

The one half of human life is generally passed in giving oneself wounds, the other in healing them. Lady M[——], whom I conveyed in my carriage to her lone empty house, left a sadness in my mind. She has not perhaps one real friend among all the numerous worldly persons calling themselves such, for whom she has sacrificed her affections and her life. Her tastes are of the most extravagant kind, and above her fortune, and her mind has been too long suffered to waste itself in desultory pursuits after phantoms, to be able to recover its tone, and derive from its own resources that interest which the world can neither give nor take away.   Yet I think her case peculiarly hard. Lady H[——] ought never to have forsaken her.   But she is one of the many who have loved and lived in vain.

I was sent for to Kensington : found her Royal Highness talking to Dr. Moseley and Lady A[nne] H[amilto]n.* I overheard her say to the latter, " Now, dear Lady Anne, take Dr. Moseley and show him the apartments above stairs."   I undertsood what that meant, and that my visit must be *tête-à-tête*. I trembled, for I fear it is in vain to do her any good.   She came to me ; and having spoken a few phrases on different subjects, produced all the papers she wishes to have published :—her whole correspondence with the Prince relative to Lady J[ersey]'s dismissal ; his subsequent neglect of the Princess ; and, finally, the acquittal of her supposed guilt, signed by the Duke of Portland, &c., at the time of the secret inquiry, —when, if proof could have been brought against her, it certainly would have been done ; and which acquittal, to the disgrace of all parties concerned, as well as to the justice of the nation in general, was not made public at the time.   A common criminal is publicly condemned or acquitted.   Her Royal Highness commanded me to have these letters published forthwith, saying, " You may sell them for a great sum."   At first, (for she had spoken to me before, concerning this business,) I thought

---

* Lady Anne Hamilton (1766–1846), one of the maids of honour to the Princess of Wales, eldest daughter of Archibald, 9th Duke of Hamilton. She was the " Lank Lady Anne " of Theodore Hook's scurrilous songs. To her great distress, a book, " Secret History of the Court of England from the Accession of George III. to the Death of George IV.," full of scandalous anecdotes about the Court, was published in 1832 under her name, but it is generally supposed to have been inspired by Mary Anne Clarke, the former mistress of the Duke of York.

of availing myself of the opportunity; but, upon second thoughts, I turned from this idea with detestation; for, if I do wrong by obeying her wishes and endeavouring to serve her, I will do so at least from good and disinterested motives, not from any sordid views. The Princess commands me, and I will obey her, whatever may be the issue, but not for fare or fee. I own, I tremble, but not so much for myself as for the idea that she is not taking the best and most dignified way of having these papers published.—Why make a secret of it at all? If wrong, it should not be done; if right, it should be done openly and in the face of her enemies. In her Royal Highness's case, as in that of wronged princes in general, why do they shrink from straightforward dealings, and rather have recourse to crooked policy? I wish in this particular instance I could make her Royal Highness feel thus; but she is naturally indignant at being falsely accused, and will not condescend to an avowed explanation. She wishes her cause to be espoused by others. This appears to me a very false pride. But were I to propose to her Royal Highness to place this affair in other and abler hands than my own, she would suppose that I shrink from the task. Now, that is not the case; whatever imprudence there may be, there is no dishonour in the service I am about to render her; let me not, therefore, seem to wish to avoid it.

Shortly after, for some reason or other, which never came to my knowledge, I was spared all further anxiety upon the subject, as other parties stepped forward, and her Royal Highness, knowing that I would not profit by the transaction, permitted her papers to be placed in their hands.

Friday, October 21st.—Yesterday, the melancholy Lady M[——] came to see me. I was obliged to go to Kensington by appointment, so I could not take Lady M[——]

with me in the carriage, and she walked away on foot.
I was quite grieved at heart for her. She was more
depressed in spirit than ever. When I arrived at the
palace, her Royal Highness was standing at the window,
evidently awaiting my arrival impatiently. She finished
reading to me the rest of the papers and correspondence,
which occupy at present so much of her thoughts.—I
have never known a more extraordinary person than the
Princess. She writes occasionally with much spirit, and
many of the copies of her letters to the Prince are both
clever and touching. Sometimes, there is a series of
exalted sentiment in what she says and does, that quite
astonishes me, and makes me rub my eyes and open my
ears, to know if it is the *same* person who condescends
to talk low nonsense, and sometimes even gross ribaldry.
One day, I think her all perfection—another, I know not
what to think. The tissue of her character is certainly
more uneven than that of any other person I was ever
acquainted with. One day, there is tinsel and tawdry—
another, worsted—another, silk and satin—another,
gold and jewels—another *de la boue, de la crasse,—que
dirai-je ? et peut-être j'ai trop dit.*

I have so often determined to write a consecutive
journal, and have so often failed, not from idleness,
which is not my besetting sin, but from the danger of
telling all I think—all I know—that I have shrunk back
into silence, and thought it better, wiser perhaps, to
forget entirely the passing events of the day, than to
record them.

After the examination of the papers, I was desired to
remain during luncheon. Lady A[nne] H[amilto]n was
the lady-in-waiting, and she was sent for to attend. I
believe the Princess has told the whole story to her, and
as she is very fond of secrets, I make no doubt she has
heard them all in their details. Then there are other
ladies who, I shrewdly suspect, have also been admitted

I   D

to this confidence. Most women, indeed, think a secret
not worth knowing, if one may not tell it to a dozen or
two intimate friends. To own the truth, I am a very
bad hand at keeping secrèts myself, and my best chance
of doing so is the great facility with which I forget them.
Nothing that does not interest my heart, or my passions,
has any great hold on my imagination or thoughts. I
am only vulnerable through my affections. My weal and
woe lie all in that quarter ; what then can it have in
common with a court ?

Saturday, the 28th October, 1811.—Yesterday, Sir
Walter F[arquhar] came and told me a curious conversation which he had held the night before with the
Prince Regent. " Well, F[arquha]r, so you were paying
your court to the Princess of Wales at Tonbridge, I
hear ? " (alluding to the day he went there last May,
when she spoke to Sir Walter.) The Baronet :—" Yes,
Sir, her Royal Highness was very gracious to me, and I
thought it my duty to shew the Princess of Wales every
respect ; but I did not stay to supper, though she was
graciously pleased to invite me ; because I thought, if
your Royal Highness heard of it, you might not have
been pleased." Regent—" What did she say to you ? "
" She asked me, Sir, why I had not advised the Princess
Charlotte to go to the sea side for change of air,—saying
' it would do her Royal Highness a great deal of good,'
and insisted upon it that I ought to do so." " And what
did you reply ? " eagerly questioned the Prince. " I replied,
Sir, that when I had last the honour of seeing her Royal
Highness the Princess Charlotte, she was in such perfect
health that she appeared not to require any medical
advice ; consequently, it would be highly improper that I
should interfere. ' Oh, Sir Walter F[arquhar],' rejoined the
Princess of Wales, ' you are a courtier ' ; and we both
laughed." Regent—" Was that all ? "—" Yes, Sir, that

was all—stay, another word I recollect; when the Princess first did me the honour to speak to me, she said 'I know you dare not, you must not speak to me'; to which I answered, 'Pardon me, Madam, I never had any orders from the Prince not to speak to the Princess of Wales."

At this, Sir Walter said, the Prince seemed pleased. Persons, however lost to rectitude, are not lost to the sense of it ; and he felt that the meaning of these words was, what *he ought to feel*, and what his friend ought to have answered. The Prince then observed, "'I hear Lady Charlotte Campbell is very tired of her situation "; to which Sir Walter replied, " That he had never known Lady Charlotte to have expressed such a sentiment." Here the conversation ended.

Sir Walter told me that by what he could gather from all the Carlton House courtiers, he thought it most likely, if any question came on in Parliament, respecting an additional allowance for the Princess, it would be favourably received.   This looks, I think, as if they were afraid her wrongs might, if not redressed, in pecuniary matters, at least, raise a strong party in her favour, and what is worse for the ministers and placemen, *against* the Prince. Unfortunately, (I say unfortunately, because the dissensions of all families, and more especially of royal families, frequently lead to incalculable evils, and often overturn kingdoms, and principalities, and powers,)— unfortunately, the Princess of Wales cannot become popular without the Prince of Wales becoming the reverse; for the odium which is taken from her, must of necessity fall upon him ; and this, in these changeable times, when the dregs of the nation are all shaken into commotion, is anything but desirable.   Who can say where discontent may end, if it once lift up its hydra head ; or whether redress of public grievances, even if they be really such, and not innovations, may not lead to the ultimate subversion and overthrow of the constitution ?   Yet, on the other hand, a blind and bigoted adherence to the past, and a venal Parliament, who are slaves to the monarch and his minions, are not less dangerous.—No, the lungs of Englishmen will not breathe freely under a corrupt government ; and, though evil spirits ever have arisen, and ever will arise, when the tempest breaks forth, yet, to submit to present evil for fear of greater danger, is not the characteristic of the nation ; though it has long shewn patience with its rulers even under discontent at their supineness.   This century will not pass without many awful changes.   We are come to a crisis.   Nothing stands still in this world— our prosperity has reached its highest point—all things now tend to change.   What leads me more particularly to think so is, the blindness of those in power.   "Whom the gods mean to destroy, they blind" ; and in all events of magnitude, whether in social life or in that of nations, the truth of this observation is exemplified.   The security, the self-sufficiency of princes and their creatures, and above all, the blindness of princes themselves, offer a forcible comment upon this remark.

I grieve to think that the Princess of Wales is obstinately bent upon bringing forward her wrongs and her complaints at this moment.   She will only, now, be made the tool of party.   Had she waited till her daughter was of age, to have backed her cause, and supported it with filial love, as well as by the influence which a young heir-apparent Queen would necessarily exercise over the minds of her future subjects, then she might have succeeded.   But as it is—alas ! alas ! all public, like private greatness, rests its security on moral rectitude ; and where that is deficient, the edifice is built on sand.   No marvel, that those who are denominated *the vulgar* should be so taken by the bait of rank and greatness.   Rank and greatness are in themselves truly admirable ; real greatness, in its original and highest sense, is an attribute of the Divinity, and earthly grandeur is the visible sign by which it is presented to our senses. The misfortune is, that there is hardly such an image of the Divinity existing as true greatness.

My pen has never before busied itself with such a subject, but my situation naturally makes me sometimes reflect upon things, from which I turn away with pleasure to the illusory world that I have created for myself—that *vie intérieure* which is worth all the rest,—and to those simple realities which nature and natural pleasures afford.

I went this evening to a friend of mine, Miss B[——]: this person, whom I have known so long and esteem so highly, has not always a winning manner, and certainly every now and then talks to her friends in a way that is not pleasant. The love that is much stronger on the one side than on the other, is always painful to witness. As to myself, the natural suavity of my manner and temper (no praise, since it is constitutional)—a suavity that I sometimes blame myself for, when it induces me to gloss over sentiments to which a more bold frame of mind would express its dislike or abhorrence,—imparts somewhat of its own nature to those with whom I associate ; and, with those of my friends in whose tempers and manners the angular and sharp predominate, I am less apt to *heurter* myself against them, than they are against each other. This I felt yesterday evening. But if my friend, Miss B[——] sacrifices somewhat to the world, it must be said to her honour, that that sacrifice is never kindness of heart or integrity of character. It is not always in our power to be generous, or to render great services ; but it is always in our power to soothe a mind and exhilarate spirits less fortunately constituted than our own ; and I do not feel it to be lost time when I have dedicated some hours to such a purpose, or at least to the attempt.

Went again to Miss B[——]. Sir Humphry and Lady Davy were there. Sir Humphry, accustomed to adulation, seems to fall into surliness or dulness where he meets it not ;—his allowed pre-eminence in the science of chemistry places him in that respect above every one ; but I never could find that there was great superiority in other respects. No person moving in the same sphere as myself, is less liable to be led away to like, or dislike, persons who are a little (more or less) vulgar in point of manner ; but there is a peculiar degree of under breeding in Sir Humphry, which is indicative of inferiority of intellect. I believe this proceeds from his always trying to be what he is not, a *joli cœur*. If every body would only be *natural !* but it is natural to some people to be affected. Lady Davy makes what I call a *douce société*. I never in my life heard her speak ill of any person ; she is frank and kind-hearted, and has much acquirement, with a wish and thirst for more, which it is pleasing to see. Anything, even a perpetual bustle after knowledge, is preferable to the careless and dreaming way in which some persons pass their insignificant lives ; pampering every appetite, and never cultivating the only spark of being they ought to be proud of, the intellectual one, without which the animals are our superiors. Yet how many of those who form what is called *good society* are sunk in this sensual sloth !

Wednesday, 28th of October.—Dined at Fish Crawfurd's,* an old epicure and *bon vivant*, but one who has seen much of the world. He has lived with all the celebrated people of his time, Madame Du Deffand, Voltaire, Hume, &c., &c., and he seems to remember with pleasure that he has done so, though gout and the consequences of indulgence render him crabbed and complaining.

* John Crawfurd, grandson of Mr. Middleton, the founder of Coutts's Bank.

His table, his house, are most luxurious, but his own
dissatisfied mind, his emaciated body, and bloated face,
give the lie to happiness. I have ever felt that old age,
even in its least respectable form, is still to be respected,
and I have a peculiar pleasure in pleasing old people.
I reckon, that yesterday's dinner was a lesson ; there
was elegance, luxury, all that can flatter the fancy with
well chosen and appropriate objects, as well as the palate,
—but pleasure—happiness—where was it?   Does it sit
at the board of the epicurean ?—is it enthroned in purple
and fine linen ?—No. A very modified quantum of
these, with vigour of mind and body, a fair and honourable pursuit, a goal in view, and contentment at one's
right hand, be it gained or not ;—these are, I believe, the
best ingredients to form the mixed good which men have
agreed to call happiness. It was melancholy to observe
this old man, in the possession of all which can gratify
human desires, and yet repining, and in fact, wretched
—a Tantalus, with the cup of enjoyment at his lip. But
there are many such,—how many ! There ever have
been, there ever will be such, so long as people live to
themselves alone.

The Princess said, that the complaints made in Parliament, of the government's not having sent over supplies
to Lord Wellington in the number, and with the celerity
he demanded them, looked like an *avant-propos* for more
complaints, and would end by Lord Wellesley's becoming
prime minister ; " then," said she, " blood and treasure
would not be spared, and the constitution and country
will be lost."

I see many other reasons for the ruin of the country,
but those who might do good are blind. Lord Moira is
sent off to India ;—I call it being sent off, for it is evident
the Regent cannot bear to have him near his person.
How few people, in any rank of life, have sufficient
nobility of soul to love those to whom they stand indebted !

Would you lose a friend, oblige him—not in the minor circumstances of life; but let the obligation be vast, and it crushes friendship to death. Lord Moira has accepted this honourable banishment, because he cannot help himself, and is ruined. But who ruined him? He lent uncounted sums of money in former years, of which no note whatever was taken, and of which he never will see one farthing in return. Yet no one pities or feels for this man. Why?—because he is of nobler stuff than the common herd. Vanity and ambition were his only flaws, if flaws they be; but his attachment, or rather devotion, to the Regent was sincere, chivalric, and of a romantic kind, such as the world neither believes in nor understands; it was a kind of affection which amounted even to a passion of the mind, and, like all passions, led him into one or two acts beneath the "*chevalier sans peur et sans reproche.*" But nevertheless, he is a noble creature upon the whole; and what can poor human nature ever be more? Formed to live in another day than the present, some men seem born too late, and some men too soon; but perhaps the only wise men are those who fulfil their course at the time, and in the manner, which providence has pointed out for them; suiting their conduct and their actions to the present, rather than indulging in speculative theories for the future, or vain regrets for the past,—neither of which can they judge with truth—for former times are seen through the medium of other men's minds, and the future belongs to the All-seeing eye alone. If the present moment be ever well employed, the by-gone, and the *to come*, will take care of themselves.

Very frequently, the dinners at Kensington were exceedingly agreeable, the company well chosen, and sufficient liberty was given to admit of their conversing with unrestrained freedom. This expression does not imply a licentious mode of conversation; although sometimes, in favour of wit, discretion and modesty were trenched upon. Still that was by no means the general turn of the discourse. Mr. Gell and Mr. Craven, in particular, though often very droll, were never indecorous. I think I never knew a man of a more kind and gentle turn of mind, nor one so humanized by literature and the particular pursuits to which he devoted himself, as Mr. Gell. He was affectionate in the highest degree, and willing to impart all he knew, (no common stock of information,) in the least pedantic and most agreeable manner ; and if ever he indulged in a joke that was questionable, it was in a manner so devoid of real vice, that the most punctilious or delicate female could scarce take offence at it. Mr. Craven likewise, his intimate friend, without possessing the strength of mind and the classical knowledge of Mr. Gell, was full of talent, and all those lighter acquirements which adorn, if they do not instruct society.

To-day, I received another letter from my amusing friend, C. K. S.*

CHRIST CHURCH, OXFORD, *October*, 1811.

DEAR [——],—What can I say to the generous return for my abominable scribbles, which you have made me by your delightful letter ? I cannot for my life think of another case than the bounty of the outlandish queen, who gave a heap of diamonds for a wash-hand basin ;—which was a sin of ignorance ;—as when Lady Strathmore married Bowes,† or C[lementin]a D[rummon]d, P[ete]r B[urrel]l. Oh! heavens, I forget myself—do not tell [——]. I wish that I had as many eyes as Fame, or Argus, or a spider, which I am told hath eight. Alas! that Lady D[ougla]s, who is the very

* Charles Kirkpatrick Sharpe.
† Mary Eleanor Bowes, Countess Dowager of Strathmore, married secondly, Andrew Robinson Stoney, of Coldpig Hall, co. Durham, who took her name. Clementina Drummond, daughter and heiress of James, Lord Perth, married, in 1807, Peter Burrell, 2nd Baron Gwydir. He succeeded, however, on his mother's death as 21st Baron Willoughby de Eresby.

reverse of a spider in every thing but her industry, hath but one !—Oh ! that I possessed as many hands as Briareus, or some of the Hindoo gods, that I might produce a weekly drawing, provided my humble efforts were crowned with such a rich reward about once a quarter, as your epistles are calculated to bestow ! But lack-a-day ! my eyes, which scarcely can be called a pair, demand a string like a doll's, in the simple operation of turning, and my fingers are about as unwieldy as an Irishman's legs in the gout. Nevertheless, I am resolved, in spite of Nature and my stars, to write, that is, to wield a goose-quill in your service, as long as I possess a little more vision than the mole, and energies that may in any measure rival those of the unfortunate sloth. In truth, the honour of any command or employment from you is sufficient to transform a sloth into a squirrel ; for I must tell you, my dear fellow, that you are one of the most extraordinary personages of the present time. Perhaps you did not know it before,—but only consider a little. In the first place, nothing can be more honourable and illustrious than your family, and your rank is suitable to it. You do not resemble some very fine and lofty persons of my acquaintance, who, however high their place may now be, had merchants and mechanics for their fathers ; and *middens*, I guess, for their grandsires. Then Nature seems to have run hiddygiddy in your formation ; for she made you noble, too, in mind, and, moreover, gave you a voice of unexampled power and sweetness,—which, in my humble opinion, is one of her greatest bestowments. And here allow me just to hint at your scientific pursuits, and, in short, whatever is praiseworthy, and fitting the true dignity of human nature ; all of which is wonderful in any body, but in one so spoiled, so favoured, I should say perfectly prodigious ! As to your more exalted merits, I shall not particularize them, my rude pen being altogether unworthy ; only this I may say, that if, according to the chances of this world, you have not always so many superfluities as King Montezuma, who reclined upon a bed of roses,—yet your pious fortitude and resignation have given a wholesome lesson to your inferiors, and added graces to yourself.

From all that I have ever heard or seen, I am convinced that you were intended to make as conspicuous a figure in

the next world as in this, and that a sentence in the funeral
sermon of Mary, Duchess of Queensberry, who was a very
exalted character, might with great justice be applied to you.
The preacher says, " But dry up your tears, my brethren, and
weep no more for this most illustrious Princess, who, though
she was a great and good Duchess on earth, is now a great
and good Duchess in Heaven." This is not very neat, but
it is all very true ; so that I may say with the clown, in
Measure for Measure, " here be truths."

Alas !—your account of London, I shall not for a great
while experience the truth of, as when I leave this place I
must repair to Scotland, where I am to remain for ages :—

> To me the gods, severely kind, ordain
> A cool suspense from pleasure and from pain.

However, as the dulness you mentioned must exist in the
mass of people, (for it cannot possibly be in you,) I must try
to extract a sour-grape comfort from the consideration, that
London is not what it was.—Meanwhile, be it known unto
you that the ingenious Mr. Shelley hath been expelled from
the University, on account of his atheistical pamphlet. Was
ever such bad taste and barbarity known ? He behaved like
a hero, " he showed to Fortune's frowns a brow serene," and
declared his intention of emigrating to America. I send his
romance, which would have reached you sooner had not an
impudent person cribbed it from my rooms. I also transmit
Octavian, and a volume of poems written by a friend of mine.
He is, poor fellow ! in the last stage of a consumption ; so
the critics should be merciful, for he will never write better,
nor worse, (which is of more consequence to brother authors,)
and a death-bed repentance of such literary crimes is as
bitter as it is useless.

Doubtless, after this cargo of Oxford goods, you will exclaim, " Enough, enough, no more of it, *de grace !* " I am
not wise in sending you such a dose at once ; for I fear that
our poetical fervours will prove little better than camomile,
only not so wholesome, and that you will never more endure
the sight of such another *bouquet*. I transmit my treasures
of Parnassus by the coach, but this shall move per post, as I
am ever dubious concerning the delivery of small parcels in
London ; and, though my books and my letters be of little

consequence, yet I would fain not appear wanting in respect where so very much is due.

I have finished your portrait ; and it is not like, so I have met the fate of all my painting predecessors.   Yet, to catch *your* likeness would not be quite impossible, if this system of galvanism could be improved, and four painters of ancient times rendered as lively by it as a pig's tail is at present.— I would rouse from his dull repose, Titian, to paint your head ; Sir Peter Lely, your neck ; Vandyke, your hands ; and Rubens for the draperies and background of the picture.— Then, perchance, one might have something worth looking at.   As matters stand, I confess I am in utter despair.

Will you deign to read of some Oxford gaiety ?—I was at a rout at the Deanery last night.   The Deaneress, Mrs. Hall, ci-devant Miss Byng, and sister to the P[——]e, a fine lady, in white satin, telling us the price of every hing in her drawing-room, from the mantelpiece to her own dickey.   We had tea and cards, and—what a Miss, whose name never reached me, called music.   After a long silence, " But where are the sweet children ?" cried a parson present ; on which, after two tugs of the bell, the door flew open, and *voilà, toute la singerie !*—a thousand little things, with monstrous mouths, hopped in, like the Egyptian plague of frogs, and surrounded the poor dean, (who resembled St. Anthony in one of his Dutch temptations,) squalling aloud for cake and tea, and I know not what.   I was glad to escape, leaving the eldest boy amusing himself with tickling the noses of all the company in turns, with a handful of dirty hog-bristles,—to the great delight of his mother, who esteems him a decided wit.   Apropos of wits, Lady [——] hath been at Lord Abingdon's, near this town, astonishing the weak minds of sundry poor youths with her vivacities.   She talked to a friend of mine of [——]'s account of the plague at Athens, which scared him sadly. He told me that he swore it was d——d fine, though he had never read a word of it.   And she played on a Spanish guitar, sitting on a cushion in the lobby by the light of the lamps, to the admiration of sundry bores, who read Sir Charles Grandison, and think a mad countess a fine thing.   For my part, I have been told that she is really not clever ; and I never could admire her looks ;—she hath such a huge nose that she resembles a hussar's sabre with the pouch and straps ;

—she's principally nose, and all the rest of her seems to belong to it. But it is time for me to have done, there being scarcely any space on the paper left for the name of

Your faithful servant.

From H.R.H. THE PRINCESS OF WALES.

I should not so soon have encroached on your time, my dear [——], but that there has happened a few coincidences which to relate to you would perhaps afford you amusement. Lord Deerhurst is quite a joke to the secret marriage of the ci-devant Mrs. Panton with a Mr. Geldi, an acquaintance of Batty's, and why it is kept a secret, and why it is made public, nobody can guess, as she was her own mistress,— or that she thought that she was public property, and that it would be essential to have an Act of Parliament to make an enclosure to become private property at a moment's warning.

Town grows every day thinner and thinner; though I had last Monday a large party at dinner; and, in the evening, a little hop for the young ladies, yet I felt how useful you would have been to make the party go off more lively and merrily. *Clan Rowland* [Clanranald], very unusually, danced with great glee the whole evening with Lady C[aroline] E[dgcumbe]; * he supped at my table with her, and I have not the smallest doubt that Hymen will soon crown that work. Lord M[ount] E[dgcumb]e looked pleased with him, and praised him to me to the skies. Poor Miss R[——] is quite forsaken by him, and I trust she will be wise enough to console herself, as Ariadne did—and not choose a Bacchus, but something more eligible to her taste.

Though Lady Harriet is very cunning and sly, still I have discovered that she is the match-making lady to her brother. She brought Lady E[lizabeth] to dinner, and did nothing but prose in praise of her. Lady G[eorgina] M[orpeth] takes her to [——], and Lord H[artington] is also of the party, and the final proposal will be made there under the shady trees, or by the placid light of the moon. The great ball at D[evonshire] House, I heard was magnificent; Lord

* Youngest daughter of Richard, 2nd Earl of Mount Edgcumbe, married, in 1812, Reginald George MacDonald of Clanranald, and died April 10, 1824.

H[artington] began the dance with Lady E[lizabeth], and she was introduced to the old Duke,* who, I hear, was very much charmed with her beauty, and I dare say this marriage will be settled before we meet again.

The H[——], Lady P[——], and the daughters came also to my party; the old lady looked like the head of a ship, Lady P[——] very embarrassed, the two young ladies, as usual, frightfully dressed—like naughty girls, with grey stuff gowns, to make them learn their lesson better the next day. The eldest danced with B[——] N[——], and the two younger ones danced together. They did not stay supper, but went away very early. I heard the next day that Lady C[——]s had sprained her ancle, which prevented her from going to dance cotillons next day at Lord D[——]'s. She sent, instead, early in the morning, for a surgeon, to Mr. Des Hayes, the dancer, and he came and said, " My Lady, je sais bien arranger les jambes qui se portent bien, mais pas celles qui sont malades " ; and so he left the room, and she was obliged to keep company with the sofa.

Monday next my humble habitation will be graced with the presence of Louis XVIII., Madame D'Angoulême,† and all the French princes, and above thirty French people, at a breakfast. My mother, and the Princess Sophia, and some old fograms, male and female, will be there to enliven the party. This is all the merriment of my budget which I can offer you to-day.

Mr. Arbuthnot looks shy and dismal. I think he must feel ashamed of his cowardice, never to have asked me to one of the many suppers which he has given lately. There have been, I hear, very charming masquerades; but I speak from report merely. " Mes beaux jours sont passés." But, be that as it may, I always remain,

Your affectionate friend,
C. P.

Wednesday, the 19th.—I dined at Kensington. All the pleasure of the party was marred by distant looks,

---

* This letter must have been inserted in the wrong place, as the 5th Duke of Devonshire died July 29, 1811.

† Daughter of Louis XVI. and Marie Antoinette, wife of her cousin, the elder son of the Comte d'Artois, afterwards Charles X.

and silence, that boded coming storms. There was Miss B[——], Mr. Ward, Mr. Knight,* and Sir James Mackintosh,—the latter, a very charming man ; but as much leaven was thrown into this society as the Princess of Wales could put into it, to make it disagreeable.

Thursday.—I went to Lady D[——]y's, where, amongst much rubbish, there were some persons worth conversing with. I met there, my old friend, Lord D[——]ley. There are some persons whom one feels to be sure friends. It is impossible for a being gifted with quick sensations to be deceived in this respect. I know not if it can be accounted for philosophically, but I always return to my own system of fascination and attraction, *sans rhyme ni raison.*

Lady M[——] came to see me.—I never saw so melancholy a proof of the extent of punishment that conscience can inflict on those who have not fulfilled the severer duties of life. The leaven of disappointment has soured all the genuine virtues of her disposition, while the acuteness of her intellect, and her quick and warm affections, have been fatally conducive to misery instead of happiness. Yet, like a wayward child that has been long indulged, I would not thwart her, or use violence to instil other thoughts to counteract the poison ; I would, on the contrary, soothe and lull her wounds with the sedative of affection before I attempted to give stronger medicines to turn her mind and views into another channel. Alas ! riches and power afford the means to do many kind things ; but who can say that when the means are ours, the inclination will remain ? The amusements of London, unless accompanied by all which can pamper and satisfy ambition, cease to be pleasures.

I learnt to-day that an old servant of my family was

* Mr. Knight, the author of a work on Taste. [Part of original note.]

at the point of death. The idea that this was the case, and that he had not perhaps sufficient means to render his transit to another world as little painful as possible, affected me. The great are not sufficiently attentive to the wants of their dependents—persons who, after passing a lifetime in their service, often die in poverty. This sometimes happens from procrastination; not from a determined neglect or a hardened indifference, but from the vague sensation that we will do to-morrow what we are not inclined to do to-day. The longer I live the more I am convinced, that to put off a good intention is generally to render it abortive

Note from H.R.H. The Princess of Wales.

All the news I can offer you, my dear [——], is a most dreadful blunder which that wonderful woman, Madame De Staël, has committed. She was in some party several evenings ago, and mistook old Mrs. B[——] for the Marchioness of Hertford. She began by assuring her " que la renommée avait vanté sa beauté et son esprit par tout le continent—que ses portraits étaient gravés, et faisaient les charmes et l'ornement de tous les palais."—Of course, you may imagine that this event has been the laughing-stock of these last eight-and-forty hours. I had the unexpected happiness of seeing my brother return; he gives no sanguine hopes at all of the restoration of Germany, and he has a very sad opinion of Bernadotte. To conclude my letter, I must only give you another piece of information, that Madame De Staël has discovered, not La Pierre Philosophale, but " that Lord Castlereagh's speech about the treaty with Sweden was the most eloquent, most rhetorical and persuasive speech that ever was made in Parliament " : these are Madame De Staël's own words. I fear this is not the way of pleasing in this country, at least not the generality of the English people. She also had a great dispute with Lord Lansdowne about the Catholic Question, which has, of course, given great offence to all the opposition. At least, he might have supposed that Madame De Staël must be tolerant; but

T. Stothard, R.A., pinxt.   I. Murphy, sculpt.

CAROLINE, PRINCESS OF WALES
From the Collection of Mr. John Lane

writing and speaking seem to be two different things with her. I will not longer dwell upon her, and only anticipate the pleasure of having an agreeable *tête-à-tête* with you on Sunday morning. Yours sincerely,

(Signed)   C. P.

[CHARLES KIRKPATRICK SHARPE.]

LONDON, *Wednesday.*

DEAR [——],—Lady M. informs me that you desire I should write; so I hasten to obey your commands, though the weather and my present mode of life are very far from propitious to epistolary exertion. Nothing but smothering heat, and parties that melt one to inanity. To go into the streets is to endure the fiery ordeal; (which none of us here at present can well abide ;) and to venture into an evening assembly is to tumble into a kettle of boiling sprats. For my part, I have endured every culinary effect of fire mentioned by Hannah Glasse, and all the newer processes of steam besides. I am in the condition of that poor Princess in the Arabian Nights, who fought so fatally with the genius, about the transformation of a monkey—(my concerns are full as apish,) and I might most justly exclaim with Nourmahal,

I burn—I more than burn; I'm all a fire;
See how my mouth and nostrils flames expire!

Thank heaven, however, I am not in love! That alone saves me from utter conflagration; for indeed, dear[——], I cannot "join the multitude to do evil," in finding Lady Elizabeth B[ingha]m, and Miss Rumbold, and twenty more, so very, very charming. Perhaps my taste is bad, and these belles are fairer than the houris; but they do not strike me; —a circumstance which can give *them* no concern, and is, on the whole, very lucky for the second son of a poor gentleman. And now, I wonder if you will care to hear about routs and such things. I shall talk a little on that subject at a venture; for you can burn this as soon as you please, or give it to your hound to mumble, if there happeneth to be no fire (as is most likely) in your chamber. But I am firmly resolved not to say one word about the disasters at Carlton

I   E

House; though I saw one miserable person brought out upon a board, and many gentlewomen worse attired than Eve in her primitive simplicity. You must have heard all these horrors long ago; so I shall begin with Lady Mary L. Crawford's ball, most magnanimously given in the Argyll Street rooms, to all her friends, or rather her enemies—as, even by her own account of the matter, she is at deadly feud with the whole world. I could admire nothing at the entertainment—not even herself. Fancy her * attired in draperies of muslin, covered with gold spots the size of a sixpence! When she reclined under that frippery canvass bower at the end of the ball-room, she looked exactly like an ill-favoured picture of Danaë in the shower of gold. To crown the whole, S[keffington],† with rouge on his cheeks and ultramarine on his nose, handed her to supper! " Sure such a pair ! "

I was one of the happy few at H[——]'s ball given in B[——]m House—a house I had been long anxious to see, as it is rendered classical by the pen of Pope and the pencil of Hogarth. It is in a woeful condition, and, as I hear, to be pulled down. The company was very *genteel* (I can't get a less vulgar word to express the sort of thing) and very dull; but all the ladies were vastly refreshed with an inscription chalked upon the floor, which each applied to herself. Within a wreath of laurel, like burdock, fastened with fifty crooked true-love knots, were the mysterious words " Pour elle." And what a sensation did these two simple words produce! First, there was such a flocking to the centre of the room— such a whispering—such a " Dear, I should like to see it ! "— " Pray, Lady Louisa, let me see it "—" Goodness ! whom can it mean ? "—and then a triumphant retreat; smiles upon every lip, exultation in every eye. It was quite amusing afterwards to ask any lady who the " elle" could be—the downcast-look of affected humility—then the little sigh of half-surfeited vanity—and then the stare of confident triumph, crowned with " How should I know ? " were delightful. After all, the true *elle* is said to be Lady E. B[ingham], for

* Lady Mary Lindsay Crawford, died in 1833.
† Sir Lumley St. George Skeffington, 2nd Bart., born 1768, a celebrated Dandy. The original note says that he was " the very wreck of a beau ; he is to be seen sometimes creeping about like a half dead fly which has outlived the summer."

whom a friend of mine is at present very sick, and carving her name upon every tree he finds in the country. But I am not quite sure that she will be Lady H[——], as I do not think that the swain looks much in love.* We had much waltzing and quadrilling, the last of which is certainly very abominable. I am not sensitive enough to be offended with waltzing, in which I can see no other harm than that it disorders the stomach, and sometimes makes people look very ridiculous; but after all, moralists, with the Duchess of [——] at their head, who never had a moral in their lives, exclaim dreadfully against it. Nay, I am told that these magical wheelings have already roused poor Lord Dartmouth from his grave to suppress them. Alas! after all, people set about it as gravely as a company of dervises, and seem to be paying adoration to Pluto rather than to Cupid. But the quadrilles I can by no means endure; for, till ladies and gentlemen have joints at their ancles, which is impossible, it is worse than impudent to make such exhibitions, more particularly in a place where there are public ballets every Tuesday and Saturday. When people dance to be looked at, they surely should dance to perfection. Even the Duchess of Bedford, who is the Angiolini of the group, would make an indifferent figurante at the Opera; and the principal male dancer, Mr. North, reminds one of a gibbeted malefactor, moved to and fro by the winds, but from no personal exertion.

Since I had the honour of seeing you last, I have been introduced to the Princess of Wales, and have dined several times at Kensington. Her royal highness has been very good to me, which I in a great measure attribute to the favourable manner in which you mentioned me to her. One night we went through all the upper rooms in the palace, to examine the pictures, and many seemed excellent in their way; but one can see little by candlelight; and there was a sad want of names,—which takes away all the pleasure of portraits. The Scotch picture, as an altar piece, is very curious; though, from the style of painting, I guess that it must have been done a long while after the death of the persons represented.

* The original edition has this cryptic note: " Perhaps that ball at B[——] House was given for one who was not permitted to attend it."

Since I have been in London I have read nothing except Miss Seward's letters, and Miss Owenson's Missionary. Of Miss Seward I am bound to speak well, as she doth so of me; and her monodies are beautiful; but the letters are naught; they abound in false sentiment, and a great many other false things. As to the Missionary, Ambrosio is his father, and Matilde his mother; but, wanting the indelicacy of papa, and the delicacy of mamma, he's a dull fellow. I could think of nothing else but poor Margaret Stewart of Blantyre,* and her presbyterian minister, while I read this book. Miss Luxina brought her hogs to a bad market, for Hilarion was little better than a beast. Walter Scott's last poem I have also seen, but so hastily that I can be no competent judge of its merits. Talking of words, allow me to recommend to you Ford's Plays, lately re-published. Some of them are excellent; the first in the series (which hath an awkward name, I must confess) and the Broken Heart, are particularly admirable. I am sure that you will be struck with them; for Ford is almost as moving as Otway or Lee,— who is the mad poet I adore, yet I can persuade nobody to read him. The History of the Somerville Family, which I have seen in MS., is soon to be printed, and that of Sutherland is to be out shortly. So much for books—saving that Sir John Murray hath found the whole correspondence of the Earl of Chesterfield, who flourished in King Charles the Second's time, in Bath House, containing most curious letters of the Duchess of Cleveland, Lady Southesk, and many other personages, whom Count Hamilton has rendered so interesting. I will try to get Sir John to publish them, for such things should not run the risk of fire, not to mention rats and mice. There is a sort of memoir of Lord Chesterfield at the beginning of the volume, in which he says his second wife died of the spotted fever or plague; but, in fact, he is said to have poisoned her in the wine of the sacrament, to be revenged for her gallantries, which were notorious: that old villain, Sir John Denham, having shown him the way, by getting rid of his wife after a fashion nearly similar.

I have written so much that I can find no room for Mrs. Dawson's masquerade, where it was said that the only good

* Daughter of the 10th Lord Blantyre, married, in 1809, the Rev. Andrew Stewart.

mask was Mr. Fitzharding in the character of Lord Berkeley ; nor Deerhurst's marriage, nor Lady O[xford]'s adventure with that rogue her brother ; but, if you will signify to me that a second gazette extraordinary will be acceptable, I shall be greatly flattered.   Meanwhile I remain, dear [———],

Your faithful servant.

Another Letter from the same.

LONDON, *Sunday*, [———], 1811.

DEAR [———],—You flatter me greatly by desiring a second number of the gazette extraordinary, which I hasten to transmit, albeit the adventures of Lady O[xford] and her brother are now what is termed in Scotland, Piper's news. But, before I touch seriously upon that legend, you must permit me to disclaim all title to the knowledge of a certain art, the first rudiments of which may be gathered from the "Academy of Compliments" and "Walton's Complete Angler."   Indeed, my dear [———], I never was accused of such a thing before ; nay, I have been told by many persons that I am too innocent of the sin, and that my fortunes in life are impeded thereby ; and I verily do believe it.   In your especial case, however, it is scarcely possible to commit this crime, except one were to give you wings at once, and—but I shall say no more on that subject, for fear of fresh accusations ; and return discreetly to my news, ancient and modern, according to the tenor of the permission through which I have the honour of corresponding with you.

Lady O[xford], poor Lady O[xford] ! knows the rules of prudence, I fear me, as imperfectly as she doth those of the Greek and Latin grammars ; or she hath let her brother, who is a sad swine, become master of her secrets, and then contrived to quarrel with him.   You would see the outline of the mélange in the newspapers, but not the report that Mr. S[cott] is about to publish a pamphlet, as an addition to the Harelian Tracts, setting forth the amatory adventures of his sister.   We shall break our necks in haste to buy it, of course crying "shameful" all the while ; and it is said that Lady O[xford] is to be cut, which I cannot entirely believe.   Let her tell two or three old women about town that they are young and handsome, and give some well-timed parties, and she may still keep the society which she hath been used to. The times are not so hard as they once were, when a woman could not construe Magna Charta with anything like impunity. People were full as gallant many years ago ; but the days are gone by wherein my Lord Protector of the Commonwealth of England was wont to go a love-making to Mrs. Fleetwood, with the bible under his arm.

And so Miss Jacky Gordon * is really clothed with a husband at last, and Miss Laura Manners left without a mate ! She and Lord Stair should marry and have children, in mere revenge. As to Miss Gordon, she's a Venus well suited to such a Vulcan,—whom nothing but money and a title could have rendered tolerable, even to a kitchen wench. It is said that the matrimonial correspondence between this couple is to be published—full of sad scandalous relations, of which you may be sure scarcely a word is true. In former times the Duchess of St. A[lban]s † made use of these elegant epistles in order to intimidate Lady Johnstone ; ‡ but that ruse would not avail, so, in spite, they are to be printed. What a cargo of amiable creatures !—Yet will some people scarcely believe in the existence of Pandemonium !

Tuesday morning.—You are perfectly right respecting the hot rooms here, which we all cry out against, and all find very comfortable—much more so than the cold sands and bleak neighbourhood of the sea—which looks vastly well in one of Vander Velde's pictures hung upon crimson damask, but hideous and shocking in reality. H[——] and his " Elle " (talking of parties) were last night at Cholmondeley House, but seem not to ripen in their love. He is certainly good-humoured, and, I believe, good-hearted, so deserves a good wife ; but his *cara* seems a genuine London miss, made up of

---

* Johanna, daughter of Charles Gordon of Cluny, married, in 1804, according to Scottish custom, the 7th Earl of Stair. He, disregarding this contract, married secondly, in 1808, Miss Laura Manners, daughter of the Countess of Dysart, a marriage which was set aside. The Earl's first marriage was dissolved in June, 1820. Miss Manners was afterwards known as Lady Laura Tollemach, and died in 1834, having never married a second time.

† Louisa Grace Manners, another daughter of Lady Dysart, wife of the 6th Duke of St. Albans.

‡ Charlotte Gordon of Cluny, sister of Johanna, Countess of Stair, wife of Sir John Lowther Johnstone of Westerhall, 6th Bart.

many affectations. Will she form a comfortable helpmate ? For me, I like not her origin, and deem many strange things to run in blood, besides madness and the Hanoverian evil.

Thursday.—I verily do believe that I never shall get to the end of this small sheet of paper, so many unheard of interruptions have I had ; and now I have been to Vauxhall and caught the tooth-ache. I was of Lady E. B[ingha]m and H[——]'s party—very dull—the lady giving us all a supper after our promenade—

> Much ado was there, God wot,
> She would love, but he would not.

He ate a great deal of ice, although he did not seem to require it ; and she " faisoit les yeux doux," enough not only to have melted all the ice which he swallowed, but his own hard heart into the bargain. The thing will not do. In the meantime, Miss Long hath become quite cruel to Wellesley Pole, and divides her favour equally between Lords Killeen and Kilworth, two as simple Irishmen as ever gave birth to a bull. I wish to Hymen that she were fairly married, for all this pother gives one a disgusting picture of human nature. Avarice in children is shocking—yet the united schools of Eton and Westminster are gaping after this girl, as if she were fairer than a myriad of Venuses. Apropos, I have discovered a Venus—a Mrs. Owen ; she is beautiful, but she looks vulgar, and is horribly affected. I think that the Adonis of this year is Grammont. He is handsomer than any body, and I know three fat ladies who are expiring through the love they bear him. Lady Barbara Ashley is to marry him, it is said.* And now admire, my dear [——], the strange change of opinion which takes place in families ! Here is a person descended from a precise Puritan, and the trumper-up of the popish plot, herself a Papist, and about to marry one ! The Count descends prodigiously, to wed such an ill-born mushroom ; but she has money and he hath not. Here is another change ; but he has much more excuse for what he does than Miss Long's pack of truffle-hunters. When Miss Porter's Don Sebastian came out, I expected to find the Margravine, Keppel Craven, (with whom the fair authoress

* She married, however, August 8, 1814, Hon. William Frederick Spencer Ponsonby, created, in 1838, Lord de Mauley.

was in love,) and many of my other friends there ; in place of which I found nothing but such heroes and heroines as might have been fashionable and common formerly, but who are wonderfully out of date and rare now ; so that circumstances gave me a disgust to the book.   As to my own romance, which you have done me the honour of accepting, I feel such prodigious qualms about its publication, that I scarcely think it will ever see the light.   When it is quite finished, you shall have it in your power, as to a perusal. The subject is certainly good, though my hero was a sad fool, and my heroine (Lady H. W[entworth]) little better than a baggage ; but I have not done it justice, and people persuade me that these mélanges of truth and fiction are pernicious, or at least worthless.   On the score of *impropriety*, you will find nothing offensive ; and the moral of the Duke of M[on-mouth]'s life is excellent, for his errors, poor soul, were venial, and his punishment most exemplary.   Lady H[arriot] never held up her head after the intelligence of his death reached her ; and his Duchess, (who was a very unfeeling woman, that breakfasted on cold haggiss,) married Lord C[ornwallis], and concluded her career very comfortably.   And here it is time that I should conclude mine for the present, as far as writing goes ;—so, with ten thousand thanks for your letter, (which I dare not call amusing, lest you should say I flatter,) and living in hopes of being honoured with hearing from you again,   I am, Dear [——],

Your faithful servant.

From H.R.H. THE PRINCESS OF WALES.

Wednesday, [——], 1811.

The accounts from Windsor certainly have been very terrifying for a few days, which has prevented my going since a week to the opera ; but the accounts are now very much the same as they were a month ago, and I feel no apprehension that it will be worse, nor, I fear, better.   My mother has been very ill indeed : her dinners have been postponed since a fortnight.   I have been much at home, and not at all the worse for having seen a few people whom I liked the best. Mr. Sharpe * would do very well, if he was not a great gossip ;

* Probably Charles Kirkpatrick Sharpe.

and there are days and times that it would be very inconvenient to have him in society. The two marriages in question are still a profound secret, and the formal proposals are
not yet made, of which I am certain. All parties are on the
point of going into the country, and before next year I believe
nothing will be settled. Mr. Macdonald is at Mr. E[dgcumbe]'s
and I suppose that it will be arranged soon. Your letter is
safely burnt, and a feu de joie made of it, my dear [——].
When the Royal visitors left me, Louis the XVIIIth could
only offer me the gout in one knee and in one toe, and Madame
D'Angoulême a swelled face * ; so that I have not been blessed
with a sight of these charming creatures. Still I was reduced
to the satisfaction of having forty, including my own family,
to this great feast. The sight was not enchanting, as it
was loaded with old fograms. My usual resource on this
occasion is to show the great apartments and the rarities
they contain.† At last, (every thing, alas ! ends,) we were
obliged to take to another resource, which was walking in
the great avenue ; and there we walked with all the plebeians,
and with all the mobs. As our conviviality was exhausted
as well as our wit, the military band supplied the sound of
our voices. We lounged there till happily the clock struck
eight, and then the party was swept away like magic.

Lord Hartington gives a great ball at Burlington House,
which is his new residence, and I suspect that this ball, which
was given quite suddenly, was for some matrimonial reasons.

Another from H.R.H. to the same.

DEAR [——],—I have lived in such a confusion since you
left me, that I don't know whether I am the besieged or

* All these ailings probably befell the royal family of France at the
command of the Prince Regent of England. [Original note.]

† This was a circumstance which her Royal Highness's enemies
laid hold of to turn to her disadvantage ; and the newspapers of the
day found great fault with the Princess for taking her guests into
those apartments, and insinuated that they were the scenes of improper
conduct, being but partially lighted ; whereas her Royal Highness
only took her company there when she had no other means of entertaining them. Thus was she often falsely accused ; and, unfortunately
for her own welfare, (though I think, in many instances, it speaks well
for her character,) the Princess of Wales did not heed what interpreta-
tion her enemies put on her actions. [Original note.]

the besieger. Lady Anne and I began by receiving an ambassador, the second day after she had been installed into
all the secrecy of our nunnery. He was sent by our gracious
Majesty; in short, it was the Vice-Chamberlain, Colonel
Desbrowe; his object being to stop my going to Windsor,
and convey a refusal to my request of having my daughter
to come to see me last Saturday. I was just sitting in Lady
Anne's room, opposite to the sofa on which she was placed,
when he was announced; she had never heard of his name,
and supposed that he was a young and fashionable beau.
She behaved like Joan of Arc in the whole of this business;
was immoveable; not a muscle of her face altered at the
eloquent speech of this knight errant. I desired him to
write it down on paper, to refresh my memory now and then
with it; but he refused. Lady Anne then took her pen, and,
in the presence of this ambassador, she conveyed his message
to paper, which he read himself before he left the room and
took his departure. I think this scene will make a pretty
figure in the Morning Chronicle or in the Examiner; but I
leave that to a much abler pen than mine.

One day I went with Lady Anne to see the English " St.
Cyr," * at Lee, where I met Lady Perceval. I think you
would have been amused for a moment, with hearing the
second Miss Grimani sing; she is one of the governesses.
Sapio and his wife also sang duets and trios with her,
and I was much gratified by the exquisite taste and great
flexibility of voice of this young person.

Poor Lady K[——] is, I fear, at this moment in great
anxiety and tribulation, as she has been absolutely refused,
under any condition, to have the house at Kensington. She
had offered to take upon herself all the repairs and finishing,
that it might prove no incumbrance to the Board of Works;
in short, *He* is a brute, and unqualified to be called a gentleman through his behaviour, this Lord Chamberlain. And
now I must tell you something else—I am so accustomed,
my dear [——], to disappointments since my childhood, that
one more or less makes not much effect upon my temper.
I am only astonished how very little chivalresque feeling is
remaining in this country; and Mr. Drummond certainly

* A school founded by and under the protection of Lady Anne
Hamilton. [Original note.]

shall not be the Banker to George IVth's Queen ; * for any historian, who would write the biography of the ex-Princess of Wales, would not a little astonish the world, in relating that she could not procure the sum of £500, at the rate of paying £500 a *year* per annum for it ! !

Letter from M. G. LEWIS, Esq.

THE ALBANY, November 10th.

MY DEAR [——],—Lord Aberdeen is a candidate for the Presidentship of the Antiquarian Society ; and I need not tell you, that I am extremely anxious to promote his success, and intreat you to use all your influence in obtaining votes for his support.

I hear that Lady [Hester Stanhope] is living at Constantinople with young B[ruce], avowedly as his *chère amie ;* and that she says nobody was ever so handsome, nor so clever, and that he is in short, and *is to be*, one of the first characters in these kingdoms. I wish him joy of his conquest, and had rather *he* than *I*.†

I send you some verses which I read in the Examiner ; I think them very witty, although very abominable.

Believe me,
Most truly yours,
M. G. LEWIS.

THE TRIUMPH OF THE WHALE.

Io ! Pæan ! Io ! sing,
To the finny people's king !
Not a mightier whale than this,
In the vast Atlantic is ;
Not a fatter fish than he,
Flounders round the Polar sea :

* The banking house of Mr. Drummond refused to advance the sum of £500 for her Royal Highness. The reason assigned was, its being inconsistent with the rule of their house to obey her commands ; but one might have supposed that an exception could be made in favour of the Princess of Wales, especially considering the small amount of the sum. [Original note.]

† Michael Bruce ; *see* Miss Knights' Autobiography, ii. p. 79. He later, with Sir Robert Wilson and Captain Hely Hutchinson, assisted Lavalette to escape from prison in Paris. The original note says that,

See his blubber at his gills,—
What a world of drink he swills !
From his trunk, as from a spout,
Which next moment he pours out.
Such his person—next declare,
Muse ! who his companions are :
Every fish of generous kind,
Stands aside, or slinks behind ;
But about his presence keep,
All the monsters of the deep :
Mermaids with their tails and singing,
His delighted fancy stinging.
Crooked dolphins, they surround him,
Dog-like seals, they fawn around him ;
Following hard, the progress mark,
Of one intolerant salt sea shark ;
For his solace and relief,
Flat fish are his courtiers chief :
Last and lowest in his train,
Tub fish, libellers of the main,
Their black liquor shed in spite :
Such on earth the things that write.
In his stomach some do say,
No good thing can ever stay :
Had it been the fortune of it,
To have swallowed the old prophet,
Three days there he'd not have dwell'd,
But in one have been expell'd.
Hapless mariners are they,
Who beguiled, as seamen say,
Deeming him some rock or island,
Footing sure, safe spot, or dry land,
Anchor in his scaly rind ;
Soon the difference they find :
Sudden, plump, he sinks beneath them,
Does to ruthless waves bequeath them.
Name or title, what has he ?
Is he Regent of the sea ?

" Having reached London, with all his honours fresh upon him, he
turned the heads of several elderly ladies, and ended his public career
by marrying a widow lady with several children."

From that difficulty free us,
Buffon, Banks, or sage Linnæus :
With his wondrous attributes,
Say what appellation suits ;
By his bulk and by his size,
By his oily qualities,
This (or else my eyesight fails),
This should be the Prince of Whales.

Who is there that may not be caricatured, when the most avowedly graceful man of his time, or perhaps of any time, can thus be personally ridiculed ?

To-day I went to see Mrs. Nugent. She is more like a corpse than anything can be that is not one. I have paid her several visits. Her conversation is sensible and composed. Whatever scandal may have formerly said against her, must, I conclude, now be silenced ; though I believe, like the Gowls in the Arabian Nights, it ever feeds upon decayed carcasses.

I see strange reports in the papers about the poor Princess. Turning her out of Kensington Palace, (for that is the true meaning of procuring her another domicile), appears to me to be the forerunner of new troubles. It is said she is to be sent abroad. How can that be, without bringing her to public disgrace ? It is further reported, that no ministers will be accepted by the Prince, except such as will further his plans respecting the Princess. Now is the time when her Royal Highness should seek for the protection of the greatest in the land. Talent alone is not sufficient to stem the tide which has set in against her. When people forsake their own position—their own station in life—to cast themselves upon the aid of those beneath them, it is an invariable rule that they fall into a pit from which none can extricate them. The latter are generally incompetent to judge of the conduct of those who are in a totally different position from themselves. There is nothing perhaps so difficult as to take upon oneself another's identity, in any circumstance or station of existence; and those who attempt this in regard to princes, must be very honourable persons indeed, not to be swayed in their judgment by party, by prejudice, or by self-interest. No royal person ever experienced this truth more fatally than the unfortunate Princess of Wales. She was alternately under the influence of all these contending powers ; and even the best of her Royal Highness's advisers, those who were honest and honourable in their intentions towards her, were not free from party spirit ; whilst others again used her merely as a ladder on which to climb to power. But then, it must be said in justice to those who tried to serve her and failed, that she frequently marred their endeavours by underhand confidences to persons of opposite principles, when she did not like a measure, and yet did not dare openly to run counter to it. This was vexatious to those who really were desirous to be of use to her, and failed of making her any stable friends with any set of political men.

The tissue of all human character is more or less uneven ; but I never knew greater inequality than in that of this very extraordinary woman. Posterity will never do justice to her memory ; for, as in most cases, the bad and inferior parts of her character were tangible and prominent to the observation, while those alone who lived in her intimate society, knew of the many good and great ingredients which formed a part of the heterogeneous mixture. A friend of the Prince, one who leant with steady affection to his Royal Highness's interests, said to me the other day, "The Princess has behaved towards me with a candour and good nature that do her honour"; (alluding to that person's never having waited upon her, for fear of offending the Prince ;) "few royal persons are sufficiently liberal to set down a seeming omission of duty, even of the most trifling nature, to its true cause, when no disrespect is intended." It ought to be recorded to the honour of the Princess, that until she was goaded to madness, she never felt any hatred against the Prince's friends, as such;—only against persons who had been her adherents, and turned from her to bow the knee to Baal, did she shew any resentment.

Returned to town—was invited to sup at Kensington —a very agreeable party, but, unfortunately, the Princess prolonged her pleasures till they became pains. No appetite for converse, no strength of nerves, no love for any individual who might be present, could possibly enable any person, *who was not royal*, (they certainly are gifted with supernatural strength,) to sit for five or six hours at table, and keep vigil till morning light. Some one, I remember, present that night, ventured to hint that morning was at hand. "Ah!" said the Princess, "God, He knows when we may all meet again—to tell you God's truth, when I am happy and comfortable, I could sit on for ever."

There was heaviness in her mirth, and everybody seemed to feel it; so they sat on. At last, we rose from table; many of the guests went away; some few lingered in the drawing room, amongst whom I was one. I was left the last of all. Scarcely had Sir H. Englefield, Sir William Gell, and Mr. Craven reached the ante-room, when a long and protracted roll of thunder echoed all around, and shook the palace to its very foundations; a bright light shone into the room—brighter than the beams of the sun; a violent hissing noise followed, and some ball of electric fluid, very like that which is represented on the stage, seemed to fall close to the window where we were standing. Scarcely had we recovered the shock, when all the gentlemen who had gone out, returned, and Sir H. Englefield informed us, that the sentinel at the door was knocked down, a great portion of the gravel walk torn up, and every servant and soldier were terrified. " Ah ! " said the Princess, undismayed, but solemnly— " this forebodes my downfall " ; and she shook her head ; then rallying, she desired Sir H. Englefield to take especial notice of this meteoric phenomenon, and give an account of it in the Philosophical Transactions ;— which he did.

I learnt the next day that three new doctors had been called in to the poor King : Monro, Symons, and J. Willis. Herberden was dismissed, and is to see him no more. It is settled, that a new plan is to be adopted :—as all the physicians now allow that the King's mind is quite gone, he is to be left to himself, except at moments of violence,—no longer to be tormented with medicine or questions, &c., &c., and only attended by the doctors who profess to treat insane persons, and by one regular physician. By all this it appears certain, that at the expiration of the year at latest, that is to say, in the course of next February, all restrictions will be taken off the Prince Regent, and he will act as King. What is to follow, time only can shew.

Heard to-day of the marriage of Mrs. Bouverie,* which event has given rise to a great deal of wit. They say that in her youth she wore a cloak, and in her old age a Spencer.

The Princess communicated to me a letter from Mr. Brougham. It is very like a conjuror's hocus pocus ; for I defy any one, and certainly her Royal Highness, to understand distinctly what it means. It is a very ingenious mystification, however :—

Copy of MR. BROUGHAM's Note.

I have seen Lord Grey, and Lord Lansdowne, and others. The Prince did not propose to Lord Wellesley anything about seeing or speaking to the opposition ; but Lord Wellesley

* Henrietta, daughter of Sir Everard Fawkener, K.B., married first, in 1764, Hon. Edward Bouverie ; second, in 1811, Lord Robert Spencer.

proposed it, and the Prince did not object.   Lord W[ellesley] saw Lord G[rey] yesterday, and to-day he saw Lord Y[armouth] and Lord Grenville—and then he saw Lord Moira, and others.   He *has* proposed several principles, in which he thinks they may all agree :—the Catholic question, and the war in Spain.   Nothing has been proposed in the order in council ; which is the chief difficulty in the opinion of many. As yet, nothing is fixed, nor has any mention been made, as to arrangements of the offices ; they are only negotiating to try to come to an understanding upon principles.   If they succeed in that, the rest will be quite easy, as far as relates to them ; and I fancy Lord Grey will be minister ; and the Prince reserves to himself to agree to or refuse the project they may finally submit to him.   The thing is still going on, and they seem to think Lord Wellesley has completely quarrelled with the old cabinet—with some (Lords Bathurst and Harrowby) irreconcileably.   I never believe in *such* irreconcileable quarrels.   The opposition (with a few exceptions) are all against their coming into office, and I am sure Whitbread, Coke, &c., will be decidedly so.

About this time, there was a talk of publishing some statements of facts, in favour of the Princess, which was got up by some of the opposition party, but which they chose to envelope in a sort of mystery ;—whether or not to deceive the Princess, or whether to serve her or themselves and their party, I never could understand.   Her Royal Highness shewed me the following sentence in a note of one of the most celebrated men of this day concerning them :—

———" The papers have been sent to me by a mysterious personage, with the view to publication.   I have fully considered the subject, and have written a *cautious* answer, which has not been called for, though I have twice advertised in the newspaper, as directed by the stranger.   I had intended to send a copy of my answer, but it is scarcely worth while ; the substance is strongly to advise publication, but accompanied with a *proper narrative*, which I have engaged a most

I   F unexceptionable' person to write as soon as required, namely, Mr. Hunt."

While Mr. [——], was busily engaged thus, as it appeared, in procuring or buying up papers, supposed to be in favour of her Royal Highness, she herself was equally busy on her part in a similar scheme; but by all I ever could make out, it was kept a profound secret from Mr. [——].

From MR. M. G. LEWIS.

THE ALBANY, *Nov.* 20th.

MY DEAR [——],—In the first place you must understand, that I have been all my life the most careful person in the world respecting letters, and that the late instances of the Duke of York and Lord Folkestone have by no means operated to produce an abatement of caution. London is still very empty, and there is nothing to be done except going to the play. Luckily that is one of my favourite amusements; and still more luckily, the few people who are in town seem to be of the same opinion; so that, whenever there is anything worth going to see, a couple of boxes are taken, in which Lady Le Despencer and her daughters, Lady de Ros, Lady Perceval, and all the men they can pick up, establish themselves, and we generally sup at Lady Le Despencer's afterwards. I have neither seen nor heard anything of the Princess, since she removed to Blackheath, except a report that she is in future to reside at Hampton Court, because the Princess Charlotte wants the apartments at Kensington. But I cannot believe that the young Princess, who has been always described to me as so partial to her mother, would endure to turn her out of her apartment, or suffer it to be done. I have also been positively assured, that the Prince has announced that the first exertion of his power will be to decide the fate of the Princess; and that Perceval, even though he demurred at endeavouring to bring about a divorce, gave it to be understood that he should have no objection to her being excluded from the coronation, and exiled to Holyrood House.* However, I only give you these as reports,

* I am confident that such a course would never have been adopted by Mr. Perceval. He was not a man to lend himself to any measures

for which I know no foundation, and sincerely hope that there is none of a solid nature. While on the subject of royalties, I may as well tell you an anecdote, which, whether true or false, has amused me very much. They say, that when the Duke of C[larence] deputed Mrs. F[——]n to make his proposals of marriage to Miss L[o]ng,* she went to her and stated very gravely that the Duke of C[larence] was willing to part with Mrs. J[orda]n, and give her place in his affections to Miss L[ong]; on which the poor little girl thought that she was intended to officiate in *the same capacity* with her predecessor : so she fell a crying, and called the unlucky ambassadress all the bad names that she could think of.

Donald Macdonald called on me a few days ago, to tell me that his brother's marriage with Lady Caroline Edgcumbe is finally settled, and will take place with all possible expedition. I am heartily glad of it. Sir John Sinclair (the Duchess of Gordon's grandson) is going to be married to the daughter of Admiral de Courcy. Lady Oxford is returned to town, to lie in. Somebody said (in allusion to the old joke about the Harleian Miscellany) that to judge by her size, this production would be a very voluminous work indeed. I have not yet seen her myself, but I hear that she is looking extremely ill, is in very low spirits, and, in short, is evidently quite chap-fallen.

You say, " I wonder what you think of Trotter's Life of Fox ? " Now I wonder that, supposing I had only read two paragraphs, you could have any doubt of what I must think ; and still more I should wonder if, supposing that I *had* read the paragraphs, you should imagine it possible for me to read two more. I contented myself with the extracts in the newspapers, which were quite numerous enough to satisfy my curiosity, and prevent my wishing to see any more of the work. The Author was a person merely taken into Fox's family because he was a relation of the widow of

which were not strictly consonant with open, upright honour. Had he been convinced of the Princess's guilt, he would not have upheld her, or *professed* himself her friend, while in secret he joined in the party against her. [Original note.]

* In 1812 she accepted William Wellesley Pole (" who," the Duke of Buckingham wrote, regarding the Duke of Clarence's proposal, " is wholly indebted to him for this acceptance "), afterwards 4th Earl of Mornington, the spendthrift and *roué*, and died in 1825.

the Bishop of Down, who was Fox's tutor; and he was only
employed (as I understand) in making extracts from different
works at Paris, which contained matters connected with
Fox's projected History.   This man has since thought himself
not sufficiently taken notice of, nor provided for by his
patrons, relations, and friends, and he is, therefore, supposed
to have published these memoirs with the benevolent intention of vexing them.   The work is evidently the production
of a disappointed man.   His late dispute with the physicians,
respecting his charge of their having accelerated Fox's death
by the use of digitalis, is sufficient to show how little he is
to be relied upon for accuracy ; and, as to his style, it is
the most inflated bombastic manner of writing that ever
yet came in my way, and would be much better adapted to
" The Sorrows of Lady Henrietta Heartbroke : being the
First Literary Attempt of a Young Lady."   Lord Holland
is so much offended, both at the manner and matter of
the work, that he will not suffer it to occupy a place in his
library, where even my trash finds room.

I have heard of nothing good in the literary way ; but I
read three volumes yesterday of the strangest, dullest, and
most incomprehensible trash imaginable, two or three passages
in which made me laugh above measure, owing solely (I
verily believe) to the writer's being half a fool, and half a
madwoman.   It is the life of Mrs. Wells,* a ci-devant actress ;
in which, among other things, she proves that the Duke of
[——] has given himself a vast deal of unnecessary trouble ;
a thing of which I never should have suspected him.   It
seems that when a person is married already, and wants to
marry somebody else, nothing in the world is necessary but
the simplest and easiest thing possible : he has nothing upon
earth to do but to turn Jew!   This is what Mrs. Wells did
with the greatest success ; and she always takes care not to
confound her personages together.   There is "her first
husband" ; and then there is "her second husband" ; and
then, again, there is "the father of her children" ; and I
assure you, of all the distinctions I ever met with, these
different distinctions are made out the clearest.   As she was
always in debt, she inveighs bitterly against the power of
arrest ; and prays devoutly, that the earth may open and

* Mary Wells (fl. 1781–1812), Mrs. Sumbel.

swallow all the *lock-up* houses. And she says that being at Hastings' trial, a citizen's wife, who had looked at her, indolently begged her to lend her the newspaper; "on which," says Mrs. Wells, "I said, loud enough for everybody to hear me, 'I'll see you at the devil first.'" Every eye was instantly fixed on the citizen's wife; she sank into her original littleness, and hastily quitted a society where she had made herself so ridiculous ! !—Addio.

Ever yours,
M. G. Lewis.

Sunday, February 23d, 1812.—The Princess Charlotte was at the opera last night for the first time, and much delighted, as it seemed. She leant over the box and bowed to every person she knew. I could not learn if she was applauded or not. She went with the Duchess of York, Lord De Clifford, and Bloomfield to attend her. Some one of her royal uncles, and Erskine, were I understand in the box.

Monday.—I was glad to hear a person, very much *against* the Princess of Wales, say, that he considered what had passed in the House of Commons as decisive in her favour, and that nothing more can be attempted to be brought against her, nor would *dare* to be attempted on the other side—for the unpopularity is extreme. The Prince Regent went yesterday in grand state to the Chapel Royal;—the first time of his appearance as sovereign. As he proceeded from Carlton House to St. James's, surrounded by all his pomp, &c., not a single huzza from the crowd assembled to behold him ! Not a hat off ! Of this I was assured by a gentleman present, on whom I can depend.

Extract from a Letter.

I was actually going to write to you about this said *insolent* drawing-room; for such it is, and will help, I think, much to raise *commencing* indignation ! but, for heaven's sake, let any one who may, advise the Princess to remain where she is, and not stir hand or foot for herself, but leave that to others, and be *assured* "qu'il s'en *présentera*." I have heard, and in a way that makes me give some credit to it, that a man unconnected with opposition, who wishes to come forward and be talked of, rich and independent, is in possession of a copy of *The Book*, and that he means to purchase a seat, for the purpose of laying this book before Parliament —to the dismay and confusion of Perceval and others of his followers, &c.

I hear, that in consequence of the Princess having gone to Windsor to see her daughter, a message was sent to her from the Regent by Lord Liverpool, to desire her not to go there again. Her reply was, that if she saw the Princess Charlotte as usual, once a week, she would obey; but if not, she thought her duty in respect to her child was paramount to all others. The Princess Charlotte *has* not come to her, and the Princess of Wales is determined to go again to Windsor. Her Royal Highness knows she will be refused seeing her daughter, but wishes to have the refusal in black and white; and also to be able to say that she did all in her power to prove her love for Princess Charlotte.

Extract from a Letter.

[C. KIRKPATRICK SHARPE.]

What you have the goodness to ask as a favour, my dear [——], I need not say I look upon as an honour; and I have finished two daubs, which I shall take the earliest private opportunity of sending to you. The one is Queen Elizabeth dancing, the other Louis XIV. and the Duchesse de la Vallière. Whichever of these unworthy performances you deem best, pray retain for yourself; for, though the Princess Charlotte is certainly a great personage, and a budding queen, and one may give oneself great airs on having done a drawing for her, yet I am a Jacobite and a Scotchman;—so I would rather have the best of my poor efforts in the possession of yourself,

than in that of the Princess Charlotte of Wales. Ever since
I have possessed eyes and ears, I have known how to appreciate the honours done me by the former. Things have gone
on rather stupidly, I think, since you left Edinburgh. There
have been some parties, where people pretended to waltz,
and imagined they were singing. Indeed, not to be above
one's trade, with some exceptions, this city containeth few
pretty, well-dressed women, and a number of Anthropophagi,
and men whose heads

> Do grow beneath their shoulders.

I had the honour of being at Lady C[——]'s one evening
lately, and saw some French country dances. I wish that
you and Miss C[——] had seen them, also ; there was every
step of a dancing duck, and the line of beauty formed the
wrong way. Pray tell Miss C[——] that the principal Vestris
was her humble admirer Charles C[——], figuring with a new
French (I presume) head, his hair being peaked up like Cor-
poral Trim's Montero cap, or some of the foretops in Captain
Cook's voyages. With this headgear, and holding his legs
like a frog swimming, he was enough to kill one with laughing ; and he never could have his fill of it—for, when any
poor Miss fell piping hot upon her chair, out of the ring, he
always handed her up again, with a kick-out of his heels
that beggars all description.

I saw Dr. A. R[obertson] there, in very good health, but still
busy with the measled children in George's Square. His
brother, an officer in the 92nd, is a very descendant of Adonis,
and all the pelisses in Princes Street are in love with him.
However, 'tis said he confines himself entirely to Miss G[——],
a lady rich in money and a hump, to which I fear Adolphus
will never find a discussing plaster—for it appears to be a
mighty obstinate tumour. She does not care so very much
for good looks, but she is extremely fond of laurels ; and
R[——] was at *** :—so she will wear his garlands upon
her shoulders ; while he will find her money a much more
comfortable and substantial thing than a night cap of green
leaves.

I saw Mr. C[——] here the other day. He is, I think,
grown fat, and has always more light in his face than anybody ; but I wish he were away from this odious town—I

mean odious with respect to young men of fortune, and indeed to young men of any sort; for I am old fashioned, I confess, in many points, and deem this place a very poison to the youthful soul. In London, young lads are dissipated enough, and thoughtless; but I never found them set up, as they universally do here, for atheistic professors of every thing foolish and impious. David Hume has left that legacy to his unfortunate countrymen; his ill-grounded reputation dazzles our college and our bar; and I actually believe that there is not one Christian—I had almost said Theist—on the benches of our lecture-rooms, or on the boards of our Parliament-House.

A propos, our *ladies* are greatly shocked with the free use of scriptural phrases in the ******, and very angry with the author on that account. For my part, as I have read a great many of the old Presbyterian sermons, I do not see those passages in so atrocious a light; for they are nothing to the wonderful things one meets with in the effusions of Peden and Cargill; whose favourite scriptural book appears to have been the Song of Solomon :—which song, by the way, I lately found in MS. in the Advocates' Library, translated into rhyme by Mistress Barbara Macky, and humbly dedicated to that most noble lady the Countess of Caithness, daughter to that thrice worthy marquess, my Lord Marquess of Argyll. And a conscientious translator Mistress Barbara was; for she leaves not out one word of her original :—but her fidelity is superior to her metre by many degrees. The Countess to whom she dedicates was twice married; first to Lord Caithness, and then to Lord Breadalbane. Her picture, extremely pretty, is at Holyrood House.

Poor B. H[——] has got such a cold that she coughs the castle rocks into ten thousand echoes, and rouses the 92d there every five minutes with the trumpet of her nose. I never saw her in so sad a condition. Not so Lady C[——]l, who is going to marry Mr. B[——]s forthwith, and seems very comfortable on the prospect. However, she will not have the satisfaction of carrying on the S[——] family; for it appears that Mr. B[——] hath a son—an unlicked lad; and I was told that, the other evening, B[——]'s old nurse (who always lives with him) and his landlady, looking out of the back windows by moonlight, beheld master salute the housemaid as they met in the cabbage garden; on which the two indignant Lucretias sallied down stairs, and fell each upon her own property, with blows as well as words—and a dreadful scene there was! Nothing like the uproar hath been heard thereabouts, since the murder of David Rizzio. They had all been very nearly seized by the police.

What became of the nymphs I know not; but Master B[——] is transmitted to the birch of the minister at Aberlady, there to mortify in sackcloth and sea-coal ashes. If I did not know your goodness, dear [——], I should beg ten thousand pardons for all this stuff; but as it is, offering my very best wishes and respect,

I rest your ever obliged, &c.

Monday.—I was shown to-day some verses by an accomplished man, which made me wish to be a free agent, and to visit the scenes which he describes so well. Mr. Keppel Craven addressed them to a lady, a friend of mine. The writer was one of her Royal Highness the Princess of Wales's most intimate friends, and she valued his acquaintance. A mind that was capable of appreciating such characters and talents as his, could not itself be devoid of taste and delicacy.

Dated Scio, *March*, 1812.

Think not, fair lady, though in foreign clime,
  'Midst isles remote, a wanderer still I roam,
That length of travel, or that lapse of time,
  Hath banished every thought of distant home :

That home where all my old attachments dwell,
  Where infant hope and young emotions grew,
Where breathe the valued friends I love so well,
  Warm in affection, though in number few.

Then lady, wonder not that when I view'd
  The lines you traced, my cheek with pleasure glow'd ;
Nor deem it strange that thus my gratitude
  Should own the comfort which those lines bestow'd.

Oh ! they were doubly welcome at that hour, '
  When solitude and sickness were my lot ;
They prov'd by words of soft persuasive power
  That, though far distant, I was not forgot.

They sooth'd my sadness, and I learnt awhile
  The transient evils of this life to bear
With patience, as I saw great Nature smile
  Upon the island she has made so fair.

In truth, this isle is beauteous to behold,
  Well worthy of the ancient poet's choice,
Who here had fixed his seat in times of old,
  And taught its shore the echo of his voice.

In yonder bay, which no rude storms invade,
  Where, hushed in calm, the billows seem to sleep,
Two Plantain trees extend their leafy shade,
  Above a spring that mingles with the deep.

There, on a rock clad with luxuriant vine,
  The Chian youths in eager number throng,
To learn the precepts of the man divine,
  Or hear the wonders of his epic song.

Mark you the woody crags that crown the wave,—
  The olive groves spread o'er the Lesbian plain ?
Alcæus there to verse new measure gave,
  And Sappho sang, and loved, and wept in vain.

Far happier he whom Teos called her own,
  The bard who drank and laughed long life away ;
Who scatter'd roses round a tyrant's throne,
  And lighten'd with his song oppression's sway.

See, in the windings of Iona's coast,
  Full many a spot enriched by classic fame ;
Behold Miletus Thales' wisdom boast,
  But prouder still of its Aspasia's name.

Observe where Ephesus its temple rears,
  The seventh wonder of th' astonished earth ;
That mighty monument, the work of years,
  Fell on the hour that gave a conqueror birth.

At nearer Chios, view the hallowed shrine
  Whose oracle the solemn silence broke ;
Erythræ, too, where, fired with rage divine,
  The Sibyl once in mystic accents spoke.

Now smooth Ionia, grov'lling lie thy fanes,
  Thy massy porticos and columns tall ;
Alone unchanged, thy genial breeze remains,
  And sighs at even o'er their mournful fall.

Beneath the marble wreck the viper hides,
  The centipede along the cornice creeps ;
Quick o'er th' Ionic scroll the lizard glides,
  While in the sculptured leaf the scorpion sleeps.

Within thy ports mute solitude prevails,
  Which arts and industry enrich no more ;
No poetry is heard among thy vales,
  No music floats along thy desert shore ;

Save where perchance some foreign minstrel strays,
  And strikes the lyre with melancholy hand ;
Or sadly chaunts in feeble notes the lays
  Which call to memory his native land—

The lays, fair lady, which you sang so well,
  Within the precincts of that royal bower,
Where beauty, talents, wit, and kindness dwell,
  And cheer the progress of each fleeting hour.

till does the wandering troubadour aspire
  To taste the joys which in those bowers are found ;
Beneath their shade again to wake the lyre,
  And hear your voice accompany its sound.

These pleasing hopes his spirits still sustain,
  And freshened courage to his steps impart ;
They bid him for those halcyon days retain
  Unmoved his friendship, and unchanged his heart.

11th May, 1812.—I know not whether to have faith
in presentiments or not ; but once or twice in my life
" coming events " have " cast their shadows before,"
in a manner almost supernatural. To-day, I experienced
the most gloomy melancholy I ever felt, without at *the
time* having a cause for so doing ; but, late in the evening,
as I was sitting with the Princess of Wales, she received
a letter ; I observed her change colour while perusing
its contents, and, covering her face with her hands, she
exclaimed, "Oh! something dreadful has happened ;
I cannot read it aloud " ; but she pushed the letter towards
me, and signed to me to do so. The letter was from
Madame de Haeckle, giving an account of Mr. Perceval's
assassination, by a man of the name of Bellingham, as
he was going into the House of Commons.—Revenge of
private injuries was stated as the cause which led to the
commission of this crime—that is to say, *conceived*
injuries. Madame de Haeckle added, " God grant this
may not be the signal for many coming woes ! "—The
panic struck us all, but no one more than the Princess.
I never saw her so deeply affected before, or since. Mr.
Lock alone declared he did not believe that the murder,
dreadful as it was, had any connection with public
events, but was a solitary instance of crime. About
twelve at night, an express which the Princess sent to
Mr. Arbuthnot returned, with a few words confirming
the truth and accuracy of the first statement ; except
that Madame de Haeckle said the deed had been committed
in the House of Commons, whereas it was done in the
lobby of the House. The assassin immediately sat down,
did not attempt to escape, and said he had no doubt
his country would do him justice, when his wrongs were

laid before the public; he was sure the laws would respect him; and, in short, used the language of a fanatic or a maniac. Mr. Arbuthnot said he had lost his best friend, and never could have his loss replaced. The whole night was spent in conjectures upon the probable consequences of this horrible event.

Extracts from Letters,
Giving an account to her ROYAL HIGHNESS of MR. PERCEVAL'S Assassination.

Though I may not be able to send your Royal Highness more particulars than you are already acquainted with, respecting the atrocious and horrible murder committed last evening, I find it impossible not to condole with your Royal Highness on an event the most lamentable that could have befallen the nation at this time. I feel it the more sensibly from its being connected so immediately with your Royal Highness, who has lost so true, steady, and firm a friend, at a time, too, when his strenuous efforts were employed to place your Royal Highness, if not in the situation you ought to hold, at least in one more proper and fitting than your present; so, at least, I have been positively informed. On the event being known, the Speaker moved an adjournment. The depositions of the witnesses present were taken immediately by Mr. Corme and Mr. M. A. Taylor, which I understand brings the act home to the perpetrator, Mr. Bellingham, a Russian merchant living at Liverpool. He also confesses the crime. The Lords voted an address to the Regent, which was immediately taken up and presented to him. Insanity is, of course, ascribed to the assassin—the motive, disappointment at not receiving compensation for losses in his trade. Lord Granville Leveson is also said to be a person of whom Bellingham complains; but his lordship has fortunately escaped. As to *what* government will now be formed, that is entirely matter of conjecture—but a few hours must decide. As your Royal Highness may probably determine to defer your appearance in public to-morrow, I shall take it as a favour if you will let me know your pleasure.

I have the honour to remain, &c., &c.
(Signed)   A. B. ST. LEGER.

Tuesday, [——], 1812.

Nothing has yet transpired of ministerial arrangements, nor is it even known whom the Prince Regent has seen ; but it is thought that the same ministry are to be continued, and that they will still venture to try their hand. The Prince Regent certainly has a mind towards Lord Wellesley, and as certainly saw him *before Perceval's death,*—I believe on the Wednesday preceding ; but whether Lord Wellesley will join with these, that is, thinks himself sufficiently strong or not, is doubtful. I dread him ! He is violent, arrogant, and haughty ! Poor Perceval as a private man is much to be regretted ; as a minister, not so ; as is most plain by the way his death is received by the people ! He would not believe in their present distress and difficulties, nor hold out any consoling hope for their relief ; and all that *has* followed, and I fear *will* follow, is in a great measure the consequence of his harsh and headstrong disbelief in miseries too manifest to be doubted. No wonder, then, if the people grow violent and unmanageable from despair, and seek remedies, alas ! where they are least likely to be found, and throw all into confusion ! I cannot, as some do, put my head into a bag, and fancy others do not see me ; or shut my eyes, and not see the gloomy prospects of the country. As to the opposition coming in at present, I neither believe nor wish it.

I last night saw at Mr. G. Lamb's several members of the House of Commons who were present, both at the moment of the assassination, and at the examination of the assassin ; and likewise Lord Lauderdale, and some of the other lords, who carried up an address to the Prince Regent. There is not the least appearance, or evidence, or indeed suspicion, of this vile act being done in concert with anybody or any party of people, or of the murderer having any accomplice. He had been in former times a ship-broker, (or something of that sort,) at Liverpool, and within these few years was resident in Russia upon some commercial business, where his conduct was eternally getting him into scrapes, and giving much trouble to Lord Granville Leveson, our then minister there. It is said, too, that he was for some time confined in that country, on account of positive insanity. At present, he seems perfectly calm, and free from any of the manners of a madman. He said upon his examination that he was perfectly aware of the atrocity of the action, but that if he was to be calmly heard, he did not doubt that he could justify it. He never attempted escape, either before or after his seizure. The Prince Regent received the address of the Lords within an hour after the event had taken place, with every due and decent expression of regret ; it was carried up to Carlton House by Lords Grey, Lauderdale, Lansdown, Holland, the Duke of Rutland, and some one else whose name I have forgotten, accompanied by all the Princes and the Duke of York, who delivered it. The address was one merely stating the horrible crime that had been committed on the person of a member of the Lower House within the precincts of Parliament, and praying a minute inquiry, and speedy justice upon the delinquent. The House of Commons, in their confusion, had adjourned without coming to any vote on the subject. You may easily conceive the effect this event must have had on all society last night in London, and how *it*, and nothing else, was talked of *universally*, with all the horror which such a catastrophe must inspire. I am sorry to add, that its effect on the mob who had collected at the doors of the House of Commons before the murderer was removed, was by no means such as could be wished— I mean, that they did not seem at all impressed with horror at such a crime, so committed, but seemed careless about the matter, and even disposed to joke ; without, however, any party cry, or any disposition to rioting.

Her Royal Highness sent for me again the next day. She repeated all that had been said the preceding evening ; and then she drew conclusions as to the future, respecting the ministry, the Government, and other public matters, with such ingenuity of combination, and so much sound reasoning, that I had a higher opinion of the powers of her mind than I ever entertained before.

"The Prince," said she, "never will have sufficient energy to change his whole set of ministers, whatever he may wish to do ; and he will merely get in Lord Wellesley, or some such person, to plaister up the rent this great man's death has made." Then she added, with an expression of feeling which excited my warmest sympathy for her situation, " I have lost my best friend ; I know not where to look for another :—though even he was changed towards me since he had become one of the ministers. Whoever is in power becomes always more or less the creature of the Prince, and of course less friendly to me. No, no," she said, " there is no more society for me in England ; for do you think if Lady H[arrow]by, and the Duchess of B[eaufor]t, and all that set, were to come round to me now, that I would invite them to my intimacy ? Never. They left me without a reason, as time serves, and I never can wish for them back again. I am too proud for that. I do not say that, were they to be civil again, I never would ask them to a great dinner, or ball : that is quite anoder affair. Mais vous sentez bien, dat to have dem in de intimate footing dey used to be on, coming every Sunday night, and all dat sort of ting, never. No, I repeat it, so long as dat man lives, [meaning the Regent,] les choses vont de mal en pire for me—for whoever comes in to serve him, even dose calling themselves my friends, are just the same ; they will set me aside, and worship the Regent. Enfin, I have had patience for seventeen years, and I conclude I must for seventeen years longer."

To hear complaints too well founded, to be low spirited oneself, to have no consolation to offer, save of a kind that unfortunately for her she has never been taught to resort to, and consequently cannot benefit from, is a very painful situation for any one to be in who is her friend. I admire her in many instances ; I honour her masculine noblenesss and magnanimity ; but I feel that we are too far apart in our habits and views, for me to be able either to divert, or entertain, or comfort her. I can listen, however ; and that is always some consolation.

She received various letters from all her intimates, filled with accounts of the tragic event ; then her Royal

Highness proposed driving to Lady Oxford's, to consult with her. I did not immediately contradict her ; but the idea of driving to Lady Oxford's at a moment when I knew that all eyes would be turned upon her, terrified me for her sake. Shortly after, she ordered her phaëton ; I know not what impelled me, but I exclaimed, " Oh ! I trust not to go to Lady Oxford ; I am so afraid, Madam, of what may be said." On looking up, I saw a rising storm upon her countenance. She affected great composure, and said with a pettish air, " Oh, 'tis all one, I assure you—let us not go " ; upon which she turned short upon her heel, and walked away in anger into the garden. I felt sorry at having been guilty of anything she deemed disrespectful. I knew not what to do, but I thought I had done what a real regard for her demanded ; so I followed her, and, when I came up to her, I saw that she wished to hide her anger, and, with a command of temper, rare in most persons, but admirable in a princess, she began talking upon indifferent subjects with great self-command, and I saw that she was determined to forget the circumstance, and I on my part resolved never to repeat the offence. After all, I knew that she would always follow the bent of her own inclinations, and nothing but an imprudent impulse of real friendship made me hazard one word of advice.

When I was first introduced to her Royal Highness she gave me her opinion upon the subject of advice, and after we became better acquainted, she said, with many flattering expressions on my character, " Now I look upon you as a friend, and we shall never quarrel if you never give me any advice." In future, therefore, I determined (and I kept to my determination) that unless her Royal Highness should call upon me to act in any business, or on any occasion, that I deemed hurtful to myself personally, I would neither contradict nor advise her—that was the province of others. Fortunately, or

I   G unfortunately, it is difficult to say which, Lady Oxford herself, came, accompanied by Lord A. Hamilton, and Lord G[re]y. These visitors prevented her going out, to commit any imprudence to which the excited state of her mind might have tempted her.

Thursday, 14th.—The drawing-room was put off, which, of course, disappointed the Princess, as she wishes to be on the scene as much as possible.

Saturday.—I was invited to Blackheath. The Princess Charlotte, as usual, at dinner; Monsieur and Madame de Haeckle, Lady Elizabeth Whitbread, Miss Whitbread, and the Dowager Lady Grey. I was sorry to see these excellent people there on this day, because I feared her Royal Highness would be blamed for inviting them to meet her daughter; as her enemies will turn everything to her disadvantage, and exaggerate every error. The Princess had been forbidden to invite any persons whatever to meet the Princess Charlotte.

THE ALBANY, *Sunday.*

MY DEAR [——],—I shall have the pleasure of dining with you to-morrow, but you will see me quite crestfallen. Madame de Staël! Oh! Madame de Staël!—" Oh! Huncamunca! —Huncamunca, oh!"—How shall I write it? She told me —she uttered it with her own lips—I heard it with my own ears—it was to my own face, which still burns with mortification, that she said it—she told me—shame checks my pen —in short, she told me—that I was—inférieur! Oh! all ye gods, inférieur! Write it not, my hand. "The word appears already written: wash it out my tears": and not inférieur merely, but *très* inférieur! Humiliating truth; can I ever survive thy declaration? What can I do? whither shall I fly? *Malheureux que je suis!* where hide my diminished head?—Hélas!—Oimè! heigh ho!—Oh dear! lack a daisy! bubble and squeak, &c., and so forth.

You may perceive that this mortification has nearly turned

my head ; let me, therefore, use what little sense I have left
to assure you that I am,

Your sincere friend,

M. G. LEWIS.

BRIGHTON.

I saw ladies Melbourne and Cowper, Lords Worcester
and Brook, walking upon the abominable Steyne, which
looks to me like a piece of ground where felons are allowed
to take the air. " Oh ! how little fashionable folks know
of rural enjoyments, or (I believe) of any enjoyment !
Lady M[elbourne] is a friend of my friends, so I am sure
there must be some fair stuff in her ; but she is sadly
encased in worldly ice. I wish I could be very fine. I
think it is a covering to all sorts of deformity ; and the
silence and grandeur of it impose delightfully upon the
multitude. The bareness and glare of Brighton put my
eyes out, and the bustle and noise put my patience out :
so Brighton is not in my good graces.

I received a letter from the Princess. She tells me
that the paper called the ——, has been bought over
by Carlton House, and that the editor, a Mr. * * *
is going to publish a correspondence, which he declares
to have passed between the Princess herself, Lady
A[nne] H[amilton], and Lord P[——], which correspondence her Royal Highness says is a forgery. She
requests me not to take the —— in any more, and likewise wishes all those who profess to be her friends, to
forbid it in their families. One of her Royal Highness's
ladies is much distressed at the continued alarms which
such threats cause to her Royal mistress ; and, in writing
to me by the Princess's desire to tell me of the above
circumstance, Lady [——] adds, that she thinks she will
not be able to continue in the Princess's service ; for
not only is it a situation of constant uneasiness, but also
of very great fatigue—such a perpetual excitement from
little causes, that, during the period of her waiting, she

never knows peace. Lady [——] is sincerely attached
to the Princess ; but she says, and says truly, that it is
impossible for her, or indeed for any one else, to be of
use to her Royal Highness ; for, if she asks advice one
day, she acts in direct opposition to it the next : and
Lady [——] adds, I foresee so much misery likely to
be the poor Princess of Wales's lot, that I had rather,
being unable to serve her, not be implicated in the blame
which will fall upon those persons who, it is very naturally
supposed, have some influence over her conduct.

Fortunately for Lady [——], the Windsor expedition,
or royal siege, is not likely to take place during her
time of waiting, for Lady De Clifford has got inflamed
eyes, and has been obliged to come to town. Princess
Charlotte * is in consequence shut up in the castle with
the Queen Grandmother, and so all will remain as it is
for the present. The Prince's going in person, or not, to
the House on Monday, is uncertain. A negociation I
hear is carrying on between Lord Wellesley, Canning,
and the Whigs, in order to turn out the present Ministry,
That would be a good deed ; but I dread Lord Wellesley
as a minister more than any other ; he is ambitious,
haughty, extravagant to excess.—Alas ! poor country !

Décember 2nd, 1812.

The Princess Charlotte was at the House, and sat on
the woolsack near the throne ; two of the Princesses
came from Windsor to accompany her. It was remarked,
that she talked and laughed much, turned her back often
upon papa,† and had a certain *expressive* smile during

* Princess Charlotte wrote to Lady de Clifford during her absence,
" We go on pretty well, considering all things, without you " ; and as
the Bishop of Salisbury (Dr. Fisher), whom she did not like, had sent her
a letter of advice, she added : " When I answered the Bishop's letter I
did all I could to make it over waite [weight]. I hope I succeeded."
† According to Karoline Bauer (Memoirs, ii. p. 221), as already
quoted in the Introduction, Princess Charlotte said of her parents :

the speech, which did not displease *all* the lords, nor
all the ladies there. The Prince, it is said, was much
displeased at her manner ; in addition to which the
Princess Charlotte *spoke* to Lord Erskine, and *nodded* to
Lord Jersey ; but those from whom I heard this seemed
to be diverted only at what had passed, and attached no
blame to her Royal Highness. The Prince was flurried
and nervous, both in going to and returning from the
House, but delivered his speech well. By the people
he was received with dead silence, and not a hat off ;—
some marks of disapprobation even, with scarcely any
loyal greeting ; only a few plaudits as he went through
the Horse Guards,—no general burst of popular applause.

There was a report of the Prince Regent's being
ill ; and I was told that the King had been, and *was*,
since Monday last, in such paroxysms, that they were
considerably alarmed at Windsor.

I have only observed the advertisement (of the letters
the Princess of Wales wished to have published) once
inserted in the Morning Chronicle, and it is not, I find,
yet generally understood as being a genuine document.
I am in hopes that some compromise may be offered
from the other side ; and the less that is said about it,
therefore, I think, the better. I dread the publication
of these epistles ; as, however great it may make her
wrongs appear—and great in my opinion they are—
yet it will give colour to a charge of breach of trust in
making letters public that were never written to meet
the public eye. This might not be an objection at a
moment of *personal* attack, or after a lapse of years,
when time brings foul and fair to light ; but this not
being at present the case, I repeat, that I dread the

" My mother was wicked, but she would not have turned so wicked
had not my father been much more wicked still." In her Memoirs,
Karoline Bauer quotes many things from this Diary as from the "Diary
of Lady Charlotte Bury."

publication of them, and think it is highly injudicious in her Royal Highness's advisers.

It appears that Napoleon has got to Wilna, and is safe, with a great part of his army. The Russian Ambassadress, I heard from Lady Warren, is making all sorts of enquiries as to the form in which she is to be presented to her Royal Highness the Princess Regent !—How will they get off this ?—I wish it may embarrass them, but fear it will not.

KENSINGTON, *Monday.*

Came here yesterday by invitation. The house desperately cold, and everything else *as bad as ever*. Was commanded at half-past two, to accompany the Princess of Wales to see the young princes, her nephews. She hates them, I don't know why, unless it is that, as she says, they are frightful. As usual, she was mighty gracious to me ; but that is because I am not curious or prying. I only wish I had ears and heard not, eyes and saw not ;—but, as that cannot be, I render myself as deaf, blind, and dumb as I can, and think myself perfectly justified in so doing.—Her Lady-in-waiting said to me, " things are grown so bad, *so dull*, so black, that if it were not for the determination, of putting a speedy end to my slavery, I could not endure it : to have, all day and all night, long complaints poured forth from which there is no remedy or relief,—nothing in heaven or earth that one can point to as a sanctuary from them !—The feeling that I tell you this, and that when in her presence I seem pleased, is a constant goad to my conscience, and would make me miserable, even if ennui and a consciousness of possible disgrace did not render me so.—All the day long her Royal Highness continues to talk of wishing people dead ; and I must not dare to contradict the wish. I have been an accomplice in murder many a time, if silence gives consent."

The Princess made many complaints of *La reine des Ostrogoths*, and long histories about the *Squallinis*, and the G[——]s, that really disgusted me. If she likes busying herself with such objects, I do not. The old ourang outang came to dinner,—more free and easy and detestable than ever,—I think of him *pour tout bien !* Then her Royal Highness sang—squall—squall ! Why invite me ?

After supper, she continued the complaints. I cannot describe how wearisome, how unavailing and injudicious the subjects of her conversation now are in general. I know so perfectly that advice or even example is totally thrown away, and that every body who gives such is detested, without benefiting her, that in the pass to which things are arrived there is only one course to be pursued, silence—and to break from her society. Regret must and ever will have place in my thoughts, when I look back on the past, and think of the pleasant days I have spent with the Princess of Wales, and recollect how cruelly she has been treated : and how recklessly she has played into her enemies' hands, by going on in a course which must ruin her character and happiness.

The persons who have gained undue influence over the Princess, have cunningly persuaded her to renounce all her former friends ; and she herself has too much sense not to be aware that the respectable individuals who were a short time ago proud to frequent her society, would not do so now ; neither would her Royal Highness invite them ; for she knows her present associates are very unfit company to be seen in her house ; so she *pretends* that she has found her old friends insincere and unkind, and professes not to like them.

The next day, her Royal Highness made a party to go to a small cottage which she had taken in the neighbourhood of Bayswater, where she could feel herself unshackled by all the restraints of royalty and etiquette.

There she received a set of persons wholly unfit to be admitted to her society. It is true, that since the days of Mary of Scotland, (when Rizzio sang in the Queen's closet,) and in the old time before her, all royal persons have delighted in some small retired place or apartment, where they conceived themselves at liberty to cast off the cares of their high station, and descend from the pedestal of power and place to taste the sweets of private life. But in all similar cases, this attempt to be what they were not, has only proved injurious to them. Every station has its price—its penalty. Princes and Princesses must live for the public; and, though it has sometimes been said that dissimulation is necessary to them, I believe it is the reverse. They are beacons set on a hill; they must be an example, or a warning; and, when they lurk about in corners, and forsake the society of those with whom they ought to associate, for that of low buffoons and characters who pander to their vanity and folly, the die is cast, and they fall rapidly to perdition. To some who have been more powerful than others, the descent has been more gradual; but from whatever I remember in tale or history, those princes have become despicable, and finally lost, who gave themselves up to favouritism and all its attendant unworthiness. By the Princess especially, a more unwise or foolish course could not have been pursued, than this imitation of her unfortunate Sister Queen, of France. All the follies, though not the elegance and splendour, of Trianon, were aped in the rural retreat of Bayswater, and the Princess's foes were not backward at seizing upon this circumstance and turning it (as well they might) to effect her downfall. As far as regards this world only, it is much more frequently imprudence, than actual crime which finally hurls people to their destruction.

All the time that her Royal Highness was going on in this idle, unworthy manner, there existed in her a half smothered compunction, which made her wish to excuse her conduct; for none can entirely emancipate themselves from blame, when aware that it is merited, or remain ignorant of the sentence which they deserve to have passed upon them by their fellow mortals. The Princess said, how ill it would appear in the eyes of the world, if she diverted herself, and gave balls and assemblies, when no further supplies were granted to her, and that she must consequently run into debt if she incurred any unnecessary expenses. Besides, unhappy as she was at being deprived of the Princess Charlotte's society, how could she affect gaiety?—would not her doing so have the worst possible appearance? would not people blame her, and say, all she wanted was to amuse herself?—" there, you see, she cares not for her daughter, so that she has company."

There was much plausibility in all this *lying*; but unfortunately, I am too well acquainted with the interior to be so deceived. To say the truth, I often wonder that the world is as easily gulled as it is by the great little people: it only proves that it is the station, and not the human being, that twists and metamorphoses every thing; but a near inspection of *Les tours de Passe-passe* reduces all the magic to mere juggling. Sometimes, I am enraged at myself for enduring to be in their society for a moment, much more so for laughing or seeming pleased; but I have the same sensation as if I was living with mad people, and really humour her as much as I would do them, for fear of the immediate consequences to myself. Yesterday, at dinner, before the servants, she told *the abominable*, that a hundred virgins had strewed flowers in the Duke of Brunswick's way, on his landing in Holland, &c., &c.

Tuesday, 11*th.*—The music mania is at its highest pitch; the intervals between singing and eating, are filled up with tedious complaints, which mean nothing, or nothing that they ought to mean. The Princess obliged one of her ladies to tell the ourang outang's fortune. It was not difficult to tell of his impudence and cunning and rapaciousness; but he would not take the hint. It was quite a relief to-day to be invited to meet Mr. Gell, Mr. Knight, and Mr. Craven at dinner; but her manner to them, especially to the two latter, would be comical in the extreme, if it were not melancholy, from the knowledge of the source whence it arises. I could not help looking with a scrutinizing glance at Mr. Craven, and I think his eyes *are* unsealed. Mr. Gell's are still close shut; but the bonhommie and truth with which he speaks to her Royal Highness, are very diverting. He talked of a gentleman who sings divinely, and who is very handsome and agreeable, and wished to be allowed to be presented to her Royal Highness; at which I saw the Princess quite furious. A rival Squallini! mercy upon us—what should we do? how should we dare to listen to any other music than that of *the one par excellence?* in short, nobody is to come into the house but Squallinis.

She told me she should sell all her plate, all her toilette ornaments given her by the King, every thing, in short, which she could convert into money—for money she must have. Another person in my place, would say to her Royal Highness, when she is detailing her money grievances, " surely, madam, if you have gained £2000 a year by putting your servants on board wages, and that you have had £1000 from another source, and that you get £1200 a year by not paying your ladies, you ought to be richer than ever,—but no, I never said one word of all this—à quoi bon?—She is absolutely infatuated: she even talks of marrying again—but never till she has tried the favoured mortal, and made him pass five times through the fiery furnace of constancy and truth: there

is an ordeal for you !—it is more truly an ordeal than
Miss Adair's.* To kill the Regent ; then go abroad,
with a court of her own making, of which the fiddler is
to be king ; this is her favourite plan. Campbell is to
write the epithalamium, and Lady C[harlotte] L[indsay]
and Lady C[harlotte] C[ampbell], the two favourites,
are to be the ladies of the bedchamber—and * * *
* * * *` "Don't you think this will be delightful ? "
she asks me.

Though the Princess was playing at chess with Lord
Palmerston, she overheard every word I said, and that
was not agreeable, though, in fact, I said nothing that
was of any consequence. I endeavoured as much as
possible to turn the conversation upon books, and upon
such books as I was aware she would not have the patience
to read. Nevertheless, from a quickness of perception,
great tact, and an excellent memory, she catches the
title of every work, and, having turned over the leaves,
has a sort of smattering of the contents, which she *hashes*
up with other people's opinions, and gives the whole *en
réchauffé*, with a *faux brillant* which imposes on the many.

As soon as these men went away, she felt a weight
removed from her. She cannot now bear to be in good
society : she calls it *dull ;* and, true enough, *good* society
is often dull—whereas, what is *called* " good " (though
often bad) is the reverse. What strange misnomers
there are in the world ! but it is possible to unite greatness with goodness ; and, at all events, it is a great merit
to bear dulness with patience.

The Princess is always busying herself with the multi-
plication-table—that is, putting two and two together.
She asked me if I thought Lady C[harlotte] C[ampbell]
would marry Mr. Arbuthnot. I burst out laughing, and
replied, " First of all, is he so inclined ?—I believe not.

* Miss Adair, afterwards Mrs. Grey, wrote a novel called the
Ordeal. [Original note.]

And, secondly, I know Lady [Charlotte] is not inclined, either for lovers or matrimony, at present." *

The Princess then held Lady C[harlotte] C[ampbell] very cheap, and returned to the old story. It is difficult to say to any persons that one thinks their principles libertine, or rather that they have no principles at all; but I told her Royal Highness, that I knew Lady [————] would never be made happy by any *illicit* attachment, and that the sting of what she conceived guilt, and the anxiety of concealment, would always make her wretched. To this, the Princess replied, "*Married love never lasts; dat is not in de nature.*" I confessed that I had seldom or ever known it do so; but that even were it the case, and that a married woman found herself obliged to resign the sweet illusions of passion, she had yet the sober consolations of esteem from others—of the applause and consideration of the world—above all, the inward peace of self-satisfaction; whereas, a woman who was a mistress, was always in danger of losing her lover, and with him she lost everything. To this, her Royal Highness had nothing to reply. I spoke merely as to the *worldly* consideration of the subject; for I knew that view of the matter would weigh most with her. I do not think she likes me when I speak thus. I assured her, Lady [————] was sincere in her principles; but she hopes she is not stedfast in them.

Thursday.—Yesterday, Mr. Arbuthnot, Mr. Ward, Mr. Luttrell, Mr. Gell, Mr. N[ugen]t (?), Mr. Fox, and Lady Charlotte Lindsay dined at Kensington. Of all these persons, Mr. Gell is, I believe, my favourite; I think he is really good, and I cannot like any one long, that has not that stable foundation whereon to rest. The con-

* She did not marry a second time until 1818, when, on March 17th. at Lady Burghersh's house in Florence, she married the Rev. Edward John Bury, a clergyman of good birth and artistic tastes, whom she had known as her sons' tutor.

versation was of that kind which most delights the
Princess—brilliant, evanescent, and devoid of reflection
—a sort of sparkling fire which only makes darkness
visible—which moves the muscles of the face to laughter,
but never dilates the heart with real joy. If flattery
could delight, I had enough of it : but it has ceased to
charm me ; for it is only intoxicating when one can bear
its trophies to the feet of a beloved object as an offering
to its merits ; 'tis nothing when it is an idle gratification
of selfish pleasure. Mr. N[ugen]t is a fat, fubsy man,
very like a white turkey-cock ; but he is a good musician,
reads music at sight, and sings correctly. Mr. Fox is
a little hideous black man, who is called clever ; perhaps
only because he bears that name ; though I am tempted
to give him credit for somewhat of reality, but it is only
upon credit, for I never heard him *say* anything that
could sanction the belief. Of all that was said, I only
remember that these persons praised Lord Byron's
English Bards and Scotch Reviewers, and declared they
were surprised it had not made more noise, as it was
the cleverest thing that ever was written. This backed
Lady M[——]'s opinion. They added that it was the more
wonderful it should be so, because his " Hours of Idleness " was remarkably weak and poor. It is curious to
hear all the different opinions that people give of each
other. On Saturday, Lord L[uca]n dined here ; he
hates Lord H[artington], and there appears to be no love
lost between them. I like the latter much the best ; he
says, Lady E. B[ingham] is an impudent, forward girl—
that she pursued Lord H[artington] à toute outrance—who
declares openly that he does not mean to have any
thing to do with her. I believe both these assertions
to be true.

People say that the unfortunate King may linger much
longer, but that, whenever the Prince does come to the
throne, he will make no change in the administration,

and that he will also totally abandon the Catholic question, in spite of having promised to support it ;—that this conduct will raise a rebellion, and that it is what ministers wish, because it will give them an opportunity to act with greater rigour, and by violence to extirpate the Roman Catholics, or at least their tenets, altogether. Others say, that as this is impossible, it will only breed a civil war. There was much talk yesterday at dinner about Mr. G[——] ; the Princess hates him ; she says, he is so mischievous and so tattling ; she added, " I could forgive him for anything he said of myself, because I have good broad shoulders ; but he calls my daughter an abandon'd little thing, and d—n me [she often swears that oath,] if ever he shall meet her in this house again. The case vas, you see, that Mr. G[——] abuse all the Royal Family to her, *vich vas* a great impertinence *as I* should say, *and she, poor little ting, vanted* to excuse *dem ;* so *wen* Mr. G[——] in his wisdom said it was pity de Duke should have his mistress here, vare de princesse was, she answered, ' *Oh Lord upon us,* vat would you have ; de Dukes cannot marry, dey must love somebody.' It would have been better had my daughter said, as one should say, dat is a subject on which I never speak ; but she is a young ting, and not prepared for such matters.—No, no, let us speak no more of Mr. G[——] 'tis such an unpleasant subject."

MONTAGUE HOUSE.—I arrived at three, found nobody but old J[——] : the horrid din continued till five, then eating, then din again till dinner at seven. I think my ears never underwent such martyrdom. After dinner, again *the music* * was continued till ten without ceasing : he was then dismissed, and I was kept till two in the morning. The Princess told me " that everything was going on as she wished—that *they* were playing her game

* With the Sapios.

—that she had the cards in her own hands," and a great many more *mystical nothings*, with which she deceives herself, and fancies she deceives others. The only facts I could catch hold of, were that Lady de Clifford had resigned, and that the Duchess of Leeds was proposed to succeed her as governess to Princess Charlotte, but that she (the Princess of Wales) as well as Lady de Clifford, had advised the young princess never to allow another governess to come near her ; a piece of advice, I conclude, which tallies too well with her own inclinations for her to disregard it. What interest Lady Clifford could have in this advice, I know not, unless it were the vanity of saying " Princess Charlotte never had any governess after me." Then, continued her Royal Highness, " Mr. Brougham has written me a letter of twelve pages, which, as soon as he returns to town, when Parliament meets, I am to send to the Regent and the Chancellor, respecting my cruel situation, and my not being permitted to see my daughter ;—to which letter he must give some answer ; but I have taken care to write a copy of it to the Ministers, also, well knowing that he would put the paper in his pocket and never say more about it."

I had nothing to do but to bow, and listen. ." Oh ! my dear [——] there will be such a crash !" " I trust it will be all for the best," said I. " Nothing can be worse," said she. " Oh ! my dear [——]," resumed the Princess, after a short pause, " there is all sort of tracasseries at Lee." Of that I had no doubt.—Such jealousies and quarrellings, Lady A[nne] fighting with Lady P[erceval], the one supporting the Sapios, the other, that is Lady A[nne], wishing to turn them out of the seminary. Then the young Miss G[——] making love to the young captain ; and the old man in a fury, and the young lover mighty cool.—" Lady [Anne]," said the Princess, " is very much attached to me, and has many good qualities, but has a love of meddling, and prying, and managing, and a want of tact I cannot endure. And, in short, 'tis nothing but little things; but in little things she is constantly doing what is disagreeable, and there is not a hole or corner into which she does not follow me— she has such a *manque de tacte*, that she wears me to death —no, I could not suffer it long."—" I wonder your Royal Highness did not tell her of your dislike to have any one in your apartment."—" No, my dear [Lady Charlotte], I showed it to her, but, to say get out, I could not." This was spoken with real good nature.

I was unwilling to add my mite of disapprobation against the poor Lady [Anne], and said what I could in her favour—and the Princess replied, " If I had a house in town, it would be very different. None of my ladies should *live in* my house. I would give Lady C. L[indsay] and Lady C. C[ampbell], a house each of their own, and this would be a good excuse never to have the ladies I do not like, as well as Lady C[harlotte] L[indsay] and Lady C[harlotte] C[ampbell], except at dinner."—Her Royal Highness said many kind things about myself and my own concerns—she praised those I love, and promised never to forget the little services they had rendered her. " You shall see, the instant I have anything in my power." One must not, however, put one's trust in princes; and, though I believe her Royal Highness intends to do what she says, I fear perhaps her opinions may change, when she has *the power* of doing what she now wishes.

Sunday.—After luncheon, I accompanied the Princess (attended by her Lady-in-waiting) to town, to the Duchess of Brunswick's. The Duke of Gloucester * was there; he received the Princess very heartily; party, as well as

* William, Duke of Gloucester (1776–1834), only son of William, Duke of Gloucester, brother of King George III., and of Maria Walpole, Dowager Countess Waldegrave. He remained unmarried until after the marriage of Princess Charlotte, being, it was thought, as an English

interested views, perhaps of the highest kind, may influence him ; but from all I can learn he is a good man,
and has the upright solid basis of religion and virtue
which distinguished the poor fallen Monarch.   The conversation between these three royal personages put me
exactly in mind of the *Margravine of Bareith's* Memoirs ;
and I think all accounts of courts, and the petty transactions therein, must have precisely the same stamp.
The old Duchess talked chiefly of the Queen and the
Princesses having visited her ; upon which her daughter,
the Princess of Wales, addressed herself as loud as she
could, across her mother, to the Duke of Gloucester, not
liking to hear her enemies, as she conceives them, so
dwelt upon, and with such complacency.   Then they
talked of the death of Lady Ailesbury, and immediately
of who would get her place in *this world ;* then of the
death of a Mrs. Fielding, and who would get *her* place ;—
upon which the Princess of Wales rolled her eyes in signal
of being weary ; though, in talking of the places she
intends to bestow if she ever has the power, she is not
at all aware that to those not particularly on the look-
out, it must be equally tiresome.—Then they mentioned
the New Theatre, and the Duke said, " Nobody but
Mr. Whitbread could have done so clever a thing."
" Why," said the old Duchess, " is he an architect ?   I
thought he was only a brewer."—Not so bad that,—
only that it was not meant to be good.   The Duke said
—" No, ma'am—only no one but he could have had so
much taste and ingenuity."   Then their Royal Highnesses
made a joke on the conveniences attached to the private
boxes ; after which the conference broke up—the kiss
of peace was given—and the Princess came back here.—
On the way, Lady A[——] was started as fresh game.

prince, a suitable *parti* if no foreign prince was selected as her consort ;
and then married, July 22, 1816, her aunt, Princess Mary, daughter of
King George III.

I   H

"Think, my dear [——], of another petitesse. Miss R. was with me, and, talking of masters, observed that she could not afford them here as she could abroad, which she regretted. 'Now,' said she, 'I want to have such a master for such a thing—but it costs so much.' 'Oh !' said Lady A[——], 'there's Mr. Bolton, the best man in the world, and so cheap, only five shillings a lesson.' Accordingly, Miss R. had this master, but found out that he had three or four guineas entrance money, which Lady A[——] had never mentioned. Accordingly, she wrote to the latter to mention the circumstance, and to say she could not employ him. Upon which Lady A[——] asks me to pay *de tree* guineas. Can you conceive! I say, 'oh! yes, to be sure,' but I tink de thing has not the sens commun, for why should I pay de masters of all de misses ? "

I quite agreed with her Royal Highness in the meanness of such contrivances.

After dinner, the Princess received a letter from the Princess Charlotte, who told her she had written to the Prince her father refusing, but in a very respectful manner, to have any more governesses, and gave the Princess of Wales an account of a dispute she had with the Queen and her Aunts about it. The Princess of Wales was in the third heaven of delight.

Her Royal Highness showed me Mr. Brougham's letter, which she is copying, that it may go to the Prince. It is a most capital letter, setting forth her wrongs ; and, providing the basis be solid upon which it is founded, her cause must be secure. No petulance, no anger, but dignity, tenderness, and propriety. Then what may they not answer ? They may say it is *all true*, if so, and so were *not ;* but if so, and so, and so *is*, why then so, and so, and so is justice, and not injustice,—and all this depends on this so and so being proved, or disproved. God grant all may be for the best !

Tuesday, 12th.—I received Walter Scott's Rokeby. I gazed at it with a transport of impatience, and began reading it in bed. I am already in the first canto :— my soul has glowed with what he justly terms "the art unteachable." My veins have thrilled ; my heart has throbbed ; my eyes have filled with tears—during its perusal. The poet who can thus master the passions to do his bidding, must be indeed a poet.*

Wednesday, 13th.—The Princess came to me yesterday in a great bustle, as though she were " big with *the fate of Cato and of Rome*." She had received another letter from her daughter :—such a character ; such firmness ; such determination ! She was enchanted. The Prince had been with the Chancellor to Windsor, and in presence of the Queen, demanded what she meant by refusing to have a governess. She referred him entirely to her letter,—upon which the Queen and her father abused her, as being an obstinate, perverse, head-strong girl. " Besides," said the Prince, " I know all that passed in Windsor Park ; and if, it were not for my clemency, I would have shut you up for life. Depend upon it, as long as I live you shall never have an establishment, unless you marry." †

" Charlotte never spoke, or moved a muscle," said the

* The original note says : " But truth must be told :—he behaved ill to a woman—and that woman her (*sic*) who was to be his queen ! From having literally set at her feet—from having, in one of the most spirited of his songs, expressed devotion to her cause, he suddenly veered round to the Regent, and never after testified the slightest remembrance of his having once courted her favour :—verily he had his reward."

† Queen Charlotte reported this scene to Miss Knight on January 16, in a way which showed her feelings towards her grand-daughter. " Our conversation was very *gênante*, till at last we got on the subject of Princess Charlotte. The Queen spoke of her with all the prejudice and enmity which she had for years imbibed against her, related to me all that had passed between her Royal Highness and the Chancellor, and considered her dignified behaviour as hardness of heart." It is no wonder, perhaps, that the Princess " hated her grandmother."

Princess of Wales; "and the Prince and the Chancellor departed as they came. Nothing could be more determined or immoveable than she was :—in short, we must *frighten* the man into doing something, otherwise he will do nothing ; and, if mother and daughter cannot do this, nothing can.—On Sunday, I shall send my letter—but I do not think gentle means will ever avail.—If we were in past times——" and her Royal Highness looked quite fearful as she spoke !

I know not what to reply, when she talks thus. What I think is most likely to ensue—and I fear 'tis what is *best*—is, that she will be set aside entirely, as a factious spirit, dangerous to the peace of the country.

Yet, after such a conversation as the above, her Royal Highness could begin squalling with S[apio] and forget her cares and vital interests, in the amusement of *frightening the air* with horrible sounds, till past one in the morning !—'Tis wonderful !—After all, what right has the Princess Charlotte to disobey her father ? Those persons who are never governed, are not, surely, fit to govern others.

I am agitated for the consequences of the intrigues that are going on. I am sincerely attached to the Princess Charlotte, but I shrink from being obliged to say, " very firm, and very fine," when I think, " very obstinate, and very wrong-headed."—If she is without shame, or fear of God or man, at seventeen, what is to become of her—of us ? Hearing of crooked ways and mean policy disgusts me, and creates a tremor, as though I were surrounded by a parcel of opera devils, shaking their resin torches in my face.

Thursday, 14th.—T. Campbell accompanied me by invitation to see her Royal Highness. About seven o'clock, a messenger arrived from Princess Charlotte, which occasioned a great bustle, and some tears to the

Princess of Wales, who is in despair, for the young Princess consents to receive the Duchess of Leeds as her governess, after all her violent objections to do so. This circumstance decided the Princess of Wales on sending off her own letter directly to the Regent per messenger. How far this sudden and premature disposal of her letter may suit Mr. Brougham's intentions, I know not. *Mais la bombe est partie*, and the mine is sprung. I fear all it will produce will perhaps be, an order to shut her up in some close confinement, allowing her to see nobody. Sometimes, I hope the best, but oftener fear the worst for this poor woman.

Friday, 15*th.*—To-day, the Princess received an answer from Lord Liverpool—only a few lines,—returning her letter to the Regent *unopened*, and saying, that he was commanded by the Prince to inform her Royal Highness, that, having some years ago declared he never would receive any letter or paper from the Princess, his Royal Highness intended to adhere to that determination; and so ended all the hopes and fears her packet had created. It seems to me that the Prince does not mean violently to attack her, for here a fair opportunity presented itself, and was not seized upon; but that he intends to let the Princess be forgotten, and to lay her by upon the shelf of oblivion. I fear parliament will do much the same. She, however, does not anticipate this. Princes have little idea, and can have little, of the very small importance of their interests and petty intrigues, out of the immediate circle of their influence; in England, especially, where even the reigning monarch is merely a chief magistrate, under the authority of laws which he cannot overpass.

Whenever there was a storm brewing, or actually raging, then the poor Princess was comparatively happy: like all restless spirits, she hoped that, as "it is an ill wind which blows nobody good," she might be the person who would derive benefit from the tempest.—But whenever there came a calm, then she had nothing to do ; and, after being accustomed to live in a state of excitement—being now let down to the quietude of common life—she suffered the depression a man feels who is recovering from intoxication.

After receiving this answer, her Royal Highness was in very low spirits for a short time. But no one feeling lasts long ; and, to do her justice, she has an indigenous courage and cheerfulness of disposition, which no provocations or vexations can wholly subdue. Had this princess been otherwise nurtured and brought up—had she, when first she came to this country, found a husband at once strict and fond, how different a person she might have been ! Her good qualities fostered, her evil ones restrained—her mind softened by cultivation, her manners regulated by decorum—what might she not have been ? But she came from a court sufficiently base in its principles, to another, where the unfortunate state of the best of monarchs occupied all the thoughts and time of his devoted consort, and the royal family, and left *her* an unprotected prey to the person who was the mistress of her husband !—To those who knew the Princess in the first days of her arrival in Britain, and the set by which she was surrounded, it must ever be apparent, that all her subsequent faults and follies admitted of great extenuation.

Saturday, 16*th*.—The Princess told me a strange circumstance, which has lately come to her knowledge, namely, that the editor of the ——, a Scotchman, whose name she forgot, told Lord Perceval, that when the paragraph announcing the publication of *the letters* came out, Mr. Macmahon went to the editor of the —— and, giving him a scurrilous piece of abuse about the Princess, desired him to put it in his paper. The former refused, saying it was actionable; and then Mr. Macmahon offered any sum to the man, to bribe him, which he equally spurned and rejected. What meanness! How these histories make one feel the littleness of human beings!

I walked to Lee. The day was fine, and I had not felt the fresh air blow on me so long, that it seemed redolent of life, and health, and peace, if not of joy and youth. There are past days that we mark in the calendar of our thoughts, by the strong sensations we have felt; while others, that have been, perhaps, replete with incident—that, in the common opinion, ought to have been more interesting—have never once returned to our thoughts. Among the former of these days was one, a year ago, when, I had taken the same walk to Lee, and when the same spirit moved within me, to see and feel—a joy I could *not tell*. This is a doubling of existence; it is a foretaste of the pure pleasures which will be for us in an hereafter. The very nature of such sensations is an impulse of " praise—it is a joy that cometh from above."

Mr. L[——] walked home with me: he is one of those beings whom we trust upon credit, and to whom we are assured we are agreeable, by those indefinable marks of courtesy and kindness which are, after all, the surest proofs of genuine good will—at least, at the moment. He talked to me of —— ; praised, and praised in a way to please. He laid the unction of flattery to my soul. I denied the charge of being——but I fear I did not do so to the purpose.—I never was made for any concealment ; partly, through weakness, partly, through the sincerity of my nature. What I love, I like to talk of, and I should like those I love to talk of me.

Sunday, 17th.—Lady De Clifford came and told the Princess all the story of the Regent's scolding Princess

Charlotte over again, and repeated what he had said in respect to her never having an establishment till she married. He had also, she said, called her a fool, and used other violent language. The Chancellor * told the Princess Charlotte, that if she had been his daughter, and had written him such a letter, he would have locked her up till she came to her senses. "Rather violent language," said Lady De Clifford, "for a coal-heaver's son to the future queen of England." Of course, there were many epithets bestowed upon the Duchess of Leeds, such as "weak woman," and "a pinchbeck duchess," &c., &c. Old Lady De Clifford was very furious, and the Princess delighted at her for so being ; but she observed to me after she was gone, that in her place she never would have taken the *salary*. I agreed. "Besides," said the Princess, "the nation would have done something for her, and it would have been in a more honourable way." It is supposed by *this party*, that the Duchess of Leeds has been placed by the recommendation of Mrs. Nugent, through the Duke of C[larence]. Princess M[ary], it is said, tells every thing to the Prince Regent, and Princess S[ophia] is the one that does exactly what Princess Charlotte chooses. The Prince had written a very cold letter to Lady De Clifford, who had also written one, as cold in reply.

This evening, there came a letter from Mr. Brougham, desiring her Royal Highness to send her letter again to the Chancellor and Lord Liverpool, and command them, as Lord Keeper, &c., to lay her petition before the Prince. It seems they *are by law* obliged to do this. The Princess has done so, accordingly, and wrote in her own name. Lord Liverpool's answer was, that he would go to the Chancellor with her Royal Highness's letter as she desired.—What will be the result ? I am anxious to know.

* Lord Eldon. *See also* the account of the scene in Lord Albemarle's "Fifty Years of My Life," pp. 117-8.

Tuesday, 19*th.*—Campbell, the poet, came to see me. His conversation always awakens thought and feeling; every thing that is *his own*, is elegant and enthusiastic. He understands not the Princess any more than if he were a native of some unknown land, and I doubt whether he would, even were I to sit down and spell *her* A B C D to him, which is impossible.

Another letter came to Her Royal Highness from Mr. Brougham, which was only a repetition of that she received from him the day before:—but she made one of her ladies answer it, standing by, and dictating a thousand trivial circumstances, without order or arrangement, and sometimes so confusedly, that Lady [——] scarcely knew whether the letter was intelligible or not. Campbell and myself talked apart, when we *could*.

Wednesday, 20*th.*—The Princess received a letter from Lord Liverpool, saying the Lord Chancellor and himself had never refused to be the channel of communication for any thing the Princess might wish to have presented to the Regent's ear; but that it rested with his Royal Highness in what *mode* he would receive such a communication: and that his Royal Highness still adhered to his determination of not receiving any letter whatever from the Princess of Wales.—Accordingly, her letter was returned.

In answer to this, the Princess commanded the lady-in-waiting to write as follows:—"Lady [——] is commanded by her Royal Highness the Princess of Wales, to desire Lord Liverpool and the Lord Chancellor will read her Royal Highness's letter to the Prince Regent without delay, since his Royal Highness adheres to his determination of not receiving any direct communication from the Princess of Wales." Lady [——] told me, she always regretted when she had to write such letters as these in her name; but royal servants ought to be considered as mere automatons.

The Princess expected Mr. Brougham to-day, but he did not come. In the evening, amongst other topics of conversation, she said to me, " oh, my dear [———], if you were to see all the curious papers I have !—I have a correspondence that passed between Bonaparte and Prince Louis Ferdinand, before the first was Emperor. It would make the world stare ; and, if it had not been for that ——, the King of Prussia, Prince Louis would now have been king of France. The fact was, Prince Louis was the cleverest and the first man in the world ; and Bonaparte, at that time, did not want to be Emperor —he only wanted to choose a proper king. Well, the King of Prussia, from his foolish notions about the Bourbons, seized upon and locked up Prince Louis. Oh, my dear, how different would have been my fate, and that of all Europe, if this had not been the case ! " How far the above is true, Heaven knows ; but it is curious.

Thursday, 21st.—Mr. Brougham arrived : his manner seems to awe the Princess ; and it is lucky, I think, from all the little circumstances, known only to myself and one other person, that he never meant *to dash in so far* as he has been obliged to do in this business. He only intended, I believe, to place the ladder against the wall, on which to mount when it was safely held ; but not to find himself, as he does now, half way up while it is tottering ;—to make her a tool of his party—yes, and not to act dishonourably either—but certainly not to run any risks for her sake. Unhappy kings, queens, princes, and princesses, ye are seldom served with any better feeling than this.

He told the Princess, that he and Mr. Whitbread both agreed in thinking that it was a most fortunate circumstance for her that the Regent had refused to read or receive her letter; and that it must go, failing all other ways, in the shape of a petition to him— last of all as a petition to Parliament. "But they are frightened to death," said Mr. Brougham, "I know; for Lord Moira has been sent to Whitbread to tell him that the Regent, being afraid he may have been led into error respecting the Princess, wished to submit some papers to him." This message by the bye came from Sheridan, who came from Lord Moira. Mr. Whitbread said he could not then stay in town to read papers, but that he should return in a few weeks, and that if they thought it worth their while they might then give him the papers, but he was sure they contained nothing but what he knew already.—Sheridan began explaining, and in fact, Mr. Brougham said, the papers by his account were merely those which the Princess has in her possession.—Another circumstance is, that Mr. Conant, the police magistrate, went to Messrs. Longman and Rees, and asked what they meant by the paragraph they had put in the newspapers, concerning a publication of letters. Messrs. Longman and Rees replied, that they meant what the paragraph specified.— Upon which Mr. Conant threatened them with the law, and foretold their ruin, and the Lord knows what. But Messrs. Longman and Rees replied, they should take care not to publish any thing actionable; and, as for the rest, they should follow their trade.

Mr. Brougham then went over the old ground, but said positively that till the Princess Charlotte was one and twenty, the Prince might even lock her up, if he chose, and had absolute power over her. How far the country would allow of such treatment, is another question. *I thought to myself*, as to that, it is the interest of all those in power to vest as much as they can in the Regent's hands, and, consequently, I have but a hopeless kind of view of the whole of this business. In as far as the Princess of Wales is concerned, they will not dare to do any thing outrageous against her, but they will keep the extinguisher over her. Mr. Brougham staid a couple of hours, and went away. The Princess is never satisfied, till she has drained a subject dry ; so she was very angry at his going so soon ;—but I perceive he keeps her in order—how fortunate !

Extract from a Letter.

Friday, January 22nd, 1813.

I am indeed anxious on the subject of this unfortunate business, and hope that the Princess will be well advised, before things are brought to extremity. Ministers, it is clear, will not bring forward any thing that is not agreeable to the Prince Regent, and, if opposition should attempt it at this time, it would be easy to give the whole the turn of a party question. This I have little doubt but that the ministry *would do*, and would succeed in, and then things would remain where they are, with the additional stigma of having been attempted to be redressed in vain. I am not saying what *ought* to be, but what I fear *would* be. Indeed, I have lived long enough in the world to have learnt, that *how* others will consider an object, is the question in all public matters where their concurrence is required, not how *we* ourselves see it, however truly. Tell me, if you know, what is to be done about the drawing-room on the 4th,—and what the paragraph means, saying that the Princess Charlotte is to be presented by the Princess of Wales. I think she can be presented by no other person than her mother, and I suppose that therefore she will not, this time, be presented at all :—am I right ? It is the general voice that the Princess Charlotte feels all the duty and affection that she ought to feel towards her mother ; also, that she declared unless she is presented to the Queen by her mother, she will not be presented at all.

Saturday, 23rd.—Yesterday, I went to see [——] ; all was well, even to her animals. What cause of thankfulness !—The vacuum in my existence, which one only circumstance can fill, still exists, and a low languor

enfeebles body and mind.—But I hope—nay, I am not
ungrateful for the blessings given.—The Princess received
a letter of twenty-eight pages, from the Princess Charlotte,
which looked like the writing of a chambermaid, and
appeared to me wholly illegible ; but she said she could
decipher it, and so she did in regard to understanding
the general meaning, but I defy her powers or her patience
to have made out *literally*, what those twenty-eight
pages contained. The whole of the matter was, that
Princess Charlotte was to remain in town, from Saturday
to Wednesday ; from which the Princess of Wales concluded, that she is to go to the Opera to-night, and
intends, if she does, to go also. There came likewise
accounts of Miss Knight's having accepted the place
of sub-governess, which the royal mother and daughter
are very glad of. The same post that brought all this
intelligence, brought a letter also from Lady Oxford,
and the Princess decided upon setting off immediately
to go to Mortimer House. Accordingly, though her
Royal Highness had not been out for a fortnight, off
she went, and her lady-in-waiting told me that when
they arrived they found, as the Princess predicted, no
one, except Lord Byron. 'Tis sickening to hear of and
see the ways of the world. The Princess immediately
retired with Lord Byron and Lady Oxford, and her lady
staid with Lady Jane. The latter is a good musician,
but sings dreadfully *out of tune*. Lady [——] told me
that she thought Lord Byron was exceedingly wearied,
and endeavoured to listen to the music, and escape
from her Royal Highness and Lady 0 [——] ; but the
former would not allow him to do so, and he was
desired to " come and sit " ; and, upon the whole, the
Princess was not pleased with her visit.

Sunday, 24*th*.—Yesterday, the Princess went to meet
the Princess Charlotte at Kensington. Lady [——] told

me that when the latter arrived she rushed up to her mother, and said, "for God's sake, be civil to her—" meaning the Duchess of Leeds, who followed her. Lady [——] said she felt sorry for the latter, but when the Princess of Wales talked to her, she soon became so free and easy that one could not have any *feeling* about her *feelings*. Princess Charlotte, I was told, was looking handsome, very pale, but her head more becomingly dressed, that is to say, less dressed than usual. Her figure is of that full round shape which is now in its prime ; but she disfigures herself by wearing her boddice so short, that she literally has no waist. Her feet are very pretty, and so are her hands and arms, and her ear and the shape of her head. Her countenance is expressive, when she allows her passions to play upon it, and I never saw any face with so little shade express so many powerful and varied emotions. Lady [——] told me that the Princess Charlotte talked to her about her situation, and said, in a very quiet, but determined way, she *would not bear it*, and that as soon as Parliament met, she intended to come to Warwick House, and remain there ; that she was also determined not to consider the Duchess of Leeds as her *governess*, but only as her *first lady*. She made many observations on other persons and subjects, and appears to be very quick, very penetrating, but imperious, and wilful. There is a tone of romance, too, in her character, which will only serve to mislead her.

She told her mother, that there had been a great battle at Windsor, between the Queen and the Prince ; the former refusing to give up Miss Knight from her own person, to attend on Princess Charlotte as sub-governess ; but the Prince Regent had gone to Windsor himself and insisted on her doing so, and the "Old Beguin " * was

* In 1788, George Selwyn writes of the Queen : " Old Beguin, as they call her, is more absurd, I hear, than ever."

forced to submit, but has been ill ever since; and Sir Henry Halford declared it was a complete breaking up of her constitution,—(to the great delight of the two Princesses,* who were talking about this affair.) Miss Knight was the very person they wished to have : they think they can do as they like with her. It had been ordered that the Princess Charlotte should not see her mother alone for a single moment ; but the latter went into her room, stuffed a pair of large shoes full of papers, and, having given them to her daughter, she went home. Lady [——] told me every thing was written down, and sent to Mr. Brougham *next day*.

There are in the newspapers, daily, long histories written, with intention to inflame the public with an idea of the Princess's wrongs, and, above all, to make it clear that Princess Charlotte could reign to-morrow, if any circumstance was to unfit her father for so doing. This is the great point with the party out of office, and which the men of ambition want to establish, in order to raise themselves. True patriotism, ture knight-errantry, where is it ? There are few minds good enough, great enough, to entertain either of these sentiments. As to Brougham, I am more and more convinced that he never meant to have risked what he has done. He is a man of inordinate ambition, and I fear of little heart : indeed, in most cases, the former generally usurps every affection.

Tuesday, 26th.—I saw Bessie R[awdo]n and her mother. The first is a very beautiful and superior creature ; the latter lives but in her daughter,† and would be a cypher without her.

* Thackeray quotes this passage thinking it means the Queen's daughters, whereas it obviously refers to the Princess of Wales and Princess Charlotte.

† Harriet, Lady Granville writes in 1817, after Miss Rawdon's marriage : " Lady William Russell is very pretty, very pleasing ; Lord William looks quiet and pleased, but a little small between his

Thursday, 27th.—I dined at Blackheath. Old [Sapio] was there, and the Princess sang, or rather squalled. Of course, those who live much with her Royal Highness must see how matters go on. It is a great pity she should be surrounded by such society ; it does her infinite harm.

Saturday.—I accompanied the Princess to the British Institution. There were not many fine pictures. One subject, taken from Scripture, that has been bought by Lord Stafford for eight hundred guineas, the painter's name, Edward Bird, the subject the death of Eli, pleased me most ; and I liked some of Barker's, particularly a woman perishing in the snow, with her baby ; and Tam O'Shanter, the horse very good, by Cooper.

The letter has been read to the Prince Regent. His Royal Highness is not pleased to give any answer whatever, says my Lord Liverpool. What is to be done now ? Brougham seems to be at a stand still. The R[——]s tell me that what the Prince is determined to try for, is a divorce. I hardly think that he will though.—Princess Charlotte would be furious, for fear of his marrying again and having a son, and putting her off the throne. The game of " change seats, the King's coming," is what she would not at all enjoy ; therefore, she would naturally make a strong party to prevent this ; and many persons dissatisfied with the Prince would side with her—not from any other motive but self-love—'tis, alas ! the most powerful one with the generality of mankind. Besides, he dare not—the clean hands are wanting

Extract from a Letter.

Date, 6th February, 1813.

I went last night to Carlton House : all very magnificent, but such a lack of young dancing men, and indeed women,

accomplished bride and *exigeante* mother-in-law, who talks all the time as if Lady William was dead :—' From the time I lost my poor Bessy.' It is clear Lord William will not love Mrs. Rawdon."

that I quite pitied the Princess Charlotte for the dulness of the ball—such it appeared to me—what must it not have appeared to youth—and *intelligent* youth ? I think her quite charming, and in all respects as to appearance, far exceeding whatever I had heard of her. I much regretted not having it in my power in any way to make myself known to her ; for possibly I should have received a gracious word or so. But I was very near her often, and could, therefore, make all my observations. Her manner seems open, frank and intelligent ; she will captivate many a heart, or I am much mistaken. I think her like both the Prince Regent and the Princess. She danced with the Duke of C[larence], that is, began the ball with him—but of that you will hear more than I can tell you. Lord Holland was there at a very short notice, as he told me, also the Duke of Bedford, Lord Tavistock, (at least I saw Lady,) Lord Cowper, Lord Jersey ; I think not many more opposition lords.

Thursday, 11th of February.—The circle of the Princess's acquaintance and attendants grows smaller every day, and I fear will at length degenerate wholly into low company. The Oxford and Burdett party prevail.

12th of February, 1813.—To-day, the Princess received the following letter from Lord Liverpool :

Lord Liverpool has the honour to inform her Royal Highness that in consequence of the publication in the Morning Chronicle of the 10th instant, of a letter addressed by her Royal Highness the Princess of Wales to the Prince Regent, his Royal Highness thinks fit, by the advice of his confidential servants, to signify his command that the intended visit of the Princess Charlotte to her Royal Highness the Princess of Wales on the following day, shall not take place.

Lord Liverpool is not enabled to make any further communication to her Royal Highness, on the subject of her Royal Highness's note.

Dated, FIFE HOUSE. *12th February*, 1813.

To which the Princess sent the following reply :

I   I

Lady A[nne] H[amilton] is commanded by her Royal Highness the Princess of Wales, to represent to Lord Liverpool that the insidious insinuation respecting the publication of the letter addressed by the Princess of Wales to the Prince Regent on the 12th of January, conveyed in his lordship's reply to her Royal Highness, is as void of foundation, and as false, as all the former accusations of the traducers of her Royal Highness's honour, in the year 1806.

Lady A[nne] is further commanded to say, that dignified silence would have been the line of conduct the Princess would have pursued upon such insinuation, (more than unbecoming Lord Liverpool,) did not the effects arising from it operate to deprive her Royal Highness of the only real happiness she can possess in this world—that of seeing her only child ; and the confidential servants of the Prince Regent ought to feel ashamed of their conduct towards the Princess in advising his Royal Highness the Prince Regent upon an unauthorized and unfounded supposition, to prevent mother and daughter from meeting ; a prohibition, as positively against the law of nature, as against the law of the land.

Lady A[nne] is further commanded to desire Lord Liverpool to lay this paper before the Prince Regent, that his Royal Highness may be aware into what error his confidential servants are leading him, and will involve him, by counselling and signifying such a command.

Dated MONTAGUE HOUSE, 15th Feb., 1813.

It is scarcely possible to read this composition without laughing. There can be no doubt of the authors, and it certainly does not do much credit to their literary or rational powers. One might have supposed that all resentment must have given way, on perusal, to the more pleasurable sensation of laughter. How that was, cannot be known, as no one was present when Lord Liverpool received it, or made known its contents to the Prince Regent, (if he ever did so.) To be serious, how lamentable that the Princess should have been betrayed by passion to trust herself or her scribes to commit such egregious folly, and to act in matters of such importance without consulting those persons in whom she partially placed confidence.   It was this *partial* and not entire confidence on her part which so often brought *them*, as well as herself, into great difficulties, and with justice disgusted those whose interest it was to serve her.   There had evidently been some hocus pocus about the premature publication of the above letter in the Morning Chronicle ; and the whole business had been ill conducted.

Copy of her Royal Highness's Letter.

THE PRINCESS OF WALES *to* HIS ROYAL HIGHNESS
THE PRINCE REGENT.

14th of January, 1813.

SIR,—It is with great reluctance that I presume to obtrude myself upon your Royal Highness, and to solicit your attention to matters which may, at first, appear rather of a personal than a public nature.   If I could think them so—if they related merely to myself—I should abstain from a proceeding which might give uneasiness, or interrupt the more weighty occupations of your Royal Highness's time ; I should continue in silence and retirement to lead the life which has been prescribed to me, and console myself for the loss of that society and those domestic comforts to which I have been so long a stranger, by the reflection that it has been deemed proper I should be afflicted, without any fault of my own, and that your Royal Highness knows it.

But, Sir, there are considerations of a higher nature than any regard to my own happiness, which render this address a duty both to myself and my daughter ; may I venture to say, a duty also to my husband, and the people committed to his care ?   There is a point beyond which a guiltless woman cannot with safety carry her forbearance ; if her honour is invaded, the defence of her reputation is no longer a matter of choice ; and it signifies not whether the attack be made openly, manfully and directly, or by secret insinuations, and by holding such conduct towards her as countenances all the suspicions that malice can suggest.   If these ought to be the feelings of every woman in England who is conscious she deserves no reproach, your Royal Highness has too sound judgment, and too nice a sense of honour, not to perceive how much more justly they belong to the mother of your daughter—the mother of her who is destined, I trust at a very distant period, to reign over the British empire.

It may be known to your Royal Highness, that during the continuance of the restrictions upon your royal authority, I still was inclined to delay taking this step, in the hope that I might owe the redress I sought to your gracious and unsolicited condescension. I have waited, in the fond indulgence of this expectation, until, to my inexpressible mortification, I find, that my unwillingness to complain has only produced fresh grounds of complaint, and I am at length compelled either to abandon all regard for the two dearest objects which I possess on earth,—mine own honour and my beloved child—or to throw myself at the feet of your Royal Highness, the natural protector of both.

I presume, Sir, to represent to your Royal Highness, that the separation, which every succeeding month is making wider, of the mother and the daughter, is equally injurious to my character and to her education. I say nothing of the deep wounds which so cruel an arrangement inflicts upon my feelings ; although I would fain hope that few persons will be found of a disposition to think lightly of these. To see myself cut off from one of the very few domestic enjoyments left me—certainly the only one upon which I set any value—the society of my child, involves me in such misery, as I well know your Royal Highness never could inflict upon me, if you were aware of its bitterness. Our intercourse has been gradually diminished ;—a single interview, weekly, seemed sufficiently hard allowance for a mother's affections ; —that, however, was reduced to our meeting once a fortnight, and I now learn that even this most rigorous interdiction is to be still more rigidly enforced. But while I do not venture to intrude my feelings as a mother upon your Royal Highness's notice, I must be allowed to say, that in the eyes of an observing and jealous world, this separation of a daughter from her mother will only admit of one construction—a construction fatal to the mother's reputation. Your Royal Highness will also pardon me for adding, that there is no less inconsistency than injustice in this treatment. He who dares advise your Royal Highness to overlook the evidence of my innocence, and disregard the sentence of complete acquittal which it produced, or is wicked and false enough still to whisper suspicions in your ear, betrays his duty to you, Sir, to your daughter, and to your people, if he counsels you to permit a day to pass without a further investigation of my conduct. I know that no such calumniator will venture to recommend a measure which must speedily end in his utter confusion. Then, let me implore you to reflect on the situation in which I am placed, without the shadow of a charge against me ; without even an accuser ; after an inquiry that led to my ample vindication, yet treated as if I were still more culpable than the perjuries of my suborned traducers represented me, holding me up to the world as a mother who may not enjoy the society of her only child.

The feelings, Sir, which are natural to my unexampled situation, might justify me in the gracious judgment of your Royal Highness, had I no other motives for addressing you but such as relate to myself. The serious, and soon it may be, the irreparable injury which my daughter sustains from the plan at present pursued, has done more in overcoming my reluctance to intrude upon your Royal Highness than any sufferings of my own could accomplish. And if for her sake I presume to call away your Royal Highness from the other cares of your exalted station, I feel confident I am not claiming this for a matter of inferior importance, either to yourself or your people.

The powers with which the constitution of these realms vests your Royal Highness in the regulation of the royal family, I know, because I am so advised, are ample and unquestionable. My appeal, Sir, is made to your excellent sense and liberality of mind in the exercise of those powers ; and I willingly hope, that your own parental feelings will lead you to excuse the anxiety of mine, for impelling me to represent the unhappy consequences which the present system must entail upon our beloved child.

Is it possible, Sir, that any one can have attempted to persuade your Royal Highness that her character will not be injured by the perpetual violence offered to her strongest affections—the studied care taken to estrange her from my society, and even to interrupt all communication between us ? That her love for me, with whom, by his Majesty's wise and gracious arrangements, she passed the years of her infancy and childhood, never can be extinguished, I well know, and the knowledge of it forms the greatest blessing of my existence. But, let me implore your Royal Highness to reflect how inevitably all attempts to abate this attachment by forcibly separating us, if they succeed, must injure my child's principles—if they fail, must destroy her happiness.

The plan of excluding my daughter from all intercourse with the world appears, to my humble judgment, peculiarly unfortunate. She who is destined to be the sovereign of this great country, enjoys none of those advantages of society, which are deemed necessary for imparting a knowledge of mankind to persons who have infinitely less occasion to learn that important lesson ; and, it may so happen, by a chance which I trust is very remote, that she should be called upon to exercise the powers of the crown, with an experience of the world more confined than that of the most private individual. To the extraordinary talents with which she is blessed, and which accompany a disposition as singularly amiable, frank, and decided, I willingly trust much ; but beyond a certain point, the greatest natural endowments cannot struggle against the disadvantages of circumstances and situation.

It is my earnest prayer, for her own sake as well as for her country's that your Royal Highness may be induced to pause before this point be reached.

Those who have advised you, Sir, to delay so long the period of my daughter's commencing her intercourse with the world, and, for that purpose, to make Windsor her residence, appear not to have regarded the interruptions to her education which this arrangement occasions, both by the impossibility of obtaining proper teachers, and the time unavoidably consumed in the frequent journeys to town which she must make, unless she is to be secluded from all intercourse, even with your Royal Highness and the rest of the royal family. To the same unfortunate counsel I ascribe a circumstance, in every way so distressing, both to my parental and religious feelings, that my daughter has never yet enjoyed the benefit of confirmation, although above a year older than the age at which all the other branches of the royal family have partaken of that solemnity. May I earnestly conjure you, Sir, to hear my entreaties upon this serious matter, even if you should listen to other advisers on things of less near concernment to the welfare of our child.

The pain with which I have at length formed the resolution of addressing myself to your Royal Highness is such, as I should in vain attempt to express. If I could adequately describe it, you might be enabled, Sir, to estimate the strength of the motives which have made me submit to it; they are the most powerful feelings of affection; and the deepest impressions of duty towards your Royal Highness, my beloved child, and the country, which I devoutly hope she may be preserved to govern, and to shew, by a new example, the liberal affection of a true and generous people to a virtuous and constitutional monarch.

> I am, Sir, with profound respect,
>   And an attachment which nothing can alter,
>   Your Royal Highness's
>   Most devoted and most affectionate
>   Consort, Cousin, and Subject,
>   CAROLINE LOUISA.

MONTAGUE HOUSE, 14th January, 1813.

This is a letter in masquerade, forced and unnatural. It is difficult to say who was its author. It bears the marks of being the composition of more than one writer. It would be convincing, were it sincere, but it is sneering and insincere. On a cursory reading, it appears dignified and temperate, but there is an under current in every sentence which might be construed into a totally different meaning from that which it conveys on its surface. Upon the whole, it appears to me to have been more likely to give offence and irritation, than to obtain any favour by conciliation and entreaty. The latter part, most especially, is jesuitical and dictatorial : it is one thing to ask a favour, another to demand a right ; it is one thing to set forth a *moral* right, another a legal claim ; it is one thing to sue as a wife, another to command as a queen. How difficult to join these different claims and make them coalesce !

But in this instance, as in most others, the happiness

and welfare of the individual were lost sight of, and she was the tool of a party. Yet it is just possible, that whoever drew up this document (destined hereafter to be recorded in the page of history) had a feeling of interest and compassion for the unhappy woman whose cause it professed to espouse,—only that feeling was subservient to their own. But there is seldom any unmixed motive to instigate human actions ;—the *bad* or the *good* may predominate, but they are both there, and are generally so commixed, that, till time has sifted the grain from the chaff, they cannot be separated.

Tuesday.—Mr. Whitbread has made the finest speech that ever was heard ; most of his auditors were *in tears,* (said Mr. Bennet,) but *all* agreed in their admiration of the manly and forcible eloquence he displayed. There was no division. He read a letter from the Princess of Wales to the Prince, written after what he termed her last triumph, and written in an humble conciliatory tone, when the news came of *another secret investigation now* going on, and the pen fell from her hands at this intelligence. The house were all electrified, say *my informants.* Mr. Tierney spoke, and Lord Castlereagh. The latter floundered deep in the mire of duplicity and meanness. But Mr. Canning made an *elaborate* speech, saying that it were better all this business should end for ever ; that the Princess was proved pure and innocent, but that if further private malice was at work against her, it would then be the duty of the house to take cognizance of the affair.

Extract from a Letter, from THE HON. A[NNA] S[EYMOUR] D[AMER].

I consider Her Royal Highness the Princess of Wales being sent abroad without a specific cause, as not only improbable but *impossible,* under our good laws ; but I do fear and believe that some machinations, in the way of trial and

THE HONBLE. MRS. DAMER
From an eng aving by Hopwood after a painting b\` G. C.

investigation, are actually going on underhand, and that real or pretended proofs of misconduct will be brought forward against her. I understand that she professes herself secure in her innocence, and determined not to give way, or make compromises, should they be offered. How all this will end, Heaven only knows. That it may never begin, I truly wish ; and, in any case, must pity her, and that most sincerely, should she be brought into trouble, for certainly she has been hardly used ; and, at her first coming into this country, when she had a right to meet with every indulgence and protection, she was vilely betrayed by those about her, who, I am convincèd, heaped lies upon lies, for the worst and most sordid purposes of their own. Imprudent she has been, no one can deny ; but *Justice* will find much to put in the opposite scale, should her case come before a tribunal. Of her being turned out of Kensington (for so, as you say, it would be) and ordered to Hampton Court, or worse, to Holyrood House, (but this latter only for *hereafter*,) still all is uncertain ; and I am sometimes inclined to hope, though I confess with no great reason, that this odious business will be put to sleep. The best thing for her, poor soul, would be the immediate death of our wretched King ; as the moment that event happens, (supposing nothing previously has taken place to prevent it,) she becomes queen, by the laws of the land :— so Perceval has positively decided ; and that would be a step and might make a difference in her treatment and be in her favour. Now, it is thought that the accusations are hurrying on to prevent that happening—I mean her being Queen.

It is certainly not the factious, and the mob alone, who espouse the Princess's cause :—the sweet charities of life, the protection of the social rights of families, are connected with her wrongs ; and if she is true to her own self duties, there will be an overwhelming force of general opinion in her favour.

The Princess is often besieged with letters, anonymous and otherwise. She showed me one of the letters the other day, from a D.D., signed with name, date and abode. It is curious, but bears rather the appearance of being instigated by private pique, than of the spontaneous emanation of any genuine sentiment of good will.   The letter was addressed to one of the Princess's ladies—the writer unknown personally to the lady.

MADAM,—Lord Eldon and his elder brother, Sir W. Scott's father, were fitters of ships in the coal trade of Newcastle. Money brought them to Oxford and the law, when no great *mauvaise honte* stood in their way; nor can it be denied that sufficient abilities in them authorized their introduction in the world by friends.   Your Ladyship, of whose proper spirit, together with that of your Royal Mistress, I am one amongst myriads of humble applauders, would, as I conceive, not object to receive anecdotes of the origin of the afore-mentioned celebrated friends.   In the letter of your Lady-ship's Royal Mistress, I noticed the word "*suborn*," and am persuaded that many lose much, (and often their lives,) by the perjury of others.   An oath, although authorized by the religion of the Church of England, was an invention of the Church of Rome, to increase the power of the powerful; in the Hebrew original of the Old Testament it is not to be found, although it is so in translations.

Christian governments have, unfortunately for society, armed their members one against another with this dangerous instrument, an oath.   With those whose belief in religion is small, an oath is a mere instrument against the enemies of the individual, or of those who can suborn him, or her; and such I should esteem Bidgood, &c., to be, and would humbly recommend the defiance of them.   Lord De Clifford as well as Lord Liverpool passed the University, during my twenty years' residence there: the Scotts are considerably my seniors.   The Bishop of Salisbury, as superintendent of the education of her Royal Highness the Princess Charlotte, ought himself to have confirmed her at the age of fourteen. A note to the Bishop of London from her Royal Highness, requesting confirmation, preparation for which should be a knowledge of the Church Catechism, so as to be able to say it by rote, could scarcely fail of being followed by an appoint-ment from that prelate to attend a private confirmation in the Chapel Royal, when her Royal Highness might properly be accompanied by her mother.   I request Lord De Clifford, who formerly knew me as fellow of the college in which his

Lordship was educated, to forward this letter to your Ladyship; and have the honour to conclude, with best wishes
for the cause and happiness of your Ladyship's Royal Mistress
and respect for your Ladyship,

Madam,

Your Ladyship's most obedient servant,

D. D., &c., &c., &c.

Wednesday.—I saw the Princess yesterday; I fear she
has been goading the sleeping lion. However, I have
heard, that when the Regent wanted the ministers to try
for a divorce, they said that it was impossible, and that,
if they attempted it, they must inevitably lose their
places. This intelligence did not come from the Princess
or her friends; so that, if it is true, that sounds well for
her cause; but everything that is reported concerning
her Royal Highness one day, is contradicted the next.
Her first letter has certainly produced a disposition in her
favour in the breasts of John and Jenny Bull in the
country; but here, alas, like all other things, it seems to
be a party question—with some few exceptions,—for
some fair judging spirits do exist. I wish the Letter to
Lord Liverpool had never been sent, but that the imprudence of his avowal of interference and advice on such
an occasion, and that of the confidential ministers, had
been left to its own punishment. It is, I think, quite
clear that nothing criminal can be proved, or most as-
suredly these nightly and daily councils would not have
been able to keep their discoveries so secret, but that
something must have transpired. As nothing comes out,
I feel secure that there is nothing to come out.

Extract of a Letter.

March 3d, 1813.

Ministers were beat last night by forty; so far I sing
Te Deum, but fear all will be again overset in the House
of Lords. The letter from the Princess was, I understand,
laid last night before the House of Commons by the Speaker,

and, after a little conversation between Mr. Whitbread and Lord Castlereagh, the subject was dropped—I conclude to be resumed in future. The letter is very good, whatever may be the consequences : I should suppose it must be Brougham's, for it is a simple and impressive law statement. The general impression seems to be, that the Princess has been harshly treated ; and it must be allowed that, unprotected as she is, she had no refuge but an appeal to Parliament ; yet, I fear no good purpose will be answered, and that the material point will not be gained—that of seeing her daughter more frequently than she has of late been allowed to do.

Extract from another Letter.

March 8th, 1813.

Pray express my most sincere congratulations on the triumph, the complete triumph, the Princess has so justly obtained. What passed on Friday night in the House of Commons made me, I confess, feel proud of my country ; which has not of late been the case with me. But what gives me the greatest satisfaction, as far as her Royal Highness is concerned, is her most admirable letter to the Prince in answer to his. That letter does her more credit than words can express, and I am heartily glad that it has appeared at this time, as I already see the impression it makes. For the present, I do trust that the Princess will remain satisfied with the sensation excited in her favour, which is what it ought to be. By remaining satisfied, I do not mean that she is to seclude herself at Blackheath, or avoid appearing as usual. For my part, I think she should in all this just follow her own inclination ; come to Kensington, go to the theatres, &c., &c., as she has hitherto done, &c.

Extract from a Letter, from the same.

Dated *March 25th,* 1813.

I must (as I hope at least) be the first to tell you, that I have heard from good authority that Sir John Douglas is, or is immediately to be, expelled by the Freemasons of this country from their society. Also, that the Duke of Sussex has dismissed him from his household. All this marks the general and honest indignation the conduct of these vile sycophants excites.

Extract from a Letter addressed to one of the Princess's Ladies.

March 26th, 1813.

Though I have not the honour of being personally acquainted with your ladyship, I feel assured that the subject which actuates this address will form an apology for the liberty I take in making it, and claim your ladyship's full and free pardon, having felt no less an interest in it than myself. On an affair of so important and interesting a nature as that which has recently been brought into Parliament, and which has gained such general attention, and from its happy termination, such warm approbation and delight, it will not, I trust, be deemed impertinent to make a few remarks. I could not, without subjecting myself to much pain, withhold expressing the enthusiastic joy which the perusal of this day's papers has produced. Will Lady [——] gratify the feelings of a stranger by conveying to her Royal Highness the Princess of Wales the warm congratulations of an affectionate heart, on the glorious victory recently obtained— a heart that has long been deeply wounded at the base conduct of the D[ouglase]s, the vilest pair that England ever knew, and who it is ardently hoped will now receive their just and highly merited punishment. Yes, revered and highly beloved Princess, the nation has long felt your wrongs and wished for redress ; but power and undue influence forbade it, until that impressive address obliged a public avowal of your innocence. Excuse the freedom of my sentiments—my heart is full, and every feeling is roused. That her Royal Highness may long live to enjoy the society of her beloved daughter, beholding in her every grace and virtue which can adorn the throne and secure the affections of the nation, is the fervent prayer of thousands. It may afford her Royal Highness some pleasure to be informed, that the patronage which she so graciously conferred on the National Benevolent Institution, has been highly beneficial to the charity ; a respectable committee has been formed, and subscriptions are daily increasing. Relying on your ladyship's forgiveness for this intrusion, I beg leave to subscribe myself, &c.

A Letter addressed to one of her Royal Highness's Ladies.

March 19th, 1813.

I do myself the honour of writing to your ladyship, to congratulate you on the pleasure you must have felt on the result of the late debates in the House of Commons. I see a variety of persons, and observe with great satisfaction that there is a general sympathy with the Princess of Wales, on the cruel persecution she has undergone; and the complete conviction of her Royal Highness's perfect innocence. Whitbread has done himself great honour by his generous defence —he has acted nobly. I wish he had been able to crush the vile snake whom her Royal Highness cherished formerly, and who so ungratefully attempted to sting her benefactor ;— that wretch and her mate have, however, covered themselves with infamy. May I venture to ask the favour of a few lines from your ladyship, to inform me how her Royal Highness endures these, which I trust will be the last efforts of calumny. It is not from curiosity that I take this liberty, but from the sincere interest which I feel in her Royal Highness's welfare.

I have the honour to be, Madam,

Your Ladyship's most obedient, &c., &c.

These letters have been taken promiscuously from the upper and middling classes, and from a large collection on the same subject, in order to give an impartial idea of the feeling which generally prevailed at that time, respecting the wrongs of the Princess of Wales.

It may be that this was the proudest moment of the Princess's troubled life; afterwards, there was more pomp and greater public demonstration of feeling for her, but then it was a storm of passion and of party, not the sober current of honest feelings, which moved justice to stand forth and defend her.

May 10th, 1813.—After all these triumphs, we are only making a charivari upon an old tin tea-kettle of a harpsi-

* The Duchess of Brunswick, mother of the Princess of Wales, died at her lodgings in Hanover Square, March 23, 1813. The Diary was perhaps discontinued during her daughter's deep mourning.

chord. Full of my own feelings and my own regrets, I yet could enter into those of hers, if there was uniform greatness, uniform tenderness, uniform anything ; but courtly ways are not my ways, and the unfortunate Princess is so inconsistent, so reckless of propriety, so childishly bent on mere amusement, that I foresee her enemies must and will get the upper hand !

Read Madame de Staël sur les Passions. What a wonderful mind is hers ! what an insight she has into the recesses of human feeling ! How many secret springs does she unlock ; and how much the woman—the tender, the kind, the impassioned woman—betrays herself even in all the philosophy of her writings ! Yet what do the other sex think of a female authoress ? With one or two very sober, but very great exceptions, it is true, that where science rather than imagination or thought is displayed, women are sneered at who venture on the public arena of literature ; and there is not a man, perhaps, existing, who does not think that those women are wisest and happiest who do not attempt that bold and dangerous adventure, authorship. I remember once a great friend of mine defended herself, (she being guilty of the fact,) by asking me what stimulus to life remained when youth and outward charms were gone, but when the affections and the imagination were as vivid as ever, and nothing was left to supply the place of that life of life to which, when once accustomed, it was as impossible to live without it, as to live without breathing ? " Men," she said, " have the camp, the court, the senate, and the field ; —but we—we have nothing but thought and feeling left ; and if we are not understood, not prized by those around us, like

Rosa non colta in sua stagion,

we scatter these thoughts and feelings to the wind, hoping they may bear us back some fruitage of answering kind.

Besides, there are many other reasons which instigate women to become authors. It is not, as men falsely accuse us, vanity, or the thirst after notoriety, which prompts the deed ; but it is generally one of two things—perhaps both together—either poverty, or the aching desire to be appreciated and understood, even though it may be by some being whom we shall never see in this world."

I was sent for this day to the palace at Kensington, to converse only on one topic—the disappointment the Princess felt at having suddenly received a message, informing her Lady Reid's house was not to be let—only sold. As this information came unexpectedly, and after she had concluded that every arrangement was settled, she supposes it is a trick proceeding from Carlton House. One might imagine such meannesses were beneath the consideration of the adverse party ; but I have known so many instances of similar littleness, that I should not be surprised if this were one.

It seems Mr. Brougham wrote to the Princess on Wednesday last, stating, that he had heard it was the Regent's intention, the moment she got a house in town, to take Kensington, and all its advantages of coal and candle, &c., from her ; for which reason he, (Mr. Brougham,) conceiving this would be of great detriment to her Royal Highness, had delayed concluding the bargain about the Curzon Street house ; and that when he went a few days after, on the Friday, to do so, he heard of the new resolution which had been adopted by the late Lady Reid's executors. What makes this the more unaccountable is, that it was specified in her will, that the house should not be sold, but *let* for twenty years, in order that the rent might accumulate for the benefit of some near relation, and that, in consequence of the will, the executors must procure an act of parliament to enable them to break it. I was requested privately (and this was what

I was sent for) to go secretly to another person, a man of business, and, if possible, on any terms whatsoever, secure a lease of the house.

This underhand manner of employing another agent, above all of making *me* an instrument in the business, distressed me greatly ; for not only is it unadvisable to be insincere, and to doubt the faithfulness of any one till he is proved false, but also, on the present occasion, it was just possible that Mr. Brougham might, with the best intentions towards the Princess's interests, have purposely prevented her from obtaining this house.

On the 11th of May I was invited again to the palace. The Princess informed me that she was in great hopes the Regent was going to Hanover. I wondered what difference that could possibly make to her. She told me there was to be a congress held, at which all the potentates were to meet, and that Bonaparte was to join them.

The Princess is dissatisfied with her daughter's conduct. She wished that the latter should have had the firmness to say, " I will go to no ball unless my mother is present at it " ; but this she does not do, and the mother of course is wounded, and thinks her child really does not care for her—which I fear is true. When this unfortunate Princess sees herself forsaken by every natural tie, and by every person of distinction once professing friendship, it is hardly to be wondered at that she should become desperate : if she does not, she will stand recorded in history as the wisest and best of her sex and regal station. But a return is naturally made to *self*, and I feel myself, as her friend, very awkwardly situated. To-day, for instance, there was that foolish Lady P[——], and her silly protégé— both very unfit company for the Princess. Dr. B[——] is clever and agreeable ; still, there ought to be another set of persons to form her Royal Highness's coterie. It is impossible not to regret that she should thus lose herself, and forfeit the vantage-ground she had so recently

I   K

obtained. Yet, for me to appear downcast, would only draw an explanation which I am desirous of avoiding. Mr. [——] came by appointment. He was pleased at being presented to her Royal Highness any how. If everybody were behind the scenes, they would not think so much of the show—but this applies to all courts indiscriminately.

It was one o'clock in the morning before I was dismissed.

Wednesday, May 12th.—Her Royal Highness graciously gave me a picture of *herself* (as she calls it !)—which might just as well be the picture of the Grand Turk, and which I verily believe was done for her dead sister-in-law, the late Duchess of Brunswick—not for herself. Nevertheless, by a little royal hocus pocus, it is now transmuted into her own portrait !—and I received it as though I believed it !—so much for being a courtier !

Friday, 14th.—Yesterday came Sir J. Owen, with the Pembrokeshire address. He is a well-looking young man. The Princess went through the ceremony with great dignity, and did the whole thing very well. Why does she not always so ? I was present at a visit her Royal Highness paid the Duchess of Leinster, when she took a china cup to her which her Royal Highness said had belonged to her mother, who was a friend of hers. What a magnificent old lady ! There is something in great age, when accompanied by sweetness and dignity, that has a peculiar charm for me. I feel inclined to honour such persons, if only for having outlived and outbraved the storms of life which they must have passed through.

> So some lone tower, with many a hue inlaid,
>   Which Time (the cunning artist) doth enchase,
> Lifts its grey head above the forest s shade,
>   And seems from age and time to steal new grace.

Now poured in the addresses from the whole of England. The Princess ought to have felt the double responsibility which such testimonies to her honour imposed upon her.

On Saturday, the 15th, came the Sheffield address. That night I dined at Blackheath, and sat up till two o'clock in the morning. The Princess read some of Mirabeau's letters on the private history of the Court of Berlin ; but every now and then laid down the book to talk on the personages mentioned therein, according to her own version of the story. This she did very well, and was extremely entertaining. Mirabeau mentions a long discourse he had with the Duke of Brunswick, about the state of Europe in that time, and adds, that it was " diamond cut diamond " between them. The Duke wanted to find out whether Monsieur de Breteuil was likely to succeed Monsieur de Vergennes as minister at Berlin.— " Ah," said the Princess, closing the book, " nobody could love a fader better nor I loved mine ; but he was a man of inordinate ambition, and was not at all pleased with only reigning over so small a principality as Brunswick. Frederick Guillaume was a very weak prince, and my fader always determined to have the whole management of Prussia. The better to bring this about, he earnestly desired my marriage with the Prince Royal, but I never could consent.—Ah, I was so happy in those times ! " I asked if he was not a very handsome man. " Very like the bust I have of him," was her reply—and that bust is, I think, handsome, but she does not. She then added,—" Things all change since that time,—and here I am."—And she burst out crying.

Sunday, 16th.—Met her Royal Highness in town, to see Harcourt House, the abode which was now pointed out to her as eligible. She was disappointed in its dimensions and appearance ;—so was I. How few persons have any idea of real magnificence ! However, it is a proper sort of house for the Princess to inhabit ; and I wish upon all accounts that she may take it.

Mr. Brougham came to her at last. His manner does not please her : they look at each other in a way that is very amusing to a bystander. The one thinks, " She *may* be useful to *me* " ; and the other, " *He* is useful to me at present." It does not require to be a conjurer to read their thoughts ; but they are both too cunning for each other. Mr. Brougham, however, gave her good advice, which was, to wait a few days, in which time, he thought, Whitbread would sound the waters, and take the bearings of all circumstances, so as to let her know whether or not she might venture to live in town without incurring the risk of losing Kensington. She wishes, and is advised, to let this place, and keep Kensington as her *villa*. That would be a very wise plan, and I hope, for her sake, she may do so.

The addresses are all going on notably : they come from every part of the country. I do hope the people may force the nobles into a more just conduct towards her ; but I look with very despairing eyes upon the state of the constitution of this country—that is to say, with regard to the continuance of its regal power,—were it not that God, who sees into the hearts, and tries the reins of men, knows of virtues that are not seen, but which, to His all-seeing eye, redeem the vices that are alone apparent to man.

The history of all courts, and all princes, from the time of Jehu unto the present day, shows them full of corruptions and vices : their very stations lead them into sin. Yet, when lately France tried to exist under an ideal form of government, greater misery ensued, and the convulsion only subsided when a more despotic power than any king's gradually subdued the tumult, and restored order by enforcing obedience. Why then should we seek for imaginary perfectibility in the laws of man ? it suits not with his imperfect essence. God sees the hearts of princes, and will perhaps maintain them in their place, in spite of all their seeming unworthiness to us. Yet sometimes I again think no—especially at this time in England.—" A house divided against itself cannot stand." The old King had many faults—I say had, for in fact he is dead, to this world,—but then he was a good and a pious man ; and the example of such has always been of powerful influence. When he dies, I fear much harm will ensue ; for there is a fermentation in men's minds, and a general system of deceit prevails, which, in regard to things temporal and spiritual, the coming power is not likely to dissipate. May God avert the evil ! It will be laid to the charge of *one*, when it does come, but it is the consequence of the hollowness and immorality of *all*.

Thursday, May 19th.—Monday was the Princess of Wales's birthday. I went to pay my respects. Her Royal Highness told me she had received a letter at half past one o'clock in the morning, from Princess Charlotte, to give notice that she was to arrive at Blackheath at two to-day, to remain for *one hour only*.* This did not please ; and *she* was pleased to aggravate the sense of her displeasure, because *we naturally like to make bad worse*, when we are ill treated. Hardly had she time to receive the Berwick address, which was delivered by a remarkably gentlemanly man, Colonel Allen, (who made her a very pretty speech from himself afterwards,) when there arrived a servant from Princess Charlotte, to say she was ordered to be at Blackheath at half past one, and back at Warwick House by half past two. There was a fresh

---

* Miss Knight writes in her Autobiography: " On the 17th of May we had visited the Princess of Wales on her birthday, but were not allowed to dine there."

cause of complaint.   Royalties do not understand having hours changed by others, though they change them when it suits their own convenience.   In general, however, they are punctual.

The Duke of Kent came, and, a quarter of an hour after, Princess Charlotte ;   the Duchess of Leeds and Miss Knight attending her.   The meeting was as dry and as formal as possible.   Princess Charlotte was rather gracious to me.   Her legs and feet are very pretty :   her Royal Highness knows that they are so, and wears extremely short petticoats.   Her face would be pretty too, if the outline of her cheeks was not so full.   She went away soon after two ;   and I left the Duke of Kent and the Princess tête-à-tête.

In the evening, singing and playing.—" Vivent les *beaux arts !* "

I do not, whatever others may say, believe that the Prince Regent considers the addresses to the Princess in the serious light they deserve to be considered ;   because he is under the influence of bad and weak advisers.   Nor do I think that, in the present state of men's minds, any immediate advantage will be gained by them to her Royal Highness.   But if she has the resolution to act with a patience scarcely to be expected, I have not the smallest doubt but that she will stand, in point of popularity, so high in this country, that justice *will* and must be done to her.

The Princess has taken a dislike to Sir C. and Lady Hamilton, and was very angry at their calling on her. Mr. and Mrs. Lock are still in favour, and dined here.

Friday, 21st.—The Princess went to town, after receiving an address from Middlesex,—a very strong one— the Sheriff and Mr. G. Byng, and some more people, all warm in her cause.   They ate luncheon, and asked a great many questions, and seemed very much interested

in all that concerned her.   The Sheriff said, her Royal
Highness had at least one consolation, namely, that the
voice of the people was for her.   God grant this may be
true—and continue !   I think, if she is but tolerably
prudent, she will get the better of her enemies.

Saturday, May 22nd, 1813.—The Princess went to town
to see her nephew at the Duke of Brunswick's, Chelsea.
I was glad to hear it, for the sake of appearances, though
I, alas ! know 'tis *only* appearance.

May 31*st*.—I have not been able for the last nine days
to write this memorandum ; perpetual late hours fatigue
me so much, and render me incapable of the smallest
exertion.

There has been *less music* lately, and the *musicantés*
have been less with her.   I am afraid, or rather I ought to
rejoice, that she has not found that society quite congenial.   The addresses have continued—Westminster is
the strongest ; Berkshire, &c., &c., have followed.   The
people certainly espouse her cause.   If it were really
virtue, or extreme delicacy, that made some people step
aside and decline her society, one should only grieve,
and could not blame ; but as it is, self-interest alone
directs their conduct, and one must despise those who
bend the knee to those only who have the power of benefiting them.   At the Opera the other night, every person
stood up when her Royal Highness entered the house,
and there was a burst of applause ; it was not so long,
or so rapturous, as I had before witnessed—for instance,
in Kensington Gardens ; but it was very *decidedly* general
and determined.   There were two or three hisses ; I
could not distinguish where they came from,—some
Carlton House emissaries, of course.   I saw nobody
and nothing, being very much moved and interested in
her reception.   I heard afterwards that the Dowager

Lady C[——]y was one of those who hissed—more shame to her. The Princess entered the house at eleven, and left it at twelve ; so that there was not much time for the people to weary of her ; and when she got up to go away, there was another applause, but she did not receive the applause as if she was pleased by it—perhaps it did not content her ; or rather, I think, the true cause which prevented her from being pleased at any circumstance that evening was, that Mr. Whitbread had written her a letter, begging that she would be very careful about *her dress*,—in short explaining that she ought to cover *her neck*. This I knew by a roundabout way. It was a bold *act of friendship* to tell her this ; she will never forget it, nor ever like the person who had the courage to give her the advice. She has many good qualities, but that virtue, Christian humility, enters not within the porch of her thoughts or feelings ; indeed, to speak candidly, it is the most difficult one to attain ; and many who think they possess it, are as far from it as the poor Princess, who openly contemns it. She absolutely wept some tears of mortification and anger, when she received this letter from Mr. Whitbread. She did not know that I knew the contents, which I rejoiced at, because it spared her another act of humiliation *before me*. In regard to myself, I have laid down a rule of conduct towards her Royal Highness, from which I am determined not to depart. This determination is, never to give advice ; because I am quite aware that it might do me much harm, and would do her no good. From a legal adviser alone can she endure a plain unpleasant truth, and she has greatness of mind enough to esteem and value the attachment of such a man *to her cause*, after the first sting of rebuke is passed away ; though such a man she never will suffer to be immediately in attendance upon her person.

On Thursday last, little Matt. Lewis came to pay me a

visit. He is such a steady friend, and so amusing, that, in spite of all his *ridicules*, I like him exceedingly.

Friday I again dined at Kensington : my cousin [——] dined there also. I am always distressed when I meet him at the Princess's, for I know he is trying *to find fault* all the time. I think, however, for once he did not succeed, and he made himself (as he ought) agreeable to his Royal hostess.

Monday, June 2d.—I met the Princess at supper, at Lord Glenbervie's : it was a dull affair, and the more so, from the Princess appearing to be very low and cross. The party did not last long ; that was one comfort. I had received *such a shock* from the accounts of the horrid murder of the poor old Mr. and Mrs. Thompson Bonar, that I was quite unfit for society ; but her Royal Highness had commanded me to meet her at Lord Glenbervie's, so I was obliged to obey. Having seen the murdered persons frequently, having been in their house, and in their very room, I had the whole horrid scene before me most vividly. It is strange to remark how the most tragic events pass under the observation of people who live in the busy world, without creating one serious thought ; they say, " shocking,"—" horrid " ; and, as soon as their curiosity is amused and gratified by the details of the story, they turn from the tale with an air of levity, and soon contrive to lose all recollection of so unpleasant a subject. The wholesome moral to be deduced from serious reflection is wholly set aside.

Mr. and Mrs. Thompson Bonar were good people : they had closed their evening in acts of family devotion ; and yet the Almighty permitted, for some wise purpose doubtless, but one unknown to man, that these innocent beings should suffer a dreadful death. What an exercise for faith and resignation ! How can any thing else reconcile such awful dispensations with the tender mercies of God ? There were few whom I heard express any serious thoughts about this tragic story ; and some contrived, even upon *such an event*, to cut their idle jokes.

Tuesday, June 3d.—I went to see Mrs. R[awdo]n ; her daughter is a beautiful girl, and very agreeable. The Princess Charlotte has taken a great fancy for her, at which I am not surprised. She told me Miss E[lphin- stone] * is not friendly to the Princess of Wales, and I fear it is so ; for, since her return to the Princess Charlotte, the latter is not half so kind to her mother. Whoever busy themselves by depreciating a parent in a child's estimation, are much to blame ; for even where the parent is in fault, the child should never know it. It is a dangerous experiment to bid the offspring discriminate where its parent is in the right, and where in the wrong. Very likely Miss E[lphinstone], did not advise Princess Charlotte not to love her mother, but she probably told her, " She is imprudent, foolish ; do not be guided by her " ; and so lessened her respect for her mother. Miss E[lphinstone], however, was on one occasion a useful friend to the Princess Charlotte, inasmuch as it was through her means that a silly correspondence into which the Princess Charlotte had entered with C[aptain] H[esse]††

* Generally known then as " Miss Mercer," the friend of Princess Charlotte, though some years older. She was Margaret Mercer Elphin- stone, afterwards Baroness Keith, and married Comte de Flahault.

† He was reputed to be a natural son of the Duke of York. He was an aide-de-camp to the Duke of Wellington, and was much esteemed in the world of fashion, Captain Gronow claiming him as his *fidus Achates*. His flirtation with Princess Charlotte is called by C. C. Greville " an atrocity of the Princess of Wales." It ruined him : he went abroad and lived at Naples until he became the lover, under the auspices of the Margravine of Baireuth, of the Queen, and was exiled from thence. Then he lived at Turin and married. He was killed at Nogent, near Paris, February 24, 1832, in a duel (resulting from a card party) by Count Leon, a natural son of the Emperor Napoleon. His seconds were Count d'Esterno, a German, and an English officer.

was delivered up and destroyed. The Princess of Wales, on the contrary, behaved very foolishly in this business ; and it gave a handle to her enemies to represent to the Regent that she ought not to be allowed indiscriminate intercourse with her daughter. They took a fiendish pleasure in laying hold of this, or any other plausible pretext, to separate the Princess from her child.

Tuesday, 10th of August, 1813.—I passed nearly an hour with Madame de Staël. That woman captivates me. There is a charm, a sincerity, a force in all she says and looks. *I am not disappointed in her.* The anger I felt at her for not taking up the Princess's cause more warmly is, I feel, fast vanishing away. The reason of this lies in my unhappy knowledge of the *dessous des cartes*—a knowledge more likely to increase than to diminish— for the poor Princess is going on headlong to her ruin. Every day she becomes more imprudent in her con- duct, more heedless of propriety, and the respect she owes to herself. The society she is now surrounded by is disgraceful.

Yesterday, when I dined with her Royal Highness, the old *ourang outang* was there, and they sang together for some time, and after that the Princess set off with Lady [——] to go to the vile *Maison de Plaisance*, or rather *de Nuisance*. It consists of two damp holes, that have no other merit than being next to the S. kennel. I was shown all over, or half over, this abominable place, and then dismissed. Lady [——] told me to-day that she was left to chew the cud of her reflections for several hours. She said, that she tried " to spit them out, for that truly they were neither nutritive or sweet." She read one of Madame de Staël's *Petits Romans*, which I had lent her, and which she told me had given her great pleasure.

Madame de Staël's *Essai sur les Fictions* delights me

particularly; for every word in it is a beautified echo of
my own feelings. Lady.[——] told me the Princess was
not content with being *next door* to the kennel, but would
go into it ; and there she was introduced to a new brother
and sister-in-law of the L[——]s. Alas ! what company
for her to associate with ! Lady [——] said she felt very
much distressed at seeing her royal mistress there ; and
thought the mother of the Princess felt so too, for that the
latter neither wants feeling nor sense. After two hours
of *music*, i.e. *charivari*, the Princess returned back again
to the other hole, and supped *tête-à-tête* with Lady [——].
This, at least, was an appearance kept up ; but Lady
[——] is terrified, for the Princess talked of sleeping at
the "*cottage*." Her Royal Highness's servants are infuriated, and there is no saying how long their fidelity
may hold out.

Wednesday, 11*th of August.*—Again I dined at Kensington, and after dinner the Princess went with Lady [——]
to Mr. Angerstein's, and desired me to follow her thither.
There was an awkward scene took place ; for Lady
Buckinghamshire, like a true vulgar, *ran off* the moment
she saw the Princess enter the room, and nothing could
persuade her to come back, instead of standing still and
making a curtsy, and taking her departure quietly.
The gentlemen were still at table. Mr. Boucheret was
the first who came out. The Princess did not speak to the
Dean of Windsor, who was there ; which I regretted, for
her sake. Lady [——] told me that she had implored
Lady [C——] [L——] to write to Mr. Whitbread, to say
it is of vital consequence he should state to her Royal
Highness that the "cottages" are already a cause of
scandal ; and, well knowing her innocent recreations, he
advised that they should take place elsewhere. Perhaps
he will not dare to give her this advice.
From Mr. Angerstein's the Princess went to sup at

Lady Perceval's. I am sorry for her Royal Highness ; I think she has sacrificed herself, and that she is really attached to a weak intriguing woman. I heard a curious story about the Duke of Brunswick. It is said that he has an intrigue with a married woman at Shrewsbury ; and, hearing that her husband was absent, the Duke set off to a rendez-vous. When he arrived at an inn there, he ordered a dinner the next day for himself and his inamorata ; but his broken English, and a peculiar air belonging to him, attracted observation ; and Mr. Forrester, son-in-law to the Duchess of Rutland, happening to be there, said to the landlord, " I am sure that is a French prisoner trying to escape " ; accordingly a hue and cry was made after him, and he was arrested. His continued bad English confirmed them in their opinion ; but he said he was an officer in the Duke of Brunswick's German legion. This was not believed ; and he, infuriated at their doubts, declared himself to be the Duke of Brunswick. " No," said Mr. Forrester, " I am certain the Duke of Brunswick is not such a frippery fellow as you are." In short, he was treated with all sorts of indignity ; but at length some one knew him, and he was set at liberty, and excuses out of number were made to him when it was too late.

I have long had a foresight of some great interior revolution in these kingdoms. All I see and know, and *do not see* but *think*, confirms me in this opinion. Speaking morally, it is perhaps better that a man should have a compensation in money for his wife's guilt, than in the blood of the offender ; but, speaking according to my own feelings, I think that were I in such a miserable position, nothing but fighting to the death would satisfy me ; for how can *gold* be a compensation for wounded honour ? It is, according to my way of thinking, only an additional affront. If a man, from the highest of all motives, Christian humility and forbearance, pardons a faithless wife, and the object of her guilty passion, then indeed he is truly great, and by his greatness alone overcomes his injuries, and washes away all stain from his character : —but to take a *price* for an injury is a cowering mean idea ! that could only obtain currency from its being part of that system of trade upon which hang our law and our prophets.

Sunday.—Last night the Princess again went to sup at Mr. Angerstein's, and unfortunately Lord and Lady Buckinghamshire were there. The latter behaved very rudely, and went away immediately after the Princess arrived. Whatever her opinions, political or moral, may be, I think that making a curtsy to the person invested with the rank of Princess of Wales, would be much better taste, and more like a lady, than turning her back and hurrying out of the room.

I wonder why the Princess treats the Dean of Windsor with such marked dislike, for he has always been respectful and attentive to her and her mother, the Duchess of Bruns-wick. It is vexatious to those who take an interest in her Royal Highness' welfare, to observe how she slights persons to whom it is of consequence for her to show civility ; and how she mistakes in the choice of those on whom she lavishes her favour. The Princess is always seeking *amusement*, and unfortunately, often at the expense of prudence and propriety. She cannot endure a dull person : she has often said to me, " I can forgive any fault but that " ; and the anathema she frequently pronounces upon such persons is,—" Mine Gott ! dat is de dullest person Gott Almighty ever did born ! "

Monday, 22nd of August.—I went and saw Lady [——]: she told me a piece of news, which it gave me great pleasure to learn, namely that *Trou Madame* exists no more, and that Chanticleer has been fairly driven off his dunghill. Lady [——] does not know *how* this has been effected ; but that it has is certain, thank heaven !— Only, I fear, that if *Chanticleer's* wings are clipped, they will grow again ; and if *his* neck is twisted, some other dunghill bird will roost on the same perch ; and it is not only disgraceful that the Princess should have lived in intimacy with such persons as the S[apio]s, but they have extracted so much money from her, that, had their reign continued longer, she would have been greatly'embarrassed. All Mr. H[——] has said to me on this melancholy subject, starts up and stares me in the face with damning truth. Even were there the excuse, though a bad one, of supposing *her heart interested* in any one person, I could forgive—nay, feel sympathy with her Royal Highness : but taking pleasure merely in the *admiration* of low persons, is beneath her dignity as a woman, not to mention her rank and station. I am sometimes tempted to wish Lord H. F[itzgeral]d had continued to love her ; for I am sure, poor soul, had any one been steadfast to her, she would have been so to them ; and though, as a married woman, nothing could justify her in being attached to any man, yet it is a hard and a cruel fate, to spend the chief part of one's existence unloving and unloved. How few can endure the trial ! It requires strong principle, and a higher power than mortals possess, to enable them to bear such a one ;— and when I hear women sitting in judgment on the Princess, (many of them not entitled, by their own conduct as wives, to comment on the behaviour of others,) and declaiming against her with unchristian severity,—some from a feeling of self-righteousness, others from political or party motives,—it is all I can do to forbear from telling them how unamiable I think such observations. Even when a woman *is* guilty, I cannot bear to hear another of her own sex proclaim her fault with vehemence ; I always think it proceeds from private malice, or a wish to appear better than others. If ever there was a woman to whom, in this respect, mercy should have been shown, it was the Princess; and those who condemn her should consider the trying, nay, almost unparalleled situation in which she was placed, immediately after coming to this country.

Who and what was the woman sent to escort her Royal Highness to England? Was there any attempt made on the part of the Prince to disguise of what nature his connection was with Lady J[erse]y?* None. He took every opportunity of wounding the Princess, by showing her that Lady J[erse]y was her rival. The ornaments with which he had decked his wife's arms, he took from her and gave to his mistress, who wore them in her presence. He ridiculed her person, and suffered Lady J[erse]y to do so in the most open and offensive manner. And finally, he wrote to her Royal Highness that he intended never to consider her as his wife—not even though such a misfortune should befal him as the death of his only child.

When the Prince made known this declaration, it does not appear that he assigned any cause of accusation against his wife. He was the first to blame; and when her subsequent follies (for from my heart I believe they never were more than follies) gave him an excuse for his illtreatment of her, it should be remembered, what an example of barefaced vice was set before the Princess when she was first married to the Prince. Unfortunately, she had not been brought up with a strict sense of moral rectitude, or religious principle, in her childhood; neither was the example set her by her father, the Duke of Brunswick, likely to give her just notions of right and wrong. She loved her father, and therefore excused his errors. From her earliest years she had been taught by the example of others, and those most near and dear to

* Frances Twysden, wife of the 4th Earl.

D. Gardner, pinxt.   Thos. Watson, fecit.

FRANCES, COUNTESS OF JERSEY

her, to consider married infidelity as a very venial tres-
pass ; and when she came to England, this notion was
confirmed by those whom she had thought most to have
honoured, and been guided by in her own conduct.   It
may be said that the person who cannot discern between
vice and virtue, and choose for herself which course to
pursue, is always to blame.   Granted ;—but surely, for a
woman *so* educated, and who had such examples set
before her, there ought to be some indulgence shown,
and some consideration made, for frailties which, in one
shape or other, are common to humanity.

While opprobrium was heaped on the Princess of Wales,
and the smallest offence against etiquette or propriety
which she had committed, was magnified into *crime*, the
Prince ran a career of lawless pleasure unrebuked, nay,
even applauded !   How true is the proverb—" One man
may steal a horse, and another may not look over a hedge."
I am not one of those who think that crime in *the one*
sex alters its nature and becomes virtue in the other.

Tuesday, 23d August.—I dined at Kensington.   The
manner in which Pylades and Orestes are treated, amuses
and makes me melancholy at the same time ; for it shows
how things *were*, and how they *are*.   The only new person
I have seen at Kensington for a length of time, is Madame
Zublibroff [Zabloukoff ?], the wife of a General Zublibroff.
She is a daughter of Mr. Angerstein's, and a very pretty,
agreeable-looking person.   Her husband appears clever
and sincere.   I am sure, by the conversation I heard him
hold with the Princess, he is a good man.   She deceives the
wife, I think, completely; but I doubt it is not so with
the husband : he nevertheless seems *friendly*, but friendly
with self-dignity.   He told her Royal Highness some
home truths, which she did not at all relish ; but, being
determined to like him, she contrived very ingeniously
to turn the subject in the light in which she *chose* to have

I   L it viewed, leaving General Zublibroff [Zabloukoff] precisely at the point whence he had set out. Accustomed as the Princess is, in common with all royalties, to see only through the medium of her own passions, she contrives generally to conceal whatever is disagreeable to her, and to have ears, *yet hear not.* So far, Bonaparte, by making a new race of kings, may perchance alter the nature of royalty : but I do not believe he will ; for the evil lies in the station more than in the individual. Yet any magistrate gifted with the same superiority of power and fortune, would, though under another title, be just as liable to the same prejudices as a king or an emperor ; and

A rose by any other name would smell as sweet.

I conceive, however, that a restless and active mind may dwell on this subject, till all sorts of chimeras enter the brain. My walk lies another way.

Wednesday.—The Princess drove to Lady Perceval's, and dined there yesterday. Chanticleer was there. It was curious to see how she thought *she hid matters* from Lady P[——]. The latter is a weak intriguing woman, who seems to me to be a mere convenience, but can see as far into a mill-stone as another, especially such a broad *barefaced* one.

Lady [——] told me, that in going out of Kensington Palace gates, by driving furiously, one of the leaders fell, and the poor little postillion was thrown off, and Lady [——] feared, at first, seriously hurt, for he did not get up for several minutes. The Princess was wholly unmoved, and never even asked how he did. Lady [——] said she could not express the hatred such want of feeling excited in her. The Princess ought not to have allowed the boy to ride on, but should have ordered him to go home and be taken care of. Instead of this, he remounted, and twice afterwards, on the road to Lady

Perceval's, the same accident very nearly happened; for, of course, the poor boy was trembling, and unable to guide the horses. Lady [——] told me she was made quite sick by the circumstance; but the resentment and abhorrence she felt at the Princess's total want of humanity on this occasion made her recover sooner than she would otherwise have done; for indignation took place of any other feeling. And no wonder! I could not understand a woman's being so unfeeling. It gave *me* also a feeling of dislike towards the Princess.

To-day I went to Blackheath, by command. Her Royal Highness was in a low, gentle humour. I walked round her melancholy garden with her, and she made me feel quite sorry for her, when she cried, and said it was all her own creation—meaning the garden and shrubbery, &c.—but that now she must leave it for ever, for that she had not money to keep a house at Blackheath and one in London also; and that the last winter she had passed there had been so very dreary, she could not endure the thought of keeping such a one again. I did not wonder at this. All the time I staid and walked with her Royal Highness, she cried, and spoke with a desolation of heart that really made me sorry for her; and yet, at the end of our conversation, poor soul, she smiled, and an expression of resignation, even of content, irradiated her countenance as she said, " I will go on hoping for happier days. Do you think *I may?*" she asked me; and I replied with heartfelt warmth, " I trust your Royal Highness will yet see many happy days." This Princess is a most peculiar person—she alternately makes me *dislike* and *like* her—her conduct and sentiments vary so in quality every time I see her. But one sentiment does and will ever remain fixed in my breast, and that is pity for her manifold wrongs.

I saw Madame de H[——]e; I think she is a good and an upright woman. Heavens! what an opinion she has of the Princess. She told me she dreamt the other night, that her Royal Highness's carriage was fired at, going down a lane, and that she was shot in the back. Madame de H[——] and I agreed on the impropriety of her Royal Highness exposing her person as she does, without attendants, in lanes and by-ways near Kensington and at Blackheath.

Thursday.—Lady [——] was sent to the cottage to fetch away books, &c., which had been left there. She heard that Chanticleer was ill. Amiable distress, interesting dénouement !—I dined at Kensington. There was no one besides the Princess, except Lady [——]. We dined off *mutton and onions*, and I thought Lady [——] would have dégobbiléd with the coarseness of the food, and the horror of seeing the Princess eat to satiety. Afterwards, her Royal Highness walked about Paddington Fields, making Lady [——] and myself follow. These walks are very injudiciously chosen as to time and place, though perfectly innocent, and taken for no other purpose than for the pleasure of doing an *extraordinary* thing. It was almost dark when the Princess returned home in the evening. She amused us very much by telling us the history of her sister, Princess Charlotte. I asked her if the report was true as to the manner of the Princess Charlotte's death. She said she did not believe it, and had even reasons for supposing she was still alive. Princess Charlotte married at 13 or 14 years of age,* and, like all princesses, and most other women, she did so in order to have an establishment, and be her own mistress. For some time she behaved well, though

* She was born in 1764 and married, in 1780, Frederick (afterwards King) of Wurtemberg. She died September 27, 1788. It is worth noticing (remembering the Napoleonic sympathies of Caroline, Princess of Wales) that her only daughter Catherine, Princess of Wurtemberg, was married in 1807 to Jerome Bonaparte, King of Westphalia, brother of Napoleon. The Princess of Wales sheltered them during their exile in her Italian villas.

her sister said her husband was very jealous of her from the beginning, and beat her cruelly.   At length, they went to Russia, and there she became enamoured of a man who was supposed to have been the Empress's lover—a circumstance which rendered the offence heinous, even though he was a *cast off* lover.   But it seems ladies snarl over a bone they have picked, just like any cross dog. The Princess Charlotte was secretly delivered of a child in process of time, in one of the Empress's chateaux. Her husband had not lived with her for a year or two, and for once the right father was actually named.   As soon as she recovered from this little accident, the Empress informed her it was no longer possible for her to allow her to live under her roof, but that she might go to the Chateau de Revelt, on the Baltic—that is to say, she *must* go : whither accordingly she was sent.   The curious part of this story is, that Miss Saunders, the Princess of Wales's maid, at this time living with her, had a sister, which sister lived as maid to Princess Charlotte, and she, after a time, came from the Chateau de Revelt back to Brunswick, saying her mistress was in perfect health, but had dismissed her from her service, as she no longer required her attendance.   She gave her money and jewels, and, after vain entreaties to be allowed to remain with her royal mistress, to whom she was much attached, M ss Saunders's sister left the Princess Charlotte.

Not long after this, word was brought to the Duke of Brunswick that she died suddenly of some putrid disorder, which made it necessary to bury the body immediately, without waiting for any ceremonies due to the rank of the deceased.   All further inquiries that were made ended in this account, and no light was thrown upon this business.   Some years subsequently to this, a travelling Jew arrived at Brunswick, who swore that he saw the Princess Charlotte at the Opera at *Leghorn*.   He was questioned, and declared that he could not be mistaken in her.   " I own," said the Princess of Wales, "from her sending away the person who was so much attached to her, and the only servant she had whom she loved and relied on, that I always hope she contrived to elope with her lover, and may still be alive." This story is curious if it be *true*; but her Royal Highness loves to tell romantic histories; so that one cannot believe implicitly what she narrates.

Saturday.—Again I dined at Kensington. Mr. and Mrs. [——] were also there. I was glad to see them at her Royal Highness's table; for, though not great personages in point of rank, they are great in goodness and respectability and talent. The Princess talked during the whole of dinner time, about her wish to procure four or five thousand pounds by giving up the lease of twenty-one years of her house at Blackheath, to whoever would advance her this sum of money. Messrs. [——] both told her it was a very good bargain for any body to enter into, but very disadvantageous for her. She insisted upon it, however, and said "she would get it done," and desired Lady [——] to write the next day, and tell Mr. H.[——] to endeavour to procure the money for her on these terms.

After dinner, the Princess, her Lady [——], and her gentleman accompanied her to Vauxhall, and supped at the Duke of Brunswick's. The evening was pleasant and amusing, but she *would* imagine that Mr. Gell was in love with Lady [——]; a very funny idea, but it annoyed her. The Duke of Brunswick is a man who has no notion of persons of different sexes associating together, *merely* for the sake of conversation and society. The only subject in which he shines is in talking of wars, and rumours of wars. He told me that the reason he could not and would not do any thing abroad was, because the Crown Prince insisted upon every person being under him, and all troops serving in the same cause making an oath to follow *him* when and wheresoever he should appoint. "This," said the Duke, "I never in honour could do ; for I do not, in the first place, feel confidence in this man ; and, in the second, I could not be subservient to him— a *faiseur d'armes*." I asked him what sort of looking man the Crown Prince is. "Very like what his former profession was," replied the Duke, holding himself erect, and gesticulating very much, and "always in this attitude,"—placing himself in that of fencing, with both arms extended. "I knew Bernadotte," said the Duke, "before he was in Bonaparte's service, and when he was only a *maître-d'armes*. He is an upstart, and, though he personally hates Bonaparte, he loves the French, and only desires to place himself in his stead at their head. He would be just as great a tyrant, were he placed in the same position. My opinion is, he would follow in Bonaparte's footsteps, and I do not think the general cause will be advanced by him."

The Duke shewed us two very curious illuminated MSS. ; one of them was a prayer-book, or rather a book of prayers, composed and written out in the handwriting of one of the Dukes of Brunswick. There were one hundred beautiful pictures in it, all finished like the finest painted miniatures, and, Mr. Gell said, executed by some great master. The binding of the book was also beautiful—of fine carved silver work. We also saw a vase twenty inches high, and ten in circumference, made of a single sardonyx, with the mysteries of Ceres exquisitely carved upon it. There was a printed account of how this vase came into the possession of the family, and its supposed age, which the author placed as far back as having been in the temple of Solomon ; but Mr. Gell said, "that is nonsense, and I hope they will not publish this in the translation intended to be made of this account ; for the workmanship of this unique vase is evidently Grecian, and of the *finest times ;* besides, a representation of the heathen deities would not have been allowed to exist in Solomon's temple." I do not know if the Duke understood perfectly all that Mr. Gell said, for his Serene Highness is somewhat bouché upon these subjects.—We were shown yet one thing more— the *Duke's bed*—which is the most uncomfortable place of rest I have ever seen. It is made of iron : there are no curtains, and only one mattress, and a sheet. He piques himself on having, he says, " sounder and sweeter sleep on that bed, than many who lie on the softest down." There is a frankness and an enthusiasm in the Duke of Brunswick which make me like him very much, notwithstanding his *ton de garnison.*

Sunday.—The Princess went to Lady Perceval's, where Lady [——] says there is no amusement ; it must be, therefore, that this intimacy is kept up for past reasons, not present pleasure—a sad consideration.

Monday.—The Duke of Brunswick came to take leave of his sister. I was present at their interview, with some of the Princess's ladies. There never was a man so altered by the hope of glory ; his stature seemed to dilate, and his eyes were animated with a fire and an expression of grandeur and delight which astonished me. I could not help thinking the Princess did not receive him with the warmth she ought to have done. He detailed to her the whole particulars of the conversation he had had with the ministers, the Prince Regent, &c. He mimicked them all admirably, particularly Lord Castlereagh—so well as to make us all laugh ;—and he gave the substance of what had passed between himself and those persons, with admirable precision, in a kind of question and answer colloquy, that was quite dramatic.

I was astonished, for I never saw any person so changed

by circumstance. He really looked a hero. The Princess heard all that he said, in a kind of sullen silence, while the tears were in several of the bystanders' eyes. How could this be so ? At length, when the Duke of Bruns- wick said, " The ministers refused me all assistance ; they would promise me neither money nor arms. But I care not ; I will go straight to Hamburgh. I hear there are some brave young men there, who await my coming ; and, if I have only my orders from the Prince Regent *to act*, I will go without either money or arms, and gain both."—" Perfectly right," replied the Princess with some enthusiasm in her voice and manner. " How did Bonaparte conquer the greater part of Europe ? " (the Duke continued.) " He had neither money nor arms, but he *took* them. And if *he* did that, why should not I, who have so much more just a cause to defend ? " The Duke then proceeded to state how the Ministers and the Regent were all at variance, and how he had obtained from the latter an order which he could not obtain from the Ministers. After some further con- versation, he took leave of his sister : she did not embrace him. He held out his hand to me kindly, and named me familiarly. I felt a wish to express something of the kindly feeling I felt towards him ; but, I know not why, in her presence, who ought to have felt so much more, and who seemed to feel so little, I felt chilled, and re- mained silent. I have often thought of that moment since with regret. When the Duke was fairly gone, however, she shed a few tears, and said emphatically, " I shall never see him more."

Mrs. and Miss R[awdo]n and Lord H[enry] F[itz- gerald] dined at Kensington. It is comical to see how the Princess behaves to him, trying to show off, and yet endeavouring to make him hate her. His behaviour is perfectly kind, respectful, and even, at times, there is a sadness in his manner, which makes me think he regrets the change in her sentiments towards him; and I am certain he is sorry to see the alteration there is in the society which frequents her Royal Highness's house.

I was for several days much alarmed by a change that I saw in the shape of the Princess's figure, and I could not help imparting the terrible fear I felt to Lady [——]. She also had noticed it; but I was much relieved by her telling me she knew for certain it was only caused by the Princess having left off stays,—a custom which she is very fond of. She ought to be warned not to indulge in this practice; for it might give rise to reports exceedingly injurious to her character.

Lord H[enry] F[itzgerald] asked Lady [——] many shrewd questions about young Chanticleer? He smells a rat: the sweet odour must soon spread far and wide. Mrs. R[awdo]n talked openly to me of this sad and disgraceful story. I felt very awkward, and very much ashamed for my poor royal mistress.

Tuesday.—Again I dined at Kensington. No company except the Sapios. Lady [——] and I sat apart, and talked together when we could hear one another speak; but the horrible din of their music hardly ever stopped the whole evening, except when it was interrupted by the disgusting nonsense of praise that passed between the parties. Interest and cunning excuse it from the low and servile; but really, to hear her let herself down so as to sing pæans to the fiddler's son, who is after all gone away from her! Lady [——] and I both agreed, it is more than human patience can bear, to witness such folly. The perpetual silly nonsense of the old buffoon, amounting often to impudence, crowns the whole.

Thursday.—I dined at Kensington. Messrs. Gell and Craven and Sir H. Englefield were there, besides Lady [——]. The Princess sat at table till we went to sleep, or near it ;—Sir H. Englefield did quite. Not that these men dislike women's society, or probably wish them away, to lose all restraint, and give way to conversation which they could not hold in their presence ; but that sitting round a table for four hours is wearisome to the body as well as mind. Sir H. Englefield went away immediately after the Princess rose ; the others remained, and were pleasant and amusing, as they always are. Her Royal Highness is very jealous of any attention being paid to Lady [——], and, if she listened to Mr. Craven singing, the Princess wanted to do the same; or if Lady [——] talked to Mr. Gell, her Royal Highness was curious, and came near to hear what they were saying ; and, when Mr. Gell attempted to teach Lady [——] to play on the guitar, that annoyed her beyond measure, and she desired Mr. Gell to " come and sit " beside her Royal Highness. I admire and am astonished beyond measure at Lady [——]'s good humour and patience.

In the course of the evening, the Princess desired Lady [——] to tell her her fortune ; and, in doing so, the story of Tiberius and the conjuror occurred to her ; and, as she told me afterwards, she could not resist telling it to her Royal Highness for her benefit. It was a comical story to tell a Princess. I do not think she was pleased with Lady [——] for doing so, though she pretended to laugh and be much amused.

Friday.—It is said Friday is an unlucky day ; and I am superstitious, and inclined to believe in these traditions ; but I never can again in this one ; for Friday was a day of happiness to me ; it brought me an unexpected pleasure ; I saw [——] and she was kind. This meeting has given me fresh courage to bear my unhappy existence.

I saw Mr. Ward ; he was in a gay good humour. How different the same man appears at different times, and in different company !

Saturday, 4th of September.—I called on Lady W[——];
she is very agreeable, and, I think, has much natural
cleverness ; but it is all wasted in *eloquence in conversation.* She leads a strange life, as to hours and customs,
which I do not think is calculated to calm her mind, or
give strength to her body. She is always in a bustle
about nothing. Many of her ideas are exalted, and her
language often poetical, but it is frittered away on
paltry subjects ; and there is a spirit of restlessness in
her, poor soul, which renders her an unhappy being.
Perhaps, were she *compelled,* by some kind but resolute
friend, to lead a more regular and wholesome life, she
might become less excited. But, alas ! she has none
such, and each day her mind is getting the mastery over
her body, to its undoing.

There was a time when I despised all notions of adhering
to any regular course of existence ; I did not believe
that such was requisite, or contributed as much as it
does to health and peace. I liked sometimes to be out
all day, and return at night to my meals. Sometimes,
I would sit up late and rise early, and at others lie in
bed for days. I did not believe that such irregularity
could injure my health, much less affect my mind. But
I am convinced now, that nothing tends so much to
enervate or excite (according to the nature of the person)
as leading this sort of unsettled life. It is the dull round
of hours for meals, and sleep, and exercise, which is most
likely to preserve health, and that calm of spirit which,
though it precludes vivid sensations of pleasure, spares
those who lead such lives many a severe pang. It was
not so once, however, with me ; and, when I look at
what I have just written, I say—Is it *I* who have thus
spoken—I who once sought with eagerness to escape
that odious " peace," which I now covet as the greatest
blessing ? It is even so.

I dined at Kensington. A Mr. Mills dined with her Royal

Highness.   I never saw him there before, and I could not discover who he is, or anything else about him, except that he has very white teeth and very festooned lips.

31st December, 1813.—In looking back upon the past there is always much melancholy reflection excited, but it is a wholesome melancholy, and I wish not to avoid it.   How little I have done or thought, that has left me a pleasant remembrance !   How much time has passed that has been wasted in idleness, and in that worst idleness, the idleness of the mind !   I know and regret that it has been so ; but I have never had the power to overcome the languor and laziness which have taken possession of my faculties.   In justice to myself, though, I must say, it is *circumstances* which have rendered me thus—it is not my nature.   Time, which either lessens or increases regret, will, I hope, bring with it healing for me under its wings ; and I have made many wise plans for the future, and framed many good resolutions, which I hope I shall be able to fulfil.

In the course of the last four months, the changes that have taken place in the political world are of so vast a magnitude, that my intellect is not great enough to comprehend them.   Holland is free ; Germany and Sweden also have shaken off the tryant's yoke ; in short, his own speech to the senators at Paris proves sufficiently Bonaparte's altered state :—" all Europe was with us, all Europe is now against us."—No more needs be added to such a confession.   We have taken all the merit of these changes to ourselves ; with what justice, I am not competent to decide.   Certainly, Lord Wellington is a great hero, and certainly, we have been partly the means of liberating Spain : but I have sometimes in my own mind doubted, whether the opprobrium thrown upon the Spaniards was not exaggerated, and whether it might not be an artful contrivance of our Government to encourage the idea, in order that a greater share of glory might attach to us ; while such a notion suited Lord Wellington's ambition, who wished to have the sole command, and whose views perhaps did not even end there. So many events in private life are so very different, when truly known, from what appearances bespeak them, that it is impossible to believe the same deceit is not practised on a larger scale ; for the passions of nations, like those of smaller communities, are, after all, only the aggregate passions of mankind individually, and are as liable to influence, and to lead to falsehood, prejudice, injustice and crime, in the great political world, as they are in the domestic concerns of life.

It has been said, that we have been the only nation, during these last twenty-four years, that has held out against the tyranny and anarchy which ravaged or confounded Europe. But when I consider our opinions and promises respecting the restoration of the French monarchy, and see how widely we now differ from those opinions, and fall short of the fulfilment of those promises, I cannot help thinking, that neither nations, nor individuals, should be hasty to enter into engagements ; since the very nature of humanity is to render all things around us mutable, and that it is utterly impossible we should not partake in some degree of the general condition. In regard to these last great Continental changes, my opinion is that if any one individual has been more instrumental than another in effecting them, it has been the Crown Prince (Bernadotte). A Frenchman himself, he knows how to act upon Frenchmen ; and, as a native of the Continent, he knows better the continental systems than we do. The weakness of all persons (with few exceptions) in private as well as in public life, is to insist upon everybody's being managde precisely as we ourselves have been managed. The narrower the circle, and the more confined the spot on

which we live, the more (generally speaking) will our
views and wills be limited, and unfit for general applica-
tion. I believe, therefore, that with one of the finest
countries and constitutions in the world, we are not calculated, as islanders, to give laws to the Continent, or
to subdue its people. Let us merely endeavour honourably to maintain our own laws and liberties inviolate,
and to be satisfied with that safe and stable power,
which our insular situation, and our internal greatness,
bestow upon us. But to subdue France, or impose
upon its people any government that is not of their
own choosing, appears to me folly. To relieve the
oppressed, as we have ever done, is noble, and becomes
us as a nation of Christians, and of good and brave men ;
but for their sakes to keep up perpetual wars with other
nations, seems to me unwise. Lending our aid to Spain
is an exception, and I view it in a very different light.
We only went with what we were at first told was the
general spirit of the whole nation ; it was not in favour
of any one family or dynasty that we fought, but for
the rights of an oppressed people, who demanded our
aid and succour. Yet even these were latterly supposed
not to desire our assistance : so seldom is it that foreign
troops are looked upon with a favourable eye, in national
warfare.

No one was so likely to be able to defeat Bonaparte
as the Crown Prince, from the intimate knowledge he
possessed of his character. Bernadotte was also instigated against Bonaparte, by one who not only owed
him a personal hatred, but who possessed a mind equal
to his, and who gave the Crown Prince both information
and advice how to act. This was no less a person than
Madame de Staël. It was not, as some have asserted,
that she was *in love* with Bernadotte ; for, at the time
of their intimacy, Madame de Staël was in love with
Rocca. But she used her influence (which was not

small) with the Crown Prince, to make him fight against
Bonaparte ; and to her wisdom may be attributed much
of the success which accompanied his attack upon him.
Bernadotte has raised the flame of liberty, which seems
fortunately to blaze all around.   May it liberate Europe ;
and from the ashes of the laurel, may olive branches
spring up, and overshadow the earth !

I wish, ardently wish, individually, for peace ; but I
wish for it also from that spirit of humanity, which cannot
hear of a land saturated with blood, and not shrink
aghast from all the desolation of heart which it implies.
My private life has been calm ; no very lively emotions
have given a high zest to existence ; and a constant
pressure has lowered the tone of my intellect, and reigned
in my imagination.   I wish to be able to leave England,
and visit foreign countries ; I long for an opportunity
to extend my observations, and to acquire new matter
for my mind to feed upon.

I check my eager longings, however ; because I know
that we are erring mortals, and that our views for ourselves are generally not those which are for our good.   I
recollect also that everything which I have earnestly
longed for has come to pass ; and yet the events thus
desired, are precisely those which have least tended to
my felicity—indeed, in many instances, have been
productive of misery.   I say, therefore, to my folly, Be
subdued ; for the wisdom of man's desire is only folly :
and to my eager wish of change, Be suppressed ; for
there are many changes which would make me miserable, and few that could make me happier.   However,
hopes and wishes must exist while life remains, and we
must act if we would enjoy.   It is only an overweening
eagerness, a repining spirit, whose gratified desires are
liable to turn to curses.   A moderated wish, made in
humble subserviency to the Divine power, cannot draw
down upon us the displeasure of Heaven.

SECTION III

SUNDAY, *January 9th*, 1814.—Yesterday, according to appointment, I went to Princess Charlotte. Found at Warwick House the harpplayer, Dizzi; was asked to remain and listen to his performance, but was talked to during the whole time, which completely prevented all possibility of listening to the music. The Duchess of Leeds and her daughter were in the room, but left it soon. Next arrived Miss Knight, who remained all the time I was there. Princess Charlotte was very gracious—showed me all her *bonny dyes*, as B[essie Mure] would have called them—pictures, and cases, and jewels, &c. She talked in a very desultory way, and it would be difficult to say of what. She observed her mother was in very low spirits. I asked her how she supposed she could be otherwise.—This *questioning* answer saves a great deal of trouble, and serves two purposes—i.e., avoids committing oneself, or giving offence by silence. There was hung in the apartment one portrait, amongst others, that very much resembled the Duke of D[evonshire]. I asked Miss Knight whom it represented; she said that was not known; it had been supposed a likeness of the Pretender when young. This answer suited my thoughts so comically, I could have laughed, if one ever did at courts anything but the contrary of what one was inclined to do.

Princess Charlotte has a very great variety of expression in her countenance—a play of features, and a force of muscle, rarely seen in connection with such soft and shadeless colouring. Her hands and arms are beautiful, but I think her figure is already gone, and will soon be precisely like her mother's : in short, it is the very picture of her, and *not in miniature*. I could not help analysing my own sensations during the time I was with her, and thought more of them than I did of her. Why was I at all flattered, at all more amused, at all more supple to this young Princess, than to her who is only the same sort of person, set in the shade of circumstances and of years ? It is that youth, and the approach of power, and the latent views of self interest, sway the heart, and dazzle the understanding. If this is so with a heart not, I trust, corrupt, and a head not particularly formed for interested calculations, what effect must not the same causes produce on the generality of mankind ?

In the course of the conversation, the Princess Charlotte contrived to edge in a good deal of *tum-de-dy*, and would, if I had entered into the thing, have gone on with it, while looking at a little picture of herself, which had about thirty or forty different dresses to put over it, done on *isinglass*, and which allowed the general colouring of the picture to be seen through its transparency. It was, I thought, a pretty enough conceit, though rather like dressing up a doll. " Ah ! " said Miss Knight, " I am not content though, Madam—for I yet should have liked one more dress—that of the favourite Sultana."

" No, no ! " said the Princess, " I never was a favourite, and never can be one,"—looking at a picture which she said was her father's, but which I do not believe was done for the Regent any more than for me, but represented a young man in a hussar's dress—probably a former favourite.*

* This probably alludes to a girlish flirtation Princess Charlotte was accused of having with Captain Fitzclarence, one of the natural sons of the Duke of Clarence, afterwards William II.

The Princess Charlotte seemed much hurt at the little notice that was taken of her birthday. After keeping me for two hours and a half, she dismissed me, and I am sure I could not say what she said, except that it was an *olio* of *décousus* and heterogeneous things, partaking of the characteristics of her mother, grafted on a younger scion. I dined tête-à-tête with my dear old aunt : hers is always a sweet and soothing society to me.

January 10th, 1814.—I read several chapters of Miss Berry's work, a Comparative View of the English and French Nations, since the time of Charles II. to the present day. I think this work a most sterling performance, and one, from the nature of its subject, as well as the grave and masterly manner in which she treats it, likely to do honour to her memory. I hear Miss B[erry] has been reproached with its being too grave ; but I think the sober chastened style in which it is written suits the dignity of the matter. A lighter pen might have found *de quoi* to have made a continuation of that most amusing and immoral work, the Mémoires de Grammont ; but where a deeper tone of thought induces a higher aim than mere wit and entertainment, surely she has chosen more appropriate means to attain her object.

It is the most severely cold weather we ave had for many winters past. I called on Miss [——]. She was full of the politics of the day, or rather I should say, events ; for truly the great catastrophe of the fate of Europe takes a higher character than that of mere court politics. There was a report that Lord Yarmouth, who was just arrived, has said, that in a few days the allies would be at Paris, as the country made no resistance to their progress. It is also said that a deputation to Louis the Eighteenth has arrived from France. Wonderful, indeed, will be the hour which sees that monarch

again seated on his throne. How far the restoration of
the Bourbons might be productive of happiness to France,
I cannot pretend to determine. Certainly, I would not
have more blood shed on their account, or on any account ;
but if the people will with one voice receive them, I believe
I have a hankering at my heart that those remaining of
the old race should resume the sceptre of their ancestors.
After all, their misfortunes are more likely to render
them deserving, than any other person might be ; and
God perhaps will now reward them after their trials.
Yet I confess, considering Bonaparte as a conqueror,
I do not know that he is worse than all conquerors have
ever been. What seas of blood they have all waded through
to gain their ambitious ends ! In spite of his crimes
and of his heartless character, I think him great ; and,
wherever there is superior intellect, I cannot help in
some degree paying homage to that divine impress. I
should be sorry that that man was shewn about for lesser
villains to hoot at ; or that he was massacred, to satisfy
the rage of an undistinguishing multitude.

The circumstance which gives me the greatest dislike
to Bonaparte, is his having put away his wife, Josephine,
whom he did not accuse of any fault, save that she did
not give him an heir to succeed to his crown. Nothing
can, in my idea, pardon this vile action ; and I cannot
understand how Josephine condescended to receive his
visits and his expressions of attachment, after he had
behaved so cruelly to her. The only thing that can
reconcile this to one's understanding is, that a woman
will do and suffer much when she loves. There has
been a little scandal reported of Josephine ; but still
it amounts to nothing more than rumour ; her husband
never accused her ; he set her aside as a useless appendage
to his state ; but he continued to profess affection for
her, even to the day of his death.

Every wife, every woman, sympathized with Josephine ;

her situation excited in her own sex universal pity.
Since the time of Henry VIII. there had been no such
instance of injustice in a monarch. Josephine was
kind-hearted, and generous; she did many acts of
charity, and was besides a very fascinating woman.
These qualities, together with her cruel fate, will make
her a heroine in history; and her rival, Marie Louise,
will stand opposed to her, as heartless and vain; for
when the people pitied her, supposing she was a victim
to Bonaparte's power, she disclaimed such pity, by
appearing happy, and pleased with the great station
to which her marriage with him exalted her.

At five o'clock I was at Connaught House; found
Lady Anne dressed out like a mad Chinese. Miss Garth
very quiet, as usual. The Princess, arrayed in crimson
velvet up to the throat, looking very well. Shortly after,
arrived Princess Charlotte and the Duchess of Leeds.
The former took very little notice of her mother, so little
that I do not wonder the Princess of Wales was hurt.
She took me by the arm and led me to the fireplace,
and I saw she was ready to weep: I felt for her. Princess
Charlotte addressed herself wholly to Miss Garth; and,
as in a few moments Princess Sophia * came, she laid
hold of her, and conversed aside with her; all of which
must have been most cutting to the mother's heart.
Oh! what an evening of deceit, and of coldness, and
of cunning!

At dinner, I had an opportunity of speaking to Miss
D[——] about the old story of the paper Mrs. N[——]
had lent to me, and which she thought I kept for some
sinister purpose. Miss D[——] said that her sister had
expressed herself warmly about me before her death.
That may or may not have been; but I was glad of an
opportunity of telling that worldly-minded woman that
I am not a spy. During dinner time, I heard the Princess

* Of Gloucester.

pouring dissatisfaction into her daughter's ear—if it
was not there already—saying, " all the world had hoped
for promotions, and for emancipation from prisons, &c.,
&c., the day of her coming of age, but that no public
testimony of joy had been shown on that occasion, and
it had passed away in mournful silence." Princess
Charlotte was considerably struck, and replied, " Oh,
but the war and the great expenses of the nation occasion
my coming of age to be passed over at present." " A
very good excuse, truly," said the Princess of Wales,
" and you are child enough to believe it ! " and so ended
all I heard them say.

Friday, 14th Jan.—Saw Messrs. G[——] and C[——]
they told me that they are both perfectly aware to *what a
low ebb* things have run.   Nevertheless, they are good and
faithful, and regret for her sake the imprudencies and
follies she is perpetually committing ; but how long the
Princess will find others so, God knows ! Lady [——]
told me she drove out yesterday for five minutes only ;
groaned and found fault, and returned ; then made
Lady [——] sit with her till seven, listening to perpetual,
wicked, and nonsensical repetition of evils, the most of
which she forges herself.   Chanticleer did not come to
dinner, which caused great rage and despair.

Saturday.—I dined at Connaught House ; Lady [——]
was ill, to my great sorrow, not only for her sake but
my own.   Chanticleer dined there.   I read a novel
all the evening, but yet his very presence is horridly
degrading.

Sunday.—I went to inquire for Lady [——] ; she saw
me, and told me she had been much distressed this
morning, for that Miss B[——] and Mr. K[——] had
called, and had been admitted to the Princess, but that

her extreme ill-humour must have been visible. Miss
B[——] told her some home truths, in a very proper
manner ; but Lady [——] said that every subject that
was touched upon—novels, public news, &c.—all were
equally displeasing or indifferent to her Royal Highness.
Lady [——] said that to her the Princess always main-
tains the language and manners of friendship and of real
liking. "This," she said, "distresses and wounds me ;
because I cannot really be her friend ; she will not hear
the truth."

"Yesterday, the Princess told her that she was of
the greatest comfort to her ; and she often does so
after conversations which make Lady [——] feel the
reverse. Lady [——] said to me that this contradiction
of sentiments harasses her more than she can express.

H[——] has engaged to advance the Princess two
thousand pounds in the course of twelve months, by
instalments of five hundred each. I *do* trust that she will
not deceive him. She is to pay two hundred a year for
the money, till the sum is paid off. I warned him sufficiently as to the paction he was entering into ; so he has
done it with his eyes open : besides, he told me plainly
she can serve him in two instances, and he expects she will
do so. The Princess sent to desire me to go to Mr. St.
Leger, as he is too ill to wait on her, and ask him to procure the lease of the house left her by her mother, from
Mr. Le Blanc, which she wants to give Mr. H. as security
for the payment of the debt contracted to him. I hope
she will get that lease ; it is the only security she can
give. Oh ! how the Princess talks of her mother, till
really my blood freezes to hear a mother so spoken of
by a daughter. And that I should listen to such conversation with apparent quietness !

At luncheon, her Royal Highness was in high spirits.
"Shall I tell you something very curious ? " said she.
I knew it was in vain to stop the tide, so I did not attempt

it. "I went one day," she continued, "in September, to walk from my house at Blackheath, with Miss Garth, to Mr. Angerstein's, who was very ill at that time. I went out the back way from my garden, through Greenwich Park, so that nobody could know me." Hem ! thought I. "Well, my dear [——], I was followed by two gipsies, who insisted on telling my fortune. I have no money, said I, but they persisted in following me, and did so till I came to Mr. Angerstein's gate : I then told them that if they would wait there, they should tell my fortune when I returned. I found them there on my return, and what do you think they told me ? " The Princess looked fixedly at me, and rolled her eyes with that quick, penetrating glance which seems to examine all the folds of one's thoughts at the same moment. "I am sure, madam, I cannot guess." "Why they told me that I was a married woman, but that I should not be married long ; and that my heart was a foreigner's, and that I should go abroad and there marry the man I loved, and be very rich and happy— they did, by G—, tell me so—and how could they know that ? "

How, indeed, unless they had been tutored to the tale ? This was to myself. What I replied aloud was, " Very strange, indeed, ma'am, but they make up many curious and nonsensical tales ; that is their trade." " 'Twas very odd," she said, looking significantly ; " was it not very odd ? " This conversation was all, save what I dread most ; and the horror of thinking I shall one day hear it, and that ere long, *et en détail*, is the most terrible thought, and makes me very uneasy whenever her Royal Highness honours me by a tête-à-tête interview. She swore to me as she was standing by the fire the other day, àpropos des bottes, that Willikin was *not her* son. " No," said she, " I would tell you if he was. No," she continued, " if such little accident had happened, I would not hide it from you. He is not William Austin, though," added she ; " but, avouez-moi, it was very well managed that nobody should know who he really is, nor shall they till after my death." I replied, that I thought it was nobody's business who the boy was, and that I, for one, had no curiosity to know. " That is for why I tell you," replied the Princess. " Then somebody ask me who Willikin is de child of. De person say to me, ' *Dey* do say, he is your Royal Highness's child.'* I answered, ' Prove it, and he shall be your king.' The person was silent after that."—I could not resist laughing, and the Princess laughed, also. She takes great pleasure in making her auditor stare. After a pause, she said, " Poor dear Willikin, I am so sorry he is growing big, but I am determined to have *another* little boy ; I must always have a child in the house." I lifted my eyes to her person ; I really fancied I saw the full meaning of her words ; but she met my glance with a steady composure which re-assured me ; for I thought no one could look so calm, so bold, were there any thing to be ashamed of ; and I replied, " But, madam, you have the same interest in Willikin that ever you had." " Oh ! yes, to be sure, I love him dearly, but I must have a *little child ;* he is growing too big, too much of a man."

The conversation then changed, for I said nothing— what could I *say*—though I thought much. If she adopts another very young child, and that the transaction be ever so innocent, still evil will be attached to it ; again her enemies will have something to say against her. Poor foolish woman ! that she should not see that, in taking another child under her protection, she will lay herself open to fresh accusations. She does not want sense ; yet such folly I never saw before in a person not bereft of her senses. I dared not tell her how imprudent I thought she would be, if she gratified this wish for a

* She made him her heir

young child. I wish she had some friend who would tell her the truth. I have often thought that her Royal Highness's having no confidants in her ladies, was a very fortunate circumstance ; and I have said this to her face ; yet, I earnestly wish that she had some wise counsellor who had influence over her.

Monday.—I dined at Connaught House. Old Ourang Outang came in the evening. The Princess went down stairs for some music, and when she came up was ready to fall with breathlessness. This lasted for some minutes, for I was sitting with my back to the pianoforte, reading ; but, on chancing to look round, I saw her look significantly to S[——] and say, " If you knew *what it is*,"— then catching my eye, she added, " so soon after dinner, to *run up down staircase.*" I looked stedfastly at her Royal Highness, but she never flinched beneath my gaze. No, I do not believe her guilty, but I wish to Heaven she did not talk such nonsense.

Tuesday.—Lady [——] told me the old Ourang and his wife were with the Princess the whole day ; that at dinner she cried and looked very ill, and said she had been so all night, and seemed really suffering. After dinner, her Royal Highness made a wax figure as usual, and gave it an amiable addition of large horns ; then took three pins out of her garment, and stuck them through and through, and put the figure to roast and melt at the fire. If it was not too melancholy to have to do with this, I could have died of laughing. Lady [——] says the Princess indulges in this amusement whenever there are no strangers at table ; and she thinks her Royal Highness really has a superstitious belief that destroying this *effigy* of her husband will bring to pass the destruction of his royal person. What a silly piece of spite ! Yet, it is impossible not to laugh when one sees it done.

Saturday, 29th January.—I dined at Connaught House, and passed three hours of dulness with Madame S[——] and the Princess. After dinner, Thomas Campbell came. The Princess did nothing but try to amuse that child Willikin, who will be a thorn in her side yet, if she lives. Campbell and Lady [——] talked and recited verses, which did not please her Royal Highness. Nothing entertains her except talking of her grievances, which always at the moment affect me, and which are, in the great outline, *true ;* but unfortunately I know all the filling up of the picture, and that is so silly, so despicable, that one becomes indignant at having one's feelings excited in favour of a cause where there is so much to blame on both sides. One can only regard it in oneself as a piece of *weak tenderness*, an animal sensation rather than a *mental sympathy*, to feel anything for evils of such a nature, and most of them of a self-constituted kind.

Sunday.—I called on Lady W[——]. She has tranquu and dignified manners, though rather cold. She was, in her youth, exceedingly handsome, it is said, and long held in thrall Lord H[——], but always with safety to her own character. Her love of *command* superseded all other love, and her husband never dared to say his soul was his own, although a very amiable man ; this cast a ridicule upon him, as it will upon all those who are foolish enough to allow their wives to usurp authority over them. Lady [——] told me that the Princess complains of being beset by spies, that she abused all her servants, especially Mrs. Robarts ; in which idea Lady [——] assured her she was mistaken.

The Princess wishes to have a lodging in the country, that she may go there unaccompanied by her household. What a mad scheme ! but, when she is determined to do a thing, who can stop her ?

All of a sudden the Princess sent out cards for a dinner party ; all the persons she invited were of the opposition. I dare say it will be said that she lives entirely with these persons, and low company ; the latter, alas ! is but too true.

To-day, I dined at Connaught House ; the Princess Charlotte was there ; she was in her most gracious mood, but appeared low-spirited. The Princess Sophia of Gloucester was also of the party ; they left Connaught House early, and none of the royal party seemed pleased with one another.

—I came to town Thursday, 24th February. I never leave home without regret ; life is so short, so uncertain, that it seems to me as if all voluntary absence from what we love most, is folly. I dined with my aunt, and went in the evening to Miss [——]. I made acquaintance with a Monsieur D'Erfeuil. He has a clever-looking countenance, but with a cast of the eye, not unlike that of the Duke of Orléans, and his expression implies insincerity. I heard that it is thought Mr. Robinson, Lord Grantham's brother, has brought over dispatches which are of a nature to force our government to make peace with Bonaparte. I am sorry for these poor deceived Bourbons, but not sorry for the peace which is talked of.

Friday.—I dined at Lord F[——] C[——]'s. It is melancholy to see one of a distinguished family reduced to living in so little and mean a house ; and the more so as he is thus reduced from a mistaken notion that he is acting rightly. And what is yet more grievous to his friends is, that it is impossible to be of any service to him, because his heart only half opens, and before one can get a place in it, it closes again. We played at dull cards. I escaped as soon as I could. I went to Mrs. Villiers, and

from Mrs. Villiers to Madame de Staël.   At Mrs. Villiers's,
I saw Mr. Arbuthnot and his bride ; she is very pretty, but
it is what is vulgarly called Pig Beauty, in English ; in
French *La Beauté du Diable,* i.e., Youth.   He is all fire
and flames and love, selon son ordinaire, and so very
proud of her !   It is rather agreeable to see any person so
completely happy.   There was, standing close by him, a
person whom, twenty years ago, he had been madly in love
with.   She had, it was said, behaved remarkably well,
but yet there was such a melancholy in seeing

> The object alter'd, the desire the same—

it was such a perfect illustration of the instability of all
human affections, that I stood and philosophised on my
own heart, and that of the rest of mankind, despising alike
the one and the other.   But this anger against myself
never lasts long : on se racommode si facilement avec ce
que l'on aime !

From Mrs. Villiers I proceeded to Madame de Staël's.
I saw there Monsieur de la Garde, Monsieur D'Erfeuil,
Messrs. Gell, Craven, and Mercer, Monsieur de Merfelt,
the Austrian ambassador, and I know not who besides.
The latter has very ugly features, but a pleasing countenance.   I made acquaintance with a Lady W[——],
just come from Paris, who has brought a packet to Lady
Hertford from the ci-devant Empress Josephine, which
packet made much noise, and raised much conjecture ;
for persons inimical to the Regent were glad to catch hold
of it as a subject of abuse.   Whether the story I heard
concerning the *presents* was true or not, I cannot say ;
but it is curious.   Lady W[——] praised Paris, its
fashions, and its society ; which latter, she says, is
peculiarly agreeable to women.

Saturday.—I dined with Madame de Staël ; there were
no ladies except Miss B[——] and Madame de Vaudreuil.

It is always delightful to be in Madame de Staël's society ;
even those persons who have been most inimical to her,
have generally been subjugated by her sincerity, her
kindness, and the charm of her conversation—which,
unlike that of any other person, male or female, in giving
out her own ideas, awakens those of her hearers, and
draws them, as it were in despite of themselves, to a
reciprocity of communication.   Thus it was that Madame
de Staël acquired a knowledge of mankind, which superseded all that books can ever teach.

From Madame de Staël's I proceeded to Lady Salisbury's.   I met there my old friend Lord D[——] ; he is
not particularly *amusing*, but he has been my friend for
twenty years, without ever evincing a shade less of kindness towards me during that long period.   It is pleasant to
have such a friend, and fully compensates for want of
superior talent.   Lady Salisbury's was a brilliant
assembly.   Lady Melbourne introduced me to a Monsieur
de Neumann, an Austrian, who seems very agreeable.
I like the society just now in London ; there are many
foreigners.   Mademoiselle de Staël is very clever and
agreeable *en tête-à-tête*, Lady [——] tells me, but she is shy
and reserved in general society ; one looks at her with
interest, as being Madame de Staël's daughter.

Tuesday.—I called on Mrs. W. Lock, to ask her how the
Princess had received my excuse which I sent for Sunday
last.   Mrs. L[ock] said she was very gracious to her, and
spoke kindly of me.   Lady E. Whitbread, and Mrs.
W[——], and Mrs. Beauclerck dined at Kensington that
day.   Mrs. L[ock] told me Lady E. Whitbread appeared
shocked when she looked at the Princess's *figure*.   Mrs.
L[ock] ascribed this to the Princess's wearing extremely
short petticoats ; but I thought, with fear, that perhaps
Lady E. Whitbread's disgust was occasioned by other
ideas ; although, considering the legs and feet which the

short petticoats display, there is more than enough to shock a woman like Lady E[lizabeth].

I dined with my aunt ; she told me a curious anecdote she had heard about Caulincourt, who [she] had hitherto held in abhorrence, as the murderer of the unfortunate Duke D'Enghien. It is said that when he was sent to arrest him, he wished to save him, and, entering the room where the Duke was, he looked round, and then full at him, as at a person wholly unknown to him ; then turning to his gens d'armes who attended him, he said—" You see the Duke is not here, we must seek him elsewhere ;—when a lady to whom the Duke D'Enghien was attached rushed into the room, and falling on her knees to Caulincourt, cried out, save him ! save him ! " Vous le voyez devant vous ; vous n'aurez pas la cruauté de le perdre." At this imprudence, Caulincourt was obliged to execute the orders he had received, and he desired his men to seize their unfortunate victim. How far this story is a fabrication or not, in order to soften people's judgments against Caulincourt, rests with future times to discover.

Wednesday, 2d of March.—I am writing from the Priory ; a far different scene of woe from that which I witnessed at Lady S[——]'s. Here every thing is to be as if no change had taken place. Poor Lord Abercorn ! he wishes to forget those he has lost ; but the remembrance of them will cling to him as long as life remains. He will not bend to the storm, but stands erect, and bids it defiance. I wish I could give him comfort, by advising him where to seek for it, where alone it is to be found ; but his heart is hardened, and he will not believe.

To-day, I received a letter from the Princess of Wales :—

Extract

Of my health I have no right to complain, but the state of suspense and the ray of hope I had for some days past have kept my mind in a constant state of perturbation; but this happy vision has vanished, and the monster is fast recovering again. Princess Charlotte I have now not seen for six weeks past. The only great news I can offer you, is Lady Charlotte Rawdon's extraordinary marriage with a lieutenant on half-pay, of the name of Fitzgerald; and the death of Sir John Douglas, which took place on the 5th of March, when exactly twelve months ago the division took place in Parliament upon his conduct. His burial was one of the most pompous ever seen, as if he had been the commander-in-chief himself, to the disgust and contempt of every body who saw that show passing; he has been buried at Charlton, to the great annoyance of the Perceval family: and so much about nothing.

I remain, for ever,

Your affectionate friend,

C. P.

I arrived at Worthing Tuesday evening. The weather was beautiful, but my mind was the reverse of serene; recollections of the past, and fears for the future, got the better of me. I dislike this place as a locale, yet it was by my own choice, I came to it. How unreasonable! Often when we say a thing is our own choice, it is the force of circumstances which drives us to the action; the will, in fact, is only in our minds; it frequently fails in the fulfilment, or is pleasing only on one side of the question, while it is abhorrent on the other. I tutored myself, however, to bear with better grace what I had determined to undergo; and, in the very endeavour to conquer ourselves, we lose some part of that irritable humour which mars our own comfort, as well as that of others.

I slept soundly the night of my arrival, and the next day the sun shone gaily, the sea looked grandly bright, and poor human nature was exhilarated. The power of employing one's faculties is the best gift of Heaven: I felt this power return in some small degree, and with it the enjoyment of existence.

On Wednesday, the 8th, I read in Stafford's library the wonderful news of the allies entering into Paris. The particulars of this extraordinary epoch in the world's history will be written every where by every pen ; but the effect it produces on the minds of individuals will be varied as the varied passions, habits, and tempers of those individuals.   On mine, it impresses the awful power of an overruling Providence, who in his own time brings to bear, by apparently very simple means, the most unexpected and incomprehensible events.   In about six months' time, the whole affairs of Europe have been changed : the storms of revolution are drawing near a close, and they have borne away, in their devastating course, many of the errors and crimes of former times, it is to be hoped ; and we may with humility conclude, this moral tempest has been designed to purify and to ameliorate mankind.   All is not yet completed ; but the hand of Heaven is peculiarly visible in this great event. The Disposer of all things will bring them to the best issue in his own good time.

Sunday, April 10*th,* 1814.—The incidents which take place every hour are miraculous.   Bonaparte is deposed, but alive ;—subdued, but allowed to choose his place of residence.   The island of Elba is the spot he has selected for his ignominious retreat.   France is holding forth repentant arms to her banished sovereign.   The Poissardes who dragged Louis the Sixteenth to the scaffold are presenting flowers to the Emperor of Russia, the restorer of their legitimate king ! What a stupendous field for philosophy to expatiate in !   What an endless material for thought ! What humiliation to the pride of mere human greatness ! How are the mighty fallen ! Of all that was great in Napoleon, what remains ? Despoiled of his usurped power, he sinks to insignificance.   There was no moral greatness in the man.   The meteor dazzled, scorched, is put out,—utterly, and for ever. But the power which rests in those who have delivered the nations from bondage, is a power that is delegated to them from Heaven ; and the manner in which they have used it is a guarantee for its continuance. The Duke of Wellington has gained laurels unstained by any useless flow of blood. He has done more than conquer others—he has conquered himself ; and in the midst of the blaze and flush of victory, surrounded by the homage of nations, he has not been betrayed into the commission of any act of cruelty, or wanton offence. He was as cool and self-possessed under the blaze and dazzle of fame, as a common man would be under the shade of his garden-tree, or by the hearth of his home. But the tyrant who kept Europe in awe, is now a pitiable object for scorn to point the finger of derision at ; and humanity shudders as it remembers the scourge with which this man's ambition was permitted to devastate every home tie, and every heartfelt joy.

I cannot recover from my astonishment, at the miraculous winding up of this complicated piece of mechanism. Still the downfall of the colossal mischief who stalked this earth in dreadful wrath, is appalling. There is a feeling of regret, unaccountable perhaps, but not unnatural, that Napoleon did not finish his career in some way more analogous to his course. He ought to have died in a manner more consonant, as it were, with himself.

How strikingly do these late events teach us, that what is merely dependent on the tricks of fortune, and the tide of popular feeling, is ephemeral and valueless ! The same mob—the same people—now call aloud for one of that race, whom twenty years ago they led to the scaffold.

Saturday, May 21, 1814.—Nearly seven weeks have elapsed since I came to this place. The intoxication of the mind which naturally takes place after any great

event, subsides of course, and there succeeds a sort of
deadness which is the consequence of excitement.   Then
comes the sober appreciation of the intrinsic value of
events.   The restoration of the Capets to the throne of
their ancestors is connected with every sentiment of moral
justice ; and the downfall of that wonderful man, Bonaparte, is also agreeable to every principle of liberty and
humanity.   But, that immediate tranquillity will ensue
appears to me unlikely. ; How can the old nobility see
all their honours tarnished, by the admission of the new,
to share with them the rights and privileges of their
order ?   How can they behold their fortunes and estates
for ever alienated from themselves and their families,
and not feel that indignation which they would be more
or less than human not to feel ?   Must not this produce
perpetual discord ?   The king, too—can he place confidence in the men who so lately served Bonaparte, and
assisted him to mount that throne from which they afterwards expelled him ?   No, it is impossible ; and they in
their turn, from feeling that it is so, will hate the puppet
of their own creation, and retain him in leading-strings,
or again hurl him from his exaltation.   To forgive and
forget every thing, are the fine foolish words put into
Louis the Eighteenth's mouth ; but who *can forget* the
murder of a brother, the dethronement of a king, the
subversion of empires, and the shedding of the blood of
millions ?   For all these crimes Bonaparte is pensioned ;
his son is presented with the duchies of Parma, Placentia,
and Guastalla ; his brother is made King of Naples ;
and he himself a kind of sovereign in an island which may
become a maritime power :—and all this is done by the
senate who are to support the throne of Louis.   'Tis an
attempt at amalgamating the most discordant elements.
There will yet be, I fear, more tumults and wars.   I
thought with great interest of the poor royal fugitives at
Hartwell, when they first heard the confirmation of their

hopes. Perhaps, that first moment was the happiest they will ever enjoy; for surely their return to their native country must have been replete with mournful, horrible recollections. Besides, the cares and miseries which are ever attendant on exalted stations, theirs must be peculiarly exposed to dangers and difficulties.

The Emperor of Austria, King of Prussia, and Emperor of Russia, are expected in this country. Great preparations are making for them. It is now said the first does not intend to come:—I think, he cannot like to show his *Janus* face. The Emperor of Russia is my hero, and everybody's hero. I once saw his picture:—if he is in reality as handsome as that represented him to be, his personal aspect corresponds with his late calm and magnificent conduct.

It is shameful how our Regent is kicking the dust in the Princess of Wales's face. There are moments when her wrongs make all her errors forgotten. There is that little vile Prince of Wirtemberg,* *her own nephew*, who has never been to see her. White's club is to give a great ball and fête; and they have given tickets to the Regent, that he may invite the *royal family*, and this on purpose to avoid asking the Princess. Was there ever anything so shameful?

The Duchess of Oldenburgh † is spoken of as a very clever woman; and I am inclined to believe the truth of the report, by the observations she seems to take, not only of our places of entertainment, but of every thing best worth seeing in this country. I understand she is a great favourite of Princess Charlotte, and gives her (as it is supposed) excellent advice about her conduct. I, however, know what a ticklish thing it is to advise princes, or princesses; and, besides, from my own observation in

* Her sister's son.
† Catherine (1788–1819), sister of Alexander I., Emperor of Russia, married, first, Prince George of Oldenbourg; secondly, 1816, William King of Wurtemberg, nephew of the Princess of Wales.

general on human nature, I am more inclined to believe in Princess Charlotte's acting according to her own wishes and impulses, than according to the advice of any one. When these tally, then it is called following advice; and the foolish advisers fancy 'tis they who do it all; just as the Prince Regent believes that he has reinstated Louis the Eighteenth, and that Europe is at his command, because one or two of its potentates come to look at England.

The Prince of Orange, it is said, wishes his wife to go with him to his own Dutch land; and so does the Prince Regent, who does not like a rising sun in his own. But report also whispers that the *rising sun* is aware of this, and will not consent to the marriage, unless she is allowed to shine in her own dominions. I believe there is more of the *woman* in her than of the queen, and that she wants to get a look at another prince or two before she makes her choice of a husband. Perhaps, also, she has still a third point in view, and that is, to play *off and on*, marry no one, and love whom she may fancy, noble or common. We may live to see strange things yet, if I am not mistaken.

I heard to-day from Miss B[——], that the Princess of Wales had been very well received, and much applauded, at the annual meeting of the National Education School; and Mr. Whitbread made her a very proper compliment in his speech. The Princess sat by the Dukes of Sussex and Kent, the first chairmen of the meetings. Miss B[——] says, the Grand Duchess is charming in her manner, and has an intelligence in her conversation quite new in the *princess* line. She dined at Devonshire House last Thursday, where she held an *awful circle* after dinner :—all the gentlemen, I hear, looked beautiful in their dress clothes.

This evening I received this note from the Princess of Wales :—

I have not seen Princess Charlotte for nearly five months. She is outrageous at the thoughts of leaving this country; and her unnatural father assured her that she should never have an establishment in this country. I expect Mr. Whitbread every moment, about this interesting subject. It will make a great rumpus in the houses, both of Lords and Commons, which I trust will accelerate his departure to the skies.—Believe me for ever, dead or alive, your most sincere

C. P.

Received a letter from Lady [——], telling me that the Princess talks of coming to Worthing. I am very sorry to hear this; for, though I do not dislike her Royal Highness's society, on the contrary, no one can be more agreeable or amusing than she sometimes is,—still, I should greatly have preferred being here alone for a short time; and, when the Princess comes, I cannot count on an hour of uninterrupted quiet. It is droll her Royal Highness should have said nothing of her intention of coming here, in her note to me. I suppose she wishes to surprise me by her Royal presence. I hope still, however, she may give up this plan, knowing as I do how many such she amuses herself by making one day, and changing another. I dread hearing the same complaints repeated over and over again; and, as I cannot be of any use to her Royal Highness, I should rather not be thrown again into her society as much as I was during the last year and this winter.

Lady [——] sent me the following letter from Mr. Gell, addressed to her, to read, thinking it would amuse me, which it has very much.

MY DEAR LADY AURORA,—At length, a letter is arrived from Keppel Craven, announcing the safe receipt of a letter from me, with an enclosure which I presume to be the secret communication of your excellency. Letters were certainly stopped somewhere, and I suppose read by Lord Castlereagh and Co., till within a few days; so, if yours contained treason, you had better take leave before he returns to England. Mrs. Thompson * has quite recovered her spirits, laughs, and is merry. I dined there yesterday with Professor Playfair, surnamed Des Dames, (like one of the guides whom you will shortly know at Chamouni,) Sir Sydney Smith, Frederick Douglas, and Keith Stuart, all of whom were very merry; not to mention Miss Berry; and the dinner went off with unbounded applause, excepting that we sat at it till past eleven. They afterwards went a junketing to Lady Hardwicke's, where I again beheld Play-fair des dames, seated between Lady Catherine this, and the Countess of that, on a sofa, to the great scandal of the discipline of the university of Edinburgh. Sydney Smith, having been long condemned to piety, and matters of fact, in Yorkshire, is now broke out quite varyingly merry in London. Ward is in Paris, looking wretched, unhappy, and angry. This we hear from all quarters. The Staël is safely lodged there, and is to give parties immediately to all the great characters,—the Emperor of Russia, L'Infini, the King of Prussia, L'Impossible, and, in short, the heroes of all ages and principles; with the intention of extracting from the mass the real quintessence and vital principle of virtue, in a hydrogen state, which she means to have ready in bottles for exportation. N.B. None are genuine but those sealed with her own arms, viz, gules, two arms a kimbo, surmounted by a Saracen's head, sable, crowned with a French pyx; crest, a cock and bull; badge, a cat and bladders. These have all been conferred by Louis XVIII. during his last visit to London.

By the bye, I saw, or rather witnessed, last night, that Mrs. Mansell, who certainly will knock out the Staël's teeth some day or other, and then she will make a pretty woman.

There is your Prince Paul of Wirtemberg,† a squinting bird, dancing and scolding the ladies, and already out of favour; nephew to Mrs. Thompson, but has not been to her. Alexander says *he will* see her. Lord Beresford is come home, and was at the Hardwickes', so I introduced the Lord B [——] to

* Mrs. Thompson. This was a name used to designate the Princess of Wales, by some persons corresponding with one another at that time. Mr. Thompson, of course, meant the Prince Regent.

† (1785-1852.) Nephew of the Princess of Wales. The Emperor Alexander did not visit the Princess ("Mrs. Thompson") on account of the opposition of the Prince Regent.

flirt with him. I kiss Mrs. D [——]'s hands, and your eyes, and if you cannot read this, it is because it is written on my knee at breakfast. Is Mrs. D [——] very angry at me for being knighted ? " Rise up Queen of Sheba." Adieu, Adieu.

Most sincerely and affectionately yours,

ANACHARSIS.

Monday, May 31*st,* 1814.—After many different changes, the Princess came here on the 26th. It was twelve at night before she arrived. The inhabitants of this town had been waiting to drag her carriage, and they had illuminated, &c., according to their abilities, to welcome her Royal Highness to Worthing ; but, at last, the lights had gone out, and the people gone to sleep, and I was not well, and fain would have been asleep, also, but I did not like to seem inattentive, and not to be there to offer my services to the Princess ;—and when at last my patience was exhausted, and I was going to bed— she arrived, all graciousness, and looking very well. The first thing she did, after a kind greeting, was to give me a detail of the late event of the Queen's having written to her, by desire of the Regent, to forbid her going to court. She then related what had been her answer, namely, *a determination* to go ; but Whitbread, without even reading her letter, insisted upon it, she was not to go ; and, in the most peremptory manner, almost ordered the Princess to copy a letter *he* had written to the Queen, which was a submissive acquiescence *respecting the two drawing-rooms* immediately in question. No sooner had the poor Princess agreed, than Mr. Brougham arrived, and told Mr. Whitbread he had completely misunderstood him, for that it was his decided opinion, that her Royal Highness should not have given up her right, but should go to court in spite of the Regent and his whiskers. Mr. Whitbread was thrown into a state of great agitation at finding he had, by his obstinacy, led the Princess into error ; and now the two wise men laid their heads together, to know what could be done to set matters to-rights, and remedy their own blunders. They thought the Princess should write a letter to the Prince in another tone, setting forth rights, and threatening complaints, which letter they had been the whole of Thursday brewing in the Princess's room.

I fear they will only make bad worse. The whole account of this transaction is to appear in to-day's papers. The poor Princess was (as usual in the midst of any bustle) vastly happy, and full of hope at the mighty things that were to accrue to her from all these court contrivances. This subject afforded matter for conversation till past two in the morning. The next day, the Princess was up and flying about at an early hour; she sent for me immediately after breakfast, and walked all over the town, and up and down the beach, until I thought I should have died of the fatigue of following her Royal Highness; and the most of the time she took my arm, and leant heavily on it. Lady [——] was not well, so I was kept in attendance the whole day.

At three o'clock, she went out for an airing; she drove by Goring and Sumpting; and, being easily pleased when in good humour, talked the whole time of the "*great event*," as she called it. Her Royal Highness descanted upon her intention of going abroad as soon as possible, saying, she thought she was more likely to be able to escape now than she had ever been; for that she hoped, and had reason to believe, the Emperor of Russia would be friendly towards her :—that she meant to ask his Imperial Majesty to bear her request to the Prince that she might leave this country. " I will tell you, my dear [——], what I expect he is to answer—that we are parted from incompatibilité d'humeur—that I am to have fifty thousand a year, and may go and come as I choose."

Poor wrong-headed Princess! I said " Yes Yes,"

to everything of course, and bowed acquiescence. But how little can I believe that the Regent will give such a reply—still less that the Emperor will interfere in this business ? The Prince hates his wife with inveterate malice ; and, if she goes out of the kingdom, it will be only on one condition, that she shall never return. And, if she does go out of the kingdom, she will inevitably be ruined. In her peculiar circumstances, as well as station, she should never withdraw herself from the public eye ; though, as it has been from the beginning of time, all potentates and public characters are desirous of sometimes laying aside their robes of state, and tasting freedom like other men, they have seldom or ever done so without losing their own station, and have not obtained that enjoyment which they sought. The sentinel must not leave his post. In the Princess's particular situation, she is more imperiously called upon than any other Princess ever was, not to absent herself from England. The English, even in these days, are unreasonably prejudiced against foreigners ; and the idea that she has resided amongst them for any length of time, will be sufficient to raise a feeling of distrust against her Royal Highness ; more especially among the lower and middling classes.

Besides, absence is such a fearful test of human attachment, that it is very dangerous to venture it. It is human nature to love those most whom we dwell most with, and who contribute most to our welfare and amusement. The person, whether a private individual or a public character, who voluntarily forsakes those over whom he ought to preside, has no right to expect the continuation of their love, or loyalty.

Had the Princess the ideas of a private individual— had she a taste for literature, or even for female employments—I could understand her wish to leave this country, and lead a private life. I should think her in that case a wise woman, and likely to be a far happier one than she could be under the most favourable circumstances of her present station. But, constituted as her mind is, she has only one course to pursue—that is, to remain in England, and to endeavour to maintain the eminence from which her enemies wish to hurl her.

The Princess told me, that she thinks the Duchess of Oldenburgh is her friend, and that she has sent her some kind messages through Princess Charlotte. The latter told her mother, the last time they met, that she was determined not to marry the Prince of Orange ;—that his being approved of by the royal family was quite sufficient to make him disapproved of by her ; for that she would marry a man who would be at *her* devotion, not at theirs.—" Marry I will," said she to the Princess of Wales, " and that directly, in order to enjoy my liberty ; but not the Prince of Orange. I think him so ugly, that I am sometimes obliged to turn my head away in disgust when he is speaking to me."

" But, my dear," replied her mother, (at least so her Royal Highness told me,) " whoever you marry will become a King, and you will give him a power over you."

" A King ! Pho, pho ! *Never !* He will only be *my first subject—never my king !* "

The Princess of Wales is delighted with this hopeful spirit, and believes in its continuance. So do I, as to the *will* of the person ; but, as to the possibility or power of the executing that will, I foresee a thousand obstacles. Besides, Princess Charlotte's inclination will vary with every wind that blows ; and I should not be surprised to hear that her marriage with the Prince of Orange was to take place to-morrow.—There is no believing one word these royal people say ; and I verily believe they do not know what they believe themselves.

The Duchess of Oldenburgh was offended, the Princess

of Wales says, at her not having sent her Chamberlain to welcome her to England, which all the other royalties had done—at least so she says *now*,—and that she (the Duchess) only awaits her brother the Emperor of Russia's arrival, in order to pay her respects at Connaught House. I much doubt this will end in smoke ; but a short time will show.

It is publicly known the Regent sent over Sir Thomas Tyrwhitt with a private message to the Emperor of Russia, desiring him to take no notice of the Princess on his arrival in England. Whether or not the Emperor is weak enough, or politic enough, to choose to submit to this dictatorial order, will soon be known.

The Princess drove about till eight o'clock, then returned to a dinner *soupative*, and sat at it till twelve o'clock. I cannot understand what royalties are made of,—they are so strong, and able to bear so much fatigue.

The next day I was again sent for to walk with her Royal Highness and Miss L[——], Lady [——] being still ill. The Princess was in much lower spirits than the preceding evening. I attributed it to her not seeing any thing in her own favour in the newspaper, but, rather, on the contrary, against her. Miss [——] told me, that Chanticleer is either gone, or going immediately, to France. I am very glad to hear it, as it will put an end to the evil rumours about the Princess, which his constant presence at Connaught House excited.

Thursday, 9th of June, 1814.—I saw Lady E[——]. Poor soul ! the operation she has lately undergone proves what strength of mind and moral courage she is endowed with. All she cares about is, that it should not be known that she has undergone this trial ! She looked quite well, and did not allude to what had happened ; neither did I, for I know she hates the subject.

As I walked through the streets, they were crowded with people waiting to hear the proclamation of peace, which was not, however, proclaimed. I dined at my aunt's. B[——] C[——] told us he had been at Carlton House the night before, where he saw all the potentates and generals, &c., now assembled in this capital. I was very glad he had been invited, for nobody likes to be left out and forgotten by those who used to receive them well, and I feared his having lived in intimacy with the Princess of Wales might have occasioned his disgrace at the other court.

I hear that all ranks, except merely those who bask in the sunshine of the Regent's favour, have expressed themselves warmly for the Princess ; and that the Prince cannot move out without hisses and groans. I am glad to think his bitterness and tyranny are mortified ; but what good will it do her ? None, I fear. The most that can happen, is her having her establishment put on a more liberal footing by the nation,—and then the Princess will go abroad, run into all sorts of foolish scrapes, and be forgotten at best :—worse will it be for her if things are there proved, which may be brought back to this country, and her whole money, hopes, and happiness, taken from her for ever. I tremble for her, poor woman, but see no daylight.

When I went to Connaught House yesterday, by appointment, I found the Princess dressed in a style as if she expected some visitors. She said, that if she did not look forward to going abroad, she should die of despair ; and, though I think her mistaken in the idea that she will be happier in a foreign country than here, and that she is wrong to indulge in perpetual murmuring, still, whenever she is in her gentle melancholy, and touches upon her crying wrongs, (for crying they certainly are,) I am really moved with indignation against the persecution offered to a princess and a woman. She read me a letter she was writing when I arrived : it was a letter to Lord Liverpool, demanding leave to quit this country, and retire whither she would ; saying, that she did not wish, nor ever had wished, to render the Prince unpopular, and that she begged permission to go abroad. The matter was spirited, dignified, and clever, but was not clothed in English language, nor free from obscurity.

I was much annoyed at her Royal Highness desiring me " to *do* this letter into English." I did not like to refuse her request, but it has much distressed me, for I shall have the credit of having composed the whole of the letter. The Princess, after some time spent in general conversation, confessed to me that she had dressed herself in a half-dress, expecting the Emperor of Russia and the King of Prussia to call on her. But the moment I told her I heard those personages had refused to go to White's, or to any public place, she said, " Then the Prince has conquered, and they will not come to see me." I saw she was very much vexed ; but she bore it with a command of temper which would have done any one honour. It seems she sent her Chamberlain to welcome them to England. The King of Prussia sent his Chamberlain to thank the Princess in return, but the Emperor has sent no one, nor taken the least notice of her, except by receiving Mr. St. Leger graciously.

It will be a shame if the King of Prussia does not visit her once at least, considering what obligations he was under to her father, who died in battle, fighting in his cause :—but perhaps *he has forgotten* this circumstance.

All goes gloomily with the poor Princess. Lady Charlotte Campbell told me, she regrets not seeing all these curious personages ; but, she said, the more the Princess is forsaken, the more happy she is at having offered to attend her at this time. This is very amiable in her, and must be gratifying to the Princess.

Thursday, 9th of June.—I dined at Connaught House. There were Sir W. Gell, Mr. Hobhouse, Mr. Bennet, and Mr. Fox there. The first was low-spirited and ill, yet amusing and kind, as he invariably is ; the other men are violently for the Princess, but I fear 'tis their politics, more than their personal attachment to her, which makes them so. I never saw Sir W. Gell so violent as he was against the present system of bowing in all things to the Regent. He said that the rights of the constitution were infringed, and that posting guards at all corners of the streets was a species of tyranny that amounted almost to a military government ; that it was the civil authorities alone that had any right to keep order, if such were necessary, in the town ; but that the next step which might now take place, was that I might see two sentinels placed at my door, and find that I neither could go in or out of my own house, if such were *his pleasure,* (meaning the Regent's,) yet no one be a bit the wiser. " Seriously," he said, " it is coming fast to this ; and I only hope some disturbance may take place to put an end to this nonsense. If other men's minds are strung to the same tone, or at all like it, I should think there would be riots."

The Princess received an anonymous letter yesterday which she put in the fire ;—the fate all such communications deserve to meet with ; for the writer of an anonymous letter would be almost capable of murder. This letter was to say, that the Prince would be killed shortly, he was such a tyrant. I do not suppose the information shocked her very much.

Princess Charlotte paid her mother a visit last Saturday, and told her that every thing was fixed for her marriage ; that she did not love the Prince of Orange, but that she must be married. So there ends all the nonsense her Royal Highness talked and wrote when she saw her mother last. It only shows what faith is to be placed in her words :—and, indeed, there is no coming at truth where not truth is.

Friday, 10th of June.—I heard Mr. Whitbread called on the Princess this morning; and Lady [——] said, she thinks he is really interested in the Princess, and feels compassion for her cruel situation, *besides* being urged by his political career to make a tool of her for his own ends. He said to Lady [——], he thought the Princess would get an establishment, and liberty granted her, but nothing more. He knows her intention of going abroad, and blames it as a very injudicious plan : but he is quite aware no one can hinder her Royal Highness from following her own inclinations ; so he has not told her how unwise he thinks her to leave England, and he, as well as all her other friends, can only hope she may be *prevented* by circumstances from taking this step ; or, still more, that the *wish* to go away may cease to exist. Mr. Whitbread has very pleasing manners in private : they are gentle, almost to effeminacy.

I dined again at Connaught House : Miss Berry, and Mr. and Miss R[——] were there : the two latter looked very *capottés*. I know they dislike the dulness which now prevails at the Princess's dinner-parties. The Princess had imagined that she could associate B[essy] R[awdon] to her fortunes, and was quite in astonishment when she found that that was out of the question. What an idea, to separate a mother and daughter !—and to suppose that a very young and beautiful girl would sacrifice her best days to the service of an *unhappy* Princess. How unlikely to find one, with similar advantages of mind and person to those which B[essy] R[awdon] posseses, willing to give them all up, to serve a person who had no claim on her ! How little does the poor Princess know human character, if she thinks to find such disinterestedness ;—nothing for nothing, in this world, is a sad truth.

Her Royal Highness has taken a dislike to Mrs. R[awdon], because she will not permit her daughter to be often alone with the Princess. Chanticleer the younger *is* gone to Paris, but the old S[apio]s are still in London, and still invited *occasionally;* but she is disgusted with their rapaciousness. This is most fortunate for her sake. She has not heard a word from kings, or emperors ;— they went to-day to Ascot Races, and are to sleep at Windsor.

Saturday, 11*th.*—I was sent for by the Princess this morning, to say that she was going to the Opera to-night, and wished me to attend her. Lady C[harlotte] L[indsay] had just left when I arrived, and the Princess complained that "her friends tormented her as much as her enemies." I found out afterwards, that this remark was occasioned by one of her friends having advised her Royal Highness not to take *Willikin* to the Opera with her.

The two Doctors Burney dined with the Princess ; Lady [——], Miss [——], and myself were of the party. There came a note from Mr. Whitbread, advising at *what* hour she should go to the Opera, and telling her that the Emperor was to be at eleven o'clock at the Institution, which was to be lighted up for him to see the pictures. All this advice tormented the Princess, and I do not wonder that she sometimes loses patience. No child was ever more thwarted and controlled than she is—and yet she often contrives to do herself mischief, in spite of all the care that is taken of her. When we arrived at the Opera, to the Princess's, and all her attendants' infinite surprise, we saw the Regent placed between the Emperor and the King of Prussia, and all the minor Princes, in a box to the right. "God save the King" was performing when the Princess entered, and consequently she did not sit down. I was behind, so of course I could not see the house very distinctly, but

I   o

I saw the Regent was at that time standing and applauding the Grassinis.—As soon as the air was over, the whole pit turned round to the Princess's box, and applauded *her*.—We, who were in attendance on her Royal Highness, intreated her to rise and make a curtsey, but she sat *immoveable*, and, at last, turning round, she said to Lady [——], " My dear, Punch's wife is nobody when Punch is present." We all laughed, but still thought her wrong not to acknowledge the compliment paid her ; but she was right, as the sequel will prove.—" We shall be hissed," said Sir W. Gell.—" No, no," again replied the Princess with infinite good humour, " I know my business better than to take the *morsel out of my husband's mouth ;* I am not to seem to know that the applause is meant for me, till they call my name." The Prince seemed to verify her words, for he got up and bowed to the audience. This was construed into a bow to the Princess, most unfortunately ; I say most unfortunately, because she has been blamed for not returning it ; but I, who was an eye-witness of the circumstance, know the Princess acted just as she ought to have done. The fact was, the Prince *took the applause* to himself ; and his friends, or rather his *toadies*, (for they do not deserve the name of *friends*,) to save him from the imputation of this ridiculous vanity, chose to say, that he did the most beautiful and elegant thing in the world, and bowed to his wife ! !.

When the Opera was finished, the Prince and his supporters were applauded, but not enthusiastically ; and, scarcely had his Royal Highness left the box, when the people called for the Princess, and gave her a very warm applause. She then went forward and made three curtseys, and hastily withdrew.—I believe she acted perfectly right throughout the evening ; but every body tells a different story, and thinks differently. How trivial all this seems—how much beneath the dignity of rational beings ! But trifles make up the sum of earthly things ; and, in this instance, this trivial circumstance affects the Princess of Wales's interests, and therefore it becomes of consequence for the true statement to be made known ; and, as I was present, I can and will tell the truth.—When the coachman attempted to drive home through Charles-street, the crowd of carriages was so immense it was impossible to pass down that street, and with difficulty the Princess's carriage backed, and we returned past Carlton-house, where the mob surrounded her carriage, and, having found out that it was her Royal Highness, they applauded and huzzaed her till she, and Lady [——], and myself, who were with her, were completely stunned.—The mob opened the carriage doors, and some of them insisted upon shaking hands with her, and asked if they should burn Carlton-house. —" No, my good people," she said, " be quite quiet—let me pass, and go home to your beds."—They would not, however, leave off following her carriage for some way, and cried out, Long live the Princess of Wales ! long live the innocent ! &c. &c.—She was pleased at this demonstration of feeling in her favour, and I never saw her look so well, or behave with so much dignity. Yet I hear since, all this has been misconstrued, and various lies told.

Sunday, 12*th*.—The park (Hyde Park) was crowded with multitudes of spectators, and all the Kings, Emperors, and grandees, foreign and English, rode and drove about, while the people flocked around them, applauding and huzzaing. Princess Charlotte drove round the ring in her carriage, and looked well and handsome. What a strange and galling sight for the Princess of Wales—her who ought to be, from her rank, her relationship to some of these foreign potentates, and her station in this country, the first to be honoured by their attentions, thus to see herself so completely cast aside ! Whilst they were in

the gay throng in Hyde Park, she drove with Lady [——]
to Hampstead and Highgate. Lady [——] told me she
was very tired of that amusement.

I dined at Connaught House. The party consisted of
Mr. and Lady Charlotte Greville, Lord Henry Fitzgerald,
Mr. Bennet, and Mr. Hobhouse. After dinner a few
more persons came, and formed a dull stiff circle; but
it was good company: therefore, I was pleased to see
there the Hardwickes, Paulets, Lord and Lady Grey,
Lord and Lady Dunmore, Lord Nugent, &c., to the amount
of fifty or sixty persons. Many more *really* intended to
come, *after* having been to Lady Salisbury's, where were
the Emperor and King, and our mighty Prince Regent;
but the crowd was so immense, they could not get their
carriages till morning.

Monday, 13*th*.—The Princess sent for me this morning.
I found her looking big with some news; but she waited
till she mastered herself before she told me she had got
a letter from Lady C. L[indsa]y, telling her that she had
heard positively from Lady Westmoreland, who had the
intelligence from a quarter that left no doubt of its truth,
that the Emperor would wait upon the Princess either
that day, or on Thursday next;—that she, Lady C.
L[indsa]y, felt certain of its authenticity, and, therefore,
took the liberty of communicating the intention of his
Majesty to her Royal Highness. The latter was delighted.
She gradually gave way to the hope which charmed her,
and said—poor soul—" my ears are very ugly, but I
would give *them both* to persuade the Emperor to come
to me to a ball, a supper, any entertainment that he
would choose."

Well—she dressed, and waited till seven, but no Emperor came. She made me remain with her all the
afternoon. I did my best to amuse her; but I am not
an amusing person at *any* time—certainly not—neither,

when I feel sad and sorry, which I did for her Royal Highness, can I exert the little powers I have of being diverting. For four hours together, it was an effort to *me* to try to seem cheerful, when I was thinking the whole time of whether the Emperor would or would not come, and whether the poor soul who sat opposite to me would be disappointed or not of the promised pleasure. Neither was it possible the Princess should be amused or interested with what I or any one else could have said when she was waiting for his visit : yet, she endeavoured to converse, and to conceal her anxiety. Alas ! I fear Thursday will be just such another day of disappointment as to-day was.—How cruel to give her a hope that anything pleasant would befall her, which people are not quite sure will take place ! Yet the persons who gave her this false hope, did not do so with an unkind intention. It was her *friend* who sent her the announcement of the Emperor's intended visit.—No wonder the Princess says, " my friends torment me as much as my enemies." *She* is not the only person who has said and felt thus. I was made to stay and dine, and, in the evening, there were the old S[apio]s (?) *pour tout bien.*

Tuesday, 14th.—Lady [——] told me, that in going slowly up a hill in the course of her drives to-day, a decently dressed and respectable looking countryman came close to the Princess's carriage, and said, " God bless you ! we will make the Prince love you before we have done with him." Another of the same class of persons cried out as she passed, " You will soon overcome all your enemies."—Such voluntary declarations prove that there is a strong feeling prevailing in her favour ; still, it is not a few kind words uttered by a chance person as she passes in her carriage, that can be of real use or comfort to her, though gratifying at the moment.

Wednesday, 15th.—The Princess, Lady [——] informed me, received a note this morning from Mr. Brandon, box-office, Covent Garden, telling her that no box could be kept for her Royal Highness at that theatre, as they were all engaged. What an answer to the Princess of Wales !—Then arrived a note from Alderman Wood, informing her, that if she chose to go to see the monarchs pass in procession to the City, he would have a private house kept for her Royal Highness for that purpose.— Alderman Wood did not mean to insult her ; it was only his vulgarity that induced him to make her such a ludicrous offer.—But what was most vexatious of all these vexatious communications was, that the Duchess of Oldenburgh and four other ladies were to be *present at the dinner*. This was galling, and the Princess felt her own particular exclusion from this fête given by the city very hard to bear, as she had considered the city folks her friends. They, however, are not to blame, as these royal *ladies* are self-invited, or invited by the Regent, and the Princess's friends had not time to call a Common Council and discuss the matter.—Immediately after this bitter pill, came another from Mr. Whitbread, recommending her upon *no account* to go to Drury-lane on Thursday evening, after having a few days before desired her *to go*. " You see, my dear," she said to Lady [——], " how I am plagued " ; and, although she mastered her resentment, Lady [——] says she saw the tears were in her eyes. " It is not the loss of the amusement which I regret, but being treated like a child, and made the puppet of a party. What signify whether I come in before or after the Regent, or whether I am applauded in his hearing or not ; that is all for the gratification of *the party*, not for *my* gratification : 'tis of no consequence to the Princess, but to Mr. Whitbread :—and that's the way things always go, and always will, till I can leave this vile country."—Lady [——] was desired by her Royal

Highness to write her sentiments, with leave to alter the mode of expressing them, to Mr. Whitbread and Alderman Wood.

I dined at Connaught House the same day, and the Princess was in wonderfully good spirits considering how much she had been vexed in the morning.—Sir W. and Lady Louisa Call, Lady Elizabeth Forbes, Mr. Craven, Sir W. Gell, and Sir J[——] B[——] were the party.—I had a long conversation with the latter; he is a kind-hearted, honourable man, but I see he is too good for those with whom he has to deal; yet, he is not deficient in sound sense or penetration. It is a pity that he indulges too much in the pleasures of conviviality. He praised the Princess up to the skies, and said he believed her to be " pure as the unsunned snow."—Then he said that he himself had been of the party all the time during the story about *Manby*, and that once when he (*Manby*) was said to have been in the boat with her, it was he himself (Sir J. B[——]), " therefore," added he, " I know the falsity of that accusation." He ended by summing up all the Princess's wrongs, and declaring she was the most cruelly treated woman in the world. She had been telling Sir J[——] of the city business, the box-keeper's message, and Alderman Wood's offer of a private window from whence she could see the show pass, and her deter-mination of going to the play next Thursday.—" I think," said he to me, " unless Whitbread gives her some very strong reasons to the contrary, she is in the right to go; but I fancy he has some good reasons, and then she must yield. Gad," he added, " if I were she, and Whitbread did not please me, I would send for Castlereagh, and every one of them, till I found one that did. To tell you the truth, I am sorry the Princess ever threw herself into the hands of Whitbread; it is not the staff on which the Royalties should lean."—" Ah ! " I replied, " but at the moment he stepped forth her champion and deliverer,

who was there who would have done as much ? " Sir
J. B [——] does not believe she was at so low an ebb ;
but he does not know all the circumstances I know, and
I could not explain them. He has been lately taken up
as a great friend of the Prince Regent ; and, ever since
he carried the King of France over, he has been in high
estimation at Carlton House, and was even made the
Prince's aide-de-camp. "It is but yesterday," said he,
"·that he held both my hands in his, and called me a
d—d honest fellow." What a pity, thought I, his Royal
Highness does not imitate you a little, and try to imbibe
some of your honesty and good-heartedness.

It is droll that there is a vast sympathy between the
Prince Regent and Princess, in their *loves* as well as in
their hatreds. Sir J. B[——] is an equal favourite with
them both—as he deserves to be ; for he is not insincere
or cringing to either of them. I think he is a friend to
both ; though he sees their respective faults.

During dinner, a note had arrived from Mr. Whitbread,
saying, that a box was reserved for her Royal Highness,
but that he implored her not to think of going. To this,
she only ordered Lady [——] to reply, by desiring Mr.
Whitbread to come to her immediately ; "if he gives
me good reasons, I will submit," she said to me, but if he
does not, *d—n me, den I go*." These were her words, at
which I could not help smiling ; but she was in no mood
to smile ; so I concealed the impulse I felt to laugh ;
for I cannot bear to be of those who wound her. The
Princess kept us all to supper, and it was past one o'clock
before we were dismissed. Mr. Whitbread never came.

To amuse herself is as necessary to her Royal Highness
as meat and drink, and she made Mr. Craven and Sir
W. Gell, and myself, promise to go with her to the masqu-
rade.—She is to go out at her back door on the Uxbridge
Road, of which "no *person under Heaven*" (her curious
phraseology) has a key but her royal self, and we are to

be in readiness to escort her Royal Highness in a hackney coach to the Albany, where we are to dress ! What a mad scheme ! at such a moment, and without any strong motive either, to run the risk !—I looked grave when she proposed this amusement, but I knew I had only to obey. I thought of it all night with fear and trembling.

Thursday, 16*th.*—Mr. Whitbread sent early to-day to Lady [——], to say he was out at Lord Jersey's ball when her Royal Highness's note was sent to him last night, and that now he begged to know at what hour she chose to see him.—She desired him to be at Connaught House at twelve, and Lady [——] was sent to speak to him for a little while, till the Princess was ready to see him. Lady [——] told Mr. Whitbread how his medicine had worked, but that nevertheless she thought it would produce the desired effect. Mr. Whitbread said he was sorry to have been *obliged* to write in the peremptory manner he did to the Princess. When she came in she gave him her hand, but received him rather drily. He then informed her who some of the persons were who think it best for her Royal Highness not to go to the play : he said Mr. Tierney, Mr. Brougham, and Lord Sefton were of opinion, that however much the Princess had been applauded, the public would have said it had been done at the instigation of Mr. Whitbread, and was not the spontaneous feeling of the people ; that the more she was applauded, the more they would say so ; and that if on the contrary a strong party of the Prince Regent's friends, and paid hirelings, were there, and that one voice of disapprobation were heard, it might do her considerable harm. " Besides," continued Mr. Whitbread, " as the great question about an establishment for your Royal Highness comes on *to-morrow*, I think it is of the utmost importance that no one should be able to cast any invidious observation about *your forcing* *yourself* on the public, or seeming to defy your Royal Highness's husband."—In fine, the Princesss was *over-ruled*. Mr. Whitbread thanked her for her condescension in listening to him, and seemed really touched when he said, " I trust, madam, you will believe me sincere, when I declare that no party interest whatever sways me in this or any other advice I have ever given your Royal Highness, nor ever shall, to the detriment of your interests." The Princess, as I am told, bowed coldly in reply to this speech, and did *not* seem to believe Mr. Whitbread's sincerity.—It is not surprising that she should doubt and hesitate before placing confidence in any one ; for she has been so often cheated, poor woman ! Yet I wish she had replied with some degree of answering kindness to Mr. Whitbread's assurance that he was faithful to her interests. She flung *cold water* on him, as it were, just at the moment when he seemed roused to energy in her cause. Alas ! how very foolish she is in all that concerns her true interests.

I dined in the evening of the same day with her Royal Highness. There was no one present except Lady [——] ; the Princess went to the Opera afterwards with her. Lady C[harlotte] L[indsay] came in during dinner, having been to Drury Lane, thinking she was there. She said she took the liberty of coming to tell the Princess that Princess Charlotte had sent for her (Lady C[harlotte] L[indsay]) that morning and had informed her that the Emperor of Russia had sent to tell the Regent that he was determined to visit the Princess of Wales, and to make his sister accompany him ; that he would do so publicly, to show his respect to her Royal Highness : and that, since the Emperor had sent that message, the Prince Regent had not spoken to his Imperial Majesty. "Depend upon it, he goes to my mother," said the Princess Charlotte to Lady C[harlotte] L[indsay], " and I sent for you to inform the Princess not to be from home." Lady C[harlotte] L[indsay] added that,

" Princess Charlotte led a very dull life, and was extremely out of spirits, and considerably hurt at the Prince of Orange's going out and diverting himself at all public places, while she remained shut up in {solitude}; and that she thought he might have refused going to Carlton House unless she was there."

The Princess of Wales had been told to-day that the match was off between her daughter and the Prince of Orange; but Lady C[harlotte] L[indsay] said, "No, madam, I do not believe so at present, but I think very likely it will be soon at an end." Princess Charlotte told Lady C[harlotte] L[indsay] that when she drives about, the mob cry out, "God bless you, but never forsake your mother." The poor Princess's eyes filled with tears when Lady C[harlotte] L[indsay] repeated this. She has excellent and strong natural feelings when they are stirred; but in general all her bad feelings are roused, and her good ones smothered, by the unkindness and persecution she meets with. There is no knowing what a different person this poor Princess might be, had she the fair play of other human beings. The Princess wished Lady C[harlotte] L[indsay], the herald of this pleasant news, to accompany her to the Opera; but her sister was ill, so she declined going. The intelligence she brought reanimated the Princess. Perhaps, it is all a falsehood from beginning to end—not of Lady C[harlotte] [Lindsay]'s invention, or of Princess Charlotte's; she herself may be deceived, or she may deceive for the pleasure of being agreeable at the moment. What a total subversion of comfort there is, when there is no truth to rest upon! The music at the Opera was divine—the house empty, of course.

Friday, 17th June.—Lady [——] told me, the Princess had shown her a letter she had been writing to Mr. Whitbread, which she intended to send, with one she has written to Lord Liverpool ; which latter she intends to send without asking Mr. Whitbread's advice. The one she addresses to himself accounts very plausibly for so doing, under the pretext of its being from motives of delicacy towards him. She says in it, that persecuted as she is, life is a burthen to her ; that her stay in this country does no person any good, and that it is worse than death to herself. She thanks Mr. Whitbread for all he has attempted to do for her, and ends by declaring her unalterable resolution to quit the country. The letter, of course, is not good English, and its mode of expression is very strange and *entortillé*. Nevertheless, there is much of that fire and determination in it, which are *great* ingredients in any character, and which she possesses. Unfortunately these qualities are not prized, or done justice to in women—they are called obstinacy and violence, except in some instances—such as in our Queen Elizabeth, the Catherine of Russia, and a few others, where power made men of them. Otherwise, as it is the interest of the stronger sex to subdue women, mentally and personally—at least, they imagine that it is so—all display of vigorous intellect in them is charged with folly, if not with crime.

Again I dined at Connaught House. There were Lord Fitzwilliam, Lord and Lady Essex, Lord Hardwicke, Mr. and Miss Grattan. Lord H. Fitzgerald and Lord de Roos were to have been of the party, but there was some mistake about their invitation, and they did not come. Lord Fitzwilliam has delightful manners—so gentle and so polite—they remind me of my dear [——]. There is a divine expression in his countenance. He is shy and rather reserved on first acquaintance, but he is not so to such a degree as to make him disagreeable. I believe Lord Hardwicke is a very good sort of man, but he is not so pleasant a person, to me, as Lord Fitzwilliam. I was sorry the Princess did not behave very

graciously to the Essexes : she is always committing
some fatal mistakes respecting whom she ought to show
favour to, and to whom she ought not ;—but she said
when they were gone, " I cannot like people who take
me up only because they are displeased with the Regent."
In this observation, there is much truth ; but, as the
Princess can play a part sometimes when she chooses,
I regret that she does not do so in regard to paying
attention to persons whom it is of consequence she
should interest in her favour.

Before the Princess dismissed Lady [——], Miss [——],
or myself, she received a letter from Princess Charlotte,
telling her mother the match between herself and the
Prince of Orange was entirely off, and at the same time
enclosing a copy of a letter she had written to the Prince
of Orange, in which she alludes to some point of dispute
which it seems remained unsettled between them ; but
Princess Charlotte does not precisely name what that
point was, and chiefly rests her determination of not
leaving this kingdom upon the necessity of her remaining
in England to support her mother. The whole letter
turns upon the Princess of Wales—it is extremely well
written and very strong. I conclude the words are Miss
Knight's, but the sentiments, for the *present* moment,
are Princess Charlotte's. This letter gave the Princess
of Wales a great feeling of affection for her daughter,
and triumph at her declaring herself determined to
remain and support her against the Prince Regent.
But then, on reflection, came the recollection that it
was calculated to be a great barrier to her going abroad ;
and, instead of this intelligence being pleasant to her,
it made the Princess so full of care and thought, that she
soon dismissed us. I know too much of all parties, to
believe that Princess Charlotte, in her heart, quarrelled
with her lover from any motive of real tenderness towards
her mother. I believe that what the Princess of Wales

told me some time ago is perfectly true, namely, that
her daughter did not at all admire the Prince of Orange,
and only wanted to be her own mistress ; and now
finding, I conclude, that end would not be answered by
marrying him, she has determined to break off the
engagement. I wonder what will ensue of her doing so.
The *Princess of Wales* will not give up the amusement
of going abroad ; and, in order to do this, I fear, she will
act foolishly, offend her daughter, and lose the advantage
of her support.

SECTION IV

JUNE, *Saturday 18th*, 1814.—I got a glimpse of my [——] once more before his departure. He looks ill and dejected. The petty torments of the moment, with the hurry and bustle of departure, overcome softer regrets, and when under the influence of the former, one is obliged to put off all tender feelings to a more convenient opportunity. This habit of drowning feeling, when too often repeated, ends by hardening the heart; and those who are constantly engaged in the bustle or business or pleasures of life, should beware of this hardening influence, lest all that is noble in character should gradually be dried up, and the sources of affection and humanity totally fail.

I again dined at Connaught House. There were present Sir William Gell, Dr. Parr, Mr. Charles Burney, and Mrs. and Miss R[awdo]n. The two latter did not come in till dinner was half over. The Princess (who has conceived a hatred to Mrs. R[awdo]n because she would not consent to have her only child taken away from her) was of course very much enraged at this circumstance. At length Mrs. R[awdon] made Her Royal Highness aware that they had been detained by the Princess Charlotte, who sent for them to Warwick House. After dinner, Mrs. R[awdon] told the Princess that her daughter had received an answer from the Prince of Orange, which the Princess Charlotte deems very impertinent. In it, he states that he could not write to the Prince Regent, and that he only hoped she might never repent her

223

determination. Upon which the Princess Charlotte wrote herself to her father, and to that letter she has received no answer. The Princess Charlotte desired Mrs. R[awdon] to communicate this to her mother. This softened the Princess's wrath, but not against Mrs. R[awdo]n. B. R[awdo]n was of course very happy, and very elated at dancing with the Emperor. That was natural. She thinks him charming ; which is natural also, whatever he may be in reality. Everybody was going to Devonshire House.—The Princess should be grateful to Lady C. Campbell for having taken an extra turn in waiting on Her Royal Highness at this particular time, as it puts her out of everything that is grand and gay.*

'. The Princess went to the Opera. She was warmly applauded, but there were one or two hisses. However, the plaudits conquered, the actors sang, " God save the King," and all the house was forced to stand up. The Princess went away before the Opera was quite finished ; which was wise ; and her Royal Highness set down Dr. Parr in Woodstock Street, and me at my own home. When we came to the end of Bond Street we passed a state carriage. At first we believed it to be the Regent's ; but afterwards we heard it was the Emperor's. I still believe it was the Regent's, as it was surrounded by guards. The mob who followed thought the same, and were groaning.

Sunday, 19*th*.—I went to Kensington to hear Sidney Smith preach. I was agreeably disappointed by hearing one of the finest sermons I ever listened to in my life ; and

---

'* * In spite of this, Harriet, Lady Granville, writes, August 9, 1816 " Lady Charlotte Campbell's daughter [afterwards Lady Uxbridge] who is just come out, is decidedly, as far as one day's experience of a person can go, the girl I should prefer [her brother the Duke of Devonshire, the best *parti* in England] Hart's marrying. She is beautiful and *dans le meilleur genre*, with the sweetest manners I ever met with. She is really quite enchanting."

I own I had expected nothing but courtly device. The Princess had asked me some days before if I did not think Mr. Sidney Smith a very fine preacher. I answered that I thought he *might* be so, but that I should suppose there was a little too much of worldliness and of stage effect in his matter and manner. She was displeased when I made this answer, and in like manner angry, when I confessed myself to have been touched and edified by his sermon.

I dined at Kensington. Mr. Nugent, Mr. Luttrell, Mr. Brougham, Mr. Ward, and Lord King, were of the party. The latter is a very dull man. I never met him here or anywhere else before, that I remember, nor can I conceive why the Princess thought of inviting him. She must have some reason ; such as making him useful ; for he is neither ornamental nor agreeable. Mr. Ward had on his *bleu celeste*, both as to his coat and his temper, and was certainly very witty and entertaining ; and I was very well amused till the conversation veered round to quizzing Mr. Wilberforce. Lord King began. He said there was a good story about Mr. Wilberforce's courtship, and that he had chosen his wife by her manner of passing Easter. Of this they made many jokes, and said the learned disputed much about the precise time when Easter was. In the evening there was a party ; good company, but not much of it ; and moreover very dull.

Monday, 20th.—I rose early to go and see the great review in Hyde Park, with my friends K[——] and B[——]. We saw the show very well, and it was a fine sight ; but I could not distinguish any individual person's appearance, not even through a glass ; for it was impossible to get near enough to any of the great personages.

Lady [——] told me Mr. Whitbread had written to the Princess of Wales, to ask if he might decidedly mention

I   P

in the House of Commons that the marriage was off
between the Princess Charlotte and the Prince of Orange,
and if he might say that it was so on the Princess of Wales'
account. Lady [——], who wrote the answer, told me
she had ventured to desire Mr. Whitbread only to say
the first; for that she thought it would have been a
great breach of confidence in the Princess of Wales, to
repeat publicly what her daughter had confided to her,
as being her own *private feelings*; and that it would have
done the Princess of Wales harm, both with the public
and her daughter, if she had allowed Mr. Whitbread to
speak of the Princess Charlotte's letter to the Prince of
Orange. " Besides," said Lady [——], to me, " I know
that Her Royal Highness wrote yesterday to the Princess
Charlotte, informing her of her resolution to go abroad,
and telling her that, as things were, they could neither
of them be of the least use or comfort to the other, and
that, after all the bitter affronts she daily received, she
could not longer endure living in this country.—There is,"
said Lady [——], " much plausible cause for all she said,
but it should not have been said at this moment; and
instead of holding her daughter's power cheap at this
time, she should have magnified it tenfold. In short,
I foresee, that instead of quitting the stage with a grand
effect, and making her *recall* possible, she will quit this
country in the worst possible manner, and sink into
ignominy in a foreign land. Mr. Whitbread is still
purblind as to all this."

I conclude Princess Charlotte is desperately angry.
She has often behaved ill to her mother, it is true; and
the latter is too quick-sighted not to be perfectly aware
that she does not care three straws for her: but still, at
present, the young Princess is following a good policy,
the elder as bad a one.

I know, and cannot help honouring the feeling that
has made the Princess of Wales often say to Lady [——],

" If my daughter love me, I love her ; I cannot bear those who are neither one thing nor t'other—neither cold nor hot in affection. If she do not care for me, why should I waste love on her ? "—Alas ! we must often in this world be content with a medium degree of affection from those nearest and dearest to us. It is hard to bear lukewarmness in those who ought to turn with love towards us ; but it is the wisest way to seem satisfied, and to assume that affection exists where it does not, rather than confess to the world that our kindred or friends fail us. The Princess of Wales, above all persons, should maintain this appearance of affection between herself and her daughter ; for if there be a hope remaining to her of future comfort or support, it is in the Princess Charlotte's appearing to protect and care for her.

My friends accompanied me to Westminster Abbey, where Mr. Whitbread had promised to get them admitted to the Speaker's house, through which it was supposed the Emperor would pass, to go to the House of Commons. Lady [——] went with me to the House of Lords. The Regent did not come, nor the Emperor of Russia. There were some acts passed, but it was not so fine a show as Lady [——] expected to see.

The King of Prussia, his two sons, and his nephew, were there. His Majesty is a good likeness of Lord Clifden, with a very melancholy expression on his countenance. He has a fine shaped head, and is an elegant, but not a dignified looking person. His two sons are little boys ; his nephew a fine looking youth.

Tuesday, 22d.—I dined at Connaught House, and accompanied her Royal Highness and Miss [——] to the Opera. The famous Grassini, old to the world but new to me, disappointed me. Her voice has no richness ; her action is, however, very fine. Like all French women, she overdoes a short waist, and makes a caricature of her person, which is indeed by nature very graceful. Sir W. Gell and Mr. Craven were the only gentlemen in the Princess's box. The dislike she has to the latter, and yet the jealousy of his paying any attention to Miss [——], is quite comical.

Her Royal Highness told me that the grand Ecuyer of the King of Prussia waited upon her, to pay the parting compliments of his royal master !—a heartfelt return of gratitude to the daughter of a man who had lent him enormous sums of money, and died on the field of battle fighting his cause ! Such are courts, and princes, and human beings !

Wednesday, 23d.—I went to see a panorama of Vittoria. It gave *too faithful* a representation of a scene of battle ; and a stranger, a gentlemanlike looking person, who was there, with his arm in a sling, and had been at Vittoria the day after the battle was fought, said it was most exactly pourtrayed. The dead and the dying were lying strewn about ; and yet, even in gazing at the representation, I sympathised with the enthusiasm of the living, and the glory of the conquerors, more than with the sufferings of the fallen. How much more must the same sentiment be excited by the reality ! how fortunate, that this sympathy in catching the spirit which flames around us, is so strongly implanted in the human breast ! The view, too, of Lord Wellington and the other Generals, *coolly* gazing around, and reconnoitring the evolutions of thousands, although involved in smoke and dust and danger, gave a grand idea of the qualities necessary to a commander, and raised the scale of intellectual glory ten thousand times above that of mere personal valour. The bravery of the mass of common men is mechanical ; but the eye which penetrates, undaunted, amidst the thunder of the cannon and the clash of contending steel, to watch for the changes of the strife, and seize upon every minor advantage which may secure the palm of victory ; and the mind which can dictate unmoved whilst death is busy around, and who itself may be the next to fall ;— *that* is the truly great power which commands our homage.

Lady [——], whom I accompanied to see the painting, lamented that the palm of glory is denied to her sex. " But not," said she, " the palm of martyrdom ! sufferings of a thousand kinds await the lot of woman—her part is more truly difficult—*it is not to act but to endure.*"

Poor Lady [——], I am sorry for her ; for she is one of those unhappy beings who had looked forward to a state of felicity such as few—none, perhaps—ever enjoy in this world ; and of course she has been disappointed. She is sensible, pious—not only in feeling but on principle —she is resigned, and strives to do her duty—but it is a hard task to teach the heart to be content, when it is not so. She is young, beautiful, talented—has many friends, many relations, is universally admired — but the idol of her love first failed to be what she had imagined him, and now he is dead. Perhaps another might have succeeded to his place in her affections ; but he did not try long enough, or earnestly enough. Again she has been disappointed ; and now, as she tells me, all she seeks is peace. Happiness, she tries to believe, is not attainable on earth ; and yet, the hope that it is, and that it will one day be hers, is strong within her,— disturbing the calm of her life, yet, at the same time, giving her courage to live. What a pity she is a " *Tête montée.*"

The poor Princess receives daily affronts : it is really admirable to witness her equanimity of temper under these trials. She is not without feeling, either. She deeply feels the indignities cast upon her ; but she is always equally kind and good to those about her, and considerate to them, though she might well be absorbed by her own sorrows.

Baron Nicolai was sent by the Emperor with a letter

to the Princess of Wales, which letter says, that he regretted extremely not having been able to wait upon Her Royal Highness, but that, under the existing circumstances, delicacy only allowed him thus to express his high consideration, &c. The Princess, Lady [——] told me, received M. Nicolai with great dignity and kindness ; she was perfectly calm ; and Lady [——] says she could not have commanded herself as Her Royal Highness did. When he was gone, she made Lady [——] copy out her letter to Lord Liverpool, which, fortunately, she consented to send to Mr. Canning before she sends it to Lord Liverpool. · She is going to give it to Lord Granville L. Gower, who is to send it to Mr. Canning.

I dined at Connaught House. The party was Lord and Lady G. L. Gower, Lord and Lady Cowper, Mr. Luttrell, Mr. Nugent, and Lady C. Lindsay. There was a very good evening party also : Lord H. Fitzgerald and Lady De Ros, Mr. and Miss R[awdo]n, Lord and Lady Nugent, Lady Rancliffe and Lady A. Forbes, Mr. and Lady C. Greville, &c. Everything is turning in favour of the Princess once more, and if she will only have patience, she may leave this country honourably ; but if she does so in a hurry, she is lost.

What a dreadful punishment is that awarded to Lord Cochrane ! Death would be preferable, I should think. He denies being guilty, and a very just and sensible man said to me last night, that he doubts Lord Cochrane's guilt. What a terrible doubt for those who have pronounced him guilty !

Poor Lord Minto * is gone !—I was never to see him more in this world. He had made an amazing fortune for himself and his children ; had returned to pass his declining years among his family and friends, in the fulness of prosperity ; and now comes death, and sweeps all his plans and hopes into the grave !

* Governor-General of India : died June 21, 1814.

Thursday, 24th.—I went to [——], and remained there till the 27th. When I returned, I was invited, on the 28th, to dine at Connaught House. Lady C[——] and Sir W. Gell were with the Princess. After dinner, she ordered travelling beds ; being still determined to go abroad. She had been out in Lady C[——]'s carriage in the morning, and was vastly amused at this little escape from etiquette.

She was, however, in low spirits ; and a letter she received from Mr. Canning did not enliven her. It stated, that as she gave for a reason, in the copy of the letter she had done him the honour to send for his perusal, that she wishes her situation to be rendered more comfortable, that reason no longer existed now ; since she was sure of her establishment being increased ; and it went on finally to declare, that the letter she had written was by no means one which Her Royal Highness ought to send to Lord Liverpool. The Princess was, of course, displeased at Mr. Canning's note, but was not turned from her purpose. She said she must speak to Mr. Canning, and wrote to beg he would come to her. Whether he will or not, is the question. Her Royal Highness dismissed us early.

Wednesday, 29th.—I went to call on Lady Glenbervie —who is going to Spa. Lady C[harlotte] told me she has consented to accompany the Princess to Brunswick, where her husband, and her brother, Mr. N[orth], are to meet her. Lady C[harlotte] said that, all things considered, she thought the Princess was perfectly justified in going abroad, but that she hoped Her Royal Highness would have patience to wait till proper arrangements could be made for her departure, and a chamberlain, &c. found to accompany her.

Again I dined at Connaught House. Sir W. Gell brought a Doctor H[olland] for the Princess to judge whether she approved of his appearance, &c. as her travelling physician. Sir W. Gell guarantees his skill. Dr. H[olland] has a good countenance and pleasing manners; and he appears clever. I was left to converse with him all the evening, and think he is a superior person : so at least his conversation denotes him to be.

Thursday, 30th.—Again Sir W. Gell and I dined at Connaught House. During dinner, a letter came (brought by a *gentleman*, as Steinman the page observed) from Lord Castlereagh, saying, that through the Prince Regent, he was commissioned to propose, as an increase to Her Royal Highness's establishment, fifty thousand a year, and that the amount of her debts was to be laid before the House. She received this intelligence without any manifestation of joy or surprise, and only said—" C'est mon droit," as she handed the letter to Lady [——]. However, that this news did give her considerable pleasure I am sure. Lord Castlereagh's letter was sent to Mr. Whitbread at the House of Commons. All the Princess's plans seem now likely to be realized. It remains only for her friends to hope that, once abroad, she may conduct herself in a becoming manner.

Friday, July 1st.—To-day, I was sent for by the Princess, in consequence of a letter which she had received from Mr. Whitbread, saying that he begged to be allowed to come to her Royal Highness at two o'clock, and advise her upon the steps which were to be taken, relative to the offer of fifty thousand pounds in addition to her income. He terms the offer " insidious and unhandsome." The moment the Princess read this note, she said that Mr. Whitbread and Mr. Brougham were again going to make war, and to throw aside all overtures towards a peaceful termination of the business. She was considerably annoyed, and walked up and down the room

several times.   At last, she said, addresssing Lady [——]
and myself, " *Croyez-moi, ma chère* Lady [——] and [——],
there is only one thing to be done, and I will do it.   It
is not *in me* to suspect evil till I see it plainly, only to be
guarded against it.   If de Princess refuse, they will say—
what de devil does de woman want ? we cannot make her
husband like her, or make de Queen receive her ; but we
can set de seal upon all our public doings of last year, by
settling upon her a sufficient sum to enable her to hold the
rank of Princess of Wales—a rank of which we tink her
worthy, and wid her rank she must hold all her privileges.
I will therefore accept—I will ; and I will do it myself."
   She then wrote two excellent letters ; one to Lord
Castlereagh, the other to Mr. Whitbread.   The one to
Lord Castlereagh, she desired Lady [——] to " *make
English of,*"—no easy job ; that to Mr. Whitbread she
allowed to go, as she said, " in its natural state and
ridiculous language,"—but the sense was good.   She
told him she exonerated him from all blame as to the
issue of the event, and took the whole responsibility
upon herself.   Her answer to Lord Castlereagh was as
follows :—" The Princess of Wales acknowledges the
receipt of Lord Castlereagh's letter of yesterday evening,
and as the proposal contained in it has no conditions
annexed to it which are derogatory to her rank, her
rights, or her honour, she accepts it unquestionably, in
order to prove that the Princess is never averse to any
proposition coming from the Crown, nor wishes to throw
any obstacle in the way to obstruct the tranquillity or
impair the peace of mind of the Prince Regent."   I
write this copy down from memory, but it is exact as
to the meaning, if not as to every word.
   I think the Princess has acted rightly in this instance ;
especially as her enemies have always said that she
threw herself into Mr. Whitbread's protection entirely
to make a disturbance, and did not wish to ameliorate

her own condition, save at the expense of the Prince's honour. This letter will prove the contrary, while at the same time, should they make conditions which are degrading to her, it will enable her to assert her own rights and dignities. But it will be time enough to complain, as she says, when these degrading circumstances are attached to the benefit.

Mr. Whitbread was surprised and mortified at finding what Her Royal Highness had done; and as Lady C[——] told me afterwards, was about to throw the Princess off altogether; but by degrees he cooled, and entered her presence. He expressed his dissatisfaction, but did so mildly, and she explained her intentions. To these Mr. Whitbread did not listen, or seem to place any faith in them, but said he sincerely wished everything might turn out for the best; there was no saying how things *might* turn out; he trusted that he misjudged the present case. The fact is, (and perhaps he hardly knows the fact himself, for we are all deceived by our passions,) that Mr. Whitbread does not like the Princess should make all the play herself; he likes the idea, that it is to him, and to the weight of his politics, she should owe whatever advantages she may reap from the present contest. This is nothing against his integrity. I believe Mr. Whitbread to be a most upright, kind-hearted man; but he has the notion which all Englishmen, nay, perhaps men of all countries, entertain, namely, that *men* only can act on the public stage of life. He has imbibed this prejudice with the air he breathes; and one cannot blame him. If I were the Princess, however, I would show him the contrary. But this I would not say to Her Royal Highness; let the deed be her own, whichever way it be done.

Saturday, July 2nd, 1814.—I dined at Connaught House. Sir W. Gell, and Mr. Craven, and the two ladies, Lady C[harlotte] L[indsay] and Lady C[harlotte] C[ampbell] were the party. After dinner came on the *mystery*,—which was quite unnecessary, but which added very much to the amusement. The Princess, in going to the Masquerade, took us down the back staircase, and out at the back-door from the garden. Mr. Craven and Sir W. Gell, and myself, walked with her and the two ladies to the Albany. It was a very fine night, and Sir William was so amusing, it certainly was very good fun. We reached the Albany without adventures or detection ; and there we dressed as fast as possible, and from thence proceeded to the Masquerade. The danger of exposing the Princess by being myself known, took away all the amusement I might otherwise have had. On our return, the Princess was so tired I thought she never would be able to walk from the turnpike to the little door of Connaught House ; and oh ! how unmercifully Her Royal Highness leant on my arm ! She did, however, get home, and I hope and think without being detected.

Saturday.—I had been desired to go to the Princess's box at the opera ; so I went, though I had much rather have remained in my own comfortable seat in the pit ; for it is impossible to listen to the music in her box, Her Royal Highness talks so perpetually and so loud ; and there is seldom any person there I care to converse with, or if there is, she mars conversation in every possible way.

Sunday.—The poor Princess is sadly teased about going to St. Paul's,—her advisers insisting that she *should* go, and all the chamberlains and deans writing word that there is no place kept for her, and that it is not in their power to give Her Royal Highness one. " It is ridicu-lous to make me always the means of making a disturb-ance for no end whatever,"—the Princess said to me in speaking of this business ; and certainly in the present instance this remark appears true enough, especially as she has no wish whatever except to go abroad. The more tranquil her conduct is, the more chance there is of bringing her wish to bear. But Brougham, &c. see the matter otherwise, and look to another source of happiness for her, (if happiness it can be called in any way,) and only wish to make her struggle and contend for.power and show in this country.

Lord Henry Fitzgerald, Sir William Gell, Mr. Steuart, and myself, dined at Connaught House. The dinner was very agreeable, and after dinner still more so ; but the poor Princess was in dreadfully low spirits.

Monday, 4th.—I was one of a party which the Princess had invited to accompany her to Vauxhall. There was no amusement in this expedition ; we were all dull, and unable to amuse each other ; and the fireworks were but indifferent. Fireworks, *pour tout bien*, will not do, even for courtiers !

Tuesday, 5th.—Mr. Whitbread told the Princess, in an interview he had with Her Royal Highness to-day, that although the House had voted her fifty thousand a year, he thought it would have a much better effect if she would write a letter to the Speaker, purporting that she did not wish to be a burthen upon the nation, and that she hoped they would re-consider the matter, and give her only thirty-five thousand. Lady [——], who was present when Mr. Whitbread gave the Princess this advice, told me she saw a gloom overspread her countenance whilst he was speaking. Her Royal Highness is not mercenary ; far from it ;—I believe her to be very noble-minded in money transactions : but she conceived this proposal not kind from a friend, and the sum not more than her due. However, Lady [——] says, that when Mr. Whitbread explained to the Princess that fifty thousand pounds would oblige her to remain in this country, and spend it where she received it, but that a less one would afford her liberty, she fell into the trap, and entered into his view of the subject with alacrity.

Mr. Whitbread then wrote a letter to the Speaker, and she copied it, but not without having previously written an ill-judged, useless letter to Lord Castlereagh, (which, as Mr. Whitbread said, was not *English*, and had no point in it,) saying, she accepted *the proposal*, but did not name the sum. This, I heard Lady [——] say, she conceived to have more point in it than Mr. Whitbread supposed ; for perhaps she intended it should be perceived that her Royal Highness was of one opinion, and her advisers of another, and hoped that ministers would take the hint and fulfil her wishes. But none of these things came to pass, if such *were* the Princess's intentions. At all events, these underhand, contradictory movements produced a bad effect. Lord Castlereagh naturally saw through the discrepancy of opinion which existed between the Princess and her friends. Lady [——] told me she wept the whole time she was out driving. Truly, I cannot wonder, for she is made to lead a wretched life. Again she said to me at dinner, " I know not who plagues me most, my friends or my enemies."

Old S[apio] dined at Connaught House. I was sorry to meet him there again, as I had hoped never to do so. The Princess treats him with a comical mixture of protection and scorn, which is very unlike what she ought to do in either way.

Monday.—Lord D[——] called on me, and asked a great many questions about the Princess. I was cautious in my replies, for I know him to be one of the Regent's *toadies*, and I have ever had reason to suspect him as one of His Royal Highness's spies on the Princess. Yet for all this he enjoys a laugh at his Royal Friend's expense, and pulled out of his pocket some very abominable verses, which he called "capital," and desired me to read. He said they were written by Miss [——]. I do not believe that they are, and I asked leave to copy them, I shall show them to Lady [——], who is Miss [——]'s friend, and will be able to contradict Lord D[——]'s statement, if it be incorrect; which I am inclined to think it is, and that the verses are his lordship's own composition.

Pour le 19me Siècle.

Soyez bien grasse, ayez cinquante ans;
Beaucoup de gorge, et bien du clinquant;
Un air dédaigneux, un fils lâche et rampant;
Un grand nigaud de mari, bas et complaisant:
Et voilà de quoi plaire un magnanime Régent!

I received a letter from [——]. She says :—

I do not see the slightest chance of our ever meeting again; which makes me horribly melancholy; especially as I pulled three strong grey hairs out of my head this morning. *Hélas! la fleur de ma jeunesse est passée!*—and as much in vain in point of pleasure, as in a *moral* sense! When I think how fast it is flying, my soul makes a kind of clutch to get away and make a little more use of life; to see foreign countries and enjoy a little of *real* pleasure; not your dull London pleasures, where you have much ado to keep your chin above the water of neglect and insignificancy; where people forget you the moment you are out of sight, and where all the charms of society and the refinements of gallantry are out of the question; but the gay, brilliant pleasures of a foreign capital, or the sylvan delight of a southern clime, under brighter skies and with more animating avocations.

You will sympathise with me in this, though you do not in most things, and think me but a wretched dry bones, inside as well as out. Who was it that said, "*Si je n'étois pas votre ami, je serais votre ennemi?*" I suppose you say that of me.

You wonderful flighty enthusiastic people have greatly the advantage of sober dry mortals like me; for we envy and admire you, though we may sometimes think you a little absurd; while the very best of *us* you think abominable, though you sometimes allow us to be wise. Don't you think I am very *éveillée* to-day? No wonder! It is the influence of Spring. Yesterday, when I got up, the first object that met my eyes was the ground as white with snow, as if it had been the first of January;—not a powdering, but an honest thick fall of snow, which is not gone off to-day; and the clouds are now doing their best to gather a fresh supply.

How I glory in the Princess's vindication to the eyes of all men! and how I am gratified at the complete mortification of her vile persecutors, from the biggest to the least. I wish she had her foot upon all their necks. It makes my blood turn to think of the degeneracy of people's feelings, their mean inventions, their pitiful, careful suspicions, and selfishness. Do you remember Mr. Burke saying, he believed that, formerly, a thousand swords would have leaped from their scabbards to defend the Queen of France?—which *leaping*, by-the-by, has been much quizzed by dull people like me. There is in England but one tongue that will wag in her behalf; yet, shame on them, there's hardly one whose heart and mind does not speak in her favour. Sneaking bodies! The days of chivalry are past; that of economists, calculators, and infidels is come; and the glory of Europe is extinguished for ever! O dull, degenerate Englishmen! If there is a spark of good feeling left, it is in the mob, who give her their acclamations, since no other atonement is made to her. The English are a noble nation *en masse*, an odious people individually. Don't you think so?

Adieu! Ever yours, [——].

July 1st.—At length I have been able to arrange my affairs, so as to be free to leave England, and go where I like. I have provided for one or two old servants; have seen [——] settled in an excellent and profitable employment; and lastly, a sad reason enables me to quit home without one regret—my dear old aunt is dead. She died a fortnight ago; since which time I have not been able to write down a word. Though her great age and long illness might have prepared me for her loss, they did not ; and when she was gone, I felt as if her death was an untimely one ; and my grief was reat in proportion. She was my last near relation : * now I can claim no nearer kindred with any one than cousinship. There is something very sad in this feeling. However little our relations may suit us, however much they may differ from us in tastes and pursuits, still there is a tie in consanguinity which nothing can ever break. We may live apart, and be long absent from them, but nothing except death can put an end to the natural affection which God has ordained between near relations.

Well—she died blessing me, my dear old aunt ; and I feel much pleasure in thinking I endeavoured to be a comfort to her. I have fulfilled all her orders to the minutest point, and now I can gratify my long-cherished wish of travelling in foreign countries.

To-day, I received an entertaining droll letter from Sir W. Gell, whom I had commissioned to find me a good travelling servant. He speaks of the Princess as follows :—

As to favour with both Mr. and Mrs. Thompson, that is out of the question. I was drubbed for executing my commissions in the aphrodisiac way, in such style ; but you are not to suppose that crowned heads are capable of distinguishing such superabundant talents. On the contrary, my constituents see my merits, and the University confers the horrors—I mean honours ; for they will not let princes do anything of the kind in mere gaiety of heart, but all is done through the ministry. Keppel Craven returns in the first week of June ; Mrs. P[——] is going to Worthing, to see Lady C. Campbell ; and so is Mr. Knutson, or Canuteson, to prevent the sea from flowing, as his ancestor, Canute the Great, did.

As to Mrs. D[——], you know, when you are gone to France I shall have a fine opportunity of retorting all your malice and your sallies, and I can trust to the lady in question.

* This is, apparently, an addition, " by way of disguise."

I seem banished from Thompson House, but she has a triumph at Boodle's ten to one. The balls at White's and Co. seem in a languishing state, but London is furiously full of parties and suppers. Only to give you an idea of what I was engaged to go to last night :—Dinner, Mrs. Lock, 2000 virgins ; Lady Douglas, music ; Mrs. Davenport, christening ; Devonshire House, supper ; Lady Salisbury's. I do not pretend to send you anything entertaining, as we write on business. Being,

My dear [——],
Your affectionate grandmother,
JOHN JULIUS ANGERSTEIN.

P.S. The signature will quite exasperate Mrs. A[——]. Tell her I am writing a pamphlet by the desire of the Classica Journal, on Troy.

ON BOARD THE [——], CAPTAIN [——],
One o'clock, 15th July, 1814.

The only ardent wish I have formed for these last two years, is now fulfilled—I am on the ocean, on my way to the Continent. There is always a degree of doubt, nay, almost of awe, in the fulfilment of our wishes ; since experience has sadly warned us how often we have wished erroneously, and how little we know what to wish for. Yet at this moment my sensations are pleasurable. The sun is gaily shining : it withdrew for a moment, as we slowly glided out of the harbour at Dover ; for a moment, too, a cloud of tender regret for what might have been, stole across my mind ; but the recollection that it is not, quickly resumed its power, and a feeling of pride and pleasure succeeded, that I was going to new scenes which would occupy and change the current of my thoughts. Perhaps, like a person excited by fictitious means, I may sink hereafter ; but the present moment is buoyant with renovated hope.

I regretted not being able, yesterday, to visit the shrine of Thomas à Becket at Canterbury, where hypocrisy paid the price of its vice by blood, and superstition

I   Q trembled in its turn, for having dared to usurp the power of Heaven to punish.

The country we traversed is rich but monotonous; the peace and wealth which seems diffused over its undulating scenery, lulls, instead of rousing the mind. The goodness of the roads, horses, and inns, leave one nothing to complain of in respect of the animal enjoyments of existence. The bustle of Dover, its dirt and noise, convey a thousand ideas to the mind, but scarcely impress one of those ideas distinctly. Its white cliffs, and bold, bare shore, seem to dare the inroad of any hostile invader, and they recall a sensation of pride to every British heart, which makes it swell at being English. Every inn was full, but I found room, at length, at *The Ship*. The quantity of travellers, and concourse of carriages, had the appearance of a fête.

Calais, five o'clock.—We had a fine passage—only two hours and fifty minutes—but having arrived within a mile of the shore could get no further, the tide being low. Our captain (rather perfidiously, I think) advised all the passengers to get into a pilot boat, in preference to waiting till eight or nine at night, and we consented. We paid through the nose, about 3*l*. sterling, for this operation, and for the noise and torment of the people who came round us, and laid hold of the ladies—hauling them out, and nearly tumbling them into the water, laughing and screaming the whole time. We landed, however, safely, but not soundly; for we were all sea water and sand. We had then to walk two miles, partly over sand, and then to climb up the wooden quay, which extends a great way into the sea. Some of the passengers found this rather difficult, especially one fat lady who had very short legs. All these inconveniences were to me' however, compensated for by the novelty of every object which met my view. I longed to draw everything

I saw, and to stop and gaze at the shops, people,
&c., &c.

While on board, I talked to the mate; his name was
Hetherden; he had one of those happy countenances
which at once bespeak one's confidence in their honesty,
and obtain it.   He told me, that the 18th of February,
1807, he was wrecked off Boulogne; the night was so
cold and stormy that one man was froze to death, standing
erect on the deck.   They fired guns of distress in vain.
As he commanded the vessel, he would not leave her,
to take to the boat, till every other soul was saved,
except four men who would drink, and who went down
below into the cabin and perished.   He himself was
rescued at last, however, and well received by the French,
though taken prisoner; and all the English were well
treated.   Some of their officers behaved shamefully,
and offended the people.   Hetherden added, " they forgot
they were in an enemy's country, and insisted upon all
sorts of unreasonable demands."

Quillacq's Hotel, Saturday.—I went to the play last
night, and heard some very good music, and not bad
acting; but the quickness of the recitation, and the
loudness of the singing, had something of caricature, or
at least appeared so to my organs, unaccustomed to
such performances.   They acted three different pieces:
La preuve Villageoise; Le Mariage d'une heure; and
Les Prétendues. The music of the first was old, but
pretty.   The second I never heard before; there were
some beautiful trios in it; but the character of the composition was more brilliant and buoyant than touching;
pathos belongs to the Italian alone, some few Scotch and
Irish airs excepted.   There were five Englishmen in the
box where I sat, mute and grave, till I made them speak
by asking them questions.   The person to whom I

addressed myself was a Mr. Davies ; and Lady H[——]'s son, Mr. C[——], sat behind, and fell asleep in spite of my eloquence. I was well amused, however, but happy to go to rest, being very tired. Monsieur Culier was excessively civil.

Left Calais to-day at one o'clock. Just before I stepped into my carriage, Lady Hamilton—the Lady Hamilton I had seen twenty-five years ago, at Naples*— sent me a message to say, that one who had known me long and well, and dearly loved those I loved [what a prostitution of the term !] wished to see me again. Yet, poor soul, I was sorry for her, and a mixture of curiosity and sadness made me desire to see her once more. I went to her apartment—time had marred her beauty, but not effaced it—and when I said " *toujours belle*," a smile of pleasure reanimated her fine eyes. My compliment was not altogether untrue, although it was a little more than reality : but such reality is not worth adhering to. Her eyes were filled with tears : she said the remembrance of the past crowded upon her, and excited them. She talked agreeably, and spoke of her own fate. In mentioning the child † she brings up, she assured me it was not her own, nor could be. When anybody assures me of a thing that may be true, and is favourable to themselves, I always believe them. It may be silly, but I cannot help it. Nor do I wish to have that wisdom which makes one doubt one's neighbour.

Beween Calais and Hautbuisson the country is flat and uninteresting; inclosures, and these are merely ditches, but no hedges ; indeed it is chiefly marsh. The soil seems very poor, and yet they do not spare manure.

---

* The Duchess of Argyll was formerly at Naples with Lady Charlotte Campbell, and not only received Emma Lyon, but was one of the chief persons in exhorting Sir William Hamilton to marry her. This he did in 1791.

† Horatio Nelson Thompson, Mrs. Ward.

Crops are chiefly wheat, oats, and artificial grasses. About a mile from Hautbuisson we reached an ascent, from which there is a sylvan view into a valley. The cottages are well built, generally of stone ; some of them very neatly thatched—a short close thatch, unlike ours, but full as neat. There is a bareness of population and a paucity of houses which, to an English eye, is melancholy. The first enlivening object or appearance of husbandry I beheld, was a woman helping a man to spread dung. She seemed to set about the occupation *con amore*. The roads are capital. I hardly found out they were *pavés*. There are mounds of gravel and small stones placed in piles on each side of the road, ready for use.

The next village after Marquise is Bois Gagnon Huit-mille, situated in a glen. From an elevation in the ground just before we came to Boulogne there is a fine view of the sea. At Huitmille I ate some of the nicest bread I ever tasted. I arrived at Boulogne at half after six ; it is a fortified town, situated on the mouth of the Lianne, in a narrow valley that opens to the sea. It has a melancholy appearance ; but perhaps the gloom of a very rainy day gave me this impression. The inn is called Hotel d'Angleterre ; and it deserves the name, if dearness is one of the attributes of an English hotel.

I walked round the Ville Haute, upon the ramparts, in spite of the rain, from whence I saw the hill where Bonaparte had organized the army with which he threatened to invade Britain, and which he afterwards led to the more easy conquest of Germany. I saw also an immense wooden tower, that was visible from Huitmille, and that looked like representations I have seen of the large wicker baskets in which Druids burnt their victims.* This tower was only a skeleton of what was afterwards

* What the writer saw was doubtless the scaffolding which was prepared for erecting the present column. [Original note.]

to be executed in stone. The *garçon de la maison*, who was my cicerone, took pleasure in relating that some stones had been already placed, which it had required forty horses to move. " *Il falloit bien qu'ils fussent des grandes pierres, celles la.*" To which I assented.

Mr. Dillon, the *seccatore*, had discovered me, and was very civil, and walked and talked till I was dead tired of him. He told me, what I had observed the day before to be in some degree true, that there is much wavering in the people's minds, and that they have received their King with great indifference.

I left Boulogne, Sunday, the 17th of July.—The river Lianne winds through a fertile valley, and the aspect of the country is more agreeable. Further on, from an eminence, there is a fine view of a rich and wooded country ; to the right, in the distance, there is some ground which has the appearance of having been a Roman camp. About seven miles from Boulogne there are two avenues leading to an old chateau, about which there is an air of romance. The quiet grey of the stones, and the dullness of the scene, conspire to make one suppose a fair lady may live there, shut up with some old guardian—or worse—married to some hated lord. The trees which form the avenues are too closely planted, yet their chequered shade seems to invite to calm enjoyment and meditation. I admire avenues. How prejudicial the love of what is fashionable is to real taste ! how much the inherent passion for novelty, when too far indulged, contributes to deteriorate from all that is truly great !

I arrived at [——], at seven o'clock—a comfortable inn. The master spoke the best English I ever heard a foreigner speak. I fancied he was English at first, but he told me he had not been in England for twenty-five years, and had remained at Samaces, doing what good he could, and saving the lives of several persons during the war ; for which he had never received the smallest remuneration, though they were all, with one exception, people of good fortune, and were now again established in their possessions.

The country beyond Samaces is rich and well cultivated. I know not if it is the effect of novelty, the too great love of which, I contemn ; but I cannot help fancying that the absence of all enclosures gives a vastness to the prospect. There is a curious sort of dark coloured marl, a few inches below the surface of the soil, which is used as manure. The women's dress is picturesque : either they tie up their hair in a conical shape, to the top of their heads, or wear caps with a high caul, and plaited wings of a large and oval form, which fly backwards and forwards, giving a characteristic and strange appearance. This, with brilliant coloured aprons, short petticoats, and some instrument of agriculture in their hands, forms a picture which requires only the artist's power to embody.

I reached Montreuil a quarter after three o'clock. Peat is made in the neighbourhood. Wheat seems almost ready for the sickle, and yet at Boulogne they complained it was so cold that the fruits of the season were not ripe. At Montreuil I went to the principal church ; they were performing high mass ; the chief magistrates and constituted authorities of the place came in to sing Te Deum for peace. The sound of the drum, and the sight of armed men, drowning the voices of the priests, and walking up in martial order to the altar, was an awful sight, and brought back the remembrance of the reign of terror. I shuddered involuntarily, and it was not till I heard the persons around me repeatedly say, " *C'est pour la paix—c'est pour la paix*," that I could get rid of the painful impression.

It is not true—at least it is not true *now*—that the lower order of catholics mutter their prayers in an unknown tongue. I borrowed a ritual of the service from a poor girl, in which the psalms, and other portions of scripture, were translated in the mother tongue. On the one side was French, on the other Latin.

Near Montreuil they hoe the potatoes with a clever machine, drawn by one horse, which runs along the earth like a ploughshare, with wheels sufficiently wide to cover three furrows, while the plough acts only on the middle one. We passed through a small but pretty and comfortable looking village. I observed there is a quantity of wood about the country. Hurdles are particularly neatly made. I coveted them for Dovenest. Dovenest! when, if ever, shall I be there again? I slept at Bernay, at the Fleur de Lis, the best of the two bad inns: dirty beds and floors; but what signifies for a night or two, when one is in health?

Monday, 18th July.—I left Bernay early. What a wonderful extent of country! no part is uncultivated, and yet there is often no habitation to be seen for miles. I saw two men labouring in a field to-day; it is quite an event in the landscape. This vast tract of country, covered with the abundance of all which is necessary to animal existence, but deficient in all that is beautiful, would be insufferably dull and uninteresting, did not a certain feeling of its greatness interpose: it seems as if it sufficed to itself alone, and that it must ever continue to do so. This, in the natural as in the moral world, is the greatest attribute with which human intellect can invest the objects of its contemplation.

I dined at Flicour, a miserable inn, and was served by two women scarcely human in their appearance. There were several pretty views from Flicour to Amiens. I reached the latter place at seven o'clock. It is a melancholy looking town, no appearance of trade or bustle, but groups of soldiers of different nations idling about, and reminding one too much of the cause of this stagnation in commerce, this silence, and this gloom.

I went out immediately to see the cathedral. It is of gothic architecture, and is the finest in that style which I recollect ever to have seen, not excepting Westminster Abbey; for although the latter is much larger, and in detail may be more magnificent, I do not think it so imposing as a whole building. The sun was setting, and we could not for some moments distinguish each particular feature, but its general effect was grand in the extreme. Who that has a heart, but must feel inspired by such temples and worship:

> What though a different law command
> A different worship in our land,
> That soul is torpid which has felt
> Unmoved, where other knees have knelt.

The pure homage of the heart is holy in all places; but in such a temple as this even the impure might feel the presence of God.

One poor woman, covered with a thick veil, knelt in deep concentrated prayer. The person who showed me the cathedral lowered his voice to a whisper, as he approached her; he felt that she was in silent communion with heaven, and that the tongue of man should be hushed. My cicerone was a decent conversible person. When I asked him how the church had escaped destruction, he replied that it had happened almost miraculously, but that it had not escaped pollution, for scenes of horror had been enacted within its walls. Much of the carved work has been mutilated, and the temple, said he, has been otherwise desecrated. "Although I speak," he added, " before the altar of God, I have seen a common prostitute brought in a sort of triumph, and carried upon men's shoulders, to be set on that holy altar. Oh! they were times which it makes one tremble to think of. But during the whole of that reign of terror I always used my own language to say Citoyenne; and *tutoyer* was then the

law, but I always said 'Monsieur' et 'Madame.'"
"How did you then contrive to escape the guillotine?"
"Ah!" he replied, shrugging his shoulders, "On parle des
miracles du temps de nos pères, et on se moque si on dit
qu'il y en a de nos jours; mais c'est la foi seule qui nous
manque; il y en a tous les jours."

I was touched with this man's conversation: there
was no cant or mummery in it, but it was sensible and
feeling.

I left Amiens, Tuesday, 19th of July. There is a beautiful natural wood, chiefly of beech, about four miles
from Amiens; but in other respects the country is flat
and insipid until you reach Bretenville, where stand the
remains of an ancient archway, of pleasing proportions.

I arrived at Paris, Thursday, the 21st of July. The Port
St. Denis gives a grand appearance to that entrance of
Paris; and the long and magnificently broad road which
leads to it, gives an air of grandeur that our English capital
cannot boast. The busy streets, the concourse of people,
and the wonderful tissue of events which have recently
happened in this metropolis, all conspire to fill the mind,
and to crowd it with a superfluity of thought; the
difficulty is to arrange and combine ideas, not to create
them.

I went in the evening to the Opera Comique, Rue
Féydeau. It is the prettiest salon imaginable. Large
pillars of marble, or what seems to be marble, support the
boxes; the pit rises in a species of amphitheatre; and
the drop curtain is the handsomest I ever saw: it is
painted in imitation of blue velvet, covered with golden
fleurs de lis; the crown on a ball, which seems embossed
in the middle, and the drapery very grand and simple in
its folds. I never saw anything in better taste than the
whole of this theatre. The performances were Le Caliph
de Bagdad, L'Habit du Comte De Grammont, and Le
Nouveau Seigneur du Village. I came in at the end of the

first piece ; the two latter were very entertaining, and the music was exceedingly good ; the people all singing in time and tune, but louder than my ears are accustomed to ; indeed, they seem to vie with one another, who shall make most noise. The principal actor and actress were excellent performers, but the whole corps executed their parts *uniformly* well, and perhaps this has more power upon the general effect of the performance, than one transcendant actor could possibly convey. No vulgar misconception or defect, in any of the subordinate players, broke the charm of the illusion. There was an exquisite duet in the last piece. I met my friend Mr. C[——], which gave me great pleasure ; I felt as if I had not seen him for years, so glad was I to meet an English friend.

Friday, July 22nd.—I went to the Louvre with Mr. C[——]. I have not time or power to enter minutely into this stupendous emporium of all that is fine in the arts. I gazed once more at the undying beauties of the immortal Venus. I felt a spark of inspiration emanate from the divine Apollo. Again the marble breathed before me, and genius once more entered my soul, with all its vivifying power. A young Bacchus, by some better designated as the Genius of Sadness, fixed my attention, and rooted me to the spot. Seen from where I stood, there is a tenderness in the countenance, a refined expression of all that is soft and sad, and yet dignified, in the half-closed lip ; the hand too seems indicative of placid reflection, the arm negligently thrown over the head, as if the soul had abandoned itself to fancy, and the body rested while the mind was far away in the excursive regions of imagination. The dying Gladiator, subdued by death, not conquered by his mortal adversary ; the fighting Gladiator, his muscles swelling with the tension of strength ; and above all these, Diana, the light, the chaste, the cold Diana, " her buskin gemmed with morning dew," scorn sitting with grace upon her lip, and all the grand severity of an unyielding nature clothing her airy well-poised figure.

It is vain to attempt a further description of countless beauties, and of all the ideas they create. To live at Paris for a length of time, and go every day to the Louvre, and see these exquisite conceptions of unrivalled art, would light the dullest soul to taste the joy which genius can impart, and raise the grovelling mind to a standard of greatness to which it would otherwise never attain. Time and circumstances tore me away.

I went to the magnificent gardens of the Tuileries; and although the building is heavy from its magnitude, it is not devoid of grandeur. The formal parterres, the statues, and fountains, are well adapted to the decoration of a palace, and from the very idea we form of the labour and art necessary to their formation, they convey no unpleasing sensation to the mind,—which is always gratified by every proof of the power of that of others. As a place of public resort it is charming, from the alternate variety of sunshine or shade, the sweet smell of the flowers, and the profusion of chairs and benches, which in our gardens are so scantily provided, and which the English public take such pains to destroy and disfigure. There certainly never was a country which had so little respect for public monuments or property, and so little love for the arts, as England.

I visited Lady Westmoreland,* and she made me accompany her all over the town. She went to every shop on the Boulevards. The variety and beauty of all materials for ladies' dress far surpasses our wares, and Lady Westmoreland says they are cheaper. Nothing

---

* Jane, daughter and co-heir of R. Huck Saunders, Esq., M.D., married (as second wife), 1800, John Fane, Earl of Westmoreland. On the death (in 1841) of her husband, Lord Clarendon wrote to Lady Granville: "Lady Westmoreland is at the Bedford Hotel at Brighton, and has told the waiter that she means to be a disconsolate widow, and is determined never to be happy again."

offends me in the Parisian ladies' toilette, except the grace-
less height and immensity of their bonnets, which are
perfect disfiguration.   How can they admire their statues,
and then endure to look at each other ?

I met the Duc de Coigni, and asked him if he knew
Madame de Coigni, with whom I had an appointment,
and was going to pay my respects to her.   He told me
she was his *son's wife, and divorced from him !*   What a
blunder of mine !

I was not able to get to the Opera till it was half over.
It was *La Jérusalem Délivrée.*   As to the spectacle, it
exceeds praise ; every scene is a picture, not merely from
its *scenic* perfection, but from the grouping of the persons,
and the nice attention paid to the most subordinate
figures ; those who remain chiefly in distance being clad
in quiet colours, to aid the deception ; and the prompti-
tude and precision with which all the changes are conducted, render it almost a magical deception.   The
dancing too is the dancing of fairies and graces ; there is
not merely one or two fine dancers, but six or eight, all
vying with each other.   The last scene, of the Christians
praying in the temple, and the falling of the walls, and the
entrance of Godfroy, and the prayers, and illuminated
heavens, with the ghosts of the departed, and choirs of
angels, &c., is almost too beautiful and awful.   I felt my
very flesh creep.   What a wonderful people these French
are, to make one feel so much, and to feel themselves
so little.   I was with Lady Westmoreland, and to my
surprise Mr. J[——]e came into her box.

Saturday, 23*rd.*—I went to Versailles.   On my way
there I traversed a great part of Paris, and was much
struck with the magnificence of the city.   I crossed the
end of the Tuileries, and passed along the Seine.   The
last bridge, built by Bonaparte in commemoration of the
battle of Jena, called the Pont de Jena, is of beautiful

and chaste architecture, and surpasses all the other
bridges. St. Cloud is situated on the side of an eminence,
which overlooks Paris, and is covered with villas. At its
base the river winds in a graceful curve. I could not gain
permission to see Versailles, because workmen were busy
in making repairs ; so I went to St. Cloud. There is an
avenue of approach, half a mile in length, to the palace,
the exterior of which has no particular excellence, but its
site is truly magnificent, commanding a view of Paris
and the adjacent country, which is well worth seeing. As
I traversed its shady alleys and entered its courts, a tide
of recollections crowded upon my mind. So lately the
footsteps of a great usurper trod the paths which now
I trod, and after the revolutionary storm had rolled in
tremendous retribution over the scenes where luxury and
pleasure had misruled, Providence has once more restored
them to their rightful possessors, after having humbled
them to the dust. What a lesson to humanity !

The views here surpass description. The ornaments of
the interior of the palace are handsome, and the gallery
is fine, but too narrow, as most galleries are.

There was a picture by a young artist of the name of
Guerin, the subject Phædra and Hippolitus. I thought
the conception of it was good, and there was more of
simple grandeur in the composition than is generally
seen in the French school. Bonaparte's bed-room possessed a strange and fearful interest ; I saw Richard's
tent in this voluptuous bed, and I thought how vain was
all the down which invited to luxurious repose. How
much more deeply was this idea impressed on my mind,
when we were informed that two attendants slept in each
of the adjacent apartments !

From St. Cloud I went back to Versailles, to visit
Trianon, a very delightful *maison de plaisance*, contiguous
to the greater palace. There are many subjects of interest there. Those which struck me most were two

pictures; one of Venus silencing the Loves, lest they should disturb the sleep of Adonis; the other, of Fortune flying over the world. The first is said to be by Giordano, and its conception and mellowness, its grace and glowing beauties, give assurance of its being genuine. The latter has a peculiar purple colouring, which I could not wholly approve, but the round and palpable firmness of the form, and its grace, commanded admiration. I proceeded to the lesser Trianon, interesting only from its having belonged to the unfortunate Marie Antoinette. An old German Swiss showed us this garden. He had been one of the Guards, and escaped the general massacre miraculously. I begged him to tell me how. " *Ah !* " said he, "*il me faudroit quinze jours pour vous le dire.*" He clasped his hands together, and appeared truly imbued with a deep and painful remembrance of those times. One could only respect his feelings, and restrain one's curiosity.

I do not recollect ever to have been so fatigued as I was to-day in walking back to Versailles; and yet the warmth which kills others animates me. When I returned home I found several invitations, one to a Madame de Vaudremont. I went to see Lady Westmoreland, and met there Lord B[———], Madame de Coigni, and Sir Robert Wilson.* The latter seems very good-humoured, but such a decided Englishman, and so loaded with prejudices, I wonder why he leaves England. When I spoke of the grandeur of Paris, he said he did not know; the generality of streets were so narrow and dirty, that he should think more of *Swallow Street* ever after. This was enough for me. I thought he should return as fast as possible to its delights. In the evening, just as I was going to bed,

* Sir Robert Thomas Wilson (1777-1849). He was a distinguished soldier in the Peninsular War. In the disputes between George IV. and his wife he became a distinguished " Queenite," and was dismissed from the army for his conduct at the Queen's funeral. He was later reinstated.

Mr. J[——]e came to see me. He is another of the same true John Bull breed.

Sunday, 24th.—I went to visit the Duchesse de Coigni, and to ask her husband if there was a court the next day, as I wished to be presented. She informed me there was, and told me I had nothing to do, but to send my name to the Duc de P[——]nne. The Duchesse de P[——]nne is now in a great situation, receiving company every night, and upon the top of the tree, after having been at the bottom. The changes in this mortal coil are rapid, and we cannot account for them. Perhaps this poor lady has expiated her errors in her former misfortunes. We cannot read the heart. Be that as it may, there she is, a great lady, and once more surrounded with splendour, and courted by all those who shunned her. Oh ! this world ! this world !

I went to the Tuileries, but could not gain admittance ; there was a mass, or a review, or some show, which prevented my seeing it. I went with Mr. J[——] and M. Delessert to the Hotel des Invalides. Of all the monuments and public buildings sacred to the memory of the great and good, or adapted to the business and pleasures of men, none ought to make more deep impression than those which are set apart to purposes of humanity. These, to a reflecting mind, possess a peculiar charm, less imaginative perhaps, but more exalting and intense, than any other. This great receptacle for the wounded soldiers, the aged or infirm servants of their country, is worthy of the object for which it is designed. I could not help comparing it with Chelsea and Greenwich Hospitals ; and I thought it more vast, but less beautiful as to its architecture. But the *intention* of the institution is the same, and that is a noble one.

From thence we went to the Museum of French Monuments—*Musée des Monuments Français.* Nothing could excuse having collected all this assemblage of relics and tombs to meet in heterogeneous confusion together, except that it was an idea of national vanity which could alone have rescued them from total destruction ; and even with this excuse I could not get rid of the impression of incongruity and sacrilege which provoked and shocked me. The sacredness of all those thoughts which hover round the tombs of the departed, and which, viewed in the holy stillness of their original sanctuaries, they must have excited, is not felt when they are seen where they are now placed. To the antiquarian, the historian, and the artist, they are certainly a fund of science and entertainment ; but still the great and higher sentiments which these monuments were intended to commemorate, are entirely extinguished ; and I doubt if the knowledge gained to science is worth the feelings lost.   ·

I dined at a Madame G[irardi]n's. I was too late, and found them all at table, which shocked me considerably ; but the master of the house came out to receive me, and accepted my apologies with great good humour. I soon became acquainted with Monsieur and Madame G[——]n, but not with their guests, whose names I never even heard. They all conversed gaily and agreeably, and I did my best to be pleasant. They talked over the politics of the day, or rather of the past, most freely. I asked my left hand neighbour if it was not rather imprudent to do so before servants. " They have always spoken thus in this house," he replied, " *On ne parle pas seulement, on babille*." The dinner was soon over, and the company rose all together, ladies and gentlemen, and went into an adjoining apartment, which opened into a garden, where we sat on a terrace, and had tea and coffee. Among other subjects of conversation, that of the present fashions in dress had its turn. I ventured to express my dislike of the high chimney bonnets, but all the gentlemen defended them, as well as the ladies, and seemed to take as lively

I   R an interest in the fashions of their ladies' dresses as they do in the affairs of their nation.

Monsieur de G[——]n talked much, and tolerably well, but with a frothy kind of manner that was truly French. He thought everything was for the best ; and all that had been, had opened the eyes of the people ; and that a Constitution formed on the basis of that of England, would now give happiness and liberty to France. My neighbour on my left hand, whom Monsieur G[——]n called *mon cher*, seemed of a very different opinion. He said that everything connected with public affairs was gradually returning to its former state, and that "*si c'etoit l'Empereur, le Roi, ou le premier Consul,*" the French people would be always tyrannized over.

I staid for an hour or two, and was well amused with the people and their conversation. One man, who was the wit of the party, and a kind of *French Ward*, told me he had been well acquainted with Lord [——] "il y avoit bien des années" ; he was very charming, he said,—"*mais d'une indolence !*"—"*dont il n'est jamais revenu,*" said I.

I drove to the Duchesse de P[ie]nne, to leave my name, and intending to pay her a visit had she been alone, but I found a great assembly at her door, and did not like to go in, so went home. There is a strange report about the Princess of Wales having written to hire Monsieur de Sebastiani's house *here*—I contradict it flatly. Fortunately I can do so, not having been informed of the circumstance—but in my own mind I fear there has been some truth in it. The cause, however, which might have induced her Royal Highness to come, no longer exists. I trust therefore she will not be so silly as to come to a court which *could* not, if it would, receive her with proper kindness.

Monday, 25th July.—I went with Mr. C[——] to see St. Genevieve and Le Jardin des Plantes. Close to the

church of St. Genevieve lives a Monsieur Chevalier, a
learned man, a friend of Mr. Craven and Sir W. Gell.
I liked his appearance and manner : he had lived many
years at Edinburgh, having fled from France during the
time of terror ; and he retained a most grateful remembrance of the kindness and hospitality he had received
in Scotland. We saw the library : it is a magnificent
room, with one or two smaller ones adjoining, which
contained medals, natural curiosities, &c., but these have
been taken away, and there are only some poor remains.
St. Genevieve is a fine building, I believe of the Corinthian
order, but is not exempt from many faults, some of which
strike even an ignorant eye, and others Mr. C[——]
pointed out, such as the columns round the cupola being
larger at the top than the bottom, which had a most
ungraceful effect. I went up to the outside of the cupola,
in defiance of the heat, in order to take a general view of
Paris. I was amply rewarded for my trouble, by beholding the grandest possible bird's eye prospect of the whole
city and its environs. This was rendered more interesting
by Monsieur Chevalier giving us an exact description of
the movement of the Allies round Paris previously to their
entrance. He said he expected every moment the town
would be burnt, and one general ruin would ensue ; but
Providence had mercifully brought this affair to a blessed
termination.

In showing us the nave of the church, he whispered
to me that Bonaparte had designed to have his statue
placed there, with an intention that it should have been
worshipped. When I remarked that I had been induced
to believe Bonaparte had restored the due observance
of religion ; he replied, " He only meant to make one after
his own fashion." " *Il avoit l'intention d'en faire une à
sa mode.*" Monsieur Chevalier's feelings lay on the other
side of the question, I saw ; and perhaps they misled his
judgment ; but certainly all the reflecting and elder part

of the community seem to partake his sentiments on this subject. After gazing at the church, its cupola, and its vaults, which latter are particularly fine, and contain the tombs, or, I believe, rather the *cenotaphs*, of Rousseau and Voltaire—for, as to the former, I heard Monsieur Chevalier say, that some of his remains were at [Ermenonville], now the country house of Monsieur de G[irardi]n—we proceeded to the Jardin des Plantes. I regretted not seeing the interior of a church called St. Etienne, close to St. Genevieve. Its exterior is beautiful : it is of no regular architecture, but it possesses that species of beauty which excites the imagination, and awakens interest. The extreme heat of the weather, the thermometer being at eighty-three, together with the quantity of sights I wanted to see, and the number of things I had to do in the space of twenty-four hours, hurried me away to the Jardin des Plantes. As I do not understand botany, and saw no beautiful flowers, I was disappointed, and did not remain there long.

Tuesday, 26th.—Monsieur Delessert took me to the atelier of a Monsieur Gérard, the person who is reckoned the finest artist in Paris. We were shown into a room in which were full-length portraits of the Emperor of Russia, of Bernadotte, of Murat, king of Naples, and a composition of Cupid and Psyche ; this last was very beautiful, and yet I thought there was a stiffness in it, a look of something not natural. There were many other pictures, but one is always hurried on these occasions, and as I was told it was the greatest possible favour to be received by Monsieur Gérard, and as Madame came and made us a visit, I was forced to employ that time in civility which I would rather have given to observation.

I asked Madame Gérard if there was no picture of Bonaparte ; and after a little demur I was shown into a small room, where the great Monsieur Gérard was himself painting. He was very polite, and showed me two half-length portraits of Bonaparte, which I think must be like : the one meagre and keen, a famished face, in pursuit of conquest ; the other, bloated and surfeited by conquest and power—both handsome, and the eyes of both miraculous. Monsieur Gérard is a little man, with a sharp, intelligent countenance. I was pleased to have seen this atelier, it being that of the best modern French painter. Monsieur Delessert is imbued with an idea of Bonaparte's greatness, which does not admit of his judging him with an unprejudiced mind.

I received several letters from England to-day. Mrs. [——] says, " The Princess Charlotte went with a heavy heart, I hear, yesterday to Cranford Lodge, (I think that is the name of the place,) Windsor Park. She has, of all her friends, only been allowed to see Miss Mercer.* Miss Knight has not been suffered to return to her. The courtiers say all is made up, but no one believes them ; how can they, while she is *a state prisoner ?* The R[awdon]s are going abroad. Mrs. R[awdon] wrote to Lady Ilchester to propose that pretty Bessy might pay her duty to Her Royal Highness before she went, but was coldly answered that she had communicated the letter to Princess Charlotte, who was just setting out for Windsor. This sad affair cannot come before Parliament, it is said, as the jurisdiction of a father is by our laws absolute till the child is of age, that is, one-and-twenty—though at eighteen the heir of the crown, as successor, may reign. Lord Stewart (Lord Castlereagh's brother) is named ambassador to Vienna. The Princess of Wales means soon to go to Worthing.

I am sorry to find, and so are all her friends, that Mrs. Thompson † is still determined to go into Yorkshire, and

* Afterwards Madame de Flahault.
† Mrs. Thompson is supposed to mean the Princess of Wales ; and Yorkshire—the Continent. [Original note.]

particularly as her son sees this in the light we do, and talks most wisely on the subject ; but, being a widow, she must do as she likes. Some circumstances too I heard from her maitre d'hotel, that I shall communicate another time to you.

Thursday, 28th, Paris.—I dined with Lady Westmoreland. There were present Sir R[obert] W[ilson], Mr. Craven, and Mr. J[——]. It was a very amusing party ; it never can fail to be so where Lady Westmoreland is.

I received another letter to-day from Mrs. [——], telling me,

The Duke of [Sussex], in the House of Lords, Tuesday last, asked some curious questions relative to the sort of confinement the Princess Charlotte is now under—Whether she was allowed communication with her friends and connexions ? Whether she was allowed the liberty of writing to her friends, &c. ? Whether the recommendation was given to Her Royal Highness last year for sea bathing, which is understood to have been given this ? Whether there is any intention of providing Her Royal Highness a suitable situation ? These questions were stated simply, without further remarks, nearly as shortly as I have set them down. Lord Liverpool and the Chancellor were much displeased at His Royal Highness, made loud speeches, but did not answer the questions.

The Royal Duke then announced a future motion on the subject, but, not having again appeared in the House, as it was expected he would, it is shrewdly suggested that *a fit of asthma*, of which he now complains, has been brought on by a sharp letter, sent to him by Lord Liverpool by the Regent's order. I believe that for the present the subject will drop, for it is thought that it is not one on which Parliament is competent to interfere.

A letter from London informs me

The fête on Thursday last at Carlton House went off uncommonly well. The round temporary building was so large, and the rooms issuing from it so numerous, that in

spite of numbers there was no crowd.   The fête was expressly
given in honour of the Duke of Wellington, whom I saw there,
and for the first time.   He is, as I have always heard, well-
looking, soldier-like, natural, and pleasing in his manner—
so he appeared to me as I stood near him, and saw him talk
to those about him.   Mr. Thompson, who of course was
there, it was remarked, did not seem in the best of humours.
The fireworks, which were to take place to-morrow, are
deferred till Monday week, they say.   Would they were over !
and so all London seems to wish.   Some dreadful accident, it
is feared, will unavoidably take place on that day, whenever
it comes.

Master Thompson,* to my great surprise, actually saw his
mother yesterday.   *Our friend*, to whom she has herself
told it, gave me this information yesterday night : whether
by permission or how, I know not.   It was a leave-taking,
as Mrs. Thompson means to leave London to-morrow.

I must not omit telling you that Sir William Gell is finally
appointed by the Princess of Wales her equerry ; and, if she
goes abroad, the final destination for the winter is Naples.
You think that *Chanticleer's* reign is over—may it be so !

Dijon, *Monday, 1st of August,* 1814.—I had been told
I was to meet with all sorts of dangers and difficulties,
and was advised to go by Voiturier, which has saved me
no expense, and I have been nearly twice as long on the
road as I should, had I posted.   All the stories I heard
in England respecting delays, and dangers, and bad roads,
are perfectly without foundation ; and, considering that
I have passed through a great part of the country which
was overrun by troops, I have hardly seen any marks of
devastation.   The innkeepers say they have *been eaten
up*, and there have been a few bridges broken, and a
very, but very few houses burnt :—having said this, one
has said all.   The harvest seems plentiful ; the people,
indeed, acknowledge it.   The earth everywhere is covered
with abundance, and there is no appearance of want of

* Master Thompson is supposed here to mean Princess Charlotte.
[Original note.]

culture ; this happy soil, indeed, requires but little care to make it yield increase.   From Auxerre, where I slept on Friday last, I passed through a beautiful country— vines, and wood, and corn, rocks crowning the whole, or peeping out in picturesque forms, or hewn into terraces, which contrasted finely with the richness of the surrounding foliage and the waving corn.

All the inns I have been in, compared with those of England, are miserable ; but they are quite good enough for the purposes of animal existence, if not enjoyment. When English persons set out from their own firesides, they must lay aside the cloak of prejudice, or they will be wretched the whole time they are absent.   I find, in the first place, that one must learn to *do everything in public*.   I do not know that I have been one moment alone since I left Calais.   The women walk in and out of one's room, whether one is dressed or not ; and there are very seldom any bars or bolts to stop their progress. They have all, men and women, (the natives I mean,) a kind of familiar politeness, which I think very agreeable. I have talked to every one I have met, and found them generally well-informed, sensible, and civil.   When I say well-informed, I must not include the subject of politics : on this head some of them appear to be comically ignorant, and many seem still afraid to speak their minds in regard to public affairs.

There are evidently two parties in France.   It appears to me, however, that if the government pay the soldiery, which they have not yet done, and devise some mode of employing them, the tide will sink of itself into the old channel.   I received, to-day, a letter from my dear friend [——].   It was a great happiness to me ; for the first week of absence from those we love or like, seems always cruelly long.   Not that I will ever allow I could learn to live without those I love, while a possibility exists of living with them ; but that the *weaning* from any habit adds an additional pang to regret. A letter mitigates this ; and I derived all the comfort from this one which it was calculated to inspire. During the few days I spent in that wonderful city, Paris, I saw more, and did more, than I ever saw or did before in the same given time :— among other things I went to court. Their courts are held of an evening, in compliance with circumstances ; and, out of compliment to the Duchesse D'Angoulême, the ladies wear no gold, or silver, or jewel, but are usually dressed in white crape or silk, with feathers or not, as they choose ; and long trains are the only distinctive mark of full dress they are obliged to wear.

This simplicity in the ladies' attire does not, however, prevent there being an air of grandeur in this court. The magnificent space, the grand entrance to the Tuileries, the staircase, the very simplicity of the women's dress in that magnificent palace, and a certain interest attached to its *cause*, produced a fine spectacle. There were few gentlemen, except those immediately *de service*. Lady Westmoreland was the only English lady. The Duchesse de P[ie]nne is now *the* great lady of Paris : her husband presented Lady Westmoreland, who, as an English lady, was received first.

The King was in an inner room, surrounded by his attendants ; he rose and said, in English, with marks of feeling, that " he should never forget what he owed to England." This touched *us* English people for the moment. The *never forget* is a great word, but one must hope it is a true one. When one ceases to believe in the possibility of truth, one ceases to believe in all that is exalted in human nature.

The women's dress is affectedly simple—white muslin, very short waists, very full petticoats : but the ugliest part of their habiliments is the high chimneys on their hats, which chimneys are covered with feathers and flowers. When fashion is subject to taste, I like it, but when it is despotic and capricious, and subverts all taste, I cannot endure it. To my idea, the more nearly women's dress assimilates to the antique, the more beautiful. Our climate and manners always demand some difference, but at present the French discard all resemblance whatever to what one has been taught to think beautiful, time immemorial. The part men take in this subject is comical : they seem to think, that from the law of their country-women there is no appeal.

Every article of living is as dear here as in England, when one passes through ; but certainly one might *live* at Paris more cheaply than in London ; and there are all the same pleasures of dissipation to be had, at a more easy rate, and in a more perfect and varied style.

Scheron, August 6th, 1814, *Geneva.*—I came from Morey, thirty miles from this, over a new road made by Bonaparte. It is magnificent, both as a work, and as affording the grandest view of the mountain scenery that it is possible to conceive ; but the whole way is a series of frightful precipices, and ascents and descents, which make one giddy even in recollection. At a place called La Fossil, about fourteen miles from hence, the first view of Mont Blanc, the Lake of Geneva, and the valley, bursts upon the sight. Descriptions of scenery seldom or ever convey the emotion the scenes themselves excite ; but it is difficult not to attempt imparting some portion of the feelings which they inspire.

This hotel is all cleanliness and comfort,—the beautiful lake and its appendages in sight of the windows. I get up every now and then from my table to look at Mont Blanc, as if it was going to run away, and that I should never see it again. It is at this moment glittering in the sun, and not one cloud rests upon its surface. It is difficult to say which is the most blue, the sky or the water, but I rather think the latter.

I am already acquainted with many persons. I have had an agreeable surprise in finding Sir H. and Lady Davy established here. I thought we never should have done asking and answering questions. Lady D. professed herself delighted to renew her acquaintance with me. I hope she is sincere, it is so pleasant to believe in such demonstrations—so much the contrary to doubt them, that it is not worth while to be an infidel. Sismond was there, author of the *Ripubliques Italiennes*, &c. &c., Monsieur De Schlegel, an author likewise, Monsieur Dumont, a Monsieur De Constant, cousin of *the* Constant, Monsieur De Rocca, and an Englishman, a Mr. Cumming, who, in point of looks, was the flower of the flock. The dinner was very agreeable—all *tumbled on* the table first, and afterwards down our throats, with an *abandon*, as to the manner of both, truly *Staelish*. It suits me vastly ; nevertheless, I cannot help seeing the *delatrement* of the *chateau*, the incongruity of the establishments, and the hideousness of *the philosophers*. I feel as if I were committing an insincerity in writing thus of a society among whom I was excessively amused and delighted, and to whom I did my best to be agreeable in my turn.

There are millions of Madame Casenoves here, of the present and last centuries ; one, the old one, very agreeable and clever. She hates *The Stael*, and knows all the *qui pro quos* of the day ; and is so cross ; it is mighty amusing to converse with her. The *ci-devant* Empress, Marie Louise, is constantly going backwards and forwards from Paris—yes, from Paris to the *Bavis Daix*, and she always sleeps here. About a fortnight ago she was here, with all her chamberlains, and the Lord knows what train of servants, ladies, &c. &c. The day before yesterday, she was here again, without any attendants save four men and one lady. I was close to her in the garden, and had not a little English *mauvaise honte* come over me, I might have talked to her, for I was not obliged to know who she was. The consciousness that I did know, prevented me taking this liberty.

I hear that this journeying of her majesty bodes no good. King Joseph of Spain, as he calls himself, wrote his majestyship, in the book in which travellers write their names at this inn : he dined at Copet. Comical enough, somebody said, all *the family* would dine there soon—but that is only a joke.

Geneva, *15th August*, 1814.—I received a letter to-day from Keppel Craven, in which he says,

All my happy plans, and the hopes of seeing you, are annihilated by Mrs. Thompson's sudden departure from England, and her requiring my attendance, which, after all her kindness, I cannot refuse ; so here you see me on the eve of setting off for Brunswick, through the worst and most uninteresting part of all Germany. I have been threatened with this event for this week past, which has been the reason of my delaying my departure, nor could I write till I was certain of my plans.

I have only received hurried scraps from Gell, who, I fancy, has had the trouble of the preparations on his shoulders, and, from these very unsatisfactory accounts, I can only make out that Lady Elizabeth Forbes and Lady Charlotte Lindsay, are in waiting, but the latter leaves the household at Bruns-wick, as does Mr. St. Leger. Gell and Dr. Holland continue, and then begin my functions, which, however, I have only promised for two months, as my mother wants me after that period, and it is impossible for me to say, with any degree of certainty, whether I can be a *permanent* chamberlain or not. I had at one time hoped I should be allowed to take my way through Switzerland, as the stay at Brunswick will be short ; and there is a project of going on to Italy, through the said Switzerland ; so I must make haste ; for by Gell's last letter, dated the 4th of this month, they were to sail on the 8th—that is, yesterday.

All this has agitated and annoyed me ; the more so as I consider the step injudicious in a *political* sense. But we must make the best of it. My sister, Lady Sefton, her husband, and family, have been here nearly a week, and this delay has enabled me to see them a little, which is some consolation.

Ever yours, most sincerely,

R. K. C.

August 16th, 1814.—I received letters from England ; one from Mrs. [——], who tells me the following news about the Princess, dated the 8th of August.

Her Royal Highness embarked, this morning, on board the Jason frigate, with all due honours—her suite, Lady Charlotte Lindsay, Lady E. Forbes, Sir W. Gell, Dr. Holland, Mr. St. Leger, &c. &c. The Princess, just before she went, wrote a letter to Canning, in which she said, that if any machinations were going on against her, were it but a *whisper*, a short time only would elapse before she might again set her foot on English ground, to defend her innocence. Canning referred this letter to Lord Liverpool, and the latter to the Prince, (as they said,) and the answer was mild—how sincere I know not—" no such thing intended," &c. &c. This may perhaps be called spirited, but I regret her thus quitting the advice of those who really wish her well, and throwing herself into the hands of others, who act only from interested views, and would be ready at any time to sacrifice her. Canning has just been named to Lisbon. Think, after all that has passed between him and Lord Castlereagh, of his serving under him ! !—for this is the case, Lord Castlereagh being minister for the department, and (nominally) naming the different foreign ministers. What can one think of Canning after this ? It is thought, too, that the whole has been an understanding, and that Canning has obtained his post in consequence of having persuaded the Princess to go abroad. That it was her wish and project we well knew, but I do think he has encouraged her in the measure, and made things easy to her—then makes a merit of this to the higher power. Be this as it may, I much (as I before said) regret the step she has taken, and fear that she may have cause to repent it in future. She received a very kind letter from her daughter just before she embarked. Poor Princess Charlotte ! she is still a sort of prisoner—has appeared at none of the fêtes that have taken place, not even at Frogmore, where the Queen (Charlotte) gave a jubilee on the Prince's birth-day; and, what is worse, she is, poor thing, really ill, and suffering from her knee. Baillie now attends her, and it is said she is ordered to the sea-side. The Prince yesterday looked better than I have seen him for years;—a new sort of head-dress, and dark clothes, with the golden fleece round his neck, which so became him, that I was in admiration of his beauty, &c. &c.

A Letter from the PRINCESS OF WALES.*

(Dated) *August 7th,* 1814.

I am on the eve of sailing, which will be to-morrow evening, as the wind is favourable, in the Jason frigate. Another brig is to carry all our luggage, baggage, and carriages. Captain King represents Jason himself. If the present wind is favourable to land at * * * [illegible] continues, we shall arrive by the 12th of August; by the 15th I hope to be at Brunswick. I intend only to remain in my native country ten or fifteen days, after which I shall set out immediately for Switzerland in the beginning of September. My intention still is to remain at Naples for the winter, but in case disturbances should commence there against Murat, of course I should prefer to be the winter at Rome or Florence—but we must not anticipate misfortunes before they really arrive, for which reason I trust for the best, to be able to be at Naples, &c. &c.

P.S. The second Prince of Orange is just arrived in London: he is of the same age as my daughter, and I should not be much surprised that this marriage would take place soon, as Princess Charlotte would certainly not be under obligation to leave her native country, [he] being not the successor, only the grandson.

Monday, 12th of September, 1814.—I have now passed some weeks at Geneva. There is a picked society of intelligent and superior persons resident in or travelling through the country; and yet, after the great stage of life in London, Paris, or Vienna, it requires to let off the

* N.B. All letters are given verbatim; the phraseology and orthography are often extraordinary. [Original note.]

gas of excitement before one can sober oneself down to the narrowed circle of "*L'imperceptible Genève*,"—one of its own citizens designated this City of the Lake. The locking up of the gates at ten o'clock, the mounting guard, and the consequential minutiæ of magistrates, who, like masters of the ceremonies at watering-places, officiate in much the same trivial points of etiquette, incline one to laugh at this Lilliput republic. And yet there is something in the good faith of its principal members, their great sincerity in what they deem the preservation of their laws and liberties, which makes one love, while one laughs at them. Not so as regards their literary and scientific republic. In no one spot, perhaps, are there more distingushed men gathered into one small focus, all nobly contending for the advancement of intellectual greatness : Schlegel, Sismondi, Pictet, De Saussure, and, at this moment, the children of other climes, but in brotherhood of tastes of the same stock, Sir James Mackintosh, Sir Humphrey Davy, &c. &c., are all congregated in one brilliant galaxy. There are many others, also, of justly famed celebrity, in the circles of Geneva ; but Madame De Stael's name, like Aaron's rod, must swallow up the rest ; and all lesser lights, before hers, will " pale their ineffectual fires.   Whatever envy and detraction may say, she is not only the most wonderful woman, but the most wonderful of human beings, that ever shed lustre on the age in which she lived. Among her own dependents, and in her own chateau, she is a sovereign who is loved, beyond all question, with a devotion that does honour to those who pay, and to her who receives the homage.

At this moment, many English are here : Lady W[estmoreland], who has a great charm about her, but never rests herself, and never lets any one else rest in her presence. As for myself, though always happy to be of use, I confess her commands, in the way of attendance, are sometimes more frequent than I can well obey; but to-day it was convenient to me to be of her party. There are some persons whom one cannot help making a convenience of.   We drove to a campagne of Madame R[——]'s about three miles from Les Grottes.   A small road leads to a terrace, from whence the beautiful scenery of the lake, its opposite shores, and the Alps, rise in all their grandeur; and the ground on either side of the Leman is finely moulded and diversified in gentle un-dulations, where vines and pasture lands intermingle their rich treasures. I know not why this scenery, more than any other, oppresses the heart with a sense of its own insufficiency to procure happiness. Is it that, calculated as it is to excite the feelings to rapture, the contrast with the dull vacuity that reigns within, is more forcibly brought to view, and renders the burthen of lonely existence weightier ? Perhaps it is—for since I came here, my own cruel fate seems more vividly represented to my contemplation; the long years of " fair occasion gone for ever by," which have blighted my youth, and will scathe my age. Madame De Stael is going, where her wishes have long been her *avant couriers*—going to Paris, the scene of her triumphs, of her ambition, of her fame; but how long will she be allowed to remain there ?—two suns cannot shine in one hemisphere.

Geneva, 14th of September.—The fine arts are at a low ebb here—here, where Nature puts forth all her majesty. This seems strange; but I believe that the very mag-nitude and sublimity of this part of creation are opposed to the imitative power of the pencil. Landscape painting is scarcely practised, except those hard, topographical views, unworthy the name of art, though it must be allowed they are faithful portraits of the features of the country; but then, so is a skeleton a faithful representative of the human form. The immense scale of the features of this country, and the abrupt contrast of eternal snow with the vivid green of the lower grounds, are not adapted to a picture, however sublime in themselves. Each particular member of the landscape takes up too huge a portion of the canvas. Besides, there may be an excitement which is favourable to the development of talent, and there may be an overwhelming sense of greatness which is the reverse. Perhaps this is the reason why there are so few artists of any celebrity in this country.

I met several very distinguished men at Lady Davy's; but the same persons are not the same in different places and under different influences; and whenever Sir H. Davy presides in a society, as usual, nothing amalgamates. It is strange, that a person so gifted, and one so justly celebrated, should so misunderstand in what his strength consists. It is very remarkable how much pleasanter all one's British acquaintance are on the Continent than at home, with the exception of a few growlers. Lord Lucan and Lord B[——] were instances of this. I observed, however, a great coldness between Lord Lucan and Lady C. Campbell. I asked her ladyship the reason of it, and she said, " It is perfectly true that he does avoid me ;—but why I know not. I will ascertain the reason, however, and if I find it out, I will tell you." Afterwards she told me, that he had only avoided her, in order not to be drawn into the society of Her Royal Highness the Princess of Wales, whose arrival here is daily expected. The reason he gave for his determination to have no further intercourse with Her Royal Highness was, that during the reign of his favour, at Kensington, she confided everything to him, and told him all she meant to do ; and that, having asked his advice upon the subject of these intentions, he had honestly replied, " By heavens, madam, since you do me the honour to ask my advice, it is my duty to tell your Royal Highness

I   S

that you will be sent a sort of state prisoner to Holyrood House,* if you act in such a manner; and you will not only ruin your own fortunes, but those of every person who may live in intimacy with you." To this she replied, that she had determined so to conduct herself. " Then, madam, I had better withdraw as soon as possible from the honour of your Royal Highness's society. I shall advise every one of my friends to do so likewise; since all those persons who are much at Kensington, must be implicated in the evil you are drawing down upon yourself." " Well," replied Her Royal Highness, laughing, " I see how it is—*you* are afraid. I am never afraid; but at all events, come to me to-morrow morning, to take your eternal adieu." " I obeyed," continued he; " she repeated her determinations—once again I reasoned with her—I told her Lady O[xfor]d was not a person with whom she ought to associate—she denied associating with her, and while in the very act of denying this, Philip, the German footman, came in, and asked whether Lady O[xfor]d was to wait in the drawing-room, or come another time. This detection of a falsehood made me think the sooner *je retirais mon épingle du jeu*, the better."

When Lady Charlotte told me this story, I had not a word to say. Alas! poor Princess, how often she has, as it were, cut her own throat.

Extract of a Letter from SIR WILLIAM GELL.

BRUNSWICK, *August 23d*, 1814.

Do not expect to have a very long letter from me: all the time I have must be devoted to business. We set out next Monday, and get to Cassel, if we can, next day, thence by Frankfort and Basle, to Geneva. Now you are to desire [——] to get a convenient situation to live in.—The Princess,

---

* Since 1746 Holyrood House had not been occupied, except, after 1796, by "Monsieur" the Comte d'Artois, brother of the exiled Louis XVIII. of France, who was allowed to reside there.

MARIE LOUISE
From a painting by an unknown artist (Gerard?)

Willikin * and Edwardind, Lady Elizabeth Forbes, Keppel Craven, and myself; Dr. Holland, Hesse Carrington, Hieronymus, the Abbé Sicard, Charles the footman, Crackler, Doctor Holland's servant,—Lodgings for all these, and, perhaps three ladies—don't know—a small party; but do not fail and write to Basle to us, *Poste restante*. Next, [——] is to look out for the best of all possible trust-worthy good maids for the Princess, as Miss Leitzen is taken ill; the maid is to be on trial at first.† Also a very good man-cook, &c. &c.

Your most sincere and affectionate,

W. GELL.

GENEVA, *Oct.* 1814.

The Princess only remained here from Monday till Thursday. I felt in that short space of time how very ill it would have agreed with *me* to have remained longer in her society. As to her mode of proceeding, (as I am really her friend,) it distressed me greatly: she was dressed, or rather undressed, most injudiciously. The natives were, as she would have expressed it, "all over shock." The suite who travel with her declare openly they fear they shall not be able to go on with her; not so much from wrong doings as from ridiculous ones. When the party were at Berne, the *ci-devant* Empress Marie Louise was there, and invited the whole party to dinner. Accordingly they went, and were received in great state. Gold plate, bearing the imperial arms, and everything *de suite*, covered the board. To sum up the whole of that extraordinary meeting, the Princess and Marie Louise sang a duet together!! That was an event of the 18th century worthy of being recorded. I wonder what Marie Louise thought of the Princess's singing? She must have been astonished.

The Archduchess Anne has a small chateau near Berne, and she also invited the Princess and her suite, who were

---

* Willikin, lately in a mad-house, the boy, concerning whom the Princess once said to a person who was giving her good advice, and informing her that evil-minded people persisted in calling him her son—"Prove it and he shall be your King." A noble speech, supposing the accusation to be false, and a clever denial, if it was true. [Original note.]

† This maid was Miss Dumont, who made such a conspicuous figure afterwards in the Queen's trial. [Original note.]

one and all delighted with the Duchess Anne, and spoke of her in the highest terms: but the Princess seems satisfied with nothing, and has a spirit of restlessness in her which belongs to the unhappy and unprincipled. Whilst she sojourned at Geneva, letters came to her Royal Highness, recommending her, in the strongest terms, not to go to Naples. Whether she will fix her residence at Florence, or Rome, seems now to be the question.

Extract of a Letter from London :—

The Princess, as you will perhaps have heard, is actually at Naples, in spite of admonitions against the measure from Lord Liverpool; and it is, into the bargain, extremely probable that there may be very serious troubles there, as the present King, Murat, seems not at all disposed to give way to the command to depart, and has already assembled sixty thousand men for his defence, and declares that he will not be sent to Elba. I believe this to be much the state of the case. The Princess will, I dare say, (but not for these two or three months to come,) have a ship sent by government, to be at her command in the Mediterranean, into which, if molested by land, she may intrepidly throw herself and escape. A house is taken for six months, at four hundred pounds,—the journey has cost eight thousand pounds, besides two thousand pounds at setting out, and other expenses; in all ten thousand pounds. The Princess writes to her man of business:—" The loss of exchange of money is quite horrible, and I have been a great loser by it; in short, I am, at this present moment, very poor indeed; but do not say a word of it to Liverpool."

I am in great haste, as I am to give a rendezvous to the Holy Pope. Little else has been talked of here but the court-martial of Colonel Quentin; and for a wonder it is a subject on which there is but one opinion,—that the officers have been most harshly used, and favour shown where least it ought to have been shown. The Princess ought to beware; she is watched by her husband; the name of a suspected person is also known: that, and a description of his person, have been sent to her by a real friend.

Affectionately yours,

A. S. D.

Wednesday, 15th.

Went with Louis Neckar to Coligny; the weather lighting up the scenery in all its splendour of beauty. We glided across the lake to Coligny without feeling that the boat moved. Above, around, below, all was beauty and sunshine; but, within—the gloom was not dispelled; I felt more powerfully that excitement is only pleasurable to the happy. I have often said, save me from monotony; but now I say, that it is better the current of life should stagnate, than to be aroused to feel all that one might be, and yet that one never can be.

When we landed on the Savoy shore, we clambered up a steep terrace covered with walnut trees and vines. Under the foliage of the former trees were seen the blue lake, the walls of Geneva, and the opposite rugged hills of the Jura, on which a light grey cloud partially rested its transparent folds. Yet all this beauty only made me feel the more utter loneliness. After ascending for some way a steep acclivity, through vineyards, we entered a low door into a park; but it had a poverty-stricken air, which is too often the case with all the beautiful *campagnes* in the neighbourhood of Geneva. Say what one will of poverty, it is an unkindly withering power, that blights the fairest, brightest scene, the most amiable of natures. A few acacias had been planted here for ornament, but they had evidently been neglected. The vineyards only are cultivated with care, because they yield fruits of increase. These were at sufficient distance from the lowly dwelling at Coligny, not to be derogatory to the scene in any of the different seasons of the year. At this season the foliage of the grape is in all its green vigour, and contrasts well with the touches and tints of autumn, which here and there tell of the rigid winter that will soon strip them of their beauty. In the humble cottage (for it is little more) which lies nestled among a bower of trees, lives Madame Neckar (her house being let for necessitous economy). This is the woman of whom Madame de Stael said, " Elle a toutes les qualités qu'on me donne, et toutes les vertus, que je n'ai pas." The world, in doing justice to the candour of this sentiment, must feel inclined to give additional homage to the eulogist who could thus nobly bestow such a meed of praise on one of the very few women who might well excite her envy. Madame Neckar is like all the women here, careless in her person, except on gala days ; careless to an unpleasant state of neglect. I should not like any friend of mine to appear attired as they are in the morning,—without stays, slipshod, *en papillottes*, or un-combed. Finery for company, slovenliness for domestic life, must always create disgust ; and the more so, as it is difficult not to annex some moral defect to this culpable neglect of outward respect to their families and intimates.

In despite of this custom, which Madame Neckar has not departed from, she is exceedingly pleasing. Her countenance is expressive of goodness and truth, and there is a composed kindness of manner, which inspires the beholder with confidence in its sincerity, and imparts the tranquillity it feels. I was captivated by this charm-ing woman, and endeavoured to turn the subject upon literary topics. Louis Neckar said I was the first stranger to whom his mother had ever avowed that she was an authoress. I could not help, as she spoke often and with the most feeling praise, of Madame De Stael, contrasting these two extraordinary women together. Madame Neckar, in the retirement of comparative solitude, prosecuting studies of a grave cast, and obtaining fame, without appearing to do the one, or court the other, —hiding her talents beneath the dull duties of household cares, and obtaining praise unsought, and apparently indifferent to her, when obtained. Madame De Stael, on the contrary, blazing unrivalled in the splendour of that brilliant intellect of which not even envy denies her the possession ; feeling that life, without the excitement of public applause, is tasteless, and that action, not contemplation, is the great good of existence.

I remained in agreeable conversation with Madame Neckar till another visitor came : and, as she is rather deaf, I thought the interest of our communion would fail if discourse became general, so I took my leave, determined to prosecute my acquaintance with so rare and so distinguished a woman.

Monsieur de Rocca * came to pay me a visit. There is an open kindliness of manner in this young man which is peculiarly pleasing. He is writing his campaign in Spain. Everybody writes at Geneva—the air is infectious of scribbling—Madame de Stael's pen inoculates all the inhabitants ; but unfortunately very few of the infected take the disease favourably.

Thursday.—I was informed Her Royal Highness the Princess of Wales had arrived. I was electrified—was it with pain or pleasure ? " Oh, that I had wings like a dove ! " My poor friend, Lady [Charlotte Campbell], was called upon to get up a ball directly, in honour of Her Royal Highness, and was obliged to drive all over the town and country to beat up for recruits ; which was not an easy matter ; so many of the English travellers wished to avoid knowing her, and somehow the natives had no mind to be troubled with royalty ; so that poor Lady [Charlotte Campbell] was obliged to take many rebuffs, and found it very difficult to get together personages sufficient to make up a ball. At last, however, this great feat was effected,

* This was the person who afterwards became so noticed as being the husband-lover of Madame de Stael. He was handsome, and had something chivalresque in his demeanour, which was calculated to turn a woman's head ; but he was not a man of any great superiority of intellect. [Original note.]

and, thanks to three Germans, who were a host in themselves, the ball took place. But what was my horror when I beheld the poor Princess enter, dressed *en Venus*, or rather not dressed, further than the waist. I was, as she used to say herself, "all over shock." A more injudicious choice of costume could not be adopted. She waltzed the whole night, with pertinacious obstinacy ; and amongst others whom she honoured with her hand upon this occasion, was Sismondi. These two large figures turning round together were quite miraculous. As I really entertained a friendship for the Princess, I was unfeignedly grieved to see her make herself so utterly ridiculous. If this is a commencement only of what she intends to perform in the South, she will indeed lose herself entirely. The next day we were invited to a dinner given by Her Royal Highness at Secheron. It might have been very agreeable, but the Princess insisted upon undue homage from two of her attendants, and made herself so ridiculous, that I determined to set off from Geneva directly, and not witness her degradation.

After dinner she took me aside, and entered upon a wild plan of what she intended to do, and where she meant to go ; then talked of giving honours and orders to certain of her suite, and made such a confusion respecting the geographical arrangements of her route, that it was enough, as she used herself to say on other occasions, " to die for laugh." Fortunately for me, a very few days terminated her career at Geneva, and she prosecuted her journey without having an idea, in fact, where she was going to, or how she should be received at any of the courts where she purposed to reside. It was really as if, in leaving England, she had cast off all common sense and conduct, and had gone suddenly mad. It was a fortunate day for me which saw her depart, and I thought it would be my own fault if she caught me again in a hurry.

Extract of a Letter from LADY [——].

After many months absence I still feel sure of your interest, because I know your own steady and affectionate nature; and, also, I think, where the sentiment of regard and admiration is very strong on one side, some reciprocity may be fairly claimed, though inadequate merit cannot boldly ask as large a portion of partiality.

I have travelled the enchanting country of Italy, to come to this delightful place, for two months of repose and tranquil enjoyment. We have seen many fine cities, full (in spite of French spoliation) of treasures and scenery which defy description, or, indeed, imagination. The union of Alpine sublimity with the charms and abundant vegetation and colouring of Italy, renders the road by the Simplon delicious, and the Lago Maggiore exceeds every other I have ever visited. The road is itself one of the worthy works of Bonaparte; and, in the hatred of tyranny, and the indignation felt for the injuries of Europe, there is still some praise due to the greatest undertaking of modern times. It is executed as excellently as it is boldly imagined; and in despite of the most inconceivable obstacles, presents as much convenience to the traveller, as beauty to the lover of nature's most sublime features.

I have been fortunate in witnessing many singular events and circumstances since we parted; and Paris on the eve of its change of government—Florence just freed from its unpopular Duchess of Tuscany—Naples not very sure of itself—and Rome, in the days of fanatic and extatic bliss, for the return of the Pope,—have shown me the varieties of human events, and the difference of national character. An excavation at Pompeii, with a royal breakfast from the Queen, who is very pretty, and was extremely gracious, formed a very curious and interesting day. The marks of wheels remaining in the streets, and, in the shops, some of the very utensils of their destination, scarcely (though Vesuvius stared one in the face) permitted the belief, that the Town had been so buried.

Two interesting pilgrimages, two following days, were to the summit of Mount Vesuvius, which is, perhaps, the object in nature that has most excited astonishment in my travels;

and our second expedition, which included a night, showed it to me in most uncommon and dread magnificence.

Rome requires no adventitious circumstances to render it eminently delightful; but, certainly, the prostrations, hysterics, screams, &c., which preceded and followed every appearance of the Pope, on his return, was a sight very extraordinary to a reasonable protestant. We mean to spend the winter in that city, where remembrances the most awakening rush on the mind in every ruin, and where the success of genius has immortalised the chisel and pencil, not of solitary instances of excellence, but of numerous artists. I never liked any place so much, yet it is rather with the dead than the living that one lives; and, of the latter, Canova alone won my friendship and esteem. I except the foreigners, who invariably do the honours of Rome to the last comers.

The strange change of events carries the tide of kings and queens strangely apart from their former territories. It is believed Marie Louise is coming to this neighbourhood, to some mineral baths; and three of Bonaparte's brothers are already fixed in this country. It is painful to see how even friendly war destroys a country; for Genoa, with her christian liberators, offers a sad scene of houses despoiled, fortunes injured, and injustice sanctioned. The Austrians of course lived free, and the commander-in-chief rather shabbily sent in the account of his baths and tooth-brushes, to be defrayed by the municipality. The having taken fifty-five pieces of the cannon of Genoa, which even the greedy and rapacious French never touched, is a more serious and deeper insult.

I am so fond of Italy, which, notwithstanding the indolence of her people, oppressed by a superstitious creed, is full of the seeds of power and greatness, that I grieve that her patrimony of fine works of art is allowed to remain where, certainly, it was taken by the violence of one whom the French now disclaim; and therefore it is pitiful to retain the prey when they reject the spoiler.

In all public events, England is my chief object, and, indeed, the proud feeling of English birthright becomes a passion when other countries and people have been seen. But why is England sanctioning unjust conditions relative to slavery, and allowing your Royal Friend to be treated with indignity,—not protecting the sacred rights of a friend and a stranger, and the national rights due to our Princess of Wales ? If you can present my remembrance to Her Royal Highness, convey, I pray, my good wishes for her health, and for all that she can claim of regard and consideration from the English people as her due, both as our Princess of Wales, and the mother of our future Queen ;—nor, indeed, can she disclaim, or we forget, the niece of our unhappy sovereign, &c.

Extract of a Letter from Brocket Hall.

October 17, 1814.

If you have had our gracious Princess with you, we have our gracious Prince here at this moment with us.   Nothing can be more agreeable and good-natured than he is.*   In excellent spirits, and looking in health and beauty, better than I have seen him for years.   He wears a certain new sort of darkish-coloured wig, without powder, that particularly becomes him.   He asked me this morning if I was going abroad.   I said, yes, that I was going in the early spring to you.

" To *Nice*,"—he immediately added, and I of course replied, " Yes, Sir, to Nice," and no more was said : but the tone of his voice was *complacent*.—Everything, be assured, that in any way, decent or indecent, relates to the Princess, is known here.   Of that I had a proof, among many others, in Lady Salisbury, who dined here, and mentioned the dress of the attendant cavaliers, and (which I was sorry for) quoted you for the intelligence ; but did not mention her authority —I mean to whom your letter was addressed : she said, you had represented the traveller as in the dress of Henri Quatre. This *not* before the Prince, as you may guess.   D.

* Besides the prestige which certainly attends on exalted station, there is no doubt that few persons ever have possessed, or ever can possess, greater fascination than did the then Prince of Wales.   He had the faculty of persuading all on whom he chose to exercise the spell or charm, that he took a cordial interest in *their* interests ; and, without allowing the person whom he so addressed to forget he was a prince, he exalted him to a level with himself, as a friend.   If this enchanting power had always stood the test of time and circumstances, it would have been not only a grace of manner, but a quality of character, that would have commanded respect, as well as ensured the affections of all who came within the sphere of his private society. [Original note.]

October 18th, 1814.—I left Geneva yesterday with regret; for its inhabitants are excellent people, and the most distinguished among them showed me every attention; almost more than enough; but this is only the ingratitude of a certain fastidiousness which I cannot wholly conquer.—Sir H. D[——] and his Lady were the most agreeable of my country-people staying there at the same time as myself. I cannot help fearing that *all is not comfortable in that ménage*. I lament that they are a hindrance to each other in their respective pursuits; but marriage is a terrific touchstone to happiness. The person for whom I felt most friendship, more even than the shortness of our acquaintance warranted, was an Admiral Hotham.* He is a delightful person, brave and gentle, and just what an Admiral ought to be. He is gone, however, to his wife and children, who are in England, and there is an end of the pleasure his society afforded me.

The Princess of Wales's visit was brief but *troublesome*. I am ashamed of the word; for she came as kindly disposed towards me as ever, and I was gratified that Her Royal Highness received a kind reception from the Genevese; but she left an unpleasant impression on their minds, by her indjudicious conduct during the few days she remained amongst them. Sir W. Gell and the two protégés, *Willikins* and *Edwardines*, were in her suite; also Mr. Craven, Mr. Hesse, Dr. Holland, Lady Elizabeth Forbes, and three ladies, Brunswickers, picked up of course on the road at the same moment when the ci-devant Empress, Marie Louise, was living at Secheron, and the whole Canton in commotion, with the wandering royalties.

* Sir William Hotham, K.C.B. (1772–1848), Admiral of the red, *m.* first, Anne, daughter of Sir Edward Jeynes, Knt.; secondly, Mrs. Pettiward. The original note says of this marriage: " their tempers disagreeing, they have separated," although she was " a lady of fortune."

To-day I received a letter from Keppel Craven, dated

NAPLES, *Sunday Night.*

I am sorry to say, dear [——], that I began with breaking through the injunctions contained in your letter, by reading it aloud, and have continued so doing after the remonstrance ; but then I was tête-à-tête with Gell, over our tea, which we have every evening like two washerwomen, and am ashamed to say, that we prefer it to the ices that were handing about in the royal box we had quitted half an hour before, and in which we had left more embroidered uniforms than ever you beheld even in your course down the Rhone.

If you expect me to give you an account of our journies, you must be disappointed ; for it is a hard task, and on retrospection it only appears like a bad dream of princes and post horses. We have been honoured and feasted to death, and these honours and feasts have come in a progressive ratio, so as to leave nothing after this place that can seem palatable ; but luckily we cannot go further. Yet, if you must have a bird's eye-view of our pilgrimage of sovereignty, I will begin with the Lago Maggiore, which, in point of beauty, far surpassed all our other visitations, though the palace was only a count's. Ma Tante Aurore * would have been in her glory ; we had honours by proxy, but in some respects they were the more satisfactory on that very account. Marshal Count Bellegarde did more probably than any sovereign could have done. At Modena a new duke and duchess sent us sweetmeats, and invited our Lady to a concert, which was all they could afford. At Florence another duke visited and was visited, but lived in too retired a way to be very entertaining ; however, we made up for that, by our own parties, which were exceedingly brilliant, and well attended by the nobility of the place, as well as all the English who were there.

We there saw a famous had-been Roman beauty, the Duchess of Lanti,† who sings far better than any titled person I ever heard. On entering the Papal territory, we flourished more than ever—never were allowed to pay for the post-horses, or to lodge at an inn, and, on arriving at Rome, were overrun with cardinals and prelates. I should have been

* Lady Charlotte Campbell, who was painted as " Aurora."
† Mistress of Prince Borghese.

well satisfied with these papishes, but we were moreover oppressed by a variety of broken-down kings and queens ; those of Spain and Etruria, a certain Duchess of Challais, of the Sardinian dynasty, Prince Frederick, of Saxe Gotha, and, I fancy, many more. Judge if we had time to see antiquities or museums, in four days, which we spent in this capital of the christian world. 'Tis true, the antiquities are very much in the style of the above-mentioned potentates— extremely mutilated remains of structures which had never been worth admiring. Not so the Pope, whom I might compare with his own church of St. Peter, as being the only thing worth seeing in Rome. We all kissed his hand, and he sent us some holy beads, and gave Her Royal Highness a firework and horse-race at Terracina, where his dominions terminate. And now you are arrived at the acmé of our glory,—a whole regiment of cavalry to escort us, the Maréchal de la Cour and sundry other great personages, sent to meet us at Mola di Gaeta, as well as the king's cooks, china, beds, &c. His own self, the next day at Areosa, one stage from this town, in a light blue and gold square coat, which, however, certainly does not look as well as ours, dined with us, or rather we with him, and he brought the Princess with his own hand into the house she occupies.

There were many other honours intended for her, which, in her name, I declined, in an *official document*, directed to the Duke of Gallo, the minister for foreign affairs, and which I suppose will some day or other be quoted in the House of Commons !

The two first days here were very arduousa : a message to the Queen in the morning—then a visit and introduction to her in form, and her return of the same an hour after— then a dinner at court, and a musical party in the evening. The following day devoted to receiving all the officers in the morning, and going to the Opera with their Majesties in their state box ; the theatre illuminated, a guard of honour, eight horses to the carriage, two ladies and a chamberlain appointed to attend : in short, for once Mrs. Thompson was fairly knocked up, and has kept the house ever since, till this day, though not at all ill.

This evening we had all the ladies of the Queen's household presented, and some English, and then went to the Opera, but only privately. We have boxes at all the theatres, and the court equipages, till our own are organised, and these must always have an equerry and page riding on horseback at each door. The magnificence and etiquette of this court are not to be imagined. The King of Naples is not good-looking, though reckoned so, but very good-humoured and civil. His Queen is, in my opinion, pretty, with an extremely good manner, and we are just now very good friends. The Princess's house is in a good situation, but there is not room enough for us all, so Gell and myself lodge out of it, which arrangement is productive of some advantages. We are much happier than we were ; but, for my part, I could not have lasted out three days more of royal travelling ; as I grew tired of all my companions, high and low, and felt that I was become at once ten years older, and what is worse, sixty years crosser ; so, had the Bay of Naples not intervened, I must have eloped.

I wish you were here instead of there, as there are real orange groves without walls, and seas without waves, and skies without clouds, (though we have had pretty severe specimens of rain,) a most magnificent theatre, and the most good-humoured set of people I ever saw, who are inclined to admire us very much. Lady Elizabeth Forbes rides the royal horses, and seems very happy, but she wants a co-adjutor. I can assure you she regards you highly, notwith-standing the deficiency of conversation between you at Geneva ; but you know I never saw you at all there. Lady W[estmorland] was very agreeable at Florence, but attributed her exit from your stage to shyness.

I believe she is at Rome by this time, as also many more of the English world, few of which are here. Dieu Merci, the Rawdons, and Davys, remain the winter there, which is quite a mistake for themselves. There are more carriages and people here than one ever saw collected in one town, and the air of gaiety is quite consoling. Gell sends you a thousand kind regards, and we both unite in being

Your affectionate friends,

R. K. CRAVEN and W. GELL.

Another letter, which should have reached me some time ago, from Miss [——], amused me on my journey.

She writes with her usual good sense, but makes a remark upon Madame de Stael which is singular, and to *me* displeasing.

Nothing can be a stronger instance of the blindness and fallacy of human wishes and expectations, than to hear your general feeling of disappointment respecting your residence at Geneva.

You give me quite the idea of having fallen into all the common-place sort of sensations and habits of life that one might enjoy in a large flat English park : and when it comes to that, I believe one could not return to the illusions and fantastic amusing expectations which filled one's imagination previously. Mine paints everything to be delightful there, with a very vague shadowy pencil ; but it appears to me that I should be a different person in my sensations altogether, were I in those countries : and yet when I hear of *you*, who have so much more *youthfulness* of spirit and freshness of fancy than myself, I must conclude that I should have grown completely humdrum in a week—should have made distresses of hard chairs, deal tables, or ill-dressed dinners—and should only have had my energies excited to make up a new dress for an assembly of five-and-twenty people in a room six feet square, lighted with six tallow candles.

Your description of Copet made me shudder : it must be pretty much like what it was in Lord [——]'s time. How dreadful to sit up and play at being sublime all day long ! I envy you everything but that : I would not have been there for the world.

Indeed, I believe I am a solitary instance, in the civilised world, of never desiring to be in company with Madame de Stael, to speak to her. At least, if any lady feels with me, she would blush to own it. I heard that *Alcandrina* (a name for the Princess of Wales) wanted you to tie yourself to her skirts abroad. That, I think, would be destroying one of the choice benefits of going abroad. I cannot conceive her being forced out of the country ; and it was highly impolitic in Her Royal Highness to leave England. It is nonsense to judge for another, especially one long persecuted ; but this voluntary exile from Britain has done her harm, even with those who take her part. It tells of such an anxious desire after mere amusements, such an unfitness for her station, such a cowardice under her sufferings, which she bore so well for a length of time !

Surely, if from no other motive but *vanity*, she might have been induced to remain in the midst of her enemies, and never to flee from them, and to be the *heroine* of the history of her time.

The letter ends with a copy of verses written by Monk Lewis, my old friend, the last time he was at [Inverary Castle], in Scotland, where Miss [——] met him to her great delight.   They are entitled,—

ST. ANTHONY THE SECOND,

A tale of wonder, very surprising, but still more true.

> ———— When the pale moon
> And silent stars shone, conscious of the theft,
> Haply they stole unheeded to my chamber.
> *Fair Penitent.*

Midnight was past, nor yet I sought my bed ;
Stretch'd on my couch, alone I lay and read.
Calista-like " *loose, unattired, and warm,*"
My night-gown scarcely veil'd my careless form ;
Nor less unguarded was my mind ; a flood
Of generous wine still thrilled within my blood,
While the soft page o'er which my fancy dwelt
Taught my whole soul in fond desires to melt.
'Twas the sad tender tale of Hugh and Anne ; *
And while their amorous woes I joyed to scan,
I felt my heart with livelier pulses move,
And all my softened soul attuned to love.

While thus I lay, lo ! voices, soft but clear,
Stole in sweet whisperings on my ravish'd ear ;
Near and more near they come—the door expands !
I start—look round—the book forsakes my hands !
Scarce can I think my senses to be right,
So bright a vision blazes on my sight !

* The Mysterious Discovery.

I   T

Three nymphs, more blooming than those heavenly maids
Who bless the Arabian seers' enchanted shades,
Pour'd their ripe beauties on my dazzled eye,
And in their midst sustain'd a huge goose-pye.
" Oh ! life is short," they sang with dulcet sound,
And moved, with graceful dance, the pye around.
" Oh ! life is short, and pleasure speeds away,
Soon fades the rose, and raven locks turn grey ;
Then wise are they who seize the passing hour,
And, ere its bloom is wither'd, crop the flower.
Oh ! come, blest youth, and share our soft delight,
Oh ! come, blest youth, the joys of goose invite !
Mark the bright blush which mantles on our cheeks,
And amorous hearts and secret wishes speaks ;
Mark the rich odours from the pye, which rise,
And speak it stuff'd with garlic, salt, and spice.
Hence with dull wisdom's saws and grave behest,
True wisdom means the secret to be blest ;
Yield, then, and say, when monks their prudence boast,
He shows most prudence who enjoys the most.

I listen'd, look'd, and long'd, by turns survey'd
Now the goose-pye, and now each white-robed maid ;
Now hunger led me towards the savoury pye,
But the fair nymphs recall'd me with a sigh ;
Now leaving *that*, I hasten'd towards *those*,
But then the pasty caught me by the nose.
Less strongly tempted, grandsire Adam fell,
Eve ruin bought with a hard nonpareil :
More powerful bribes did Satan *here* produce,
My Eves were *three*, and season'd was the goose.
Could I resist ?   Oh ! no ! I yield, I cried ;
When, lo ! my guardian genius at my side
Clapp'd his white wings, and bade, in colours true,
Next morning's breakfast shock my mental view.
How shall I bear the just and stern rebuke
Of Tom * the abstemious and the stoic duke ? †
How moral scorn, immaculate surprise,
Will flash through Garthmore's supplemental eyes ! ‡

* T. Sheridan.   † Duke of Argyll.
‡ Mr. Graham. of Garthmore, wore spectacles constantly. [Original note.]

What wrath will furious Mr. Toms display !
And, Oh ! ye gods ! what will Miss Dickson say ?

That last appalling thought re-nerved my mind—
Avaunt ! I cried, and thrice my breast I sign'd ;
And thrice I named Aurelia in my prayer,
And thrice I kiss'd the bracelet of her hair ;
That powerful charm prevail'd : their cheat made plain,
Demoniac shrieks exprest the tempters' pain ;
Sulphureous flashes from the goose-pye broke,
The seeming nymphs were wrapt in flame and smoke,
To brimstone hue was changed their white attire,
And all their petticoats were flounc'd with fire.   .
Swift up the chimney past the infernal flight,
And all the vision vanish'd from my sight.

SECTION V

CONTINUATION OF·JOURNAL

AT Lyons I met the two Madame de C[——].
The young one is a woman of marked
features, not handsome, but has a considerable deal of character in her countenance.
They proposed to take me out in their carriage, which I
accepted, and accordingly we went to view the general
appearance of the town. I had not leisure to enter into
any of the public buildings, but we drove along the quays,
and saw the confluence of the Rhone and Saone, and
beheld the beautiful banks which rise by the side of the
latter river. The flat plains which skirt the Rhone are
not so picturesque. The Cathedral of St. John is a fine
building, and has suffered little from time and the storms
of the Revolution.

I dined with Madame C[——]. Her husband is the
most unpleasant-looking and unpleasant-mannered man
I ever met :—little in his person, his head flat and square,
and his hair sticking out like an unfledged sparrow. He
seemed to consider he was conferring an honour when he
addressed me, and hummed a tune between his teeth all
the evening. Poor T[——] C[——] was evidently much
worse than when I last saw him, and though I affected
to talk of meeting him again at Nice, I have no hope of
doing so. It is difficult to know how seriously or how
lightly a person in his situation wishes one to consider
his malady.

We went to the play : the " Magnifique," by Gretry, and the " Nouveau Seigneur du Village," were performed. The actors were very indifferent, and they acted as if they had been going to sleep : but no wonder, for although the theatre is attended every evening, it is entirely as a place of resort, and no one ever pretends to listen to the performance, much less to applaud. This indifference in the audience must of course produce the same feeling in the actors. I ventured, however, to applaud once, and, as if the people had suddenly been touched by some magical wand, they all began to applaud one after another. It is comical to observe this awakening from lethargy, and the effect it produced on the poor actors. Madame de C[——] remarked this, and it was not my own fancy suggested the idea, how easy it is to give an impulse to public feeling ! There is something gratifying, and something humiliating, at the same moment, in the reflection, that the sympathies of our fellow-creatures are so easily aroused to a unison with our own, and yet as readily turned towards those of the next person whose interest it may be to excite them to a feeling probably the very reverse.

We revisited the cathedral next morning. I expressed the sense of religious awe with which such buildings, particularly those of Gothic architecture, always inspire me, and, in the enthusiasm of the moment, I said something in favour of the Roman Catholic religion, whose imposing forms captivate my fancy. Madame de C[——] replied, shaking her head, that it was the worst of all modes of worship ; "would to heaven that the Revolution, qui nous avoit emporté tant de choses, eût emporté celle-la." "And why ? " I said. "Because it leads to all sorts of mischief." "Certainly," said her mother-in-law, looking round at some poor persons kneeling in different parts of the church ;—"certainly they are more religious than we are." "Religious ! " rejoined the other ; " they pray here for a few minutes, and return to all sorts of vices and crimes."

I think this remark was intolerant ; for, if indeed ill-disposed persons avail themselves of this veil to con-science, the good, as in all other religions, remain good, and do not pervert the meaning of the promise held out alike to all Christians, of pardon in return for penitence. An indolence of tongue, and dislike to all dispute, made me silent ; but in the evening again, at the Opera, the men-tion of Madame de Stael's last work, " Germany," led the conversation to serious subjects. Madame de C[——], who appears to me to be a clever and deep-thinking person, admired the whole of it without reserve, and said, she thought nothing could be more luminous than the manner in which Madame de Stael spoke of the different systems of metaphysical philosophy ; and the only thing she regretted, was, that some extracts of Kant's writings had not been inserted.

I have myself read his works, and I think nothing can be more lucid than his style, or more easy to be understood. Madame C[——] went on to say, that she conceived Madame de S[——'s] ideas upon religion, the most pro-found and the most true she had ever heard ; in fact, she said, nothing is more probable than that one universal religion should at length be brought about, as the scripture promises, by the influence of some of those intermediate sects which are not allowed to belong to the Established Churches.

In the gospel we are there decidedly promised one uni-versal peace and one universal gospel ; and by what means are we most likely to obtain this ? By some of those modifications of our religious worship which we condemn. The Roman Catholic is too bigoted, too cruel in its doctrines, to admit of any tolerance. The Episcopal is too proud, the Presbyterian too stern : some other then must interfere.

Madame de C[——] then continued to discuss some remark I made upon the fault found by the curious, not with the book, but with the author ; as they alleged, that the sentiments which pervaded Madame de Stael's Allemagne, were not her own, but differed entirely from all she had ever thought or written previously, and were only assumed opinions to suit the fashion of the hour. I had said, that in repeating this insidious remark, I desired not to be implicated in having framed it, for that I knew Madame de Stael to be incapable of suiting her sentiments or feelings, even to expediency, and that I perfectly believed in her sincerity, and did not think an opinion less deserving of acceptance, because it was one adopted from conviction, even allowing it had not always been that which she professed. "I do not consider at all," observed Madame de C[——], "the author of a book, but only the work itself abstractedly, and I think the work we are now speaking of is one of the most perfect and most extraordinary, to be a woman's writing, I ever read."

Madame de C[——] praised Miss Porter's " Scottish Chiefs," and said, it quite *montéd* her imagination about Scotch persons and Scotland. Had she known the excellent and high-minded authoress, she would have added an additional note of praise on the rare character of the writer.

Madame de C[——] gave me an instance of sincerity in religious profession, in a person who, after having enjoyed all the luxuries and pomps of the world, and the pleasures which they bestow, and incurred great blame from her conduct, had, whilst still young and extremely rich, forsaken the world entirely, and dedicated all her wealth and time to the poor. It was Madame de Kruitzner, [Krudener] personally known to Madame de C[——].

The next day I left Lyons, and embarked on the Rhone. I lodged at a miserable cabaret, called Le Mulet Blanc, at Vienne. The women who attended us were very civil, but the landlord was extremely rude and exorbitant in his charge for his miserable fare. He told my courier that *les Anglois* had done him much mischief, and they should pay for it.

When daylight discovered to my view the beautiful Rhone, winding majestically through its high vine-covered banks, with the remains of some Roman antiquities peeping out occasionally, I forgot all animal inconvenience in the mental enjoyment of such a scene.

In an old tower, at the top of the hill, my cicerone informed me there lay the remains of a Scotch lady who died at the cabaret where I slept, of the name of Sterkey, and that a man who was her husband, or who called himself such, had erected a mausoleum to her memory ; but, in the time of the Revolution, it had been destroyed. The circumstance of a foreigner being buried at the top of that high mountain, in unconsecrated ground, far away from friend or relative, and the melancholy manner of her death, furnished matter for imagination to work upon. Perhaps she fell a victim to unholy and unhappy love ; perhaps—in short, I imagined many things about the poor lady who lay beneath the green sward.

My old cicerone, who called herself Veuve Giroux, entertained me all the way with her eloquent lamentations on the horrors which she had witnessed during the times of revolutionary fury, and subsequently of ambitious tyranny, it was impossible not to sympathise in her unaffected expressions : she tossed her withered arms about with that impressive gesture which genuine feeling never fails to inspire. It is from observing such natural impulses of the heart, that all descriptions of the passions should be copied ; if they have not been actually felt, it is impossible for imagination, however vivid, to impart even their reflected image. "On n'osoit dire la messe," (publicly,) said Veuve Giroux. "Yet some few did so. I always went, and rien ne m'est arrivé. I was baptized dans l'Eglise, and I like to say my prayers there.   I never felt afraid of the armed men."

Between her lamentations she called to a child, (belonging to a family who had come in the same boat with myself,) saying, " Prenez garde, ma mie," as it ran carelessly on the edge of the precipice.   It seemed as if tenderness was the burthen of her song, and after such personal miseries, it was the more amiable, for they are apt to harden the heart.   How much people lose of the knowledge of human nature, who never mix but with one circle of persons !

I inquired for the famous tower of Pontius Pilate, which, by tradition, is said to have been situated here ; but there are no remains of it now.   The cathedral in the town is of gothic structure, its principal front richly carved and much ornamented, but the interior is dilapidated, the chapels destroyed, and the fine gloom which clothes such ancient piles with a vestment of grandeur, is entirely lost, by some pious souls having painted the walls of a bright blue and white.—I rested afterwards at the house of a Monsieur Loriol : he was an old man with a white ribbon in his button-hole, and a good-humoured countenance, which became ten times more beaming upon our informing him, when he made the inquiry if I knew the Lady K[——] as he called her, that I was acquainted with her.   " Ah ! " said he, " she is an excellent lady ; she lived here eighteen months, and made drawings of all the ruins in the neighbourhood.   She had a very cross mother, but was herself a most amiable person " ;   and then he showed me two of Miss K[——]'s gifts to himself, a pocket-book and snuff-box, of which, with some Derbyshire spar, he seemed very proud.   On one side of his apartments was hung a picture of Bonaparte, (a copy of Monsieur Girard's portrait of him,) and on the other, as a pendant, a likeness of the Pope.   This arrangement put me in mind of the old song of Bartlemy Fair—

"Here's the Tower of Babylon, the Devil, and the Pope," &c. &c.

The next night we disembarked at a small village called *Bœuf*. On my admiring the carving of an ivory crucifix, hung in the sitting-room of the carbaret, the landlady told me she had been obliged to hide it till very lately; "but," said she, "strong as man's oppression is, religion is stronger." It is gratifying to find that the demoralization which the Revolution has caused in all classes of society, has still left some unpolluted, and steadfast in their faith. I have met with several striking instances of this fact, but chiefly amongst the low-born.

The next day there was an awful thunder storm. One peal reminded me of the dreadful thunder-bolt which fell at Kensington Palace. I never heard so loud a one since, but yet no harm was done, neither did any bolt fall this time. Certainly the extraordinary storm which happened when I was dining at the Palace at Kensington, might in other times have been deemed a forerunner of the poor Princess's troubles. The declaration of the King's hopeless insanity, the establishment of the Regency, and consequent desertion of the great and powerful persons of the realm from Her Royal Highness's society, which immediately followed, were but too true a fulfilment of the omen.

To return to my Journal.

The next night I stopped at St. Vallière. Again my landlady was a pleasant, communicative person, and, as usual, spoke of the tyrant Bonaparte, and the misery his reign had brought upon the country. The Veuve Gardon informed me she was by birth an Irishwoman, her maiden name O'Farrel. She was not handsome, yet had some of the attributes attendant on beauty; good teeth, a thick and richly coloured lip, sensible eyes, and marked eyebrows. The tone of her voice, too, was mellow and flexible at the same time. She told me she had sent one of her children to a place among the mountains, where there was a race of persons who had never been civilized. Among these she represented the conscription to have been borne with the greatest impatience. The desertions were so frequent, that after families had paid their all to ransom their children, and when the soldiers ventured to take them away again by force of arms, the parents said, " There—you will have him—there he is—he shall not desert again," and often shot or stabbed their sons to the heart.

At Avignon I found several letters, one from the Princess of Wales, giving an unsatisfactory account of her poor royal self (dated Milan).

Je viens de recevoir votre charmante lettre—toujours encore de Genève. Nous sommes très bien ici. L'Opera est superbe, et Le Marechal Bellegarde poli pour nous, au possible : beaucoup d'étrangers, et surtout Monsieur Ward. Ce Lundi le 18 je quitte pour Florence, et puis a Rome, jusqu'a ce que ma frigate arrive pour me garder a Naples. J'ai justement recue la nouvelle que Le Roi De Naples (Murat) à recu l'ordre de L'Empereur D'Autriche et les Alliés, de quitter son Royaume d'abord. Si tel est le cas, qu'il céde la place tranquillement, je m'y rend d'abords. Si non, il faudrait s'etablir à Palermo pour l'hiver. Je vous regrette toujours d'avantage. Car on me néglige beaucoup à la Maison. Le reste du monde est fort agréable, et me comble d'attention. Demain je penserai bien à vous—car il y'aura au Théâtre un Bal Masquè. J'en espére beaucoup, adieu. Écrivez moi bien bientôt.

Mademoiselle Dumont * est bonne fille, cependant elle n'a point inventé la poudre. Mais tout và bien. Croyez moi pour la vie, votre très sincere et affectionné amie,

C. P.

* Mademoiselle Dumont was hired for the Princess by a most respectable person in the family of Lady C. C[——]l; but either she was not, in the sequel, proof against the temptations she was exposed to, or else she must originally have been of *doubtful character*, as her subsequent conduct was not what it ought to have been. [Original note.]

Letter from MR. KEPPEL CRAVEN.

Dated thus—NAPLES, *New Year's Day*, 1815, of which
I wish you many happy returns.

MY DEAR [——],—Colonel D'Arlincourt, who I hope will
put this into your own hands, will tell you that he left us all
well, and how agreeable we are. But as he will not be equally
descriptive of his own merits, I must beg you to believe they
are very great, as you will soon discover, if he gives you
time. His wife also is a most charming person, and we all
doat upon her, and mean to take care of her during his absence.
If you ask him what is done at Naples on New Year's Day,
you will find that it is wonderful I can write even one line to
you ; but Her Royal Highness is so fatigued with a masked
ball she gave last night, that she has wisely curtailed all her
share of the performances till the evening.

I have only been to the *Te Deum* at the Royal Chapel with
E[——], and have a little while to dispose of before dinner.
After it, the Princess will hold her usual Sunday court, which
is expected to be more than usually brilliant, and then proceeds to the Palace with all her suite, to accompany the King
and Queen to the Opera in their state box. The theatre is
illuminated on the occasion, and of course everything very
magnificent. All the male part of the court wear Henri
Quatre dresses, which are so entirely covered with embroidery
that ours, whatever figure they might have cut on the Lake
of Geneva, merely look like smock-frocks at the foot of
Vesuvius.

Last night Her Royal Highness gave a masked ball at a
small villa of the Queen's, where there is a very pretty garden
actually in the sea. It went off very well, and there were
many quadrilles danced by parties, which gave the whole
thing an air of gaiety, quite unknown in our climate ; but
you will judge what an atmosphere this is when one can
walk out *à la Vauxhall* in an illuminated garden on the last
night of the year. The Llandaffs are here, and a few more
English families, who all pay the *properest* attention to Her
Royal Highness ; and, indeed, situated as she is with the
court, they must do so in their own defence, but at the same
time I give them all due credit for it. I had a letter from
Lady Westmoreland a few days ago, but I conclude she, or

Lafond, fe., delt.   Choubard, sculpt.

JOACHIM MURAT AND HIS WIFE CAROLINE BONAPARTE,

Lady D[——], or some of the English that are there, have written to you. I hope they will not come here; for except the present company, and the *two Lady Charlottes*, I do not wish to see any more Britannic faces here while we stay.

I am happy to say we go on well. There have been clouds, but they were all *interior*, and I believe none of the natives are at all disposed to blame, but on the contrary, strive to do their utmost to please and to amuse. I am quite determined that it is the only place to live in, and am only fearful that *we* shall be tired of it, sooner than *I*. Gell is in waiting, or would have written to you. Her Royal Highness writes, I believe, by Colonel D'Arlincourt.

Believe me ever,
Your very sincere and attached
K. C.

From the PRINCESS OF WALES.

Ce neuf de Janvier, a NAPLES.

Depuis hier j'ai recu votre seconde lettre, de la date du quatorze Decembre. Je me trouve fort malheureuse qu'aucune de mes lettres ne vous sont enfin arrivè. Vous scavez combient je vous suis sincèrement attachée, et combien je desire en tout temps et lieu de vous le prouver. Je crains que vous ne m'accusè de negligence, et peutêtre d'oublie : ne croyez rien de tout cela, et croyez seulement que la Poste est vraiment horrible, et d'une incertitude affreuse. Au reste, les lettres sont tous lu partout, avant qu'il passe, et puis sont copié ; les miens sont envoyés pour la critique de L'Angleterre, pour etre reveu, et corrigé. Ce qui me fait trembler chaque fois que je prends la plume en main. Soyez tres persuadé que Naples est actuellement tout rempli d'espions. J'en connoit plusieures, qui sont caché, et les autres qu'ils se montre publiquement. Quad même, je mene la vie la plus tranquille du monde, et ne suis lier avec personne. Les mœurs sont bien stricte actuellement, et il y'a beaucoup d'etiquette partout ; ce qui à ainsi fait changé Naple, en fait d'amusement, et qui me conviens, car il est triste comme je sent mon cœur.

Je n'ai pas encore reçu une ligne de ma Fille. Ce qui m'inquiete beaucoup. Monsieur St. Leger est le seul personne qui m'écrive. Le climat est bien doux, mais beaucoup de pluie, et d'humidité, mais cela me conviens. Au reste, je suis si charmée d'être etabli quelque part que je me contente de tout bien aisément. Lady Oxford n'est pas ici a la mode du tout. La Reine ne peut la souffrir ; ils sont dans des embarras terrible pour de l'argent, et j'ai été obligé de lui donner mille ducats en present. Elle compte de vendre la plus grande partie de ses diamonds a la Reine. Ont la trouve nullement plus belle ici ; ont parle d'elle comme d'une personne qui est absolument passée. Lady E[——] est appele La Petite Folle. Elle court apres tout les hommes, et surtout apres notre Roi. Ce que la Reine n'aime guère. Mais cependant il n'y a pas le moindre espoir de trouver un mari ici, et encore moins *de filer le parfaite Amour*. Nous avons . . . (words illegible) toute ma cœur Aussibien que la petite *basse cour*, et je ne la vois jamais. Je dine bien des jours pour cette raison seule dans ma petite Coquille à m'instruire, et mene une vie contemplative : je pourrois écrire une volume. Cher . . . si j'etais sûre que ce chiffon vous arrivà sans que cela fut lu. Mais comme l'incertitude est la *base* de notre existence, il faut agir en consequence. Ecrivez moi souvent et tous ce que vous faites. Le bon K[——] sera toujours le bien venu. Le Sieur Priam vient d'arrivé ici. Lady Westmoreland n'arrive qu'au printemps ; les Hollands, et les Bedfords aussi. (Some words illegible.)

Je propose faire un petit voyage par mer aussitot que Lady Charlotte Lindsay arrive ici. Et peutêtre je vous recontrerez a Genes ou a Marseilles pour l'automne, pour vous ramener ici au mois d'Octobre. Voila des plans de bien loin. Je donnerai milles écus pour une heure de conversation, mais combien c'est cruelle que je n'ai pas une etre à qui ouvrir mon cœur. Mais soyez toujours bien persuadée qu'absente ou presente vous etes toujours près de moi, et que je languis bien apres cette heureux moment, et que je suis pour la vie votre affectionné,

C. P.

Letter from MRS. D[AMER ?].

Dated LONDON, *Jan. 10th*, 1815.

DEAR [——],—First I must begin by all best wishes for your happiness, this and many succeeding new years. Then I have to tell you, that I now, since my last letter, have every

reason to believe that you will find no difficulty in passing
your time where you please, without troubling the Frigate
for a conveyance, and that your excuse on the score of health
will be readily accepted.

H[——] read me a letter just received from Mrs. Thompson
to Col. St. Leger, saying how much she enjoyed her present
residence, where she "led a sedentary life." She would
"have him come to her, with all his family," but not a word
of the means so to do ; which I think clearly indicates that
all her present invitations are mere flourish, and from a
conviction that they will not be accepted.

Mrs. Thompson's most agreeable head servants are both
leaving her ; (I doubt not a sort of mutual intelligence ;) but
they are leaving her. The one is going to meet his mother,
and the other, I believe, returning to England ; * only Lord
[Mr.] H[ollan]d remains, who, she says, is "a great comfort
to her." One other man, I should suppose, also remains ;
but of him, in these last accounts, I have heard nothing. I
leave you to make your own comments on all this. You will,
I think, hug yourself to think that you are out of this mess.

I saw the most entertaining letter possible, from C[——]
to B[——], in which he describes, in the most ludicrous way,
not only the bustle, but the perpetual whirl, of the journey
and of Naples. This is well contrasted with Mrs. Thompson's
"sedentary life."

Have you heard that the Besboroughs and Ponsonbys were
nearly lost in their passage down the Rhone ? It is odd that
C[raven] should not in his last letter have mentioned his intention of coming away ; but as he said that all letters to certain
persons in particular are opened by the N[aples] government,
this accounts for his not saying all he might otherwise. Mrs.
Thompson's letter was positive as to his and his friend's leaving
her.

Letter from MR. GELL *to* [——,] *at Nice.*

Dated NAPLES, *Jan.* 19*th*, 1815. A very hot day—looking
over the sea—and in waiting.

MY DEAR [——],—After so many months and years, I
have at last heard from you ; but as you accuse me of

* Mr. Craven went to meet his mother, the Margravine of Anspach ;
Mr. Gell desired to return to England.

negligence, I cannot help retorting by a hint that you only wrote to me because you find yourself obliged to enclose a letter to my address. Oh! thou most fair, yet false of thy sex. I have heard from my aunt, Mrs. D[——], and have every reason to believe that I shall have the fortune at last, for her letter is very kind; and if she joins you in the spring, as she threatens, "too much familiarity breeds contempt," and, therefore, the fortune must inevitably be mine.

As to any lady's account of a place, whether there is society or not, or whether the climate is good, no person who has seen so much of the world as I have, makes much account of it, for there are a great many English here, who, for a long time, found out there was no society at Naples, and that the climate of London was equal, if not superior. Blind as they are, what is one to say to them, except to cite the utter impossibility of having a masquerade in a garden on the night preceding the first of January (as we had here) in London, and showing one's own invitations to dinners and suppers; not to mention places where one can go without invitation whenever one pleases? You may depend on it, you and all the English are strange animals. Here is arrived my sister-in-law's sister, Madame De Polier Vernaud, from near Lausanne, who either knew you or heard of you there this summer, but of course little good, or I would let you know. As to Lady Charlotte Lindsay, she is quite come into favour again; but whether because I did not write to her, or not, I cannot tell.* The truth is, that I have been coming for her every day, for these two months, in a Neapolitan frigate, to Nice, as it was thought she would be afraid of a foreign ship, alone, till at last news of two ships of our own arrived, so I wrote to her to say, I really can advise all good Christians to come to Naples; for, excepting houses, everything is very cheap, and a good carriage costs only, with coachman included, 12s. 6d. per day.

Mrs. Thompson had an idea of hiring Lady Oxford's house next door, and persuading Lady C. Campbell to come and occupy it. I wish Her Royal Highness would try and make

* The Princess of Wales was ridiculously jealous of Sir W. Gell's liking or paying attention to any one else, more than to herself. [Original note.]

Ma Tante Aurore accept this invitation; it would do very well, if the said Oxfords quitted it. The Oxfords say that they can live perfectly well for 3000 a-year, provided they have *only* what is necessary; but a carriage is included in the said necessaries, and a tutor for the ugly boy, and a doctor for the naughty girls, besides all the furniture they spoil or destroy, which cannot be trifling; and four thousand dresses, with gold embroidery, for the little Alfred; and last, but not least, many dogs, who have not left one corner of the carpet nor a single silk chair, without holes.

Inspired by these awful reflections, my paper seems to be finished. I see, every day and every hour, more reasons why people should never marry, and why I shall never be in love with a lady of fashion. I see sighs and tears lavished on one, and as quickly bursting and dropping from another. No; in spite of those smiles of Lady C[harlotte] C[ampbell], which might seduce one's weak heart for a moment, I shall never be really in love with her. Tell her so, and, that she may give way to all those elegant effusions of sentimentality in her next letter, which so eminently distinguish her from the other inhabitants of the civilised world. Add, that my judgment will not be perverted by the state of my heart, which is adamant, and I shall be able to give her excellent counsel, where prudence, patience, chastity, temperance, and the best of the virtues of northern climates, want of opportunity, and barren hills, are required. We expect Lady Charlotte Lindsay daily. Love to Lord and Lady Glenbervie. Oh! fie, Mr. Douglas?

Your most affectionate aunt,
ANNA TAYLOR.
Alias WILLIAM GELL.

Tuesday, 21st of February, 1815, *Nice.*—Read some Italian letters of Gallileo's and Raphael's, more for the names of the writers than the matter of the letters. How dull they are! how many letters written by less extraordinary persons, are ten thousand times more interesting. I went to visit Madame Davidoff, and Miss M. M[——] came in whilst I was there. The former told me the Princess Grassalcovitch had confided to her,

I   U

that at first she had preferred Lady S[——] to all the other English ladies here, and had been prepared to like her from what the Duchess of B[——] had said in her praise, but that latterly she had liked Lady C. Campbell best, and thought her more natural. Nuts to me! It is always sweet to hear one's friend praised. Went out to walk: a fine day, but no inspiration came to me. Passed the evening in reading Sismondi, &c.

Wednesday night, 22nd.—I received two letters from the Princess; one brought by a gentleman of the name of [——]. It was by way of being a letter of introduction from Her Royal Highness to me, but such a one as, I suppose, nobody was ever himself the bearer of. I laughed heartily when I read it, in the presence of the person, but endeavoured to be as polite as I could, and he fortunately remained in ignorance of the bad character the Princess had given him. Here it is :—

Letter from the PRINCESS OF W[——] *to* [——].

Dated NAPLES, *ce de* [—] *Fevrier,* 1815.

MA CHÈRE,—Je vous annonce mon arrivè a Nice pour le moi de Mars, ou je me flatte que je vous trouverai en parfaite santè, et je ferais des arrangements finalement pour notre retour pour Londre, qui sera pour l'hiver prochain.

Adieu, croyez moi pour la vie,

Votre affectionée Amie,

C. P.

P.S.—Le porteur de cette lettre est une personne qui ne dit jamais la verité: il est un Espion de la Cabal!

Another from the same to the same.

MA CHÈRE,—Je suis domicilié ici, depuis le huit Novembre, un peu fatiguée du long voyage, et de mes companions de voyage d'infortune. Ma maison est placé rue La Chiaja, comme je suppose que vous avais déjà entendue par Mr. Craven, et vous vous rappellerez bien autre foi de cette promenade de la Villa Reale. La situation est superbe, et la

maison est elegant. Je trouve Naples nullement cher a
vivre, et si je reste ici avec £18,000, j'aurai fait tous les
depense et extravagance, possible. J'ai deja donné un grand
bal au Roi et a la Reine, et un bal en masque le dernier jour
de l'année ; et avec 1800 ducats ces fêtes, qui (comme ont
m'assure) etè tres splendide, ont été payè.

Il y'a beaucoup d'Anglois ici. Lord Sligo, Lord et Lady
Landaff, le General Matthew, et beaucoup de jeunes hommes ;
Monsieur Perceval, fils du feu ministre ; je les voi tous les
semaines une foi, chez moi a un grand diner ; il vont donnèr
la semaine prochaine,* un grand bal au Roi et a la Reine ;
car apres la declaration de Monsieur Vansittart, le Roi Murat
à eté reconnu par l'Angleterre, et il le merite bien, car le bien
qu'il a fait au royaume, n'est point a dire : il est aussi adoré
que la Reine. La Reine est extremmement jolie, spirituelle,
fort affable, et fait les honeurs de la cour parfaitement bien.

Le Roi est beau, gai, polie, toujours gracieux, et faisant
toujours des actions genereux, car il est le Dieu de la bien-
faisance. Je me trouve bien ici sur tout les rapports. La
societé est excellente, beaucoup de beaux Messieurs et infini-
ment de jolies dames a la cour du Roi et de la Reine. Comme
je suis établie ici pour quelque temps, j'ai deja ecrit trois
lettres à Lady Charlotte Lindsay pour la faire venir ici, ou
avec les Glenbervies ou avec Mr. F. North, pour passer quelque

* This is most probably the ball of which Madame de Boigne writes :
"During the previous carnival, which she [the Princess of Wales]
had just spent at Naples, she conceived the idea of inducing the resident
English to give a subscription ball to Murat. The scene took place
in a public hall. At the moment of Murat's arrival a group of the
prettiest Englishwomen, dressed like goddesses from Olympus, advanced
to receive him . . . and conducted him to a platform where the
curtains opened and showed the spectators a group of symbolical figures
including Renown, a character sustained by one of the pretty Harley
ladies. Glory, who was represented by the Princess [of Wales], even
more ridiculously dressed than the others, tripped forward, took a
feather from the wing of Renown, and wrote in large golden letters
upon a panel which she held the names of the different battles in
which Murat had distinguished himself. The spectators roared with
laughter and applauded, while the Queen of Naples shrugged her
shoulders. . . . I heard the story of this performance from Lady
Charlotte Campbell, the last of the ladies of honour to abandon her.
She wept with vexation as she spoke, but her story was only the more
comical in consequence. It was necessary to have the heroine before one
to appreciate the ridiculous element to the full." [Memoirs, ii. 40-41.]

temps ici. Au printemps je me propose de me rendre par
mer. Si jamais ma frigate arrive a Rome, le Roi m'a offert
son palais de Farnesè pour ma demeure, ainsi je crois en
profiter. Je n'ai fait que passer six jours a Rome et n'a fait
que courir apres les curiositès et antiquités de l'ancienne
Rome : je me propose aussi de me rendre par mer a Génes,
de voir Venice, et les Iles Grecques, et puis de revenir a
Naples au moi d'Octobre ; j'ai n'ai jamais recue des lettres
de la main propre de ma fille, ce qui me chagrine beaucoup
quand même je n'ai fait que de lui écrire plus de cent lettres
depuis mon depart. Je serai tranquile ici si ce cuysante
chagrin ne n'avrèz point mon cœur. Mais tel va le monde :
quand un est finie, il se trouve un autre cheminant tout pret
à prende sa place. Il y'a aussi tout pleins d'espion ici : un
certain Monsieur Zuriton, un palfrenier, frère du Colonel
Zuriton, du 10 regiment De H[——], et ajoutè a cela des
Messieurs qui voyage sous un titre si honorable, et qui mêmes
s'en glorifie, car il n'en font pas même le moindre secret a
ce sujet.

Voila comme les Anglois sont connu, puisque même ils se
vante d'avoir un poste si honorable a supporter. Mais bouche
close : ce sont des vrais misères. Je vis tranquilement et
ce n'est que depuis quelques jours que je commence a sortir.
Dans les societiés privés la Princesse Belmonté m'a donné
un superbe bal, et la Princess Caramanico une autre. Les
ministres du Roi qui sont de ce pays sont amiable, et on
beaucoup d'esprit, et donne chacun des bals masqué, tous
les semaines qui est le Mecredi. [*illegible*] au theatre de St.
Carlo, outre les bals.

Je me retire toujours de bonne heure ; tous commence a
huit heure, et jamais des soupers, il ne sont pas ici de modes,
ainsi a onze heure je me trouve au lit : les autres personnes
dancent jusqua trois heure du matin sans jamais souper, ni
s'asseoir. Il y'a beaucoup d'etiquette à la cour, ce qui rend
la societé un peu *formal*, la decence est poussé a un point que
même Whitbread et Lady Elizabeth en seroit edifié : dites
tout ça a Madame D[amer ?], elle ne reconnoitera plus Naples,
pour les mœurs ; aussi beaucoup d'Anglois le trouve une en-
droit forte ennuyante quand même il sont obligè d'avouer,
que la societé ici est infinement plus agréeable qu'a Paris
aujourdhui.

Pour l'economie je vous avoue que je crois vraiement que vous et toute la famille de votre cousine pourrai vivre pour la moitié de ce que ca coute ailleurs, j'en suis bien sûre. J'espére que vous viendrai au mois d'Octobre. Je payerais le voyage par terre ou par mer, comme cela vous convendra le mieux. Monsieur Hesse heureusement part dans trois jours. J'èspere que Lady Elizabeth se rentournera avec lui, si Lady Charlotte Lindsay est arrivé ici a temps. Monsieur Craven j'èspere aussi sera loin chez sa mère qui se trouve a Marseilles : enfin cette cour *grecque* et philosophe sont dans l'interieur des vraies tyrants et des hommes fort peu fait pour faire les honneurs d'une cour Anglaise.*

Adieu, je vous supplie de faire mes plus tendres amitiés a tout la monde qui se rappelé de moi : Mademoiselle Dumont est bien bonne fille, et nous sommes toujours tranquilement ensemble.

Croyez mois pour la vie votre très affectionè,

.C. P.

I am sorry to see by these two strange incoherent letters, that the poor Princess is as unsettled in mind and purpose as ever. Her complaint of her attendants being " des vraies tyrants," tells me what she means by that expression. I dined with M[——], and as we were sitting after dinner, listening to a journal, which she was reading aloud, to my astonishment the Prince and Princess Grassalcovitch came in. The latter had been so very ill that they had put her ashore at Ville Franche, beyond which point they never got ; and he said that he was determined they should proceed by land. I was glad to know these people were safe, and to see them again. We always begin to know and like people when we are just about to part, it may be for ever. M[——] and I were sorry when Madame De Corvesi and Monsieur and Madame De Neuburgh were announced. She is a pretty little civil person, with a sweet gentle tone of voice, and

* These foolish, unreasonable complaints of persons whose presence did her honour, and whose attachment to her was sincere, were the offsprings of a diseased mind, and foretold her downfall. [Original note.]

more of the *jargon du monde* than have the people here. They sat on for a couple of hours, and told ghost stories and murder stories, and had I not been taken up with attempting to draw, I should have liked them very well. I was too unwell to do anything that required vigour of mind. Read a little in bed before I went to sleep, and so ended the day.

Thursday, Feb. 23rd.—I went to see Lady Glenbervie. I think her better for the present, but in a very precarious state of health. Lord Glenbervie is going on Saturday to Genoa and Rome. Lady S[——] wishes to go to Genoa with Lord Bradford, but it is thought her lord does not like that arrangement.

Friday, 24th.—Paid a visit to Lady W[——]; was shocked at the nonsense she talked to me about my friend's verses, which Miss M[——] had read to her. I felt really provoked. Lady W [——] was not satisfied with the unaffected and genuine spirit of piety which reigns in them, and is their chief merit, but wanted them to be converted into a dissertation on theology, an exposition of the Christian religion, and, in short, to become a sermon. I was confounded, but told her that really the subject was not sufficiently serious to build such a structure upon ; and that religion was not the theme that had given birth to my friend's verses, although the theme itself had elicited some religious sentiments. I felt disgusted, and walked directly to Lady S[——], but did not find her at home, so I proceeded to Lord and Lady B[——]. Their conversation made me feel more stupid and foolish when I left them, than when I went into their house. The society of some persons produces a lethargic influence. Dined at Lady S[——]'s, played at cards, and was weary of myself and of all the world. Mem. A bad sign of the state of my own mind.

Sunday, 27th.—Allowed spleen to conquer me, and made myself and my best friend unhappy thereby; was very sorry for it, and suffered justly. Went to church: a good useful sermon on the value of time, which, (in spite of Mr. O'B[——]'s calling it the *valloo*, with sundry other ridiculous mispronunciations,) produced some wholesome effects on me. I endeavoured to write and read at home, but the machine was out of order, and would not play. Received a visit from Monsieur D'O[——], the most agreeable man I have been acquainted with here, of this country: he brings me all sorts of books, and has much pleasant conversation. I passed a bad night, repenting my spleen; did not sleep, and rose sadly worn out—" Better not do the deed, than weep it done."

Monday, 28th Feb.—I went to get some plants for Lady C. C[ampbel]l, at a Chanoine Grosson's, who has a romantic house about two miles up in the mountains. A disagreeable stony path leads to the foot of a steep, which is covered with pines and cypresses; a turn to the right, through an archway, conducts along a sort of wide passage formed on one side by a rock, on the other by a screen of cypresses, to a little chapel; through apertures cut in this screen, a delicious prospect presents itself: the Bay of Nice, the blue sea bounding the horizon on one hand, the Alps towering in gradations of cultivated mountain, till they end in snowy peaks on the other. The terraces of olives, vines, figs, and other fruit trees, intermingled with the cypress, the caroubier, and the almond now in flower, rising in gradual amphitheatre around, present a magic scene. The blemishes which disfigure this beautiful landscape on a near view, are unobserved in looking at it from a height.

The inclosures of high stone walls, the miserable state of decay of the houses, the filthy odour of manure, are thus avoided. The Chanoine led us from this passage round to another terrace, and through a little formal garden into his house. The garden was cut into parterres, divided by patches of orange trees; and a small marble fountain played in the midst; but inside the house there was an offensive smell, as is the case in every habitation at Nice. Upstairs, the room was clean; one or two small etchings hung upon the wall, of tolerable taste, but a number of family portraits, sufficiently hideous to scare the eye, disfigured the apartment.

From the window, the same enchanting scenery presented itself; the whole place bore a character of interest; and romance might have peopled the scene with delightful persons, but reality only presented the Chanoine to view. He showed me a small piece of sculpture in wood, representing flowers, beautifully carved; and then, pleased with my admiration of the site of his house and garden, he took from a closet a case containing his best apparatus of glasses, and a bottle of very delicious white wine. There was a mixture of courtesy and coldness in his manner, which was peculiar. From the sitting-room he opened a door which conducted to a large space, or open corridor, covered only in summer by a trellice of vines, and surrounded by a stone seat, on small buttresses of the same material. Projected from the walls on stone brackets, were some busts of not inelegant sculpture. One of them, a female head of a Cleopatra, was very well executed; and a lesser one, representing a male head, which the Chanoine said had been found in the neighbourhood, I thought was remarkably good.

Through his bed-room, a low and concealed door, covered by a curtain, opened to a small chapel. I was struck with a feeling of interest difficult to explain; here, then, in this narrow secluded abode, was united all that was dear to the heart or soul of man. Piety might pour its orisons to the ear of Heaven ; reflection's still voice might commune undisturbed ; regret might hallow the remembrance of past pleasures ; hope might anticipate those yet in store. In short, with a rapid glance, and in one hasty sketch, I ran over the life of mortals, from the cradle to the tomb.

The Chanoine next conducted me up a steep path to a rock composed of marble and gravel, that overtops his house. There is a sort of gorge scooped out by the hand of nature, which he has planted with innumerable cypresses, pines, and other evergreens :—it is a strange and lovely solitude. He was well pleased with my admiration of its beauty. He told us he had been an emigrant for ten years ; that in the time of Robespierre's tyranny, two of that monster's brothers had lived at Nice ; and that during their reign he had returned to see his paternal home in secret, and had escaped with difficulty, in the middle of the night, by flight to an opposite hill, which he pointed out to us, and which was at that time entirely covered with trees. Among these, in a cavern, he had lain concealed for some time. He was supported by the charity of a poor woman, who brought him food for many days ; at length he escaped again into Tuscany, and ultimately had been brought, by Providence, to enjoy his own possessions in peace. I left this Chanoine and his romantic abode, with a firm determination to return there. In the evening I went to Lady B[——]'s, and played loo with her and Lord B[——] and the two consuls.

Tuesday, 29th Feb.—Paid a visit to Madame D[avido]ff.* She is very agreeable. I do not quite understand her character, but feel sure she is good. Went also to see Lady S[——]. She has very odd manners, and sometimes

* A Russian, *née* Orloff, wife of General Davidoff.

appears to me quite unsettled in mind. She tormented my dog. Certainly, educating other people's children and dogs is a thankless office, at best.

Thursday, 2nd March.—Took notes from Miss Plumtre. Finished the first volume. Received visits from Mr. D[——], P. Bradford, Captain H[——]. Mr. D[——] sat them all out. He talked about the propriety of letting dying people know, or not, their actual state of danger. He convinced me that it was right to do so ; but I fear in some cases, where no previous preparation of mind had led the person to serious thoughts, or imbued them with proper feelings, I should not have courage to awaken their conscience to the stings of remorse. "Yet how much more cruel," replied Mr. D[——], after I made that answer, "to allow a dear one to die with his or her sins unrepented of, and go to an eternal suffering, where the worm dieth not, and the fire is not quenched."

His opinion was the right one, and should I ever be in a situation to fulfil such a duty, painful though it would be, I should endeavour to fulfil it. I walked out, and felt an oppression of melancholy for poor Lady G[lenbervie] ; for though I am but slightly acquainted with her, I am told she is very amiable, and unfeignedly attached to her poor husband, from whom she is about to part. That her present hour of trial excites the sincerest sympathy, I am sure ; she has the prayers of all the good people here.

Every idea was for a time chased away to-night by the entrance at Miss M[——]'s of Madame D[avidoff] and Lady S[——], with the wonderful news that Bonaparte is at Grasse, accompanied by, some say five, some six, some eight hundred men. That he is there, is a fact ; the Prince of Monaco passed this day, on his way to his own little principality, and saw him. This event is as astonishing as if it had not been probable. Who could think he would remain at Elba quietly and be a good boy, because he had been whipped, and put in a corner? I never believed it, and yet now I am all surprise.

A number of small vessels were seen off Nice this morning, and several jokes were made about them. Nobody guessed how serious was the cause which spread their sails. They brought Bonaparte and his troops; and where is he going to? That no one can tell. France must be his object; and surely he never would set foot on its land, unless he had pretty well ascertained that many persons would give him a kind reception. Whether he will remain at Grasse till other forces join him, or whether he will march immediately to the interior of the country—what he will do, in short—is the greatest point of interest to all the world, and to us who are now so near him, especially.

This indeed is an event to stir the stagnating blood. How many at this moment may be in all the horrors of a sanguinary night, if he has organized his plans and traced his path in blood; if the fearful Revolution is to be acted over again! But God forbid! Policy more than cruelty must be at his sword's point. But he cannot be on foot for nothing, and without a fearful struggle he cannot regain any point of his ambition. In each event, those who look most for succour to the Power of Powers, will be those who have least to fear. I think of my friends in England, who will personally be anxious for us, not knowing how quiet poor little insignificant Nice is. They may imagine some scenes of bustle here, from which at present we are quite free.

Friday, 3rd March.—To-day, I heard that Bonaparte has issued proclamation, saying his eagles are on the wing, and will soon light on the spires of Notre Dame. He is said to have set off at two o'clock yesterday, and marched twelve leagues, to a place called Castellane.

Nice, I should think, is a nook of great safety.   I am glad to be here, and my insignificance is my best security against all personal danger ; but I should not like to see others exposed to fear ; I am grown so frail, body and mind.

Horses and carriages have been going out of the town all night, I suppose to join Bonaparte.   The commandant has forbidden any person to cross the Var.   But what signifies his half dozen of grasshoppers ? are not there passes over the mountains fifty ways, by which Bonaparte will be joined by all those who are so inclined ?   Conjectures as to his means and measures are endless ; but that they are great, I cannot doubt, for his all is at stake. Perhaps the Congress has decided points to which Austria will not agree, and Austria may now be ready to pour her troops on France.   Perhaps too Bonaparte may be desperate, and may choose to set his last hazard on this cast.   His character, however, is not that of headlong valour ;   policy and prudence have always supported his ambition.

Saturday Night, 4th March.—I went yesterday to town, to gather all the reports.   Called at Madame de Corvesi's, thinking she might have heard from Paris, but she was gone on a *quête*, and my *quête* was in vain.   Called next at La C[——]'s.   I found him foaming with rage, because he had not been allowed to sail to Genoa the preceding night.   This vexed him particularly, because he had hoped to be the first person to bear the news to Mr. Hill at Genoa, and he ascribed his not being permitted to do so to private spite in the Comte D[——], for fear he should precede the Estafette of the former.   All this littleness in the midst of great concerns, is the law of earthly things.

I heard that Bonaparte landed on Wednesday, at or near Cannes.   The next day he sent twenty-five or thirty of his soldiers to Antibes.   These were questioned who they were and whence they came. "We serve our General." "And where is your General?" "On the high road." This farce did not last long, of course. They were soon known. They were, perhaps, expected, but the form of taking them prisoners was gone through, though they were allowed to walk about, even without being disarmed. They seemed rather there as friends than foes. It is impossible to think mere inertness should have thus favoured Bonaparte. There must have been some decided sentiment at Antibes in his favour. In the meantime he landed all his troops, to the amount of a thousand men, twenty cases of ammunition, &c. He did not sleep in Grasse, but bivouacked near it, and marched on the next day to Castellane, where he distributed proclamations to the different ranks of people, prefects, soldiers, &c., saying that he was not come to hurt or oppress the people, but to restore the glory of the French nation, and to make his faithful subjects happy ; adding that his eagles are flying from steeple to steeple, and will soon perch on those of Notre Dame. These proclamations are bombast, and presumptuous in the highest degree.

I had heard that he had made this presumptuous declaration before ; Monsieur De Condole, the French Consul, now here, confirmed the truth of the report. M. Condole is just returned from Antibes, where, he added, the Prince of Monaco had been stopped ; that Bonaparte asked him if he knew him, to which he replied, "Certainly, Sir, as I have served under your Majesty." Bonaparte inquired where the Prince was going ; " à mes Terres," was the reply. "Et moi aussi, je vais aux miennes," said Bonaparte, with a forced smile of assumed gaiety, and added, with a sneer, " I have begun a very good road for you, Prince, but I suppose the king of Sardinia will finish it." Then taking away a couple of the Prince's horses, without asking it as a favour, he dismissed him, and told him he might continue his journey.

The Prince of Monaco was glad " *d'en etre quitte pour la peur*," said Monsieur De Condole ; he also told me Bonaparte pays immense prices for everything. Some of his soldiers damaged a vineyard : the people to whom it belonged asked an exorbitant compensation, which was immediately granted. The same for a horse which he wished to purchase at Castellane. In short, he seems to lack neither men, means, nor money. In the evening I saw Lady G[——]; she talked of this great event, and conjectured till conjecture could go no further. She agreed with me in fearing that this last effort is one that will cost the world much blood.

Saturday night.—Went about seeking news, but could find none. Heard only what I knew before, repeated with the variations which everybody makes in telling a story. In the evening I walked with Madame D[——] to Lady S[——]'s. More suppositions, till Madame de St. Agathe came in, and spoke very good sense upon the subject, and informed us that she had just heard from the Commandant that sixty men from the garrison at Antibes have deserted, and one of the officers with them, who was fearful of being one of the prisoners. It is also said, Massena and his troops are in motion, but whether on the offensive or defensive cause, seems unknown.

Sunday, 5th March.—Went to church. The Arch-deacon preached a very good sermon, on the non-existence of faith without works, and the inefficacy of works without faith. Went afterwards to visit Madame Rivière. I had a curiosity to look at her pretty niece, a Miss Fells ; a woman as white as an Albinoise, but with sense and sweetness in her countenance, and the bluest eyes I ever saw. I thought her pleasing, particularly from an expression of open sweetness on her forehead. The conversation turned upon Bonaparte, of course. Nothing new had transpired, not even lies. When I was at Miss M[——]'s, Madame D[——] and Lady S[——] came in. They did not know whither to go, at least Lady S[——]. She has the disease of ennui, but let no one say it ought not to be pitied. He who knows all things will surely have mercy upon the sins it engenders, especially if there is any attempt at conquering it.

Monsieur D[——] came to me in the evening, bringing me more books. He is a very intelligent man, and, above all, seems to have a placidity and a spirit of tranquillity and content which diffuse serenity around. Certainly every human being possesses influence in the circle in which he moves ; he should, therefore, seriously consider whether it is employed in a baneful or a salutary manner. In that very consideration there is matter of useful and of interesting employment.

Monday, 6th March.—Saw a large vessel opposite to my windows. Went out immediately to inquire what she could be. Heard it was the Aboukir, commanded by Captain Thompson, sent from Genoa in pursuit of the small frigate in which Bonaparte had escaped ; and could not help thinking they were a day after the fair. They knew at Genoa as soon as we did, of the lion's being out of his den. Lord Glenbervie wrote to his Lady, saying he should not proceed from Genoa till he knew that all was quiet at Rome and in Italy.

He seemed to be quite at ease about us, knowing this spot is out of the line of Bonaparte's business, and that we are all safe here. There are reports from Genoa that Murat has sent, or is sending, troops to join Bonaparte on the confines of Switzerland ; that the latter has turned aside from Grenoble, and, taking the route by Barcelonette intends to proceed round towards that country, to unite his forces with Murat's. As he knew nothing of the decision of the congress respecting the new-made Sovereign, one cannot draw any conclusion as to the probability or improbability of this measure. I am inclined to give it credit, and am extremely sorry for it on every possible account.

Poor Sir Stephen Glynne died yesterday, about four o'clock. His death, by every account, was truly christian. He resigned youth, fortune, love, all that makes this life a life of felicity, without a murmur. He received the sacrament, and breathed his last in that firm and pious trust which religion alone bestows. His widow is now the one to be pitied.

I was again sadly disappointed yesterday at receiving no letters. Came home low ; read, but my thoughts, in spite of myself, wandered in sandy deserts, where no well-springs of joy are to be found. Visited Lady S[——], and found her ill. As soon as Lord S[——] came in, she began quarrelling with him ; and cried and lamented herself till I felt quite distressed. There are some people who cannot be at peace, or who are never content unless under the excitement of some excessive joy or misery ; and Lady S[——] is one of these. She is not satisfied with her brilliant portion in life, her kind husband, and her children. What can please her, since these do not ? She is doing all she can to make the latter odious characters and leading them to hate her. I think in this she will certainly succeed.

Tuesday, 7th March.—Lord S[——] paid me a visit. He is so desœuvré, and has got such a desœuvré partner, poor man, that he is really to be pitied ; but I can do neither of them good, and I wish they would not both make me their confidant about nothing at all ; for that is the fact. Oh ! if some real distress or heart grief were to come to them, how could they bear it, when they find their present pleasant lot hard to bear ?

No news of Bonaparte ! Conjecture about him and his doings is fatiguing, yet one cannot lay it aside. It is a week to-day since he arrived at Cannes.

Wednesday, 8th March.—Received a letter from Mrs. D[ame]r, saying all London was up in arms, at an official notice having been made to Lord Liverpool that the Princess of Wales was to return to England in May. The letter announcing this intention, and one also to Princess Charlotte, formed, it seems, the contents of those letters Her Royal Highness desired me to forward to H[——] on the 10th of last month. How strange that she should not have written a word of this to me ; on the contrary, should have told me that she should meet me in October, at Genoa or Marseilles.

Certainly there are two wonderful people in the world, the Princess of Wales and Bonaparte ! Of the latter, there are a thousand and one vague reports, many of them very puerile and vain ; such as his being cased in armour, which was discovered by men who lifted him upon his horse ; his drinking very hard, &c. &c. Other reports, of more consequence, (if they are true,) state that some English vessels have fallen in with others which were conveying troops and arms from Murat to join him ; that Massena has set a price on his head, and declared him and his followers outlaws ; that there has been a conspiracy at Paris ; that fifty people have been shot. It is very difficult to know the truth anywhere at any time ; but here, and at this present moment, impossible. Played at loo at Lady S[——]'s in the evening, whilst Bonaparte was playing for kingdoms—let us hope *only* playing. Ainsi va le monde ! du sublime au ridicule, il n'y a qu'un pas.

Thursday, 9th March.—Sang ; should like to sing oftener. Walked with Lord B[——] to my favourite

I   x haunt. He has all the suavity which supplies the place of information; all the polish of manners which implies refinement of mind. I know not if the force of vigorous intellect, or high-wrought genius, be there. I should think not; but for a time, on s'en passe.

Dined with Mr. B[——]. There were, of women, Lady E[——] A[——], a perfect Argus, with eyes behind, I believe; Miss B[——], very like a doll in a barber's shop; both like things in a bad dream; Mrs. D[——] and her daughter, starch-looking persons, harsh and full of angles, mentally as well as bodily. An old Mr. D[——], very like a gentleman; his son, a beautiful young man, with fine soft features, but quite a lad; Col. C[——], that epitome of self-consequence and vulgarity; Mr. K[——] a little haberdasher, or clerk in a counting house; and Sir Somebody Something, with a crooked face, formed the party. B[——] has a gentleness of manner that I rather like.

I sat next Col. C[——] and Mr. D[——]. I tried to make acquaintance with the latter, and found him very conversible and intelligent. He gave me an account of his going down the Rhone, with his family, and their being nearly lost. How awful it must have been; in an instant they were up to their throats in water, even sitting upon the barouche box of their carriages; and had it not been for a small boat, whose crew saw and came to their relief, they must have all perished.

After dinner, came Captain Aidy, of the Partridge frigate, who arrived to-day, and brought in his vessel Col. Campbell, *alias* Sir Neil Campbell: we were all anxious to hear what he could have to say for himself.

Sir Neil did not come, but pretended to have business with the Commandant and the French Consul. Captain Aidy stated that since October he had been stationed off Elba, to be at the disposal of Sir Neil Campbell; that the latter had frequently made excursions, and lastly had gone to Leghorn.   That on the night of the 26th, he, Captain Aidy, had seen Bonaparte's frigate quite tranquil in the harbour, without any appearance of bustle or preparation.   He had accordingly sailed to bring back Sir N. Campbell ; and when they returned, they found Bonaparte, his troops, and arms, had left Elba two days. In consternation, they landed, and found Madame Mère, the mother of Pauline, and Madame Bertrand, wife to the General.   Captain A[——] and Sir N[eil] C[ampbell] told them that Bonaparte would certainly be taken and killed immediately ; but they seemed quite secure of his success.

At three o'clock on Sunday, Bonaparte shut the gates of Elba.   At nine o'clock, he was towed out of the harbour of Ferrajo, and immediately a favouring breeze sprung up, and wafted him at once to the shores of Provence, without opposition.

At best this is a blundering business ; and I should think either Sir Neil, or the ministry, or both, must answer for it with their heads, or at least with their reputations. All that is said by way of excuse for Sir Neil Campbell, does not appear to me to exonerate him from the greatest blame ; indeed, I cannot fathom the whole affair, and do not wonder foreigners throw the blame on the whole nation.

Friday, 10*th March*.—Lady Glenbervie is far from well.   I wish Lord G[——] were well, to nurse her. I received a visit from Sir Neil Campbell.   Lady C[——] C[——], whom I had just been visiting, told me he was a handsome man, and so he is.   His eloquent defence of his conduct certainly made me view it with a more favourable eye than I had done before, considering it with the eyes of my understanding only.   His conversation, as nearly as I can remember it, was as follows :—" I was never placed about Bonaparte as his gaoler.   I was a commissioner, on the contrary, appointed by the English government to provide him with everything he could want in his island. For that purpose I had the Partridge, stationed at Porto Ferrajo, to obey my orders; but I had no men, no means whatever to prevent Bonaparte's doing whatever he chose; and as the latter had a small frigate, a bomb vessel, and several small boats with a thousand soldiers at his command, I certainly could not be supposed to have any power to prevent his leaving the island whenever he might be so inclined.

"As far back as October last, I wrote to Lord Castlereagh, stating my belief that if the allies did not pay Bonaparte the salary they agreed to give him, he would make some desperate attempt. Since that, I have been aware that he had constant communications with Murat. I also informed our government of this circumstance. I have been frequently absent from Elba, not conceiving myself under any engagement not to be so. The last time I left the island, I saw that everything was perfectly quiet, and in its usual state. When Captain Aidy came away, on Saturday, the 25th, all was apparently as usual. The soldiers were amusing themselves making a garden before the guard-house, and in Bonaparte's brig there was no appearance of any preparation whatever for sailing. Captain A[——] came to me at Leghorn, to take me back there.

"However, some rumours reached me at Leghorn, which alarmed me, and I waited on the French consul and the English. The latter did not give these reports the least credit, but the former did. I hastened away, but, unfortunately, my intelligence led me to believe that Bonaparte might have fled to Italy; and to Porto Caprai, therefore, we took our course. When we got there, we heard that such and such vessels full of men had been seen to the westward of the shores of Provence. These answered to the description of Bonaparte's little fleet. In all anxiety we turned, therefore; but I thought

it best to take Elba in our way, to ascertain the fact of
his flight. We were becalmed; and when we reached
Porto Ferrajo, Bonaparte had been gone two days. I
left the Partridge at the outside of the port, and told
Captain Aidy that if I did not return in two hours, he
might conclude I was detained prisoner, and make the
best of his way to give the intelligence. As I approached
the shore, I saw none of the great caps, none of the usual
soldiery, but what he calls 'gardes nationales,' in
their room.

" I was received by some of the under persons in command, and requested to be led immediately to General
Bertrand. 'General Bertrand is not here.' ' To General
Oudinot'; 'he is not here either.' ' To the Emperor.'
They looked uncertain what to say. ' Very well, I see
how it is; you need not be so discreet. I knew this
plan long ago, and you may depend upon it they are
all taken prisoners by this time.'

" I thought it best to pretend this knowledge, in order
to appear of some consequence."

Just as I write these words, [——] tells me, Barzotti,
music master, has ridden by, and says, our English officer
told him, Bonaparte is taken, with four hundred men.
I do not believe it, and go back to my narration.

" Who is in command here ? "   Sir Neil told me, was
his next question. " I was answered, 'Monsieur [——].'
' Lead me to him.' ' What are your intentions ? '   Sir
Neil said, as soon as they met, ' Do you mean to submit
to your lawful sovereign or not ? '   ' What sovereign ? '
·' The allies, who placed Bonaparte here.' ' I know of no
sovereign but Napoleon,' replied Monsieur [——], 'and
I have means to defend the island, and shall use them.'

" I had nothing to do but to bow, and say it was well;
that I could remain no longer at Elba; that my frigate
waited for me, and that I must be gone immediately. I
thought, however, that I would endeavour to learn all

the intelligence I could, and called at Madame Mère's and the Princess Pauline's.* They both declined giving any information, if they had any to give. They said they were in the greatest anxiety, and, on the contrary, so far from giving me any news, they requested me to give them some, of their brother.

"I spoke as if I was well acquainted with his plans, whereas I was in perfect ignorance of them ; but I could observe that whenever I mentioned Italy, they seemed much relieved. Princess Pauline took my hand, and, pressing it to her heart, desired me to feel how it beat with anxiety ; but I could not perceive any symptoms of alarm, and, being in haste, I shortened my visit as much as possible.

"Delighted to find I was not detained prisoner, I sailed to Antibes ; but still in a pitiable state of uneasiness of mind, for I was aware how much the imprudence of the nations would be laid to my charge, and how much circumstances might make me seem guilty in the minds of thousands."

Sir N. Campbell coloured violently as he said this, and I was sorry for him. Then he added, that he was going into France, but should return this way, and so we parted.†

All these particulars, however, do not lessen my surprise at the conduct of our ministers, as well as at that of the allies ; and I regret that one of my countrymen

* Princess Borghese was doubtless very beautiful, but her manners were those of a petite maitresse giving herself the airs of a crowned head. Many were the really great ladies who waited in her drawing-rooms, and did not blush to be subservient to her caprices. [Part of original note.]

† If it be true that Sir Neil Campbell was the heart prisoner of a fair lady at Florence, that may account for his having watched his prisoner at Elba so ill. Certain it is, Sir Neil Campbell seemed very anxious to prove that he was not to blame in having permitted the escape of a man on whose liberty the fate of Europe depended. [Original note.] He died in 1827.

PAULINE BONAPARTE
(*From a pastel in the possession of Mr. John Lane*)

should have accepted the place of a sort of petty spy over even Bonaparte. Better, far better, to have been his appointed gaoler, and known by the prisoner himself to be such, than a spy in the disguise of a friend to provide for his wants.

I think Sir Neil feels thus himself, and regrets having accepted the office. Many circumstances respecting this affair will, I doubt not, be made known by time, which brings foul and fair to light ; but at present there is a mystery enveloping the whole of this wonderful business.

Saturday, 11*th March.*—No confirmation of the good news, but all the English feel confident that Mr. King and Sir Neil Campbell will bring us the intelligence that Bonaparte is certainly taken. They say it is impossible for him to escape ; he is surrounded by troops. Bonnet is a small village, quite encircled by mountains, and he never can make his way over these, with an army, while the enemy are in close pursuit. Monsieur [——] reached Lyons on the 8th, and Massena sent off five thousand men from Marseilles. What can Bonaparte's handful of men do against all these ? Oh ! it was a desperate impulse, almost madness, I should think, which induced him to make this last attempt for his liberty.

Sunday, 12*th.*—Went out with Lady S[——] and Miss M[——]e. We went visiting ; amongst other places to Madame Villegarde's *campagne*—such a place ! a miserable house on the high-road to Turin, more like a dirty ale-house than a gentleman's chateau, with some ill-growing trees, cut into shapes, before it. The door was opened by a wild-looking man ; the dust blew through the empty passage, and made a cloud which we found it difficult to pass through without being blinded. We were shown, or rather left to find our way, up a ladder-like staircase, to a dirty room, the floor of which was strewed with rags and filth, where we beheld La Marquise De Villegarde, in dress and in person, like an old witch. She took us in great haste, leading Lady S[——] by the hand, into an inner room, in which were two beds, covered with caps, and gowns, and *breeches* of the Marquis De Villegarde, and various other things, strewed together in disorder. "Ah!" la Marquise exclaimed, "how terrible to receive you here!"—Of course we made the civil; but Lady S[——] was so disgusted with the disagreeable smell which prevailed in the Marquise's apartment, that she would not stay a moment. I was much pressed to return; and the old lady said she would tell me my fortune, and many curious things.

I had heard before that she was learned in the *black art*. I declined having my own fate foretold, but promised to pay her another visit. We met Madame Davidoff, and we all walked to the promontory of Leucate,—as I have christened that beautiful walk among the olive-grounds, extending beyond the port towards Monaco. The locale is such as one would have supposed the Lesbian maid might have chosen, when she plunged into the ocean.

We saw a quantity of ammunition that the Sicilian regiment in the English pay brought with them, in carts each drawn by four fine grey horses, which they were driving to the Place Vittoria. This excited our curiosity, and I questioned an English soldier, but he either knew nothing, or would communicate none of his information.

Tuesday, 14th.—Yesterday evening, Mr. King and Sir N. Campbell arrived. Sir N[——] would positively *say nothing*, only sent his apology to Mr. B[——], with whom he was to have dined, informing him he was to embark immediately. Mr. King declared the news was as bad as possible, but would not say what it was. This put all the inhabitants of the Fauxbourg in a fuss; but some of them concluded that it was only the ignorance of Sir Neil Campbell and Mr. King, and not any real knowledge of facts, which made them cast an air of mystery over their journey. I passed two hours with Madame De Villegarde ; she showed me a small library of curious old books on the black art. This woman gave me the sort of entertainment one feels on reading a German novel full of horrors and wonders ; our reason despising our imagination all the while, for being diverted. There was quite sufficient basis for romance and mystery in all she said and all she showed me. Among other things, she told me that she herself had seen gold made, with her own eyes, and had partly been initiated into the mysterious process ; " but much," she added, " must be gone through, much must be known, before the slightest knowledge of that wonderful thing called the philosopher's stone can be understood."

" There," said she, opening five or six mystical books interspersed with strange prints and drawings, and hieroglyphics, " these are the elements of that study, but you will not understand them any more than if you looked at any unknown language." I read some of the letter-press of the cabalistic books, which indeed appeared to me nonsense. Madame De V[——] looked wise and pleased, because I listened to her, and she said, if I would study any branch of the occult sciences, all her works on those subjects were at my disposal. I thanked her, but thought what a waste of time such a study would be, and left the old lady with a poor idea of her powers of divination, and a thorough contempt for the *black art*. The only curious *fact* I ever heard of the Marquise's having predicted future events, was, (as Lady Charlotte Campbell told me,) that, several months ago, when every one thought Bonaparte safe at Elba for life, Madame De Villegarde laid out the cards, and read by them before Lady Charlotte, that Bonaparte would first be victorious in a great undertaking he contemplated, then occasion tears and mourning, and finally die himself overthrown and taken captive. This certainly was a singular prediction, but it might have been foretold without any assistance from supernatural information.

Wednesday, 15th.—To-day I received the following letter from the Princess of Wales, dated Rome.

CHÈRE [——],—J'ai eu le bonheur de recevoir deux lettres de vous avant mon départ de Naples ; depuis hier je me trouve a Rome pour m'embarquèr à Civita di Veccia, pour me rendre a Livorne. J'espére que la peur vous a pris, et que je vous y trouverai. Lady Charlotte Lindsay et Monsieur F. North, sont de la partie. Mais comme Lady Elizabeth Forbes est resté a Naples pour ce rendre a Londre pour quelque mois, je serai absolument sans dame ; ainsi je vais proposer a Lady Charlotte Campbell de venir a Livorne dans ma frigate, avec toute sa famille et Mrs. Damer, pour nous rendre a Gêne, ou je compte de rester quelque temps et de voir quel tournure les affaires politiques prendront, *car le Lac de Como* est mon point de vue pour mon establissemen, si Napoleon me le permette—ainsi si Mrs. Damer veut accompagner Lady Charlotte, je serai trop heureuse de l'avoir chez moi. Si Lady C[harlotte] ne peut pas se rendre a Livorne avec toute sa famille, je veut lui offrir de prendre sa fille aineé pour etre ma *bedchamber woman*, et lui payer deux cent pounds, par ans.* Si Miss M[——], l'ami de Lady Charlotte, voudrai accompagner Miss Campbell, je serai charmé de l'avoir quelque temps chez moi, pour trois mois ; je lui ferais un present et payerai son voyage de retour ou elle voudra se trouvér ; mais il faudrait quelle vien avec la fille de Lady Charlotte, et sans femme de chambre. Ah ! comme je serai charmé de vous revoir. Combien de choses j'ai a vous dire et vous communiquer. J'ai le cœur bien gros, mais bouche close

* What an idea, to suppose any mother would allow her daughter, especially so young a person as Lady C. Campbell's daughter was at that time, to accept such a situation ! The poor Princess, who did not want for discernment, must have been aware that the request was one very unlikely to be granted by any parent, considering the *mala fama*, or, to say the least of it, *trumpery* reputation which her Court had obtained since her residence abroad. [Original note.]

pour ce moment.   Croyez moi pour la vie, absente ou presente, toujours votre sincère amie.   · · ·   ·   ·

C. P.

I showed Her Royal Highness's letter, as she desired, to Lady C. Campbell, who, of course, rejected her offer of making her daughter the Princess's *bedchamber woman*; but she said she would endeavour herself to meet the Princess at Leghorn.   I replied to Her Royal Highness's letter, by saying I regretted she was compelled to ask here and there, for persons to attend her; and ventured, for the first time, to give her a piece of advice, which, I fear, would offend; but the impulse was too strong within me to endeavour to serve her, that I could not resist breaking through my rule, which had made me such a favourite with the poor lady.   I besought Her Royal Highness to return to England; I represented to her the troubled state into which it was to be feared the Continent would soon be thrown, so that no place might shortly be safe from one hour to another; and besides that, I felt sure it would be wisest for her own interests that she should return and take possession of her station and situation in England.

For God's sake, Madam, lose not the place you hold in the British people's hearts, by too long absence from them. Live amongst them, spend your money amongst them, and they will stand by you to the last.   Live abroad, and be surrounded by foreign servitors, and, I fear, the English people's affection will not stand the test of a long absence, or of your showing a partiality to foreigners.   Remember the *prejudice* John Bull bears them.   Excuse the freedom of my speech, Madam, and I implore your Royal Highness to believe, that sincere attachment makes me express this opinion, though reluctantly.   If you are *always under the public eye of the English nation*, no lies can be invented, injurious to your honour or happiness.   Return to Britain, choose from some of the worthiest of her nobles, persons willing to be, and deserving of being, your attendants; keep up an interest in your child's heart, by living in the same country, partaking of the same interests with her, and, I venture to say, your Royal Highness will not repent of the determination.

Once again, I beseech your Royal Highness to forgive the liberty I have taken in writing to you thus freely.

I shall be ready, at all times and places, to obey your commands, and remain,

Madam, your Royal Highness's
Most faithful and obedient humble servant,
&c. &c.

Such was the answer I made to the Princess. She never gave me any reply, and did not follow my advice. I hardly hoped she would; but I have reason to think she was not displeased at the time, but only contemned my opinions as insignificant. It is a vain endeavour to serve Her Royal Highness.

Lady Glenbervie told me the melancholy and almost incredible news, of Bonaparte's being at Lyons. At Grenoble all the inhabitants declared themselves for him, and some regiments had joined him. He got there, it appears, without any interruption, and was at Lyons on the 9th. This awful news was transmitted by telegraph to Turin, and from Turin to Genoa, from whence it reached Lady Glenbervie. She added to this news the scarcely less surprising intelligence in another way, of the Princess of Wales being expected at Genoa every hour.

I went to Lady S[——], who did not know any of these tidings; and when she heard that her lord, not master, had been acquainted with the whole business the day before, she burst forth into a torrent of invectives, and said that when confidence ended between man and wife, there was a total end of every tie. She made a fine tirade, which stunned me, for she spoke, or rather screamed, so loud, that I expected to see her fall into convulsions. Lord S[——] defended himself by saying that her nervous state of mind was so great, he feared to agitate her, and intended to break the matter by degrees. After this quarrel Lady S[——] said she must go to bed, and I left them.

Early this morning I went about to gather up the news, and found all the English, as if with one consent, were setting off different ways, in order to get back to England. Most of them were flying to Genoa, where, from the number of troops, and through our minister, Mr. Hill, and Lord William Bentinck, it was supposed we should find greater protection than here, with poor old Comte D'Osasque. In the meantime, Madame Davidoff and I went to the commandeur, to make friends with, and consult him, what we had best do for ourselves. Madame D[——] waited not to ask if he was at home, but walked straight forward into his apartment. The appearance of calm despair which he betrayed in his whole countenance and manner, alarmed Madame Davidoff considerably. He told us that Bonaparte had passed Lyons, that twenty-six regiments had deserted from Monsieur and gone over to his cause ; that when Monsieur rode along the lines and made the men a speech, exhorting them to do their duty, and crying Vive le Roi, a dead silence pervaded the whole rebel rout. At length one of the officers came forward and said, " Prince il est trop tard, tout est fini : the honour of France has been sullied, we are going to avenge her disgrace. The Emperor is the only sovereign we acknowledge." Monsieur fled, with about forty or fifty men, to Paris.

The commandeur promised to inform Madame Davidoff the moment there was any occasion for her to leave this place. Monsieur D'Osasque said he was afraid there was not a hope left that Paris would resist. I accompanied Madame Davidoff to Lady L[——] B[——] : she has a pleasing manner, but her religious sentiments are too bigoted, and her endeavours to convert Mr. [——], a gay young man, a friend of her husband's, were too much

of that school which is *sujet à caution*. Lady L[——]
said she looked upon Bonaparte's being permitted to
return, as a punishment for the allied sovereigns having
disputed about their own petty points of interest, and also
as the means of extirpating the Catholic religion, against
which she seemed quite furious. This violent zeal for our
own mode of worship, where the great points of christian
faith and trust are the same, appears to me intolerant
and blameable. I did not suffer my opinions, however,
to impede Lady L[——]'s eloquence.

I dined at Lady S[——]'s with the Consul D'Espagne
and the Consul D'Angleterre, and that most disagreeable
man, Col. C[——]. The nonsense that was talked at
dinner put me out of all patience ; and making jokes on
the most awful events and dispensations of Providence,
seems to me the dullest as well as the most senseless and
unfeeling conduct.

Thursday, 16th March.—I have determined to remain
here until war is absolutely at the gate, and I shall then
go to Geneva ; for I dread returning to England, and
many circumstances combine to make me doubtful
whether or not I shall ever bring myself to go thither
again. I saw Lady Glenbervie, who is all anxiety about
her husband. Went in the evening to Lady S[——], who
is all gall to hers.

Friday, the 17th.—Lord S[——] called on me to tell
me that Colonel Bourke had four transports at his disposal, and as his regiment was ordered to go over the Col
de Tende, and to occupy that part of the country, these
transports were to return to Genoa, and should take his
family, or any of his English friends, for nothing ; but
that they would be obliged to sail twenty-four hours
after he left Nice. Lord S[——] begged me only to make

this offer known to Lady Glenbervie. The reason that Colonel Bourke wished it to be kept secret, was, that he apprehended all the English who are flocking here from Marseilles, &c. might apply to him for conveyance to Genoa, and bring him into some scrape, as he could not be of use to them all. I declined the offer of this conveyance to Genoa, as it appeared probable, from the recall of troops, that no present apprehension was entertained for this place.

There were flying reports all day of Bonaparte's having met with some check, and his being driven back to Lyons. It was also said that Louis XVIII. was riding about the streets of Paris, and saying he never would quit it but with his life—that Soult had been discovered in a conspiracy, and that he had been shot. But all these were only vague reports, which could not even be traced to their reporter.

I went with Lady S[——] to pay visits. She was all bustle and delight at leaving Nice, caring little for the cause, like a child freed from a dull bondage. Her mind is very desultory ; she is not devoid of capacity, or rather, of quickness ; but it is *a garden full of weeds*, a most confused assemblage of rank and overgrown evils. Colonel Bourke, whom we met, told me his destination was changed, and that he and his troops were going straight to Genoa, and that he wished I would avail myself of his offer to convey me thither ; but Lady Glenbervie, who is here alone and unprotected, having asked me to remain, I should feel myself quite a barbarian to leave her, till her husband returns to her.

She read me a letter from him to-day, written Tuesday last, in which he says that Monsieur de Revelt, governor there, has desired him particularly to remain a day or two longer. Lady Glenbervie reads the sense of these words *mystically*, and supposes that they expect some attack to be made there, of which however they are not certain, and may not speak, but that they wish Lord Glenbervie, before he leaves Genoa, (with the intention of bringing her back there,) to be acquainted with the truth. This may or may not be, but I rather think Lord Glenbervie is only amusing himself, however late in the day.

Reports came to Madame Davidoff, through a German here who has a brother at Leghorn, who wrote him word that Murat is at Florence. This tallies with the notion of an attack being contemplated at Genoa. Spent the evening at Lady Glenbervie's, with Lady W[——] and Lady S[——].

Saturday, 18*th March*.—Lady S[——] made sure of setting off the next day, by packing up her children in Colonel Bourke's transport, and sending them to Genoa. The Archdeacon and Lady Waldegrave decided to go over the Col de Tende : they were to set off on Monday ; the B[——]s also, and Mrs. S[——]. This was a general breaking up of the English colony, and I felt melancholy to be the only one who was tied by circumstances to remain, whether I would or not. No letters seem to pass through Paris—an additional cause of vexation. I received a letter from the Princess,

Dated 15th March, 1815, CIVETTA VECCHIA.

MA CHÈRE [——],—Je me trouve depuis deux jours à Civitat Vecchia, ou j'attende ma frigatte de Naples, La Clorinde, qui doit directement me mener à Livorne. Lady Charlotte Lindsay et Monsieur F. North sont les seules personnes qui m'accompagne, mais ils sont obligée de me quitter alors pour ce rendre en Angleterre. Madame Falconniere, la femme de mon banquier, qui est avec ses deux petite filles pour ce rendre en Suisse pour voir ses fils, elle pourra bien ce rendre jusqua Nice en cas que ma lettre que je vous ai ecrit à Rome ne sera point arrivé.

Hélas ! combien de choses j'ai a vous communiquer. Mon plan ainsi est de rester dans la maison de Lady Charlotte Campbell à Nice pour deux jours, mais le petit Guilliaume et Mademoiselle Dumont nous avons tous nos lits, ainsi une chambre, est tous ce qui est necessaire Mes gens je les enverrais dans une auberge, et Madame Falconniere peut d'abord ce rendre dans une auberge, puis ce rendre en Suisse. Je pourrais alors faire quelque arrangement avec vous, où de prendre une maison près de Nice pour jouir de votre societé et de celle de Lady C. Campbell, ou de nous rendre a Gene, ou j'avais deja pris une maison en cas que Napoleon ne resistoit plus. J'ai quitté Naples dans la plus grande vitesse possible. Lady E. Forbes se rende en Angleterre— Monsieur Craven chez sa mère a Paris—Monsieur Hesse pour l'Angleterre, et je crois que Sir William Gell reste encore quelque temps a Naple. Je deteste Naples, et ne compte jamais d'y retourner, sur tout les rapports, mais enfin bouche close pour ce moment.*

J'espére que Lady Charlotte Campbell aussi bien que sa fille seront contente de mon arrangement de la prendre comme bedchamber women, avec l'appointement de deux cents par annee. J'attend Monsieur St. Leger et sa fille bientôt, ainsi j'aurais assez de monde autour de moi.

Votre tres sincere amie,
P. C.

As usual, the poor Princess wrote the above letter evidently in a state of excitement, and was considerably annoyed at being forsaken by all her English attendants. I fear she will never retain respectable persons about her, for she is unreasonable in her demands on their services, and leads so desultory a life, and oftentimes one so wholly unfitting her dignity as a woman, (much more as Princess of Wales,) that those most attached to her can least bear to witness her downfall; which this *wandering mania*, without a proper aim or object, is very likely to effect.

I spent the evening at Lady S[——]'s. Madame de

* The sudden alteration in Her Royal Highness's mind respecting Naples, seems at best very capricious, and, by all I ever heard, was totally without any rational foundation, as every one showed her attention and respect, till her strange, unaccountable conduct caused them to leave her society. [Original note.]

Corvesi was there, and related all the horrors of the first
Revolution, which she witnessed. I felt ashamed of not
feeling more regret than I did at bidding Lady S[——]
adieu, for she has been kind and hospitable to me. Yet
she has made no way in my heart, or even in *my liking*.
She does not care whether she has or no ; and so we
both parted without any sorrow, though we have lived
in intimacy for a length of time. I received a note
from the Duchess of [Devonshire], desiring me to take
lodgings for her and Lady B[——]h here, from Wednesday
next.*

Sunday, 19th March.—Mr. Vivian preached a very affect-
ing sermon, taking leave of his congregation. We, that
is to say, almost all the English, received the sacrament,
and parted in peace. After church, I received the farewell visit of Mr. V[——], and, while he was talking to me,
a stranger entered with a letter from the Princess of Wales.
I was confused and awkward, as I always am at the

---

* E[lizabeth], Duchess of [Devonshire] completed her reputation for
being a clever woman, by performing the part of ambassadress, under the
rose, from the court of England to the Papal See. One of the occasions
on which she exercised her sway over the Pope was, when the Queen
Caroline (which she was then become) returned to Rome the last
time on her way back to England. The Duchess prevented his Holiness
from showing Her Majesty the smallest civility, and he refused her
a guard of honour, or any of the honours due to her rank. It was a
weak and servile trait of character in Pius VI. to allow himself to
change his conduct towards the Queen, whom he had formerly received
with so much courtesy ; but Cardinal Gonsalvi it was, who probably
regulated him in this, as in most other points, and he was, as is well
known, subject to the Duchess of [Devonshire], who was desperately in
love with the Cardinal. Whenever she saw him approach, her whole
frame was in trepidation, and no girl of fifteen ever betrayed a more
romantic passion for her lover than did this distinguished, but then
antiquated lady for the Cardinal. It is to be doubted whether he
returned the tender passion ; but his idea of the Duchess's consequence
at the English court induced him to " *se laisser aimer.*" [Part of
original note.] The original note recounts the story that Elizabeth,
Duchess of Devonshire, was the real mother of the 6th Duke of Devonshire, who passed as being the son of her friend the first Duchess. She
married the 5th Duke in 1809, three years after her friend's death.

mention of certain royal names.   The person announced
himself as Mr. M[——], and the letter was merely a note,
saying she meant to be at Nice in May, and to return to
London for next winter.   This last intelligence gave me
pleasure, but I fear she will not keep to her present
determination.   Then, at the bottom of the paper was
written in broken French—The bearer of this is a spy,
and does not speak a word of truth, and is altogether
odious.   This is the second time Her Royal Highness has
sent persons to me with similar letters of introduction.
I had very near laughed in the man's face, when I read
the comical letter of recommendation he brought of
himself.

Mr. M[——] proved to be *such a talker*.   I never heard
his equal.   I thought myself obliged to ask him to come
to me the ensuing evening.   He did not go away till my
dinner was on the table ; and if it had not been for Lord
B[radford], who came to take leave of me, I do not think
he would ever have left me.

Lord Glenbervie is returned at last.   He looks as gay
as a lark.   Ah ! it is always the poor women who suffer,
who lament in the absence, and who fear even in the
presence, of those they love.   Lord G[lenbervie] knew no
public news, and was determined to go to Genoa ; because,
he said, there was better fare to be had there.   Lady
Glenbervie, too sick and too English to enjoy anything
but home, thought only with pleasure of getting thither,
and of Genoa being a step to that desired haven of rest.
I was *not able* to be amused by Lord Glenbervie.

Monday, 20th.—Every body left Nice to-day ;   and
although nobody was very dear to me, I felt a good will
to all, and a sad melancholy at being left alone, as it were,
in a state of suspense.   There is a hope of better public
news, that is to say, of a successful resistance being made
by the allied powers.   Mr. M[——] passed the whole

evening with me, and rattled till I felt not to have an idea left.

Tuesday, 21st.—Walked to Ville Franche, by a romantic path, of mountainous and picturesque beauty. The corn and beans that are springing up under the olives, the fruit-trees in luxuriant blossom, the flowers blowing among the corn, narcissus and anemonies in wild profusion, presented an enchanting scene. I met Madame Davidoff, and we rowed across the Bay of Ville Franche. A Miss E[——], the governess of Madame Davidoff's children, a poor quiet little personage, who seems estimable, but very miserable, accompanied us ; yet not miserable through Madame Davidoff, but because a governess's is always a miserable situation, and she detests the Governor.

If she be a superior person (and who would like to place an inferior-minded one about their children ?) a governess is apt to gain such an influence over her pupils, that the mother becomes jealous. Then the governess is treated like a servant, and as if she were not fit to live with ladies and gentlemen, though she is chosen to bring up the dearest objects of affection. It is a hateful *métier* to those who have to fulfil it ; and if the mother is a good, feeling person, it is painful to her to have to treat the governess with coldness, and to keep her at the distance marked out between the holder of that office, and the elder members of the family.

When I came home, I met Mr. Stanford, who told me Lady B[urdett] * was arrived. In the evening I called on her and Lady L. B[——]ly, who has not yet left Nice ; but neither of them could receive me, so I went to the Miss Langston's and could have listened to their good instrument with pleasure, had it not been for the tiresome clack of Mr. M[——].

* Lady B[urdett], one of Mr. Coutts' daughters, a very amiable person. [Part of original note.]

Wednesday, 29th March.—This last week, one of my overcoming periods of returning sadness stopped my pen. Suspense, astonishment, dismay, have all combined to make me feel that common daily notes were trivial and insufficient to express my state of mind. Lady Elphinstone, her sister, a tutor, her boy and girl, and Lord and Lady Malpas, and her sister, a Miss Campbell, are also arrived.

The Duchess of D[evonshire] has postponed her intended journey hither. Public news still uncertain. One hour one report takes the lead, the next, another, till conjecture is baffled, and belief is wholly suspended. Yesterday it was confidently asserted that Bonaparte entered Paris on the 20th, at night ; that not a blow was struck, or a resistance made, but that he entered amidst acclamations and rejoicings : that he had published various proclamations ; some saying that Prussia should pay dearly for its conduct, and that Austria also should be punished. As to England, he added, " England is our friend ; we have nothing to fear in that quarter." (How invidious !) Other manifestos declared that Marseilles was " hors de la Loi." It was added that Napoleon was to be crowned on the first of May ; with many other particulars ; but nothing was known certainly of the King. Some said he had fled to Brussels. In the evening, however, the whole of this news seemed very doubtful, as no authentic account had been received by the Commandant, or none that he would acknowledge. What was as agitating to my private interests was, hearing the Princess had arrived at Genoa, by a letter from Lady Glenbervie, written on Good Friday ; alas ! giving me such accounts of everything on that score, as made me tremble.

SECTION VI

CONTINUATION OF JOURNAL

ON *board the Clorinde, Captain Pechell, Sunday, 2nd April,* 1815.—Who knows what a day may bring forth ? The very next day after that on which I last wrote my Journal, I spent the morning in gazing at a large vessel that was on the horizon, without any presentiment that it was to convey me away so soon. Mr. Denison and the Consul came to visit me ; the latter informed me that this vessel was the Princess's frigate, the Clorinde, and was arrived at Ville Franche, to convey Lady Charlotte Campbell and her family to Genoa.*

The Consul brought me several letters, one from the Princess, and one from Lady Glenbervie, both requesting me to accompany Lady C. Campbell.

What a multitude of contradictory emotions rapidly chased each other through my heart ! The secret wish

---

* The arrival of the Princess of Wales at Genoa is thus described by Mme. de Boigne : " The next day we saw in the streets of Genoa a sight which I shall never forget. There was a kind of phaeton constructed like a sea-shell, covered with gilding and mother-of-pearl, coloured outside, lined with blue velvet and decorated with silver fringes ; this was drawn by two very small piebald horses driven by a child who was dressed like an operatic angel with spangles and flesh-coloured tights, and within it lounged a fat woman of fifty years of age, short, plump, and high-coloured. She wore a pink hat with seven or eight pink feathers floating in the wind, a pink bodice cut very low, and a short white skirt which hardly came below her knees, showing two stout legs with pink top-boots ; a rose-coloured sash, which she was continually draping, completed this costume. The

I have long felt to go to Genoa was in some degree checked by the doubts and fears of the ultimate good of this wish being gratified; besides, on a first hearing, the idea of my being conveyed away in a moment seemed impossible. I took my letters, and read them with a palpitating heart. The note from Captain Pechell recommended my going on board immediately, as he said Lady C. Campbell intended to do so; and another note, from a Captain Campbell, who commands the Tremendous, the flag ship at Genoa, desired the Clorinde might not be detained above an hour. I wrote, therefore, declaring my inability to obey Her Royal Highness's summons, unless the Clorinde could wait till Saturday; and when I went to Lady Charlotte, she said she should be very glad not to leave Nice till that day, as it was extremely inconvenient to her and her family to set off so suddenly. We were kept in suspense till evening, when Captain Pechell came to Lady C[——], where I dined. Madame Davidoff entered at the same moment, with one of her " Wells ? "

I expected to see a certain tall *pata pouff* son of Lady Pechell's, and to my astonishment I beheld a very well-looking young man, but a perfect stranger. I felt confused, from the nature of my own hopes and fears; but when Lady Charlotte made known her wish not to go away till Saturday, he immediately agreed to wait till that time. Our destiny was now decided on this point, and Lady C[——] dismissed us all early; and the next day we were all busy preparing for our departure.

carriage was preceded by a tall and handsome man [Bergami] mounted upon a little horse like those which drew the carriage; he was dressed precisely like King Murat, whose gestures and attitude he attempted to imitate. The carriage was followed by two grooms in English livery and upon horses of the same kind.

" This Neapolitan turn-out was a gift from Murat to the Princess of Wales, who exhibited herself in this ridiculous costume and in this strange carriage. She appeared in the streets of Genoa on this and the following mornings." [Memoirs, ii. 39–40.]

My physical as well as mental nature is always much affected by any variety of events, particularly by the fulfilment of those which I have myself wished for, or endeavoured to bring about. I scarcely could persuade myself that my departure was so near at hand; for although I had long thought it possible the Princess of Wales would send for me, I did not imagine it would be at this moment. But thus it ever is through life, and death itself arrives as unforeseen, as unprepared for, as all that precedes it. From the instant I heard the news, universal confusion succeeded in my occupations and hours, and I neither slept nor ate till yesterday, at four o'clock, when we embarked. My feelings are always roused to regret, at leaving a place where I have passed some pleasant hours; and the general state of public affairs is so unsettled and awful, that to leave a quiet spot, one little likely to be disturbed by the general commotion, or any scene of horror, to go to one which, if war becomes general, cannot fail to be the scene of strife, made me feel nervous. Captain Pechell is well-looking, and has pleasing manners.

In the morning, before I embarked, I walked all over Nice, to take leave of those I knew, many of whom had showed me not a little kindness; Mesdames De St. Agatha, De Cezolles, &c. &c. I met the Denisons, who, through the means of Melise, their drawing master, had leave to go and see Madame De Sevigné's picture. I requested to be of the party, and accordingly, wearied as I was, and full of cares, I took the opportunity, and beheld, in an old room full of cobwebs and dirt, this famous woman's resemblance. It speaks for itself, and must surely be an original. It is very like the one at Strawberry Hill, but has more truth and less affectation in the expression. It is not a face of regular beauty; the nose is even coarse; but the mouth is beautiful, and the eyes lustrous; the whole countenance is expressive of refinement and tenderness. How much I regretted not having attempted to copy it all the time I was at Nice! but I had put off doing so from day to day, and felt, for the hundredth time, that procrastination is our great and fatal enemy. I might have learnt to draw, I might have copied this famous picture! "I might have been"——whereas, what am I, and what have I done? Alas! alas!

I should particularly have liked to have had her picture; for of all the generations who have praised Madame de Sevigné, and commended her writings, I am certain no one has ever entered more completely into the sentiment of her delightful letters than myself. It is melancholy that no similar instance of so perfect a love between parent and child has since been upon record. Doubtless, very many a true and devoted affection has subsisted between such relations, who have not chronicled their love on paper, in the middle or lower classes; but when do we hear of the like amongst the great? Oh! for a Madame de Sevigné and a Madame de Grignan in these days! How the publication of such a correspondence as theirs would please me. It combined all the romance of love, with all the sober stedfastness of affection.—

> Full many a gem of purest ray serene
>   The dark unfathomed caves of ocean bear;
> Full many a flower is born to blush unseen,
>   And waste its sweetness on the desert air.

I hope and believe there are thousands such instances of love, that do not transpire to the knowledge of the world; but I should like that such a one should be discovered and brought to light.

I looked at Nice with interest, on the day we embarked. It was a beautiful evening. I felt a tender regret at the idea that I looked at it for the last time. The last time! there is a fund of sadness in those words.

What a magnificent thing a forty-eight gun frigate is! how grand, how imposing! It is a command which must inspire a certain confidence in the commander. That mastering of the elements is a noble prerogative; and when gentleness and suavity of manners accompanies strength, one feels respect for the being who unites these qualities. It would seem to me (as far as a cursory view of character can give a fair estimate) that Captain Pechell possesses them.

We had the finest possible weather, and remained on deck till we got under weigh, gazing on the slowly receding shore. After tea we went again on deck: the stars appeared gradually in the heaven, till it was richly spangled with their trembling light. A few sparks of fire ran upon the ripple of the wave, and we glided imperceptibly along the coast of the maritime Alps. The scene, the circumstances, and my own situation, together with reflections on the public history of the time, the wondrous convulsion in which the ambition of a single individual has thrown the whole of Europe,—filled my mind with thoughts too numerous, too vast, to be defined.

Monday, 3rd of April, on board the Clorinde.—I slept, but it was a sleep so disturbed, so unlike that which steeps the senses in forgetfulness, that I scarcely felt refreshed. Walking on the deck, and feeling the fresh breeze, gave me a new vigour. Lady Charlotte Campbell is a sweet-mannered person; I should not say she was a happy one. Her children are a fine family: Miss Eleanor Campbell, I think, will be a beautiful girl, and they are all peculiarly agreeable for such young persons.

Lady C[——]'s friend, Mademoiselle La Chaux, is clever, and must have been handsome. I like the Captain and his brother very much; they convey the idea of being good and respectable persons. They both draw prettily and have good taste for music, although no scientific or improved knowledge. I conversed with Captain Pechell, who seemed to have formed a sad opinion of all the doings at Naples. Without implicating any one, I made my own way of thinking sufficiently known, to prove that it had nothing in common with the situation I held. This I was glad to do, and thought it but justice to myself.

I heard, among other strange inuendos, that the Princess of Wales wanted to go with Murat to Ancona, and that nothing but his positively refusing to receive Her Royal Highness, prevented her going thither. She then embarked at Civita Vecchia, which was the worst place, it seems, she could have chosen, as they were obliged to row out several miles to sea, and it was eight days before the Captain could get near enough to take her on board !

It is known, I am sorry to say, by every one, that she has quarrelled with Sir William Gell, and Mr. Craven, and Lady E. Forbes. In short, things, I trust, are going to change during Lady Charlotte Campbell's and my reign, or else we shall be obliged to suffer much, and ultimately to quit her service. Lady C[——] was much distressed to hear all Captain Pechell related, and the opinions he expressed about the poor deluded Princess. I cannot help hoping that Her Royal Highness will be influenced by our presence, and the force of circumstances, to better and wiser conduct; and, indeed, I think she has suffered enough to have disgusted herself with her late behaviour. She has nothing for it but to go home to England ; but if she goes home, it must not be by sea, or we cannot accompany her.

Tuesday, 4th April, 1815.—Still on board the Clorinde. After an anxious night, I rose to pass the same sort of desultory day. I like my captain and his brother very much, and feel more acquainted with them than if I had been years on shore, and had no particular subject of interest to have made us acquainted. A selfish feeling of being under his care for a time, produces that sort of interest which long intimacy in other cases alone produces. Captain Pechell, in particular, has a respectable, good countenance, and a gentleness of demeanour, which is an excellent substitute for courtly manners.

We danced on deck, and I was surprised at my own security, and my ability to dance, as there was a considerable motion, and the wind constantly against us. But the scenery was so beautiful, and the weather so fine, I found the time too short which I passed on board the Clorinde. The Captain, too, enjoyed the voyage. He told me confidentially that he had not done so when carrying Lady O[xfor]d and her family; and that the behaviour of the young Lord H[arley] * had very much shocked him.

Wednesday, 5th April, 1815.—Still on board. All was doubtful as to our arrival; a heavy rolling sea and little wind; what wind there was being against us. Sometimes they said we should reach Genoa that night; sometimes that we could not. The latter proved the case. But we came within seven or eight miles of the city, which was illuminated, and appeared like a magical crescent bending round the bay. The circumstance of this illumination made us guess there was bad news; bad for our way of thinking. Either Murat had entered, or the Pope had fled thither, as it was reported he was to have done. I looked, till from fatigue I could look no longer, at the beauty of the illuminated town; and after one more tedious night, we anchored in the harbour of Genoa, about ten o'clock on Wednesday, the 5th of April.

For the first time in my life, reality exceeded imagination. The magnificence and beauty of this town,

* Edward, Lord Harley, born 1800, died January 1, 1828.

its situation, its gay and clean appearance, (so unlike all other Italian towns in that respect,) exceed description. The city is built on terraces, which descend to the sea-shore. The form of the bay is that of a crescent, which is terminated on either side by rocks ; on one of which the principal part of the town is built, the cathedral, &c. : on the other, the lighthouse. Orange, evergreen oaks, oleanders, and other trees and shrubs are mingled among the marble palaces, and the hills rise in grand amphitheatre at the back of this enchanted scene.

I came on shore first with the Captain, in his gig. The Princess of Wales's palace is composed of red and white marble. Two large gardens, in the dressed formal style, extend some way on either side of the wings of the building, and conduct to the principal entrance by a rising terrace of grass, ill-kept, indeed, but which in careful hands would be beautiful. The hall and staircase are of fine dimensions, although there is no beauty in the architecture, which is plain, even to heaviness ; but a look of lavish magnificence dazzles the eyes. The large apartments, decorated with gilding, painted ceilings, and fine, though somewhat faded, furniture, have a very regal appearance. The doors and windows open to a beautiful view of the bay, and the balmy air which they admit conspires with the scene around to captivate the senses. I should think this palace, and this climate, and its customs, must suit the Princess, if anything can suit her. Poor woman ! she is ill at peace with herself ; and when that is the case, what can please ? Still there is a soothing power in this soft breeze, which, in despite of every circumstance, lulls the mind for a time into forgetfulness. Certainly there is no place which, from its climate and its customs, combines so much to deaden mental suffering as Italy ; but these contribute, even to a fearful extent, to an indolence of body and soul, which, though it gives *temporary relief*, is inimical to a healthful vigour of mind. And when we are aroused from that state of mental torpor into which it casts us, and are obliged to return to a ruder climate, or endure some new trial, or perform the active duties of common life, it is too often found that Italy and its opium have done harm in a moral sense, if not in a physical one.

What a long digression from my Journal! I am often ashamed when I read over what I have written, to see how I allow my mind to wander, and my pen to note down so many of its vagaries. Yet I never have resolution to amend the style of my diary. And why should I not indulge myself by giving way to my feelings? One must confide in some one, or in something; and though it is very melancholy to be obliged to have recourse to the latter, still it is a comfort to have no secrets from one's Journal. It is this entire confidence, and this alone, which renders it a pleasure to keep one.

The Princess received me in one of the drawing-rooms, opening on the hanging terraces, covered with flowers in full bloom. Her Royal Highness received Lady Charlotte Campbell (who came in soon after me) with open arms, and evident pleasure, and without any flurry. She had no rouge on, wore tidy shoes, was grown rather thinner, and looked altogether uncommonly well. The first person who opened the door to me was the one whom it was impossible to mistake, hearing what is reported; six feet high, a magnificent head of black hair, pale complexion, mustachios which reach from *here to London*. Such is *the stork*.* But of course I only appeared to take him for an upper servant. The Princess immediately took me aside, and told me all that was true, and a great deal that was not. The same

* Bartolomeo Pergami, known in England as Bergami, formerly a subaltern in an Italian regiment and recommended to the Princess of Wales by the Marchese Ghislieri. She thought him, according to Madame de Boigne, like her hero Murat, and showered every kind of favour on him, making him, from her courier, her chamberlain.

decoction of mingled falsehood and truth is in use as heretofore. Oh! that some one would break the vial, and spill the vile liquid which she is using to her destruction in this world, as well as in the next!

Her Royal Highness said that Gell and Craven had behaved very ill to her, and I am tempted to believe they have not behaved well; but then how did she behave to them? Besides, she began telling me such stories of them as made me sick, and that I in no way believe; which immediately proved to me that she was lying, from the littleness of her heart.

Hell has no fury like a woman scorned.

All this I laid to its right account; but it made me tremble to think what anger would induce a woman to do, when she abused these her best friends for their cavalier manner of treating her. If there was any cause of complaint, I am sure it was brought about by her own conduct, and I lament that it should have been so.

"Well, when I left Naples, you see, my dear," continued the Princess, "those gentlemen refused to go with me unless I returned immediately to England. They supposed I should be so miserable without them, that I would do anything they desired me; and when they found I was too glad *to get red of 'em,* (as she called it,) they wrote the most humble letters, and thought I would take them back again; whereas they were very much mistaken. I had *got red of them,* and I would remain so."

Then came a description of the King and Queen of Naples, the stable boy, and Buonaparte's sister. *He* was all delightful, *she* was false and furious. The stable boy was a prince in disguise!

As to public news, the Princess repeated what I had heard before, that the Pope had fled hither, i.e., to Genoa;

that Murat had declared the independence of Italy;
that he said, if the King of Sardinia gave up Genoa, he
would not attempt to take it ; that he wished for nothing
so much as the friendship of the English ; and that he
hoped the Princess would *agréer* his letter to Lord W.
Bentinck, which was to this effect. She then proceeded
to show me a note she had received from Murat, a mere
sugar-plum, not ill-written, but beginning " Madame,
ma chère, chère Sœur," in quality of one king treating
with his fellow sovereign. She also read me her answer.
Such an answer ! Certainly not unclever, but so flippant,
so much beneath her dignity, so strange, and so wild, that
I think if it remains upon record, it will afford one of
the most curious specimens of royal letter-writing that
ever was written. I cannot say how vexed I am at every
fresh instance of the Princess's folly ; and whenever she
commits herself on paper I am doubly annoyed ; for
though so full of faults, or rather, to call them by their
right name, vices, she has a noble and kindly nature ;
and I always return to her education, to the example
set to her by those who ought to have guarded her youth,
not to have exposed it to be sullied by every degrading
circumstance that could contaminate her character.

She has heaped benefits on Lady C. C[ampbell], and
sent her a thousand ducats in hard cash as soon as she
arrived. Lady C[harlotte] told me this, and spoke with
gratitude and affection towards our poor mistress, though
she confessed that it was painful to owe gratitude where
esteem could not cancel the debt. " Yet," added Lady
C[harlotte], " I hope my services are of some use to Her
Royal Highness, and that the balance is pretty even
on the score of obligation."

After my long *tête-à-tête* with the Princess, we walked
out on the terrace from her boudoir. This terrace
commands a view of the harbour of Genoa, the city
placed around its beautiful crescent, and all this seen

through trellises of oleander and various creeping plants, trained in good order round these lattice works; at the feet of which are beds of every kind of flower, all now in full bloom and fragrance; and at the ends of the different walks are marble fountains of classical designs, and quantities of the purest springs constantly descending from sources in the rock above, and refreshing everything with their cool and translucent waters. From this terrace you ascend to another, and then another, till you reach the wood above. The wood consists of the most beautiful evergreens, and various shrubs and plants of lighter foliage, scattered throughout. There is an ascent by a winding path to the summit of the rock above. I only went half way, but intend to explore further some day; only this part of the grounds is locked up by the Giant, and without applying to him, there is no entrance—a circumstance, together with his guardianship, which must lessen all enjoyment of the scene. From the same story on which one of the lady's bedrooms is placed, there is an egress to a terrace, which Her Royal Highness calls Lady [——]'s terrace. It is very beautiful, and there is a large fountain on a broad marble pavement, where one might pass hours and days of happiness in a scene truly enchanting, were it not for that vacuum in the heart which demands other aliment than the mere gratification of the senses.

Lord and Lady Glenbervie dined with the Princess, as did Madame Falconet and her two daughters, who seem to be quiet, decent people, but very like chambermaids.

Thursday, 6th of April.—Breakfasted at the palace. Had I any occupation under the sun, I would prefer it to that of waiting upon this royal lady; but, having none, I am glad of this one, unsuited as it is to my taste in every way. I walked through this most beautiful

I   z

of all towns.   In saying this, I do not throw out a chance expression : it appears to me to be, as I say, the most beautiful of all towns.   I walked through the Strada Nova and Novissima, Bocca Negra, &c. ; passed the Doria palace, famous for its history, but reckoned the least splendid of the palaces.   These streets are a succession of palaces.   Large porte-cochères open into corridors supported by columns, and others into spacious courts, from whence flights of marble steps, covered with statues, ascend to the apartments above ; and in the midst of these staircases are fountains and large vases of flowers, placed on the sides of the bulustrades. Almost every palace has its garden, and there is a lavish magnificence expressed in every feature of the place, which seems to say that liberty and commerce are the foundation of all greatness.   The refinement of classic elegance and pure architecture is not found here ; but such grandeur, such picturesque effect, such wildness of magnificence, and such a scorn of gold, are impressed on every object, that even taste itself leaves its nicer discrimination, to feel all the romance of unfettered fancy, and loses its fastidiousness in admiration.

I went to Lady S[——] ; found her very kind, but *he* was kinder than she (I mean Lord S[——]).   Lady S[——] and Miss M[——] were going to see the Pope.   There has been some little affront on the part of the Princess towards his Holiness.   I met Lord B[radford].   He has a kind and affectionate manner, and evinced it so very strongly towards me, that I cannot choose but like him. He walked about the town with me, then dined with the Princess, who likes him exceedingly ; so does or did her royal husband, the Prince.   He was the friend of Mrs. Fitzherbert, and could, I should think, reveal many a curious anecdote.   I have often observed that the Prince and Princess of Wales have a strange sympathy in their loves and hatreds.

Friday, 7th April.—The Princess received a visit from Lady W. Bentinck, accompanied by Madame D'Osmont,* the French Ambassador's wife and Madame D'Auloyne, [de Boigne] or some such name, her daughter. The first is a very cross-looking personage, and the Princess's manner of receiving her did not lessen this crossness. For some reason or other, or more likely from some caprice, Her Royal Highness chose to treat Madame D'Osmont like a dog ; hardly spoke, and what she did say was dry and disagreeable. When these persons were dismissed, Lady W Bentinck was desired to remain a moment alone with the Princess ; so Lady C. Campbell and myself, who were in attendance, accompanied Madame D'Osmont into the ante-chamber. The latter said, if the Princess had not a mind to receive the French Ambassador's wife, she need not, but that it was quite unnecessary to be so uncivil. I made an excuse, saying, Her Royal Highness had many private subjects of annoyance, and that I was sure some unpleasant news must have been the cause of making her so silent. And this excuse was in part true, for she had received letters from H[———]

* *Née* Dillon, wife of the Marquis d'Osmond. Her daughter, Madame de Boigne [Memoirs, ii. 41 *et seq.*], gives this account of the interview : " It was necessary to go and pay our respects to this merry-andrew, as her position required. She hated us as she considered us hostile to the King [Murat], and gave herself the petty pleasure of great rudeness. We went with Lady William Bentinck at a day and hour fixed by her. She kept us waiting a long time, and at length we were admitted to a green arbour where she was lunching, dressed in an open dressing-gown, with Bergami to wait upon her. After a few words to my mother, she attempted to speak nothing but English to Lady William. She was somewhat disconcerted to find us also taking part in the conversation, from which she had hoped to exclude us, and was thus reduced to speaking of the virtues and the royal and military talents of Murat. . . . We were in no way tempted to renew the acquaintance. She insisted that my father had helped to secure the order for her departure, an utterly false assertion. If the Government had been urged by any one, it was rather by Lady William Bentinck, who was greatly weary of her. Lord William and Mr. Hill [who had' gone off specially to Turin] were spared these annoyances."

about money matters, which considerably embarrassed her. Madame D'Osmont replied, with bitterness, " Yes ; I should think she must have many *private causes* of disturbance."

"Murat is advancing rapidly," observed Madame D'Osmont, after a pause. I looked grave, and affected not to understand. Shortly after, I changed the conversation, and expressed my own sentiments. She caught my hand, and said, warmly, " Thank you—thank you, for that." I forgave her former crossness. Soon after, Lady W. Bentinck came out, and they all went away.

The Princess made known to me her wild schemes of travelling· on, and on, to the Lord knows where, and complained bitterly that Lady C. C[ampbel]l had declined remaining in her household, and said, when Her Royal Highness left Genoa, she would give up her situation. The Princess asked me then, " Who shall I take along with me ? " I ventured to name Miss M[——]e. " I think she will do." Yes ; because she knows not what else will. She told me Lady W. Bentinck was a very meddling woman,* and why ? because she had not forwarded a letter she gave her to Murat. " But she shall know that I never take advice. I have a banker at Florence, and a banker here, and will write to my banker at Florence, to give the letter, which I will inclose to him. By G—, when I will do a thing, I *doot*,"—and she walked to and fro.

Monsieur de La Rue was announced. Her Royal Highness desired him to talk to me while she wrote some letters. We walked in the beautiful garden, but he is a tiresome man. Lord Glenbervie always dines here ; a very great comfort.

The Princess held a sort of a drawing-room in the evening, which was respectably attended, and went off

* *Née* Lady Mary Acheson, daughter of Arthur, 1st Earl of Gosford.

very properly. Among the persons who came to it, were the Queen of Etruria, and the Archduke [? Grand Duke] Constantine.

Saturday, 8th April.—I went with Lady Glenbervie to a Signor di Negri, one of the nobles of Genoa. He is a poet, an improvisatore, and a musician. His house and garden are a little terrestrial paradise : never did I see such an enchanted spot. It only wants the comfort of sofas and chairs, to make it quite perfect. One terrace above another leads to grottos, bowers, trellises, from all of which different views of Genoa present themselves, in exquisite points of beauty. Flowers innumerable embalm the air.

Signor Negri improvisèd at our request. It was the first time I ever heard verse poured forth in spontaneous numbers. The wonder at that power, and the answering flame of poetic fire with which it inspired me, all combined to inebriate my fancy. I had but an imperfect understanding, however, of his lays. The theme Lady Glenbervie gave him was The Poet's Paradise. He commenced by an apology—went on to call the beauties of spring to his aid—and then made allusion to some of our poets, Dryden and Milton, from whence he very ingeniously descended to praise the female part of his audience. I do not believe there was anybody present but Dr. H[——] who knew much about it. Nevertheless, I admired his talent, though I did not think his subject well chosen. He played well on the harp ; but what pleased me most was, that Signor Negri told me he had been at D[——]. I felt proud to tell him it was the place of my forefathers ; those honourable forefathers of whom I may justly feel proud. He admired the grandeur of its scenery, although so different in its character of beauty from this. And on my saying, " We also can boast of poetry and song," he named Ossian and Burns, and immediately began reciting some lines in praise of Ossian's Malvina, which he said he well remembered. His voice was rather melodious, but nothing more.

I do not think he *excels* in any of the accomplishments he professes, but he loves them all with the ardour peculiar to his country. He reverences the arts, and pursues them with an *estro* that does one's heart good. What a pity it is that those who are endowed with the mechanical power of skill in small things, often lack the enthusiasm and feeling which others, who have less handicraft and head, possess in such a pre-eminent degree. Lady C. C[ampbell] sang a Scotch song to him in return, which he did not much care for, because the words were not particularly fine, and he regards music only as the vehicle of poetry.

A Monsieur and Madame D'Amiser, or D'è Amer (I know not which) dined at the Princess's. She is a Neapolitan ; he is a French general, who served Murat, and is attached to him, but, owing to some dissatisfaction, leaves the court of Naples, and is returning to Bourdeaux. I was left to talk to him *en tête-à-tête*, and found him a very sensible, agreeable man, more like a solid quiet Englishman than a foreigner. He is only thirty, but might be any age, from his appearance. I never saw so old-looking a person for his time of life. He spoke reasonably about politics ; said he had never known the Bourbons, and was too young to have formed any attachment to them ; but, had he once sworn fidelity, he never would have been so vile as to have forsaken their cause. The evening was tolerably agreeable.

Sunday, April 9th, 1815.—Went out at eight o'clock, to see the Pope perform mass in the cathedral, but was too late to be able to see any part of the ceremony. The church was so crowded, there was hardly room to squeeze through the middle aisle. We met, however, the Pope's secretary, who directed me very civilly, through a low door, into an adjoining house belonging to some Cardinal, where the Pope was to go after mass to take refreshment. The soldiers who lined the way, at first refused me admittance ; but some one cried out " Inglese, Inglese ! " and immediately we had way made for us to pass.   I went up stairs to a large apartment, where many others waited besides myself ; and there I saw *La sua Santità* pass close by me.   He is a little man, and bowed with age, but of a noble aspect, and a peculiar serenity of countenance. After he had passed by, I was not satisfied with so cursory a glance, and waited in the hope of being presented to him. My friend, his secretary, came forth and desired me to pass into an inner room, a place of greater honour, within two of that in which the Pope was eating cakes and ices. I did so ; and I believe I should have been presented at him, had not Dr. Holland unfortunately observed thto Lady C. Campbell and Lady Glenbervie, whose party I joined, were attendants of the Princess of Wales—thinking that would gain us all more favour.   But the title of the poor Princess's attendants conveys no reflected grandeur, but the reverse.   I have often remarked this lately with regret ; and in the present instance I fancy it is particularly obnoxious ; as the Pope at first showed Her Royal Highness every sort of respect, paid her passage through his dominions, &c. : and on returning that way she wholly neglected him, besides committing some other egregious offences.   Accordingly, a message was sent to say the Pope could only receive ladies at his own palace.   We were obliged, therefore, to depart unsatisfied ; but he sent us out some iced lemonade, which he had blessed, by way of comfort.

After this we went to our own service.   It was not performed with that holy and reverent feeling which I have of late witnessed at Nice : still it is gratifying to meet with our own mode of worship in a foreign land.

The Princess drove out in the afternoon, and made me

accompany her. She uses a shewy equipage, with the courier dressed up, riding on one side, and a man like a puppet-show man riding before Willikin on the other. She has small cream-coloured ponies, fit only to drive about a park in. Her Royal Highness never goes to see any of the many objects worth seeing here, and never drives through the streets, but confines herself wholly to the delights of the garden at the back of the house. When she goes beyond her own grounds, she only drives on the road called S. Pierre D'Arena, for about six miles. A most beautiful road it is. Lady Glenbervie dined, as usual, with the Princess ; a great and continued comfort. I have never yet been able to detect any impropriety of manner, or even familiarity, towards the courier yet ; but I live in fear every moment of having the horrid stories confirmed before my eyes. I should far rather go on doubting, than be convinced of their truth. The rascal—for such I am sure he is, in the way of cheating Her Royal Highness—is very handsome. I have never hitherto observed anything with regard to him, as I did with the singers. I hope the whole is a lie.

The Princess had evening prayers on Sundays, and some of her English attendants were present. I wish she would attend church ; it is a pity she does not, I may say, even for form's sake ; it would be a blessing to all that wish her well, that she should mind the outward duties of a Protestant Princess.

Monday, 10*th*.—Went early in the day to see the Brignole palace, Il Palazzo Rosso. There are four magnificent apartments on each side, on the ground floor, called after the four seasons, with appropriate decorations, and ending in a gallery named " The Life of Man," which idea reminded me of Shakspeare's Seven Ages. Above this range of apartments is another suite, which are let, and are just now occupied by Lady Dalrymple. There are several good pictures : one, the Rape of the Sabines, by Valerio Costello, a Genoese painter ; and two half-length figures of our Saviour and the Virgin, by Guido. There is much sweetness in the expression of the countenances, but little grandeur in the figures. Two portraits by Vandyck ; the one of Antonio Giulio Brignole Sale, on horseback, and his wife ; both magnificent specimens of the artist. The horse's head, and the dignity of the male figure, striking. An unpleasant picture (in the conception of the story) of Christ turning the changers out of the Temple, by Gian Francesco Barbari, *detto Il Guercino da Cento ;* with a want of heavenly grandeur in the figure of the Saviour wholly unbecoming the sacred character ; and two large pictures by Michael Angelo Da Carravagio ; the resurrection of Lazarus, the subject of one ; that of the other taken from Tasso, of Saffronia and Olinda at the stake, Clorinda on horseback. These formed the collection. The figure of Clorinda is beautiful ; her hand resting on her horse's neck, is very lovely ; but she is made the principal figure, and yet is placed in the corner, and so much in the foreground, that half her form and that of her horse alone is seen. There appears to me something ill contrived in the general arrangement of the composition, but it is a pleasing picture, and one I would willingly have carried away. Its companion is in my opinion wholly *manqué :* the figures hard and ungraceful, and no sense of awe is inspired in beholding it.

These rooms have all painted ceilings. If not by the first masters, they are very tolerably executed, and give a richness to the general effect of an apartment. In those called the Four Seasons, there are magnificent frames to the mirrors, carved in various rare woods, in the most exquisite manner—birds, and insects, and flowers, and fruits, and hanging foliage, after the manner of our Gibbon. In the *Camera detta del Inverno* there hangs a large picture, reckoned fine, by Paolo Da Verona : the subject, Judith cutting off Holofernes' head. A black slave holds the sack in which she is depositing it. The only remarkable circumstance I observed in this picture was, the exact resemblance I saw in its colouring to that of Sir Joshua Revnolds.

Tuesday, 11th of April, 1815.—I went to call on the Princess Grassalkovich. I like her and her Prince vastly. I found it difficult, however, to *twist* the state of things into anything like respectability, and they ended by saying Lady Glenbervie and Lady C. C[ampbel]l were very good, to remain in their situations. This, alas ! is the melancholy account I hear of my royal friend. They detained me so long I was nearly too late to be in waiting to receive the King of Sardinia's chamberlain, who paid his master's respects very politely to Her Royal Highness. He had a long conference with her : so also had the King of Prussia's chamberlain, Monsieur De Raudel. These persons were telling her the public news when I entered, and I evidently saw it did not please her. They said it was impossible for Murat to pass the Po ; and I am sadly afraid the Princess had some foolish mad scheme in her head about him ; which frightens me more than the rest of her doings. How much more was this increased when Her Royal Highness asked me, as soon as these chamberlains were departed, if I thought Lady Glenbervie's and Lady C. C[ampbell]'s health was equal to a journey ;—which preface ended by telling me, that next week she intended to go to Venice.

" An affair," said she, " my dear [——], of ten days ; *two days* to go, *two* to come back, and four to remain there." *

---

* Her Royal Highness was not very exact in her calculations ! I once heard her ask what o'clock it was ? Her page, Mr. Steinman, answered, " Eight o'clock, please your Royal Highness ! " " It does not please me," said she ; " it is only six o'clock." " Certainly,"

Four days sufficient, in her estimation, to see Venice !
The Princess added, that the whole expense of this
junket would not be more than a thousand *louis-d'or ;*
and she holds that sum cheap for a mere fancy !   Then
she is going to change this house, and go to some other,
which she is to see to-day or to-morrow.   Captain Pechell
is to row her round in his boat to the other side of Genoa.
How strange, how wild, are all her thoughts, words, and
actions !   I really think she has *a bee in her bonnet*.   I
hope yet something may change this plan.   The idea of
her crossing over a part of the country so near the seat
of war, and of being prevented from getting back here,
terrifies us all.

Wednesday, 12th of April.—We, that is all Her Royal
Highness's attendants, held a council of war at Lady
Glenbervie's, and decided *that the ladies, at least, should
refuse to accompany* Her Royal Highness to Venice, as
it was most improper to set forth, not knowing if we
should be allowed to return.

If she is bent on this excursion, she may choose to go
with some of her attendants ; but I trust she will be
persuaded to defer her intention to a more fitting season.

I went to see St. Cyr, one of the most beautiful churches
in Genoa, perhaps the most so, in respect to the richness
of its decorations.   It is all marble and precious stones ;
the pulpit is inlaid like a gem ; and the ceiling is richly
gilt and painted.   From St. Cyr I proceeded to St. Ambrosio.   This church contains the finest picture in Genoa,
the Assumption of the Virgin, by Guido.   The subject
is magnificently managed, and contains, in fact, two great
ideas—one of earthly, the other of heavenly things ;

replied the well-educated page of honour, " it is only six o'clock, then ;
as your Royal Highness commands it should be."   This was almost
as characteristic an answer as was made by the Cardinal de Rohan
to the Queen of France, when Her Majesty commanded him to execute
some difficult order—" Madame, s'il est possible, c'est deja fait ; si
c'est impossible, ca se fera."   [Original note.]

but they are so well blended together, that they become
one grand whole. The lower part of the picture consists
of the apostles, in various attitudes of admiration and
adoration : the upper is a semicircle of angels and arch-
angels, seated on clouds, and winging their way to heaven.
In the midst is placed the Virgin, clothed in white drapery,
her hands meekly folded on her breast—her eyes cast
upwards—and the whole head foreshortened. One arm
seems to stand out from the canvas. The figure is grandly
simple. The whiteness of her garment is at once splendid
and yet mellow ; her attitude natural, yet graceful in the
extreme. There is no *trick* of beauty either in her attire,
her air, her expression. She is worshipping supreme power
in spirit and in truth, and is borne by angels to supreme
beatitude. The whole tone of the picture is one grand
solemn tint : the lights fall from the radiance which
descends on the Virgin alone, and are thence led off
subordinately upon the other figures. Many of the angels
are of exquisite beauty and lightness : one of the principal
ones to the right, in particular ; and beside that one, a
little behind him, is the head of a cherub, with hands
joined in the attitude of prayer. A thousand minor
beauties might be seen in this picture, but we had only
a certain time to gaze and to admire, and I was desirous
to look at the others. Two more, said to be by Rubens,
and in his style, are in the same church ; one over the
altar, of the Circumcision ; the other of a Jesuit curing
one possessed, and bringing to life a dead child. Of these
two pictures I prefer the latter, though there was something grand in the composition of the former : but the
angels, and palms, and cherubim, in the air, did not
please my eye, after those of Guido. There is a streaki-
ness in Rubens's manner of colouring his back-grounds,
and a red unfinished tint on his fingers, not to mention
the fat flabbiness of his women, which I dislike. All these
faults are much less observable in the picture of the Jesuit

healing the sick and bringing to life the child, than in any
work of his I ever saw. The *Possédé* is truly "*maniac
and demoniac*," and the figure of the woman foreshortened
(in the right corner of the picture) bending over the dead
infant, expresses all the passions she is supposed to feel ;
although the face is scarcely seen. This church, like that
of St. Cyr, is encrusted with marble ; the ceiling richly
gilt and painted. Part of the cupola is destroyed by
damp, or some other cause ; perhaps by the revolu-
tionists ; for in this church, in the middle of the building, was placed the dreadful guillotine :—the doors of the
church were shut, but the victims were led to their fate
along the galleries, and by the passages which were destined for the organist or singers. God forbid such times
should ever return ! I shuddered at the recollection.

I went to the Doge's Palace, now the Royal Palace.
The great room of audience is the finest space I ever
beheld—a hundred and thirty feet long. In the times
of general desolation, the marble balustrade which surrounded the gallery that runs round the top of the room,
and the statues which decorated it, were destroyed ; so
that now their place is supplied by an iron rail and casts !

I was delighted to learn from Lady Glenbervie, when
I returned to the Princess's palace, that before Lady
G[——] made known her determination about the Venice
expedition, the wind had veered. Her Royal Highness was in perfect good humour, and said, "It don't
sinifies, some months hence will do just *so* well." "So,"
said Lady G[——], "the burden was off my spirits without
quarrelling."

The King of Prussia's chamberlain dined at the royal
table. He is a very agreeable, eccentric man, and seems
a good person. He reprobated, but in the mildest manner
possible, the interest that the Princess expressed for
persons whom it scarcely *suited her to know*, and said,
"what will become of her own interests, if such are her

principles ? " I said what I could in extenuation. He asked me how long I had been in Her Royal Highness's service, and if I never had quarrelled with her. " Ah ! c'est bien," he said, when I answered him—" c'est merveilleux." Then he proceeded to speak about religion, and my opinions thereon seemed to please him so much, that he exclaimed, " C'est beau, c'est vraiment beau ! ah ! je vous remercie," and he took my hand, and pressed it.

This man is quite original, a singular person to be about a court. He is full of fire and enthusiasm, and of good and devout principle ; in person old, ugly, and dirty. "Cependant, vous êtes protestante," said he to me. This " *cependant* " diverted me, but I replied, " Surely all Christians are of the same religion, although they differ in points of form." Again he was pleased with me. We were not, of course, allowed to converse very long together. We were called to the royal sofa, and the topics of discourse took another turn. Sometimes Monsieur [——] opened his eyes wide at the Princess's declarations ; and Her Royal Highness enjoys making people stare, so she gave free vent to her tongue, and said a number of odd things, some of which she thinks and some she does not ; but it amuses her to astonish an innocent-minded being, and really such did this old man appear to be. He won her heart upon the whole, however, by paying a compliment to her fine arm, and asking for her glove. Obtaining it, he placed it next his heart, and, declaring it should be found in his tomb, he swore he was of the old school in all things. He had a great deal of varied anecdote and conversation, which was very amusing. Was he sincere ?

Thursday, 13th April.—I wrote and read all the morning : it rained, and there was no going to see sights. The only event of to-day was the receipt of one of my friend Gell's unique letters, which are always a treat.

⌐ MY DEAR [————],—Mr. Tringsberg has requested me to enclose to you a letter to the Princess's cook, Mrs. Grundy Thompson, maker of stews and sauces. Be¸pleased to deliver the same. I received a letter from you at a moment when it was quite impossible to answer it, for we have been all sent to Coventry by the rest of the world ever since poor King Jehoiakim set out on the conquest of Italy, which has had the fate every one prophesied, and has been the ruin and destruction of many worthy people. We have been taken, murdered, sacked, bombarded, threatened, executed, pillaged, and everything else which is usual in conquered states. Yet though I have feared much from the populace, I have suffered nothing as bad as two fits of the gout which I have had during the fortnight in which we have been so maltreated, and under which fits I still labour, with my foot over a caldron of boiling water, under which is a hot pan of coals. Lord ! how it burns ; and the flannel which is around it emits the odour of burnt pens ; which, if you ever were a school-boy, and had toasted in a candle, you would remember to have found very agreeable. I smell the ascending odour of a lamb and tortoise in a brazen caldron boiled.

Brass lies above, and brass below, the flesh.

This was the answer which the Oracle of Delphi sent to King Crœsus, when he sent them the question of " What's my thought like ? " to try whether the Pythian was up to snuff or not. However, you never could have guessed what I was doing, if I had not told you. Craven is gone to the opera, to see the illumination for Prince Leopold Calfsheadsky, a Polish Prince, who is to be there. We have seen some delightful interviews between friends and relations, just come from Sicily, after so long a banishment. I should think at 'least ten thousand kisses have been given in the course of the day, and many miles of maccaroni eaten on the happy occasion. Among the good things, I saw the mules landed from a transport, who kicked, brayed, and then flew on shore in the manner here shewn,* thinking they had done it all by dint of genius themselves.

⸰ In the original letter there is a ridiculous drawing of an ass, hanging suspended in the air by cords, and a man pulling it by the bridle down to the earth. [Original note.]

Oh! my foot, it is regularly boiled, like potatoes in a patent steam kitchen; besides which Carrington has just given me a pinch. I recommend the gout to all married couples, when they are too happy for this world.

If you had been here lately, the news of all that has passed might amuse and interest you; but as it is, I must tell you that I hear *the Queen is furious* about going to Trieste, though they have it under her own hand, that she wished it. Captain C[——] had the management of it, but is not at all to blame. On the contrary, the Queen's negociator, by trying to be too cunning, has overreached himself. Some people called him Count Mosbourg; others, Count Noseberry. Talking of Berrys, those cruel traitresses have never written a line to us since our departure—faithless jades as they be; though I offered to conduct them to Nice, and many other civilities, besides marrying them all, which they lost by going to stride over Scotland, in a snow-storm, trailing after them that good old man, their father, under pretence that he wished once again to see the heath where he was born. Really too wicked! Mrs. Damer, how could I send your marble to Nice, London, or elsewhere, when you have been blockading us by sea and land for the last two months? As to files, I have got one or two; but the robbers who conquered Mrs. and Miss R[awdo]n, took them among the other valuables, so that only these remain, which they threw in Knutson, Schomandtrenè, or Canutson's face, when they found of how little value they were; while he, good man, was occupied in preserving what he calls *Paley's figs*,—which, by the strict scrutiny of a jury of matrons regularly empannelled, was discovered to mean the gentle Bayley's wigs.

What a beautiful house we have got, the envy of Lady Westmoreland, who drank tea with us last night! At this moment the moon is just rising over the bleak barren hills of Sorrento, and faintly gilding the lofty rocks of Capri, while the waves in gentle murmurs break on the terrace of the Francarilla garden below my balcony, which is covered with a profusion of roses and carnations. Ah! Maria! what a scene! But here comes Eustace and his Classical Tour, to tea. I must leave the window and its romantic delights, for the charms of hyson and souchong; not to mention curds

from Ischia. Shall I help you ? Would this last question
were not a joke !

If this is brought to you by Count *Leeching*, patronize him,
being a friend of mine, who will I think entertain you. Give
my love to my fair and lovely friend, and tell her I wish
the house of A[——] may reign triumphant on the shores of
M[——] and I[——], and when, seven years before the end
of the world, a deluge shall drown the nations, may Columbus'
Isle still swim above the flood, though the sea should at one
tide cover the green-headed I[——] and Ireland.

Ever thy friend—I would say *best*, did I dare, my dear
[——], at least I may say, not thy *worst*,

GELLINO.

I send you some verses, excuse the freedom.

Another Letter from SIR W. GELL.

MY DEAR [——],—Not having been at home when your
note came, and finding that it was infinitely too hot to send
any unhappy Christian to toil through the sun and up your
hill, I would not send you an answer ; but my servant has
discovered that you have a penny-post of your own, which
conveys things to you in the course of some weeks, so I
shall fire at it. The Gazette contains a decree, awarding to
Guglielmo Papre, the small sum of 500,000 ducats (about
100,000*l.*) which he has most magnanimously *refused*, saying
that what he had done was for the universal good, and not
for filthy lucre. Also the officers of the Avellino army were
promised a step of promotion, which would have made a
great difficulty, as the rest of the army might have also
claimed it ; but they have all refused to accept it. Finally,
all have refused the orders, and ribbons, and stars, with
which they were to be rewarded, and all from a spirit of
patriotism and *tolderolitility*. It is said the militia have
also refused four Carlines a day to take them home. One
would give them ten to go. The money comes out of a fund
of thirteen millions, found concealed for his most gracious
Majesty the Doctor, and the florid Duchess. This hoard of
money secures for this revolution what has always been
wanting in other revolutions, money for immediate use,
without having recourse to pillage through necessity.

I   2 A

Of the ships seen through your glass we have no accounts.
Have you seen the Queen's " Green Bag," now before the
house of Lords ?   It begins thus :

Since the law of the land has established the thing,
And Judge Blackstone declares " the Queen equals the
   King,"
As I always must think that a generous nation
May desire to know who gave first provocation,
Which the household of Royalty turned upside down,
And which threatens the credit and peace of the Crown,
I do tie all my evidence up in a bag,
And present, like my husband, my Royal Green Bag.
Mein Gotts ! or, my Lords, I believe I should say,
What right has my husband to drive me away ?
Do they think with their Oliver, Castles, and spies,
To make me sit silent to prove all their lies ?
Let them send all their carles to Milan and Rome
To hash up a story to publish at home,
Or their Browns to spy Como and Lombardy round,
And expend—for the nation—twice ten thousand pound.
Such plots and such plans, I may safely defy,
For *Brown* ne'er can blacken the *white* of my eye.
While their Redens and Omptedas charged with commission
To hunt me through Europe without intermission,
Have only exposed, when they drove me from Rome,
The meanness of those who employed them at home.
At one great distance off, and one great while ago,
I lived safe *wit* my fader at Brunswick, ye know ;
And although it be not the most favoured of lands,
Because 'tis surrounded with deserts and sands,
Yet many fine things may still Brunswick adorn,
Though the stupidest place that God ever did born ;
And de mens might be brave, and de women be good,
Though they feed on sour-kraut in a palace of wood.
So my *fader* took part in all wars and all quarrels,
And my *moder* she scold and take care of my morals ;
So she gave me the Bible, but pinn'd up some pages,
Not suited, she said, to all girls, nor all ages ;
But I knew all good Christians should read all dat book,
So I unpinned the pages and ventured to look.

Then she call me one day, and she tell me fine tales,
Of how I should surely be Princess *von Vales*.
I talk of my heart, but she tell me 'twas just
Like de preach to de wind, for 'twas fixed, and I must ;
But she tell me my husband not send for me yet,
Till the nation consented to pay off his debt.
So I soon found my hopes and my pride tumble down,
And was sold to *my husband* for less than a *crown*.
So I leave old mamma, which I like very well,
And quit, without crying, both Brunswick and Zell,
Forget Rostock, and Klopstock, and Weimar, and Schiller,
With Professor Fonfrarius and learned Von Miller ;
And I *tink* to myself, though the thought was in vain,
I'll be whipt if ye catch me among ye again.*

I cannot remember more of the Green Bag. Some say
Tommy More, some Sir Harry Englefield, some Southey, and
some Campbell, is the author.

Ever yours,
PETER PROUD.

Friday, the 14th of April.—I cannot recollect how the
morning passed—in nothing *tres marqué*, I am sure. In
the evening there was a circle as formal and dull as
possible, but still I was glad to see such respect did still
exist towards Her Royal Highness. Lord W. Bentinck
talked a great deal with me. There is something so
kindly and good in his manner ; and I remembered too
my first childish fancy of friendship for his brother, the
Duke of P[ortlan]d, which gave the conversation some
interest. Like dreams long forgotten, these recollections
sometimes recur ; and when, as in the present case, they
were wholly pure and pleasurable, they cannot fail of
coming back with a " charm under their wings "—for we
can only be said to live when we have been excited to feel.

* These verses appear to have been written at a later period than
that of the Princess of Wales's sojourn at Genoa, but they came in
at this part of the Journal, and I have made it a rule not to displace
the MS., but merely had it transcribed as it was given into my hands.
Indeed, it matters little where the above clever lines are introduced,
for they would be welcome anywhere. [Original note.]

After the people went away, the Princess kept me up till very late, talking over her grievances with her ex-chamberlains. I could not help thinking, whatever were Her Royal Highness's faults, they must have been also to blame. The spirit of expediency, which I had hoped found no dwelling-place in their minds or hearts, must have led them to think it wisest to leave her service ; but they should have attended her till she got others. Among many stories too shocking to put on paper, and which, I make no doubt, were mostly, if not all, lies, the Princess told me one of the minor but meaner kind, with such detail of circumstance that my faith was staggered. It was nearly as follows : Some time about Christmas, Sir W. Gell came to me and said, in his cavalier manner, " Craven and I want two coats, and your Royal Highness must give us thirty ducats to buy them." " Very well," I said ; and soon after I sent for Siccard and told him. Siccard said, " surely your Royal Highness is mistaken ; Sir W. Gell must only have referred to his salary, which has been due such a time, and is now owing to him." " Very well," I replied, " but you'll see it is not that." I took the sum, however, which Siccard put up in paper, determining to give it him myself, which I did accordingly, on going to the opera. He said, " Do you know I was very near returning the sum you gave me ? " " Why ? " " Because it is not at all what I meant ; I meant to have thirty ducats for my coat." I did not answer a single word, but I gave it him, and then told Siccard. " Is it possible that a gentleman can do such things ? " said he. " Amen," said I, in my own person.

Abashed and astonished, I own I cannot believe this ; I am sure it was false ; and yet there was an air of truth in it which terrified me for my friends. How very dangerous to be near such scenes !

> To mingle with the bad, and make us run,
> oo near the paths which virtue bids us shun.

I went to bed confused and doubting, and with that uncomfortable impression which the fear of finding out human faults, and frailties in those whom we imagined good, always imparts.

Saturday, 15.—I was made to accompany Her Royal Highness to see a house, and we had another scene of another kind. The poor little cream-coloured ponies are only fit to drive about a park, and they were made to scamper up a very steep and slippery road. This longing for perpetual change is the longing of a disordered mind, which loathes all it possesses. Why seek another house when the one Her Royal Highness is now lodged in is so delightful ?

. Mr. R[——] dined afterwards. During the evening he was not, of course, allowed to talk with me, but was called to the sofa, and forced to amuse the Princess. He was made, for this laudable purpose, to relate a story which was most horrid, not fit for the *lowest* or most immoral society.* Lady C. C[ampbell] and Lady G[lenbervi]e did not know which way to look, and their distress made us all look grave ; which displeased the Princess, and her countenance was immediately over-spread with a scowl, which is always very painful to witness   I cannot conceive how a man of any taste or feeling could be persuaded, by any royalty, to utter such things in the hearing of any woman ; and I doubt if the ladies should not have risen and left the room.

Sunday, 16th April.—I went to church : heard a very fine sermon. The text was taken from the Psalms. Missed the verse, and could not find it, but the meaning was, that evil company corrupts good manners. After

---

* It may be said, in excuse for the Princess, that she certainly did not understand English thoroughly ; and, in her quest after diversion, she encouraged everything which created a laugh, without often knowing the real meaning which excited it. [Original note.]

what had passed the preceding evening, it came home to me in a most forcible manner.

I went to see Lady M[——]. M[——] told me, seriously, that W[——] B[——]l, who is just arrived, would like of all things to be one of the Princess's lords of the bedchamber. I thought this was one of the greatest pieces of good fortune which ever befell her, and hastened, on my return home, to communicate the intelligence, conceiving she would jump at it; and so she did, only she hoped Lord M[——] might; in which case she would prefer him, because of his having a *handle* to his name. I told Her Royal Highness frankly, that I did not think *he* would. I am certain he would not. In short, if she loses this opportunity of securing such a respectable attendant as Mr. B[——]l, she loses every chance of building up again her fallen house. But I did not give Her Royal Highness one word of advice, for I know it to be useless. Lord Malpas and Mr. B[——]l dined with her. We walked afterwards in the garden, but it was too cold and dark to enjoy it. The Princess did not go beyond her own terrace. 'Tis evident to see, she is afraid of those she ought to despise.

Dreadful news came from France: the tricoloured flag is said to be flying at Marseilles and Toulon, and the poor Duc D'Angouleme is beaten—some say he is taken. How Heaven has scourged that house! surely it ought to be a lesson to princes, to all mankind indeed, not to deserve, at least, the wrath of Supreme Power.

Monday, 17th April, 1815.—Captain Pechell sent the Princess word that he was obliged to go to Lord W. Bentinck, and could not attend Her Royal Highness upon her intended water expedition: so she would go by land to see the house she had heard of. Captain Pechell came, however, saying his business was over sooner than he expected, and he could obey her commands ; but the Princess entered the room where we were waiting, in a very cross humour ; said she would not be made a fool of twice in one day ; then waited not for the boat, but walked down to the quay. She was also displeased at the idea of Captain Pechell's firing a salute, and would not allow it, so another boat was dispatched back again to the Clorinde, to forbid their doing so, and at last we set forth.

The palace we went to see was called *Paradis*. It certainly commanded a fine view, but had not been inhabited for many years, and was so old and so melancholy that I dreaded the thoughts of the Princess having it. There was a small house, called *Le Petit Paradis*, more dreadful than the large one, which I saw Her Royal Highness thought would be a convenient *Trou Madame*. We walked four miles ; and Her Royal Highness was very tired : it blew freshly also, and Lady C. C[ampbell], who is a great coward on the water, was nervous, and unfortunately said, " Well, Madam, I do for your Royal Highness what I would not for any relation. It is a sacrifice I would not make for them, to come in an open boat in such a wind." She was angry, and said, " Then you should never travel, Lady Charlotte." We were much amused by the latter pinching me and Dr. H[olland], (between whom her ladyship was sitting,) from fright. I think Lady C. C[ampbell] is a little smitten with the handsome Algernon Percy. She said to me, " His voice and looks are supremely interesting " ; and she talked to him the whole night.

Tuesday, 18th of April.—Went to see the Institution for the Deaf and Dumb, under the direction and tuition of Arzarotti. I never was more delighted or instructed. Hitherto this divine institution has been carried on by gratuitous subscription · now, the King of Sardinia has promised to establish a fund for its support. It consists of twelve girls and twelve boys. We only saw the boys : beings who by their naturally defective organs seemed destined to pass a life in worse than heathen darkness, a merely brutal existence, have been by the care and ingenuity of the benevolent and learned Arzarotti brought into life and light, and are become sensible on the subject of their being, here and hereafter. They replied, by a wonderful process, in writing, to various questions which were put to them. They were made to find out and write the names of all the ladies, and proved beyond a doubt that they had not only acquired a certain set of ideas, but that their intellectual faculties were as intense (if not more so) as those of half the persons who walk about the world with all their senses given them in a state of perfection. I regret that I did not follow the process sufficiently clearly to set it down. I shall go again, and give a more distinct account of the manner in which this miraculous effect is brought about.

Lady W. Bentinck set me down at the Palazzo Durazzo. There was a large dinner party : the Bentincks, Col. Le Moine, Bourke, and Hosted. The Princess was only gracious to the first two of these persons, and was very angry with Lady C. C[ampbell], because she talked a good deal to Lord W. B[entinc]k. She cannot bear her to have any *conversation suivie* with anybody. I suppose it is for fear they should ask questions about herself. Her Royal Highness might put entire confidence in Lady C[——], for she is very trustworthy. I sat up late, writing the following verses. It is long since I have felt the *estro* of poetry, or any other pleasurable *estro* cheer my heart, and I welcomed the result, however weak and mediocre it might be, with the joy one feels on the return of a long and absent friend.

TO ARZAROTTI OF GENOA,

THE SUCCESSFUL INSTRUCTOR OF THE DEAF AND DUMB.

O gifted mortal, who with hallowed zeal
Hast taught thine own to live in others' weal,
To thee I pour, in secret fervent lays,
Spontaneous homage of sincerest praise.
Whoe'er hath seen thy works of love, nor felt
That Heaven to thee its purest spirit dealt ?
Afflicted Nature feels thy high command,
And through a mortal's, owns the Almighty hand.
While warring nations raise th' embattled host,
And in the voice of tumult peace is lost,
Gazing on thee, and thine, we soar above
This world of strife—to realms of joy and love.
Whoe'er hath seen and can forget the face
Pregnant with fire and intellectual grace,
The eyes upraised, and fixed on Heaven their bent,
While every muscle worked with high intent
Of that poor youth who late inertly trod,
Himself scarce better than the senseless clod ?
Who can forget, nor own the man divine,
Who gave that countenance with grace to shine ?
Th' unconscious objects, who of speech bereft,
And hearing's senses, have scarce a semblance left
Of that high origin from whence they sprung,
Cimmerian darkness round their beings flung,
By thee are called to life, from hopeless night,
To the clear day of intellectual light ;
From the drear silence of their torpid state
They wake to be—to feel, in faith elate,
That when this transitory scene is o'er,
A life to come will lasting life restore.
Nor they alone shall swell the grateful lays ;
Their parents' hearts record the note of praise :
Re-echoing there, it sounds in tender strai:
And gives to listening Heaven thy name again.
Say ! who hath taught them everlasting truth ?
'Tis thou, blest guide of their unhappy youth !
Thou, Arzarotti ! man of meekness, thou,
Who mak'st the little great, in life, seem low ;

Thou, who when every sense shall fade away,
And the great light of this our earthly day
Dimly shall shine before thy closing eye,
Unfading brightness wilt behold from high
And in the glory of celestial songs]
Shalt list that heavenly music which belongs
To those who passing from this earthly sphere,
In realms of living light hosannahs hear!

Wednesday, 19th.—Wrote and read. Mr. Percy and
Mr. Wilson called on me. As I fear there is no hope of
W[——] B[——]'s being taken at his word, I sounded
Mr. W[——] to find out if he would accept this place
about Her Royal Highness, which has gone a-begging
to be filled up, till I am quite vexed and ashamed of her,
poor soul! to find on how low a footing she has placed
herself. Mr. W[——] would like it, but I see he dares
not, for fear of the B[——]'s.

Lady W. Bentinck brought a Comte Somebody, whose
name I never heard, but some minister from his Majesty
the King of Sardinia. The Princess thought she did
wonders for Murat, by talking politics to him the whole
time.

We had Mr. R[——] and M. D'[——]a to dinner. I
cannot conceive why Her Royal Highness invites the
latter little sneaking fellow, who is a decided enemy to
her, and a spy, set over her by the Prince. I was very
glad that her dress, conversation, and manners, happened
by some *lucky chance* to be all perfectly proper ; so that
unless Monsieur D'[——]a told lies, he could not say
anything was improper.

Passed this evening at the Palazzo Durazzo. If the
Princess were ten times more foolish and ill-conducted
than she is, I should still wish her well and try to uphold
her : for any one so *persecuted* should be protected. Let
England try her. If she be found unworthy of her station,
let her be turned out of it at once, and her name never

mentioned again ; but if she is not, let her live in peace. This the Prince will not permit. There is a vindictiveness in his character which makes it quite odious.

Thursday, 20th.—I went with the Princess rumbling about nine miles out of town, to see a deserted palace in a village ; a melancholy cut-throat-looking place, where we shall all die of the pip, and Her Royal Highness too. That is my only hope of escape, for she seems at present to fancy removing there.

Lord Malpas, Mr. W. B[――], Mr. Percy, and Mr. Wilson, dined at the Palazzo Durazzo. The Princess pretends to think Mr. Percy very ugly : that is, because he is precisely otherwise. I wonder how he likes courtly favour. She told some excellent stories, but then, as usual, she degenerated into all sorts of idle talking, and she encourages laughing at the expense of propriety and delicacy. We went to the Opera late. For the first time the music was indifferent.

It is reported that Bonaparte is levying a great force to conquer Italy. There is better news once more from Toulon and Marseilles : they are said to be hoisting the white flag again, and the Duc D'Angouleme is supposed not to be taken, but, on the contrary, to be at the head of an army.

Friday, 21st.—Two Monsieur Durazzos—a little and a big—both equally disagreeable in appearance ; Lady Dalrymple, Lord and Lady W. Bentinck, Lord and Lady Glenbervie, dined at the Princess's. The storm in her temper, which has lasted nearly three days, and which was on Monday at its height, has subsided. I am really anxious about Madame Davidoff, who I fear must have been a prisoner in some bad inn ; that is the best thing to hope for her. I read Montaigne and Metastasio. Captain Thompson, of the Aboukir, called on me : he is an agreeable person. I went to a ball at a Comtesse [——], and was rather bored till I talked to Lord M[——].

Saturday.—The Princess drove out to the dreaded house at Nevin. Thank my stars she did not take me, but was accompanied by Madame Dumont and William. Monsieur De Negri called ; I walked out with him. Went to the Doria Palace, to view the grand remains of that magnificent man's magnificent ideas. The gardens descend to the sea, from whence he could embark or disembark in his galleys. A superb fountain in marble, around which sit eagles as large as life, ornaments the middle of what has been a noble formal parterre. It is loaded with decoration, and not in classical taste ; but it is grand, and the marine horses are spirited. Above the palace, which is of vast extent, rise other gardens. A colossal statue, seen from afar, stands in these gardens, like a gigantic genius lamenting the fallen greatness of the republic of Genoa. All here is on a vast scale.

The Princess dined at five o'clock, because she expected the Ex-Queen of Etruria at an early hour in the evening. Her Majesty is the Queen of Spain's daughter, ci-devant Arch Duchess of Parma. She is a woman of low, heavy form, which appears still more so, because her legs, if legs she has, are so short, that she is like a *walking torso.* I never knew before why it was high treason to say a Queen of Spain had legs. Her face is sensible, though ugly. She only passed through the apartment where we were, to the Princess's room, her son and daughter following. The son is a beautiful boy—which is very odd. The two ladies-in-waiting are two monsters to look at. The Comte Guicciardini, a descendant of the Florentine historians of that name, is a well-looking, *fattish, blackish* man, speaking horrid French. This Queenly visit, for which we were all dressed to the utmost, lasted about three quarters of an hour. The boy and girl—I beg their pardon—Prince and Princess, sat with them, and the four royalties passed out as they had passed in, and so ended that farce.

I went on Sunday, with Lady Glenbervie, to see an institution which has commenced, and is still supported, chiefly at the expense of the Fieschi family. It consists of a hundred and thirty poor women, who support their community by various works. We only saw, of their performances, artificial flowers ; but if they sell all their works as dear, no wonder they live so well. I never saw anything better kept or arranged than their abode. No English charitable Institution, that I ever saw, was more clean or comfortable in its arrangements.

The Princess had at dinner Madame Morando, Lord Malpas, W. Burrell, Lord Strathaven, W. Palmeda, the English Vice-Consul ; but it was a gloomy, dull affair.

Friday, 28*th*.—I have had nothing to write worth keeping a note of, for a week past ; all has been tolerably smooth. To-day I took a delightful walk into the country, among green hills, that put me in mind of D [——] and its neighbourhood. To my surprise, Lady W. Bentinck, who I thought was at Milan, called on the Princess. They met a courier from England, which made them turn back hither. This courier brought news which makes everybody sorry. Lord William is recalled. No troops are to remain in Italy, except in garrison towns ; and Lord William is considered as of too high rank to remain here, when we have so small a force. There is also a rumour that we are to make peace with Bonaparte ! Lady William and her husband have paid the Princess great and kind attentions. They are excellent people, beloved wherever they go ; and I wish Her Royal Highness valued their countenance and support as highly as it deserves ; but she is so foolish, so regardless of what is of vital consequence to her interests, that it is pitiable.

Lord and Lady Glenbervie dined here to-day, but they were not coaxed as usual. She was (I mean the Princess) in a dreadful humour. Monsieur De La Rue sat by her. After dinner, Her Royal Highness went to return the Queen of Etruria's visit. The little crownless King came down a hundred stairs, I believe, to meet our Royal Lady. Up they went again : and, as usual, passed into an empty room, where they sat by themselves. I found out that one of her Ex-Majesty's ladies is not so ugly. She is married to the Chamberlain Guicciardini, and is his sister-in-law. After endeavouring to talk Italian, and their paying me compliments upon the same, (the reason, I suppose, of my change of opinion,) back we came again home, the pretty little King handing the Princess down stairs as he had done up.

I was called by Her Royal Highness into her secret chamber, where there was a fire, though the thermometer was at eighty ; but she makes cosmetics and dirt pies, and there were various pots and pans boiling. What a droll amusement ! *au reste*, the apartment was comfortable enough ; filled with all sorts of things, the oddest mixture of finery and trash, which, by the way, all royalties are apt to like. Now a bit of cut-out paper ; now a gem ; now a *papier maché* box ; now one of jasper ; such is usually the decoration of their tables and cabinets. She showed me all her *bonny dies*. I was in a better temper, but not right. Though it was eleven when she dismissed me, I could not resist going to Lord William Bentinck, to hear Major Andrèossi, who sang like an angel. I never heard anything sung so well, not even by the *chanticleer*, in point of taste. He is besides a handsome man, highly considered by Lord William Bentinck, and reckoned an excellent officer. I heard every word he pronounced, and he sang with so much feeling and so much nature, that I have had him in my head all night. What a ridiculous way of expressing myself ! Shame on such *slip-slop* language ! I ought rather.to say, the sound of Major Andrèossi's voice is still in my ears, and his sentiment and feeling touched my heart, and have left an impression on it which, I think, will never be utterly lost. I would ask leave to introduce him to the Princess ; his presence in her circle would be a great charm ; but I am so afraid of ever making any one known to her, for a thousand reasons.

Saturday, 29*th*.—To-day I received the following from my friend, K. Craven.

Dated NAPLES.

DEAR [——],—Having at length a chance of sending you a letter safely, I will not let it escape, and must express my satisfaction at hearing that you were with Her Royal Highness at Genoa. I shall not attempt to describe the strange scenes we have witnessed here, and which have not ceased—the downfall of an usurped dynasty, and the restoration of a legitimate one. Still less shall I venture to decide under which of these the country is most likely to prosper, or its natives are to be happy. I always augured ill of the *late* King's imprudent eruption with Italy, but did not foresee the business would be so speedily concluded. His Queen, whose behaviour has gained her universal applause, I may say, admiration, sailed this morning for Trieste, which she has chosen in preference to England. Our Port is full of English men-of-war and transports, and the town of Austrian troops, whose presence contributes not a little to the public tranquillity, which, however, has been chiefly maintained by the civic guard, who have distinguished themselves by preventing the pillage of the palace and most of the nobility's houses, and saved many fortunes and lives. Of the latter, however, a considerable number have been sacrificed, in repressing the criminal endeavours of a set of beings that scarcely deserve the name of human.

On Sunday last, the day that the Queen went on board, and before the Austrian troops came in, the danger was at its utmost point ; and I can assure you that we passed several very unpleasant hours, both in the day and night. Since

that, it has been on the decline, and I trust will continue so
until the King's entry, which may, perhaps, afford some
opportunity for a renewal of irregularities ; but I believe
all precautions will be taken that human foresight can devise.
He (Ferdinand) is expected about Sunday next, and cannot
well arrive before, as the ship that is to carry him from Messina
only went from hence the day before yesterday. His son,
Prince Leopold, entered with the Austrian army, and gives
universal satisfaction to the apostates, or penitents, whichever you may please to call them ; in which number almost
all the first families are included. The army is annihilated,
and without much actual loss in battle, as it is estimated it
never amounted to above three thousand men ; but the
moment the first defeat was suffered within the frontiers,
want of provisions, desertion, private quarrels, jealousy
among the chiefs, want of confidence in the leaders, and all
the other evils that can disorganize an army, spread themselves through this one, and soon put an end to it, leaving a
few generals only, to make a capitulation. You may, perhaps,
know that previously to this the Queen had signed a con-
vention with Captain Campbell of the Tremendous, giving
him up the men-of-war, all the stores, and putting herself
under British protection. The King returned, and staid one
day, during which a new and liberal constitution was proclaimed, which ended this tragedy something in the manner
of a farce ; and in the following night he made his escape,
no one knows exactly how. And now you have a pretty
correct outline of the whole transaction. The country is in
a state which I fear it will be difficult to retrieve it from :
the provinces without any administration ; the inhabitants
refusing to pay taxes, and even rents ; some towns in Calabria
themselves independent ; free corps of vagabonds and dis-
banded soldiers roving about in all drections. The very
vicinity of the capital is so infested with these men, that it
is dangerous to take a drive a mile out of it. All this in the
midst of the most lovely climate and the most beautiful of
countries ; Vesuvius majestically smoking above it all, and
Pulicinello continuing his facetious career with undiminished
perseverance and activity.

For my part, I am as I was when her Royal Highness left
this, still waiting a summons from my mother, which I have

now a possibility of obeying, as the communication will be open either by sea or by land; though I fear the latter may be attended with inconvenience, if not peril. I wrote to you and Dr. Holland about a month since, and Knutson engaged to get the letters conveyed: you are the best judge whether he succeeded or not. He is still here, with all the English I then mentioned; and as they were all so bent upon going away, when it was not possible to do so, I imagine they will all stay, now that there are no difficulties about going. Lady Elizabeth sailed about a fortnight since, and, I trust, is by this time safely landed in France. Gell and I made a short excursion to Ischia, which reminded us so much of the Grecian Islands, that we think of going again; and the Bedfords and Lady Westmoreland talk of doing the same. I am very well, but poor Gell's gout attacks him so frequently, that I am really seriously annoyed, though not alarmed, by it. It is a fact, that without any regular fit, he is generally three days in each week without being able to walk at all. Lady Burghersh arrived yesterday, and they inhabit the house her Royal Highness had. Ours is the delight of our existence, being the most comfortable, quiet, and gay residence I ever was in, and the envy and admiration of all visitors. We generally have a tea party every evening. We have just been embellishing our terrace with a treillage of cane-work, and have millions of flowers both there and in our garden. The Oxfords are going, but I know not where, and I fancy in that respect they are not wiser than myself. I shall now take my leave, only adding, that a few lines from you, addressed to the care of Monsieur Falconnet, banker, will very much oblige

Your sincere friend,

TELEMACHUS.

—I went to see Madame Davidoff, who had arrived the day before: she had very narrowly escaped being drowned. I was quite happy to see her again. I walked with her to Lady W. Bentinck's, and to Lady Sandwich's and Glenbervie's, where I left her.

On my return to the Palazzo, the Princess sent for me. I found Her Royal Highness sitting with Monsieur De

Negri, in her dressing-room (though called such, there was no appearance even of a toilet ; her *real* dressing-room was separated from this apartment by an ante-chamber). He is in high favour : she was showing off all her wit to him. I found out afterwards it was because he was a Milanese, or had Milanese *possessions*. Why that should affect her, I know not. She has decided to give a great ball on Monday, which allows nobody time to get their clothes made. All are to be asked who do leave, or who have left, their name for her. The Princess did not come down to dinner, having a head-ache. Lord and Lady Glenbervie, and Dr. Holland, and myself, had a very merry dinner. Afterwards we wrote all the invitations ; then were called to the royal presence, and kept up very late : *voilà les plaisirs de cette Cour.*

Sunday, 14th May, six o'clock in the morning, Genoa ; in bed. Scoglietto Palazzo Durazzo.—A fortnight has passed withou my writing, and this fortnight has been the most busy time. It is ever so. What is most worth remembering we are no longer calm enough to profit by. During this fortnight the Pope came to the Princess—a circumstance so singular that it became quite interesting. Her Royal Highness received him on the steps of her palace, and, after he had sat with her for about half an hour, during which Lady Glenbervie and Lady C. Campbell had time to fall in love with the almoner, the good old Pontiff went away, blessing all whom he passed. The scullions and cooks came out in a crowd to kiss his toe, which they did most audibly. The Princess followed the Pope down stairs ; and when he descended the grass plots to his carriage, and was told she was still there, his Holiness turned and made the most graceful bow I ever saw. His countenance is so fine, and his figure so venerable, I felt quite a Catholic ; or rather, I felt the respect due to respectable age.

In this short space of time I have laid up remembrances without regrets, except that the fortnight is past. I went twice again to the Brignole Palace, and to the Pope's present residence, which is truly magnificent ;— corridors, gardens, marble terraces, from whence there are fine views of the sea—and everything that grandeur can give to make locality superb ; not the petty grandeur of silks and satins, although that exists also in the interior, but the really sublime circumstances of all that constitutes greatness. The picture I admired most in this palace was the Death of Seneca, by Lucca Giordano. Its opposite neighbour, the Gorgon's head, I did not at all admire. The Adoration, by Lucca Doranda, one of the early painters, is more curious than gratifying. Judith with Holofernes' head, by Weilings, has too much indifference in the female countenance. There is another of the same subject in the palace where the king of Sardinia is lodged —a much finer picture. Cupid bending his Bow, by Annibal Carracci, a copy from Correggio, is an odd conception ; for the Cupid is so very serious he must meditate some deep and lasting wound, there being nothing playful in his mien. Rembrandt's portrait by himself is a fine picture ; but he is always so much the same, there is so much method and trick in his greatness, that it almost ceases to be greatness. A head of our Saviour, by Carlo Dolce, is one of the most beautiful and melancholy pictures I ever saw. It makes one's blood run cold. What must the painter not have felt who represented that sacred head in such a state of suffering ? The Madonna, its companion, is not equal to it. There is a grand composition by Tintoretto ; but the representation of the Almighty is always offensive and almost impious. " Eye hath never seen him."

Another day I went to the *Alberghi dei Poveri*, where one thousand three hundred and nineteen poor are supported in peace and plenty. It is a glorious establishment.

There is a small bas-relief of Christ and the Madonna, by Michael Angelo, over the gateway of this hospital. The head of the Saviour is beautiful. There is a yellow tint in the marble which is truly like the marble of death. The Virgin is not so striking ; but still there is a world of sweetness in the sorrowful smile with which she gazes on the Saviour.

One day the Princess of Wales went to visit the King of Sardinia, who had come sneaking here in the dark one night, because he could not help himself ; and while the royalties were together, I looked at some of the pictures. The Judith, which I mentioned before as being much finer than either of the pictures of the same subject at the Brignole and Durazzo palaces, is a grand work of art. There is an air of hurried motion in Judith's figure, as though she said, " If it were done, 'twere best 'twere done quickly " ; an appearance of terror, lest she should not be able to hold the head, makes one better able to endure the subject. Joseph's bloody garment displayed to his father, was also a good specimen of the master ; and a Virgin in grief, by Carlo Maratti (though I think him in general an indifferent artist) is a very touching composition ; her grief is so deep, so resigned. The tremulous motion (if I may be allowed the term) in the lip—the pallid colours that appear to float through the skin—the redness of the eyes—above all, the languor which pervades the whole, struck me forcibly, and render it a most superior production. I could have gazed for hours at it. One only circumstance lessened its beauty —its indefinite size—being neither large enough for life, nor small enough for miniature. The companion picture, Herodias with John the Baptist's head, had the same fault ; but it is a minor fault after all ; and the latter is wondrous in another way. The deep tone of the colouring, its fleshy roundness and force, demand sovereign admiration ; but it does not excite the tender interest which makes one long to wipe the tears and console the sufferer, as in the case of his weeping Virgin.

And now I must end about pictures, and palaces, and transcendant Genoa, to be engaged in all the hurry and bustle of an immediate departure. The Princess hears that the oaths of homage are to take place at Milan sooner than was expected, and Her Royal Highness set off at three or four this morning, to go thither as fast as horses could carry her ; to fly from herself, and seek in pleasure that happiness which exists in the soul's peace and content. I went to bid Madame Davidoff good bye, and did so with regret, which was not diminished on hearing from Miss Esterly, that General Davidoff is now attached to another woman, an unmarried person, a *Princess Byron ;* * that she lives in the Empress's family, and is protected by her Imperial Majesty.

The general has flown in the face of the whole imperial family, and has sued for a divorce from his wife, having presented a petition to the Emperor to this effect. Miss Esterly said, that often for months together, General Davidoff would not look at his own children ; that he hated them ; that his poor wife has been at his feet with all his children, to conjure him not to be divorced from her. She has such a sentiment of deep religion, that she conceives it to be breaking a sacrament, according to her doctrine, of the Greek church ; and, in short, her leaving her country was all in order to get him away from the object of his fatal passion. In vain ! Now, Miss Esterly says, she is waiting for every post to bring her news of his having quitted her for ever, and that her situation is truly deplorable. This is a melancholy history, and I could not leave Madame Davidoff without a lively sympathy for her sorrows ; they are so true, so noble, that they excite compassion without any blame being attached

* Probably of the family of Biron de Courlande.

to the sufferer, as is the case, alas ! too often ; for instance, in the unhappy Princess of Wales.

The Princess returned in two or three days, and once again she paid a visit to Monsieur de Begnis' delicious garden. How sad to look at scenes of wondrous beauty for the *last time !* To look at *any* object for the last time which has afforded us interest, is always painful, but at such transcendant loveliness, at such a scene, where fancy has once more floated in spheres of pleasure, it is doubly mournful. Above all, when the *locale* is associated with an individual—when a dear voice has echoed in that spot—a beloved footstep been listened to as it advanced to the place of rendezvous—there, where friendship and love have held sweet converse together, making a temporary paradise, into which the spite and malice and sin of the Evil One have entered not ;—then it is indeed a bitter parting. I looked at this garden with infinite tenderness. I bade its soil be fruitful ; I bade its flowers bloom in undiminished luxuriance ; I bade the sun to shine on it, and the flowers to refresh it. All this looks very foolish on paper—what piece of sentiment does not ? but so long as a third eye does not glance over the words, it matters not ; and I would fain keep a record of these feelings.

I dined at Lord William Bentinck's ; sat next Mr. Andrews, a pleasant man. Lady Barbara and Mr. Ponsonby, Mr. Milner, Mr. Catanelli, were the party. Mr. Catanelli has a remarkably sensible, agreeable face, and I am told is very superior in all things.

Walked to the Palazzo Durazzo, breathing the odour of orange flowers, and loitered late on the lovely terrace.

Rose at daybreak to see Her Royal Highness depart. I have a foolish dislike to saying good-bye to any one, and I never felt sadder presentiments than when I bade the poor Princess farewell. I could not follow Her Royal Highness. I did not wish to do so ; but when we part from persons who have shown us individual kindness, be their faults what they may, we remember only that they were good to ourselves, and the pang at saying farewell, and the throb of one's heart as one exclaims a grateful and a hearty " God bless you ! " is a very keen anguish.

A few hours after, I also left the Palazzo Durazzo. And now farewell Genoa, but not farewell the memory of thy enchantments !

VERSES WRITTEN ON LEAVING GENOA, 1815.

GIVEN ME BY LADY [——].

I thought the dreaming hour was gone—
That sad reality alone
Had traced an arid path, whence I
Life's furthest verge could plain descry ;
But I have trod on fairy ground,
Where sweet illusion scattered round
Fresh flowers, to make me lose awhile
The sense of fortune's frown or smile.
Then let me gaze, and gaze again
On scenes whose power to banish pain
Have come with such a gentle force,
I cannot trace their unseen source ;
But which, in memory's tablet placed,
Will ne'er by others be effaced.
Can I forget thy crescent bay,
" Thy palace pride "—thy gardens gay,
Whose hanging terraces invite
To climb the sweet luxurious height ?
Can I forget thy silver sea
Whose circling zone of majesty
So sweetly clasps its " city bride,"
As if it had not love beside ?
Can I forget ? perhaps—alas !
For memory fades and objects pass ;
But deep impressions of delight
Remain, when these shall fade in night.
Transcendent Genoa ! can I leave
Thy wondrous beauty—and not grieve ?

The vague enchantments, visions rare,
Which hover in thy magic air ;
The quiet walk—the blaze of noon—
The balm of twilight—night's calm moon
These stamp their glories on the soul,
And scorn of time to own controul.
Transcendent Genoa ! take the tear
Which, trembling, starts unbidden here,
For soon thy magic will be gone,
Thy beauty and thy influence flown.
To-morrow's sun once more for me
Will light thy splendid imagery,
And then—Farewell—ah ! since for ever,
'Twere better I had seen thee never.

SECTION VII

CONTINUATION OF JOURNAL

SIMPLON.—In the midst of clouds, and rain, and cold, on the top of the Alps; a good fire my only consolation. Here I am, out of the region of sunshine and pleasure, transported once more to all the *morale* and' all the *physique* of a cold climate, and the dull duties of common existence. Heavens! what a contrast! I passed a winged fortnight at Milan. To go over it day by day, I cannot—to pass it by in silence, impossible. Arrived at Milan, Monday night, the 15th, about nine o'clock. The Princess of Wales knew I was to arrive, and sent for me to the Opera, whither she was gone, without any English attendants whatever. I was too much concerned for her not to obey her summons, and therefore drove to the *Gran Teatro Della Scala*. I arrived as the performance ended, and had only time to make my bow as the Marquis de Ghisilieri was handing Her Royal Highness into her carriage. With her unvarying kindness to me, she had the complaisance to return into the theatre, that I might have a *coup d'œil* of it in all its glory. It was the finest building of the kind I ever saw; and being lit up for the Archduke of Austria, it had an imposing effect. Still, the illumination was partial; for though the lustres on the outside of the boxes were lit upon that occasion, the back parts of them were in shade.

I was sorry to observe that the Princess had no lady in

attendance upon her ; but the Marquis Ghisilieri, who is a man of high rank and charming manners, was all respect and attention to her. Some persons made a bad joke, and said his being at the *head of the police*, was an additional circumstance in favour of his being an *attaché* to Her Royal Highness's court.

Everybody has heard of, and so many have seen, the cathedral at Milan, that it may seem unnecessary to dwell upon it ; yet one word I must write, not by way of regular or historical description, but merely to please myself, by living over again, as it were, my first visit to that beautiful shrine. The dignity of its structure, and the rich, yet quiet, beauty of its white marble walls and gothic pinnacles, are more in accordance with my feelings of a place of worship than the painted roofs and inlaid altars of the churches of Genoa. I walked repeatedly round the beautiful screen which circles the high altar. A thousand brilliant rays of coloured light darted through the painted windows, and danced over the pavement, giving animation to the statues, which appeared, to a fanciful view, as if just starting into life. I sat down on a bench to contemplate the scene, and tried to define the sentiments to which it gave birth : in vain. So I suffered myself to look and to enjoy—to shut out the past and the future —and was satisfied—to be. I gazed delightfully on one of those fortunate accidents of light which fell on two of the statues. The illusion was magical ; it produced that once-to-be-seen effect which, like some happy circumstance in life, illumines certain spots of existence with colours too vivid and too etherial to last. *The same thing never returns.*

I proceeded to ascend the highest pinnacle of the cathedral, and was well repaid for the trouble ; for although these *mappe monde* views are not the most beautiful, it is gratifying to embrace a vast expanse of country at one view. There is a latent sense of imaginary power in

standing on an elevation, which is undoubtedly gratifying.   Amid the most elaborate and beautifully-executed
tracery of gothic ornament, spire, and foliage, and scroll
innumerable, covered by statues, and glistering white in
the unclouded atmosphere, I looked over the rich plain of
Lombardy, far as the eye can reach.   It is bounded only
towards the north by the vast chain of Alps, whose
romantic outline forms a barrier which might well seem
impregnable, and yet has not protected the beautiful
Italy, which it vainly encircles.   As the eye wandered
over the most luxuriant plain, the scene of so many wars,
so many disputes, who could forbear wishing that the
nature of mankind were less selfish, and that instead of
monopolizing the possessions of others, each nation and
people would rejoice in the prosperity of each other ?   But
the world must be regenerated before this can take place.

I quitted the cathedral of Milan with regret.   I have
seen it since often, but it has never been the same
cathedral to me.

Extract of a Letter from Milan.

The Archduke is here receiving the oaths of homage, and
all Milan is in a state of festivity and confusion ; balls, masquerades, &c. &c.   The Princess is received in great state,
and applauded wherever she appears.   The first night of
my arrival, Her Royal Highness went to the theatre ; the
second, to a great court ball, which was certainly the most
magnificent fête I ever beheld.   The vastness and solid
splendour of the apartments reminded me of the entertain-
ments described in the Arabian N'ghts.   The Grand Duke
met the Princess at the door of the saloon, and walked round
the endless suite of rooms with Her Royal Highness, followed
by their respective attendants.   Some gentlemen, as well
as ladies, are appointed to form part of her *cortège* wherever
she goes ;   and there is a proper court etiquette observed
towards her, which must be gratifying to her, or ought to be.

Yesterday afternoon there were games in the amphitheatre
built by Bonaparte.   The immensity and beauty of the

building are very striking. It can contain, it is said, thirty-five thousand persons, and in its arena are performed various games, after the manner of the ancients—chariot races, foot races, &c. In two hours' time it can be filled five feet deep with water, for Naumachian games; but on this occasion, chariots, men, and horses were the amusements of the hour. The spectators sat in the amphitheatre, with umbrellas only to shade them from the sun; but the Grand Duke and the Princess sat on two state chairs, under a magnificent pavilion, supported by pillars of the Corinthian order, (stolen, by-the-by, from some church,) and the Maréchal Bellegarde, and all the Austrian court, attending upon the royalties. The Duchess of Visconti and some other lady waited upon the Princess of Wales. Every person in this vast assemblage was dressed in the most splendid array. Flowers, feathers, diamonds, glittered and waved around. Twenty-five thousand persons and upwards were said to be present. Certainly every part of the vast building was filled with spectators, and yet you might have heard a pin fall. The graceful outline of the oval structure, as wide, but not nearly so high, as the amphitheatres of the ancients—the Alps rising in yet more glorious amphitheatre than any formed by mortal hand, in the background—completed this extraordinary and indescribable fête.

Letter from KEPPEL CRAVEN.

I cannot let [——]'s letter depart without adding a few words to you; not to apologize for not answering your two last, which I received some time ago, but to give you some account of your friends in this part of the world, who are not few in number; as, besides our two selves, there are E. F. Knutson, Lady Westmoreland, Irvine, &c., and I dare say many others. I wish you were of the party, as, in point of English, we are much better provided for than during the winter; and in every other respect this place is to me perfection, and I don't know how I shall ever tear myself from it. I expect, however, so to do, by a summons from my mother, unless she comes to Italy, which her last letter indicated a wish to do: but I have been somewhat uneasy about her, as she was at Marseilles, which, in consequence of the Duc D'Angoulême's presence, held out the longest in favour of the Bourbons.

The English that are here are very uncertain what steps to take ; and I fancy many would have taken flight some time since, had not the fear of banditti been stronger than any other ; and indeed poor Irvine * will, I hope, write you an account of his adventure with them, which will interest you much, but which must have been as unpleasant a piece of romance as ever befell a poor traveller : but you will be happy to hear that the said banditti wore green velvet jackets, with a power of gold buttons—and white hats looped up with ribbons innumerable.

Elizabeth, who sends her kind regards to you, is going to set off for Paris with a certain Countess Waleska [*sic*— Walewska], of whom Her Royal Highness will give you an account ; and with her I consider her quite safe. From France she will probably go to England.

Gell and I have the most comfortable and, we think, the prettiest apartment in the whole town, which is the admiration of all our countrymen. We give them tea every evening, at any hour from eight till eleven—as, if we are not at home, the tea-pot is : and we generally have very good company, headed by Ward, who is in a kind of honey mood, which renders him an universal, and I must add, unexpected favourite.

The beauty of the country just now is not to be described by pen ; but I hope peace will enable you to judge of it next year, for I never mean to leave it again, except perhaps for a short time, if I am able, &c. &c.

Yours most sincerely and affectionately,

K. C.

HOLLAND HOUSE, *Dec.* 8*th.*

MY DEAR [——],—When we have once determined on taking an important step, we are glad of the suffrage even of an insignificant person in favour of it ; and though I am afraid that you have known me too long and too well to have much confidence in my judgment, on the other hand, you must by this time be too thoroughly persuaded of the warm

* Mr. Irvine was one of many persons who were attacked by the banditti between Rome and Naples. He escaped with his life, but not without being severely wounded. [Original note.]

and sincere interest which I take in your welfare, to doubt
that if I rejoice at your having taken any particular step,
it can only be from my believing that it is likely to contribute
to your benefit and pleasure. I therefore take the liberty of
telling you that I am very glad of your accepting [——]. I
have lately seen a good deal of your future mistress, and am
persuaded of her possessing many estimable qualities. She
is extremely good-humoured and obliging, and seems very
much attached to the persons in whose favour she conceives
a prepossession. She is by no means *exigeante;* at the
same time, no little attention is lost upon her. She seems
grateful for the slightest indication of good-will towards
her, (probably, poor soul! the ill treatment which she has
at times received since her arrival in this country has made
such doubly acceptable to her,) and she is generous; indeed
I may say profuse, in her manner of returning it. She reads
a great deal, and buys all new books; is very fond of music,
and the play; has boxes at the Opera and both the theatres,
which Her Royal Highness attends frequently. She has
concerts often at the palace, with the best performers; is
fond of having persons of distinction at her table, either for
rank or for political and literary merits; and I need not
tell you, that her ladies are all most agreeable persons. Lady
Glenbervie and Lady C. Lindsay are *pétillantes d'esprit,* and
Lady [——] will please you infinitely. * * * I know you well
enough to assert, upon my own authority, that the above
is exactly the sort of society which you would have chosen
for yourself. The *gêne* of a court attendance will be less
felt by you than by almost any body else; as I know few
people who have been more in the habit of sacrificing their
own inclinations to those of the persons with whom they
were living; and the Princess, by her manner of speaking
of you, seems prepared to like every thing you say and do.
To be sure, I have endeavoured to *clear up* her ideas on this
subject, but I cannot say with much success; she seems
most obstinately prejudiced in your favour. Into the bargain, I confess it will give me great pleasure to see you placed
in your proper sphere,* and occupying a situation in which

* What a mistake Mr. Lewis made in wishing his friend such joy
at the appointment about the Princess of Wales! for though what
he said of Her Royal Highness's society at *that time* was true, and

you cannot fail to appear to so much advantage. Her Royal Highness has for some time past been so kind to me, that gratitude for her attentions must necessarily render me a partial judge : but even, making all possible allowance, I cannot help flattering myself that you will have reason to be satisfied with your new situation.

There is no news of any kind. Mr. R. Walpole has been tapped for the dropsy, and is considered as being in a very dangerous state.

Ever yours,
M. G. LEWIS.

Letter from HER ROYAL HIGHNESS THE PRINCESS
OF WALES *to* [——].*

DEAR [——],—I resume my pen again. By the franc which you received on Tuesday, you have seen that Lord Byron was of the party on Sunday ; and he was really the hero of the party, for he was in very high spirits, free like a bird in the air, having just got rid of his chains. He intended still to go abroad, but where, how and with whom, he is quite unsettled in his mind about it. I am sorry to mention, that his last poem upon " The Decadence of Bonaparte," is worthy neither his pen nor his muse. So much about him. We sat down seventeen, and the dinner was as merry as any party of the sort could go off. Everybody was determined to be good-humoured and witty. Even old Borringdon did " son petit possible." After we had left the gentlemene and we ladies sat round the fire, equal in number to the nine Muses, a German flute-player, of the name of Foust, came to assume the place of the demigod Pan. He worked much upon the feelings of Lady Anne, who was quite enraptured.

that it was a very agreeable one, *it was no feather in any body's cap* to have been in that unfortunate lady's service. On the contrary, so vindictive are all members of the R— F— in their feelings towards her even to this day, that nothing would induce them to have any person in their households who had ever been about the Princess. No *worldling* ever served Her Royal Highness ; and even those who were personally attached to her, and felt her wrongs, were at last compelled, one by one, to leave her service. [Original note.]

* The following letters really belong to an earlier part of the book, but are placed here—an instance of the haste and carelessness with which it was put together.

She went close to the sounds of his flute, looking strangely
into his face, as if looking him through and through. Upon
the other virgin's heart, Miss Hayman,* he also had much
effect. She took out her pair of spectacles, and went to the
pianoforte to accompany this bewitching flute. Lady Anne
acted the pantomime the whole time the music continued.
I could admire neither the one, nor the other. This heathen
god is deaf upon one ear, which occasioned him to produce
a great many false notes, and I was too happy when released
from this cacaphonie.

On Monday, as I mentioned to you, I had a little children's
ball in honour of my nephews, little Princes Charles and
William.† Twenty couple never were better fitted for
dancing, for beauty, and skill. Lady Anne presided at the
head of the large table appropriated for the children. There
was no dancing after supper, but fireworks, which made the
conclusion of the evening. I confess I was as tired as if I
had danced also, from the noise and from the total want of
any real good conversation with the grown people. I think,
in general, people are grown more old and dull since the
two years I have not met them. Nothing but the wine at
table exhilarates their spirits, and the high dishes takes
them out of their [*word wanting*]. But I am glad to assure
you that I have now done my duty for this year, and shall
not be troubled again. I wish to God for never with any
sight of them.

Yesterday I made morning visits to Lady Glenbervie and
Lady Charlotte, at the Pheaseantry; this evening I go to
Covent Garden, and to-morrow to Drury Lane, to amuse
Willy, and to take away from the dreadful dreary and long
evenings I passed with *La Pucelle d'Orleans*. Everybody of
my acquaintance almost is gone to Paris. Mr. Ward went
on Monday; the Pools went, like conjugal felicity, to Paris
also, and took their only petit fruit d'amour, Emily, with
them. Lord Lucan has sold his house in Hamilton Place
to Lord Wellington: the former is going abroad for three

* This lady was a fine and rare specimen of English character:
rough in manner, right in principle, blunt in speech, but tender in
heart; kind, true, and trust-worthy; with a love for, and true understanding of music, in which she was a proficient. [Original note.]

† Prince William was afterwards the reigning Duke of Brunswick:
on the deposition of his brother, Prince Charles.

MADAME DE STAËL.
From an illustration in "Juniper Hall" by Constance Hill

years, with his whole baggage of children. I say amen, as probably I shall never see them again, for which I shall not weep. The Emperor of Russia is expected in the course of a fortnight, and as he has visited the Empress Josephine at Malmaison, he can have no objection to visit the Regent's wife at Kensington.

Miss B[——] intends to pay you a visit with the brothers. I wish I could as easily as my thoughts do, convey myself to you. You may say a hundred things to a person, but it is impossible to put them all upon paper. You can express your thoughts, but not your feelings, which is my present case. What do you think of the " Wardour," by Madame D'Arblais ? It has only proved to us that she forgot her English ; and the same suspicion has arisen again in my mind, that " Evelina " was written, or at least corrected, by Dr. Johnson. There is nothing out worth recommending in either language. I understand that Madame De Stael has been much offended at the Regent not inviting her the evening Louis XVIII. was at Carlton House. She now laments much that she never came to pay me a visit, and sacrificed me entirely to pay her court to him. She is a very time-serving person. She is going to Paris immediately. A long letter of congratulation was written by her to Louis XVIII., and paying all possible compliments, after having abused them, and done the Bourbons all the mischief in her power. She is a very worldly person, and it is no loss whatever to me never to have made her acquaintance. I shall return to my little nutshell next Saturday, the 30th, and shall feel myself much more comfortable, and not so damp, as in my present habitation, and to live like " La dame de qualité qui s'est retirè du monde." Adieu, and believe me,

Yours most sincerely,

C. P.

Extract of another Letter from HER ROYAL HIGHNESS
to the same.

I wish you would persuade Lady Augusta Charteries * to come and be my lady of the bedchamber for six months ; and in case a great change in my situation should take place

* Lady Augusta Charteris, daughter of Francis, Lord Elcho, married, 1819, Warner, Lord Rossmore.

I

2 C

which would enable me to go abroad, to take her then with me. She would either take the six months waiting at once, or divide them in three months, just as it would be convenient to her, as I have good reasons to think of preparing myself, one day or another, for my journey abroad. The late great events on the Continent enable now everybody to go over there, and the living there will be so much less expensive. I can only assure you, that 2000*l.* of English money would make 12,000*l.* upon the Continent. I had lately occasion to transact some money matters abroad ; 300 dollars just make 50*l.* English money, so that I could be very well and very comfortable in a fine warm climate, and liberty into the bargain. I came to the royal menagerie on Tuesday, the 19th, not from idle want of variety, but from duty, mixed with very little inclination, to be civil to the very uncivilized society of the metropolis. The following day I had a great dinner of twenty people. The chief objects in the picture were the Duke of Gloucester and the Princess Sophia, and the Greys, Lansdownes, Cowpers, &c. In the evening every one who left their names at Connaught House ; though many repented of their civility, and sent shilly shally excuses for not attending the party. Thank God, the dreadful bore was over by twelve o'clock ; the curtain dropped, and I retired in the green-room to my solitary den.

The other three days I saw nobody except the Prince Condé, who was the only gentleman who showed the least urbanity in taking leave of me. I did not hear or see any - thing of the farce with the white cockades, neither * * *

*   *   *   *   *

Everybody wore white favours for three days following, and any stranger arriving in the metropolis would have supposed that the whole country had been married, and I have said, que cetoit le marriage du * * *, uni pour la premiere fois en Pall Mall. We have now a right to expect wonders from that quarter. So much about nothing.

You may easily imagine I have not seen the Duchess of Oldenburgh, and I have also no curiosity to see a Kalmuck face. I shall have to-day Mr. Canning's party to dinner, which will enable me to get a *franc* for all this random of mine. To-morrow I give a children's ball for my little nephew, whose birthday it is. I have invited all the fathers and mothers who have children for that occasion. I am afraid it will be dreadfully dull for the old folks; and then I have concluded for this year of our Lord 1814 with the great and dull world, and shall only devote my hours and days to my especial friends. The Ossulstons have followed Louis XVIII. Mr. Craven is gone in the same packet, commanded by Sir J. Beresford, in which the King is lodged, to Paris. His mother sends him to the King of Prussia for the pension as Dowager Margravine to be paid, and even the arrears. His stay will be six weeks, but I am afraid unsuccessful with regard to his commission. Heaven bless you, my dear [——].

C. P

Extract of a Letter from HER ROYAL HIGHNESS THE PRINCESS OF WALES *to* [——].

The great news most talked of is this great state prisoner retained in the prison of Vincennes. I, in my own mind, am convinced it is the Dauphin, with which I should be delighted, but particularly to see completely the nation made an April fool of by *this scham king*. I am only afraid it would involve the nation in a civil war, as these old gouty fellows would not like to remove the crown so easily. How many regrets about the Saint-Esprits and the garters will be expressed, which, after all, was a very rash action of two old foolish noddles The English nation has at all times been made April fools of, but never so completely than this year of our Lord, 1817.

The Prince Hereditary of Orange has been sent for in great haste, and arrived on Saturday evening, incog. I have not yet heard or seen anything of him. He is to persuade his fair bride to settle in Holland. After she has refused to receive the Duke of York, who was to bring her such a message, they suppose that all-powerful love will make Princess Charlotte yield to leave her native country. But I trust that for once she will be steady, as she would involve herself in more difficulties in future, if not even lose her crown; which I think would be a very bad joke, in consequence of too much obedience before marriage. *O tempore, O mores!* Since Saturday I am in town again; and I feel myself much more comfortable from having performed my arduous tasks at the royal menagerie. Lady Westmoreland called on me one morning, and is going abroad directly. She is always going somewhere or anoder. I call her de perpetual motion. A Mr. Malcolm sent me a second edition of his " Sorrows of Love," for which I had paid him years ago ; and also two copies for the Regent and Princess Charlotte, both of which I sent to her ; and desired Mr. Malcolm to write to the Duchess of Leeds to get paid. I certainly never shall give him another shilling for his trash of poetry. He should send a fourth volume to Lady Hertford, as I think, in the present predicament, it would be acceptable, as it contains the " Sorrows of Love."

Pray believe me ever your affectionate

C. P[——].

A copy of a letter from Lord Liverpool previously to Her Royal Highness's departure from England ; written in the Princess of Wales's hand.

FIFE HOUSE, *July* 28*th.*

Lord Liverpool has had the honour of receiving your Royal Highness's letter, and of laying it before the Prince Regent. Lord Liverpool is commanded by the Prince to acquaint your Royal Highness, that he can have no objection to your Royal Highness carrying into effect the intention announced by your Royal Highness of going to your native country to pay a visit to your brother the Duke of Brunswick, and that it cannot be the wish of the Prince Regent to interfere in any plan which may be formed by your Royal Highness for your present or future residence ; but His Royal Highness will be satisfied that you should exercise your own discretion as to residing in this country or abroad, as may be most convenient to you. Lord Liverpool has been directed further to inform your Royal Highness, that the Prince of Wales does not wish to throw any impediment in the way of any arrangements which you may be desirous of making respecting the house of Her Royal Highness the late Duchess of Brunswick, or of any other part of your Royal Highness's private property ; but various considerations must prevent the Prince Regent from appointing Her Royal Highness Princess Charlotte ranger of Greenwich Park at present, or of permitting her to reside in the house at Blackheath.

Lord Liverpool is commanded by the Prince Regent not to conclude this letter without noticing the two circumstances mentioned in your Royal Highness's letters—of the rupture of the negotiation for the marriage of Her Royal Highness Princess Charlotte with the hereditary Prince of Orange, and of your Royal Highness not having received a visit from the allied sovereigns and other illustrious personages before they left England. With respect to the first of these points, Lord Liverpool is commanded to say, that from the course of the transaction itself, the Prince Regent cannot consider the peculiar circumstances of your Royal Highness as having formed the obstacle to that marriage. Upon the latter point, Lord Liverpool is commanded to acquaint your Royal Highness that no obstruction was placed by the Prince Regent in the way of the allied sovereigns, or the other illustrious personages, visiting your Royal Highness before they left England.

A short note from the Princess herself accompanies this copy of Lord Liverpool's letter, which Her Royal Highness sent to her friend. She says, " I send you the *best* letter I ever received from that quarter. I can now do what I like, go where I choose ; *I have got leave*, and feel quite happy." Poor soul, what a mistaken view of the subject ! Her husband was too glad she should leave the country ; it was what he most wished for. He well knew there was no peace for him to be expected whilst there were " two Harrys in the field," and a Prince and Princess of Wales, situated as they were with regard to each other, could not fail to be a thorn in each other's side ; so that the Regent was delighted to see her depart. At the moment, however, the receipt of Lord Liverpool's letter gave Her Royal Highness pleasure. She looked forward to release from restraint, and rest from bitter words and cruel mockings ; and it is not surprising she contemplated with satisfaction going to a foreign land which promised her enjoyments she missed in England.

Extract of a Letter from LADY [——].

I saw the Princess of Wales to-day. Her Royal Highness informed me that the Duke of Kent had just left her, having announced a drawing-room, which is to take place on the 16th. This great event was settled the other day at Carlton House. The old Queen did not like it *at first*, or pretended not to do so, but was at last *obliged* to consent. It will be the most curious thing in the world, if it actually does take place; but I have my doubts. The thing is so extraordinary. That an old *Dowager Queen*—for, in fact, she is a dowager as long as the poor King is set aside, from a *living* death—that she, I say, should give a drawing-room and gaieties, when there is a Princess Regent, whose business it is to do so, seems very extraordinary, and likely to excite the rage of John Bull.

Extract of another Letter from the same to the same.

MY DEAR [——].—*Chanticleer is fairly routed and terrified off his dunghill*, and *Trou Madame* exists no more. How this blessed change was brought about, I cannot say; but all wild, common birds have a great abhorrence to some pets of their own kind; and, by all I can devise, it has been successfully managed by them. One thing certain is, that I have had nothing to do in the matter; but that so it is, and it is most fortunate. Of course, at the Palace, things go on as usual; but that matters not, in comparison.

I passed a pleasant evening last night at Woodland's, where I found the *Sweet Williams;* but I must, perhaps, give you *the key to that lock*—a written pun, and such a one, demands an apology. Well, there was also there a General Zabloukoff, who married a daughter of old Mr. Angerstein's. He and his wife are just imported from Russia, and the former, as an eye witness of the campaign there, was very entertaining. He related horrors that made my flesh creep; and it is quite curious to hear (by his account) how very nearly Bonaparte escaped: but *a miss, you will say, is as good as a mile.*

A Letter from the same to the same.

Here we are, in what I call *trou Madame*, at seven o'clock in the fine August evenings, to be immured, for a *certainty*, till half-past twelve. It is a trial of patience. This has been the case three evenings out of five; and I find, from my predecessors, that this was the case for a fortnight together. I own it is very disgusting, and the more so to me, from my feelings being constantly oppressed by *goodness* for which I cannot return unmixed gratitude. I know you will enter into all my feelings upon all accounts, and it is a relief to express them to you, though at present I beg you not to reply to my communications. As long as I choose to be what I am, I will be it faithfully and according to my station; but I have been sadly *goaded* these last four days, and should not be surprised if I could not bear it much longer. However, do not be afraid of my doing anything *suddenly or violently*. Enough of this subject, perhaps too much, on paper.

Messrs. Gell and Craven dined at the Palace, and made two evenings pass pleasantly; but I can see that they are not what they were to the Princess. Gell is so *de bonne foi*, that I do not think he has discerned how bad things are become; but his friend has, in some degree, and I see him turn away in pity, but contempt. Alas! alas! for my poor mistress! it distresses me to see her doing all to sink herself.

The Royal Dukes pay Her Royal Highness great court. The Duke of Kent was here yesterday: he told the Princess that his regiment, which has been engaged in this last affair at St. Sebastian, is cut to pieces; the whole of the grenadiers killed. I feel more than usual horror at this carnage, for many of his men were drafted out of the —— Militia, and several officers whom I knew, poor fellows!

I suppose you have heard that it is thought the Prince of Orange is to be placed before Princess Charlotte, to see if he can find favour in her sight. This is to be managed by means of a breakfast, given by Lord Liverpool, at which the Queen's *most gracious* Majesty is to be present, and, of course, the young one; but the latter wrote word to her mother that she would not go. This, I believe, is only by way of pleasing the Princess of Wales, who, for some reason or other, does not like the idea of this marriage. Perhaps she does not wish for *any marriage*, for fear of a new and greater influence over her daughter than any that has yet been.

Princess Charlotte hates her grandmother *; and, tell

* Queen Charlotte, called already "Queen grandmother," the dulness of whose virtuous court has never been sufficiently insisted on.

it not in Gath, but I am sure she has no partiality for her father; so that, to *spite them*, she takes her mother's part. I wish I could think she had a better motive for so doing. Perhaps I wrong Princess Charlotte; but, as I at present view her character, it seems to me a selfish one; tyranny, and the love of power, the master-passions of her mind. But her mother will not long have any influence over her, if she continues the same frivolous and disgraceful mode of life which she has indulged in lately. But no human power can check her course, be it right or wrong. There is a propelling force in the Princess of Wales's own heart and fancy, that urges her to do whatever she wills, and bids defiance to reason, or to the fear of God or man. This is all I can pick out of my brains to-day: and little and dull is the *all*, my dear: but I trust the assurance that I am yours, affectionately, will be welcome to you.

Extract of another Letter from the same to the same.

FLORENCE.*

Though I know you do not interest yourself about gossip, I must tell you that there is a most curious story afloat (I do not vouch for the truth of it), saying the Duke of [Devonshire] is not the Duchess's son. The Duchess, it was said, substituted her friend Lady [Elizabeth Foster]'s child for *her own*—the present Duchess's, that is to say: consequently, the child thus imposed on the world as a son and heir to the honour of the House of [Cavendish], is no son and heir. There were strange doings in that house, if report speaks truth. If this story be true (and that there is some truth in it I do believe), many persons will suffer shame and loss. It seems Croft, the man who attended poor Princess Charlotte in her confinement, was the only person in the secret, and was sent for from London to Paris to attend the Duchess of [Devonshire] when this Duke, or, rather, no Duke, was born; and this man has lately shot himself; which some persons have attributed to his evil conscience. Lord [Burlington] would then be Duke, were his story proved true. She is coming to Rome, it seems, and, it is supposed, to extract

* From the allusion to Princess Charlotte's death (November 6). this letter must have been written in 1817, or later.

the truth out of the Duchess: *cosa difficile assai*, unless it be true that she is turned Catholic, out of love for Cardinal G[onsalv]i, and that fear compels her to make a clear conscience.

Among other English news, I heard to-day that Lady [———], Lord A[———]'s sister, has run away from her husband. This shocks me, for I knew her intimately. She loved her husband dearly, passionately, when I knew her ; and nothing was wanting to their felicity except children. It is horrid to think of crime without any excuse to palliate it : and where is this poor lady's excuse—who forsook the man of her choice, and one who seemed tenderly attached to her, and with whom she had lived for twenty years !

Lord A[———]n is dead. This is even a still more fearful event ; for, from all I have heard, he was little prepared to die. In a letter I received to-day from Lady [———], who was an intimate friend of his, she tells me the following curious particulars relative to his end. " One morning, when he met Lady A[———]n at breakfast, he said, you know I am no coward, not afraid of ghosts or such idle fancies ; but if I were to live a thousand years, I would not pass such a night over again, or see such sights as I saw last night." A short time before his death he also said to his wife, " you think I am quite well ; but I tell you I am not—I am dying." And when his physicians had held a consultation about his health, Lord A[———] charged them to tell him their exact opinion, and they did so, informing him that his life was certainly in imminent danger. He did not appear at all agitated, but ordered his coach and four, with outriders, and went out driving. Some say, that as Lord A[———] was lifted out of his carriage on his return home, he died ; others, that he lived through the night ; but altogether, adds Lady [———], I never heard a more awful account of the close of a life. I hear Dr. H[———]y * implored Lord A[———] to see him, and permit him to talk on religious matters, but he obstinately refused the request. No one knows what was the disease of which Lord A[———] died. Sir T. Lawrence's expression to a friend was, " I looked for Lord A[———]n in his arm-chair, and could not see him, he was so shrunk."

* Now Archbishop of C[———]y, formerly tutor in Lord A[———]'s family. [Original note.]

I regret Lord A[——]n's decease, for the sake of my friend Lady [——], to whom he was very kind ; and also he was friendly to the unhappy Princess of Wales.

Now, as you kindly wish me to do so, I will say something about myself ; but it shall be as little as possible, for I have nothing to tell you that can be interesting or agreeable to hear. The day is beautiful, and it has done me some good to breathe its genial breath ; but do you not know that feeling of contrast, of painful contrast, between the beauty of a first day of spring, and the wintry cold that is in the heart—that sighing of the soul which says, " I, too, *might be happy* " ; but I am absent and miserable, and can taste none of this gaiety of nature. Heavens ! how beautiful the clustering domes and towers of Florence looked—its distant frame of hills, its many-coloured lights ! I went to the Santa Croce, and enjoyed the greatness of its recollections. The tombs of the two Aretins are very beautiful : the marble has acquired that mellow tint, at once so brilliant, so transparent, and yet so subdued, which I admire more than when it is very dazzlingly white ; and I like the design of those monuments. I am called away by visitors, so must bid you farewell for to-day, my dear friend. Yours, with every kind wish for your happiness.

From the same to the same.

FLORENCE.

. have heard nothing more about the D[evonshire] story, except that the mother and son (if such they are) appear to be living on very happy terms, and the story is said to be hushed up by a promise on the part of the Duke, that he will never *marry*, or *pretend to present an heir*. What an agreeable compact for his Grace ! I heard a great deal of the first Duchess, from a man of business, to whom she was frequently indebted for assistance in pecuniary matters. He gave me a curious autograph of her's, which I copy and send for your amusement. It makes one marvel to think how a high-born lady could ever lay herself under such disgraceful obligations. The Duke always behaved to her with the greatest kindness and generosity. But then, to be sure, he knew *she* knew his peccadillos ; so it was, *Tais toi, je scais ; tais toi, je scais,* that made them bear with one another. What a disgraceful bargain! yet it is one very frequently made by great folks. Here is the Duchess' letter.

[COPY.]

Dated LONDON, 18th Dec, 1779.

Mr. D[——]ll having lent me two thousand six hundred and fifty pounds, I do hereby promise to pay him two hundred and fifty pounds every three months, at the usual quarter days, and continue to pay that sum quarterly to him or his heirs (allowing five per cent. interest, and five per cent. for insurance of my life per annum), until principal, interest, and insurance, shall be fully paid.

(Signed) G[EORGIANA] D[EVONSHIRE].

My agreement is, that in case the Duchess does not pay me two hundred and fifty pounds quarterly, that I shall acquaint the Duke of D[evonshire] with this transaction; and her Grace has promised, in case of her death or other accidents, to leave in writing a request that I may be paid, as I have lent her the money to relieve her from play debts, under a solemn promise that she will not play in future.

(Signed) J. D[——].

This is a very curious letter, and a melancholy record of the folly of this great Lady, who was one of the best-hearted persons in the world. I have often heard it told of her, that if she had money set apart for pleasure, or for the payment of debts, and that some individual came to her in pecuniary distress, she would always relieve him or her, and leave her own difficulties unprovided for. Oftentimes she was wrong in so doing. One must be just before one is generous. But it is impossible not to be charmed by the kindly impulse which made her, without a moment's hesitation, shield another from distress. Alas! it is frequently thus. Those who are amiable, are often not estimable; yet, I fear I lean to the former, with a weak partiality, for which I have repeatedly blamed myself.

To-day I heard a most romantic story, one which, if it was narrated in a novel, would be called exaggerated. But there are often romances in real life which far surpass any fictitious compositions. Madame [——] told me that her sister, Mrs. T. B[——], persecuted her since the death of her parents; and when she discovered her attachment to her present husband, at Naples, she made it the means of turning her own brother against her. They could not lock her up, as her fortune was very large, and independent of them; but they contrived to imprison her *lover*, and carried her off to Malta. From thence they sent her to England, to an uncle. To tell you all the story is now impossible; suffice it to say, she escaped from the people who had the charge of her. The very day she arrived at Portsmouth, she dressed herself in boy's clothes, and got, unobserved, to Calais; but when the passengers landed, she had no passport, and they would not suffer her to go on shore. It was night, and she was in despair; but, by the light of a lanthorn, she beheld a man, who appeared like a gentleman, walking on the pier. She threw herself on her knees to him, appealed to his compassion, and told him her story. He took pity on her, and procured her a passport, but only as far as Paris. Madame [——] had only seventy pounds with her, for her brother had the power of stopping her income, under pretence that she was mad, and about to disgrace her family. Obliged, therefore, to husband this sum, lest it should not carry her to Naples, where her lover was imprisoned, she at length, after great difficulties, obtained the necessary passport, and the ninth day reached Rome. There she was told by a Neapolitan that her lover was released, and gone to London in quest of her. She turned her steps back again, and caught him at Milan; but only saw him for two hours, for he said, " They will tell you that I marry you for your fortune; that I do not love you; and therefore, till every shilling is settled upon yourself, we must not be united. Go, return to England; have that matter arranged, and I will come and claim you in England." Accordingly she did so; they were married, and after a trial of two years, pronounced themselves happy in all except the persecution of her friends, and the mode in which they have tied up her fortune, so that she cannot live as she would wish.

Are you tired of this long story? I have not imparted to it the interest which Madame [——] did in relating it to me, with heartfelt energy; and she made me look with admiration, even at her little ugly self, as she sat beside me, while

I thought on how much she had undergone of trial, and how nobly she had combated against the mean tyranny of her relatives. To be sure, it seems astonishing that Madame [——] should have gone through so much for love of her ugly husband, insignificant in mind, body, and estate, as he appears to others ; but love (which like a piece of water in an ugly landscape, which reflects a thousand tints of beauty, and redeems a common scene from its monotony) endows the beloved one with fair qualities, which exist only in the reflection of passion's mirror. Blessings on the power which creates this magic charm ! In truth, love is the sun of the human heart, without which it is a dark abyss, joyless and arid.

I am ashamed of this rhapsody ; do you forgive it ? I said I was disappointed in Florence, when I first arrived. I must make it the *amende honorable*, and tell you that I am now very fond of this place. Again I cannot resist a simile : like an ugly person, whose outward appearance repels at first sight, but in whom, after longer acquaintance one discovers innumerable merits of head and heart,—so have I learned to know and value the locale of Florence as it deserves.

You must be weary of reading this long letter. Perhaps you have not had patience to read so far ; but let your eye glance over the last words, which are to assure you I am affectionately your friend, and may your heart re-echo the feeling !

From the same to the same.

FLORENCE.

Your letter from Brieg has this moment relieved me from some anxiety. I began to be afraid you had lost yourself in regions of " thick ribbed ice," or broken your neck over a precipice in your pursuit of glory after the Chamois : so that, on all accounts, your letter was most welcome. If you have ever wished for my friend and myself in the course of your tour, I assure you we have as frequently returned the compliment ; and I often say to myself, when I am tempted to walk about into strange-looking shops, in quest of prey, as well as in viewing things of high and sacred fancy,—when [——] comes, I shall avail myself of his protection and taste, to indulge in the latter. Often, too, at night, when I long to enjoy the moonlight, I think if I had a comfortable, quiet sort of an arm to protect me, I should like to wander about as chance led me ; and I have fancied that something of similar taste, perhaps of similar *distaste*, might make *you* not an unwilling companion.

Perhaps you think I am going to tell you of the Gallery of the Palais Pitti, the Academia, the Santa Croce, &c. ; but not a *bit* of these things shall I pretend to write of.   Flowers, feathers, silver tissue, jewels, golden ornaments, pomps, and ceremonies, and bridal attire, are all I am competent to give you in description.   Yesterday I went to the nuptials of the Grand Duke's daughter with Prince Carignano.   The ceremony took place in the Duomo, at ten in the morning. The church was illuminated, or, rather, I should say, spangled with thousands of waxen tapers ; it was hung with crimson and gold ; decorated with draperies of various sorts ; and all the spectators—those admitted with the court, at least— in the most splendid attire.   The women were magnificently and tastefully habited ; the men, as fine as finery could make them.   The forms of male costume exclude the possibility of beauty.   The bride (the victim, or the beatified— who can say which ?) was gorgeously arrayed.   A long veil nearly covered her whole form.   This was taken off at the foot of the altar, when the ceremony began.   She is a young girl, of sixteen ; fair and gentle in appearance ; her husband not ill-looking, but nothing particular, in his form or face, to attract or repel.   I thought the whole scene imposing ; and the Roman Catholic rites (do not despise me for the confession) are *very often* grateful to my feelings.   There is something very awful in the reflection, that two beings are binding themselves for ever, to the performance of the most sacred duties, the fulfilment of which, inasmuch as regards the heart alone, does not always depend upon themselves. That word, " *for ever* "—it always thrills through me.   I was not gay while I beheld the ceremony I have been describing ; but I was interested—interested even to bodily fatigue.   At night we went to a great *apartimento*—which means court— at the Palais Pitti.   The Palace, the arrangement of the attendance, the quantity of servants, guards, &c. far exceed our courts.   The women in general are not to be compared with our English beauties ; but there were two or three that commanded admiration, and looked like fine works of art started into life.

To-night is a night of rest, I am glad to say, for my health is not strong.   To-morrow there is a ball given to the court, by Madame Brignole ; and there are to be more fêtes given by the Grand Duke.   I shall be glad when this racket is over.   My friend, however, enjoys foreign gaieties so much, that I have a pleasure in seeing him well amused.   One pleasure I myself enjoy exceedingly,—the Opera.   The singers are not particularly good ; but the orchestra is fine, the choice of the music tasteful, the ballet quite delightful. In general, I care not for dancing ; but it is an historical ballet, taken from a story in Macchiavelli, of the Guelphs and Ghibellines.   The enthusiasm of the people was so great on hearing this the first night, that they absolutely roared and shouted, although the presence of the court ought to have silenced all but royal applause, according to etiquette.

Well ! so much for what, perhaps, you care not about ; but can my letter be entertaining to you ?   Are we well enough acquainted, that I should chatter securely, and be certain of not wearying ?   Our acquaintance is of such a recent date ; yet, somehow or other, my fancy has stepped over time, and I imagine myself, at least, a very old acquaintance of yours ; in consideration of which, I use the privilege of being tiresome.

I think I like Florence ; I think I shall love Florence ; but what I dreaded is now come to pass ; the Alps, the Appenines, the Ocean, they rise in all their majesty, and with treble majesty, before the eyes of my imagination, to make a barrier, that seems to shut me out from England ; and though I would not displace this barrier, the contradiction of human nature makes it more than fearful to me. In the act of travelling, distance and absence are less felt ; once settled, remembrance and fancy are living agents, and the survey they take is exaggerated—most cruelly exaggerated.   But this will pass, for does not everything pass ? and then I shall love Florence.

Have you voted me a teazing woman for giving you a commission to bring me artificial flowers ?   It was a comical commission, certainly ; thanks for the real ones.   There are beauteous ones here, but I have nobody to choose them for me. Will you sometimes charge yourself with this office in my service, whenever we meet, which, I hope, we shall ; if not here, elsewhere. I am reading Macchiavelli's History of Florence. Lorenzo, by Roscoe, has been taken from me by a tiresome Englishman, Mr. [——]. What a nice occupation it would be to illustrate the latter work ! I do not think Lorenzo's poetry very well, or very literally, translated.

I had some letters from England to-day, telling me that Lady [Coningham] has completely gained the summit of her ambition, and has all the honours paid her of the [Regent's mistress]. Did you ever happen to hear that she once openly declared she would arrive at that goal one day or another ? She has reached it,* and may it prove all she thinks it is worth ! But what a false notion of happiness and honour !

I wonder the remembrance of a La Vallière never crosses the mind of a woman, when she seeks for unhallowed and joyless love ; nay, Lady [Coningham] need only behold Mrs. [Fitzherbert] and Lady [Hertford], and tremble, lest such should be her own fate.

I hear unsatisfactory accounts of the poor Princess of Wales. I am afraid she is going to destruction ; not an English attendant left, and the vile Italian cormorants are ruining her, both as to finance and reputation. Is there no hand can be outstretched to save her ?

Yours, &c. &c.

* Joseph Jekyll wrote, February 10, 1820 : " To-morrow I dine with a rural queen, Lady Conyngham, who will not triumph. 'Tis l'esprit faible contre l'esprit fort of Lady H[ertford]." She did " triumph " however

Lightning Source UK Ltd.
Milton Keynes UK
UKHW021917010121
376217UK00007B/54